Building Christian Character

Building Christian Character

*A Devotional Guidebook through the Elements
of Christian Character for Children and Adults*

by Blair Adams

*Can be used for children with the character curriculum
chart designed to accompany this book*

Second Edition, Expanded and Completely Revised

Colloquium Press
Elm Mott, Texas

Note on Scripture Quotations:

Scriptures, unless otherwise indicated, have been quoted directly from the *Holy Bible: New International Version* or the *New King James Version* with the exception of the name "Yahweh" in place of the title "LORD." The *NIV* is copyright 1973, 1978, 1984 by the International Bible Society. Used by permission of Zondervan Bible Publishers.

Library of Congress Catalog Card Number 89-51225
ISBN-0-916387-55-0

Published by

Colloquium Press
info@colloquiumpress.com

P.O. Box 869 • Elm Mott, Texas 76640

Printed in the United States of America

For you know that we dealt with each of you
as a father deals with his own children,
encouraging, comforting and urging you
to live lives worthy of God,
who calls you into His kingdom and glory.

(1 THESS. 2:11-12)

Even a child is known by his doings.

(PROV. 20:11, KJV)

Dedication

To Regina,
a wonderful wife and mother,
for whom I first started this book
as an aid in raising our 10 children,
who are now using it to raise theirs.

CONTENTS

To Parents and Ministers

This book has been designed to help parents and other ministers in building Christian character in children and disciples. Thus everywhere the word "child" is used, it can read "natural child" or "child of God." It is normal then that, as ministers and parents have prayerfully studied this book and used it in instructing their charges, most testify they come to see how it applies to their own lives as well and that this has sometimes become an uncomfortable or even troubling "two-edged sword." If you do stand in a mentoring relationship to others, don't let this discomfort cause you to throw off any conviction you yourself might feel as a child of God working through these pages. Rather, let God change your life as well and thereby more effectively use you to disciple those under your care and even perhaps others beyond your immediate sphere of abiding relationships. Don't be discouraged, then, if you feel God chipping away at the unfinished work of your own life. Rather, shift your eyes from the chips on the floor and toward the finished masterwork "conformed to the image of [God's] Son" (Rom. 8:29). Then be encouraged that God loves *you* as His own child just as you love your natural or spiritual children.

In fact, as you work with this book, why not *deliberately* measure yourself against the plumb line of His Word (Amos 7:7-8)? Why not examine *yourself* to see if you stand in the same relationship to God and His order as you require (or at least should require) that your children or flock stand in relationship to you? If parents or pastors find themselves falling short, no help lies in saying, "Yes, I'm a hypocrite for asking of my children or others what I refuse to give myself. So I'll stop requiring this submission." Rather, we should repent and bring our own lives in line with God's Word.

If we actively participate in the Word God speaks to us, His character will emerge more clearly than ever in us as well as in our children and the members of Christ's Body generally.

Most of this book can be *directly* ministered to children, and at least part of *every* topic can be so ministered; but parts of the book are written for the parent or minister who can then put it into their own words to meet the need at the level the recipient can understand.

THE GOAL OF GODLY CHARACTER

To Be Like Him

Christian child rearing, or discipleship in general, does not aspire to develop talents, gifts or intellectual knowledge prior to everything else. Although we cannot dispense with these, to nurture character takes primacy over all else. For instance, most parents, even unbelievers, have in mind some sort of image or another that they envision for their children. As Christians, we want to impress—that is, allow the Spirit to work through us to impress—a very definite and specific image into the hearts of our children: the character of the Lord Jesus Christ. His life declared above all the nature of God—redemptive love. The pure, spotless character of Jesus perfectly reflected this love. God has commissioned us and our children to walk in perfect step with the heartbeat of God's love. This demands an intimate, living relationship with Him. This unfolding and growing intimacy with God through His Spirit allows us to increasingly become one with God as we, too, manifest His image in His love and wisdom. What is true of children is also true of disciples in general.

Jesus Christ manifested God in human flesh. He was our example of a human being wholly at-one with God—the Son of God. Our own supernatural experience with the same Spirit that conceived Jesus (Matt. 1:18; Rom. 8:4-14) marks our entry into His sonship as we move toward oneness with God (John 17:21; Gal. 3:26). We and our children, as well as all those under our nurture and care, have been destined for the same sort of relationship with God that the Man Jesus of Nazareth fully personified (John 10:30; Phil. 2:5-8). So the education of children or of believers in general aims for a life wholly committed to the God laid in a trough and made to bleed. The lives and characters of all who would follow Him will be consumed by God's love, shaped by His truth, submitted to His purpose, disciplined by His will and in every way conformed to His image.

Education comprises far more, then, than merely teaching someone to do and to know *about* certain things. Above all, it involves what the person *is*. This truth bears the most important sense in which God establishes His dominion "in earth as it is in heaven" and makes us to *be* in His image, to "*be* witnesses" (rather than merely "do" witnessing). God has designed every facet of our lives to reflect the pristine purity and goodness of His own holy nature. Godly character stands as the highest prize in Christian education, whether of children or adult disciples. Every task placed before us serves ultimately as the means—the potter's wheel and kiln, the blacksmith's anvil and bellows, the spinner's carder and spindle, the weaver's shuttle and loom—through which God supremely transforms and crafts us into His image. While parents and pastors should encourage those under their care to excel in all they do, the Bible warns against a kind of knowledge that puffs people up (1 Cor. 8:1). True knowledge, Christ-centered knowledge, does not puff us up (1 Cor. 8:1-3) but nurtures humility as it brings us to recognize our complete dependence on the Giver of all true wisdom and, indeed, of every perfect gift. Such knowledge builds us up in love, and such an attitude enables our charges to live lives authentically guided by God's Spirit, worshiping Him all their days in both Spirit and Truth. All believers, young or old, must find God's forge of character and walk through the coals. If we succeed in everything else but fail here, then we have failed God, our children and God's flock. If we succeed in this area, then we can succeed in every area of child rearing or pastoral care.

Tamim is the Hebrew word translated "complete," "perfect" or "whole" in Genesis 17:1 and in many other passages of Old Testament Scripture.* *Tamim* men and women, people of integrity, wholeness, consistency (Gen. 17:1) stand as the goal we seek. The Biblical view does not see children as already whole but, as with all human beings, fallen and fragmented by nature. So wholeness or integrity of heart, mind, soul and strength in people is no casual or small event. It begins with a powerful supernatural experience and proceeds only with diligence, love and care. All of this can only come as the fruit of a vital relationship of covenantal oneness with God, with God's people and with God's creation. Yet wholeness and integrity stand as benchmarks of Christian character. Oneness (that is, the wholeness, completeness and integrity of the One God of Israel Himself) is the foundation of Christian character just as it is the foundation of Christian truth.

> "The most important [commandment]," answered Jesus, "is this: 'Hear, O Israel, *the Lord our God, the Lord is one.* Love the Lord your God with all your heart and with all your soul and with all your mind and with all your strength.' The second is this: 'Love your neighbor as yourself.' There is no commandment greater than these." (Mark 12:29-31)

> Hear, O Israel: *Yahweh our God, Yahweh is one.* Love Yahweh your God with all your heart and with all your soul and with all your

---

* For example, Gen. 6:9; Deut. 18:13; Ps. 18:32; Ps. 101:2, 6; Prov. 2:21.

strength. These commandments that I give you today are to be upon your hearts. Impress them on your children. Talk about them when you sit at home and when you walk along the road, when you lie down and when you get up. Tie them as symbols on your hands and bind them on your foreheads. Write them on the doorframes of your houses and on your gates. (Deut. 6:4-9)

Hidden in these scriptures lies the message upon which everything in God's kingdom rests. Jesus Himself declared the *first and greatest commandment* begins with the revelation that God is One. This greatest of all commandments begins with the word *hear*. So we must first open our ears, come under the hearing of (the literal meaning of the New Testament Greek word *hupakouo*, which we translate as "obey"), this revelation of divine wholeness, of God's absolute integrity, His oneness. Then Jesus tells us that we must love this one God with *our* whole being. Obedience to this commandment ensures that our love for God, and therefore for others, will conform to the image of the living Word coming from God's Spirit, the Word that consistently expresses and reveals God and informs us as we come under its hearing.

Here, Jesus has quoted Moses' words recorded in Deuteronomy 6:4-5. Then, turning to Leviticus 19:18, Jesus tells us that we must love our neighbors as ourselves. After giving us the first commandment, Deuteronomy 6 proceeds by then telling us in verses 6-9 that we must impress God's commandments upon our children. As the following pages show, to impress the commandments upon those under our spiritual care means to teach them to love God and their neighbors as themselves. Paul said:

> Let no debt remain outstanding, except the continuing debt to love one another, for he who loves his fellowman has fulfilled the law. The commandments, "Do not commit adultery," "Do not murder," "Do not steal," "Do not covet," and whatever other commandment there may be, are summed up in this one rule: "Love your neighbor as yourself." Love does no harm to its neighbor. Therefore love is the fulfillment of the law. (Rom. 13:8-10)

We can only love others as ourselves when God's commandments are first pressed into the softened flesh of our own hearts as God shapes us into vessels through which His love can flow to others. When we serve those we see, we serve the One we cannot see (1 John 4:20; Matt. 25:40). When we take on the form of a servant, as Jesus did, His character increasingly impresses itself into our lives through our self-sacrificial service.

> If you have any encouragement from being united with Christ, if any comfort from His love, if any fellowship with the Spirit, if any tenderness and compassion, then make my joy complete by being like-minded, having the same love, being one in spirit and

purpose. Do nothing out of selfish ambition or vain conceit, but in humility consider others better than yourselves. Each of you should look not only to your own interests, but also to the interests of others.

Your attitude should be the same as that of Christ Jesus: Who, being in very nature God, did not consider equality with God something to be grasped, but made Himself nothing, taking the very form of a servant, being made in human likeness. And being found in appearance as a man, He humbled Himself and became obedient to death—even death on a cross! (Phil. 2:1-8, NIV, KJV)

To truly put on the mind of Christ, esteeming others more highly than ourselves, looking out for their interests with the same concern that we look out for our own, is to take on the form of a servant and be increasingly conformed to Christ's own image.

Without doubt, the fallen human will cannot do this work; only the dynamic power of the Holy Spirit can bring this change in a human life. Our will must therefore be broken so that an opening comes into our lives through which the Spirit can first fill, then lead and guide, us into Christ's own life. Only then can His commandments be *impressed* upon us and upon our children. Hebrews 1:3 declares Jesus to be the "express image" or the "exact representation" of God's Being. These words translate the Greek word *charakter*, the root of our English word *character*. When the minter of currency stamped an image on a coin, transmitted an impression, the Greeks used this same word to describe this process. Character, in brief, is something *impressed* upon us, stamped by the weight of life's burdens, cares, responsibilities and even suffering or pain as all those come to us in the context of God's love and blessings, pressing Christ's life into our inner-most nature. And we likewise want to see impressed upon our offspring, "stamped" within them—until their nature entirely conforms to it—the image of the Lamb of God (Rom. 8:29). Herein, then, lies the meaning of the injunction in Deuteronomy 6 that we "impress" the words of God upon our children, that we do our part as God's servants to conform their character to God's essential nature revealed in Christ's self-sacrificing love. The Biblical injunction that parents must impress the words of the Law "on your children" meant, in other words, that the Law was to be *internalized*, written or impressed upon human hearts (Jer. 31:33; Heb. 10:16). A child's very character was to be conformed to God's Word by being conformed to the image of the Word made flesh in the life of Messiah. This was, of course, the promise of the New Covenant (Jer. 31:31-34; Heb. 8:7-13; 9:15). The Spirit has now come to New Testament believers to dismantle stubborn barriers of the flesh so that God's Word can imprint His nature upon us through "the obedience that comes from faith" (Rom. 8:4; 1:5).

Yet, as so much in life shows, only form can hold the content that fills up human lives, and not just any form will do but only the form through which *God's* love flows.* Since this love does not originate with us, how can our children or anyone else learn to love the Lord with all of their hearts, souls and strength unless channels exist through which God's love comes to them and through which they can then also express that love? And herein lies God's reason for a form: in this case, it is a character curriculum (literally, a "racecourse") of His Word that can show our children that channels do exist through which at every moment of their lives they can express the love that God gives them. As we will see, through the channels of daily relationships and responsibilities, people serve their parents, their brothers and sisters and other members of the community. They concretely manifest the love and grace of God as it moves through their lives to others.

Children who channel their hearts and minds, in word and deed, to the service God has given them will see these channels of covenant relationships and functions begin to serve as living forms to shape them into Christ's image. A life moving ever toward more perfect submission to the service of Jesus, where His character is impressed increasingly upon us, becomes the irrefutable evidence of our covenantal oneness with God. Such a oneness with God is a life in the Spirit, and if we actually live by the Spirit, its fruit will overflow our lives to feed others.

> So I say, live by the Spirit, and you will not gratify the desires of the sinful nature. For the sinful nature desires what is contrary to the Spirit, and the Spirit what is contrary to the sinful nature. They are in conflict with each other, so that you do not do what you want. But if you are led by the Spirit, you are not under law.
> The acts of the sinful nature are obvious: sexual immorality, impurity and debauchery; idolatry and witchcraft; hatred, discord, jealousy, fits of rage, selfish ambition, dissensions, factions and envy; drunkenness, orgies, and the like. I warn you, as I did before, that those who live like this will not inherit the kingdom of God.
> But the fruit of the Spirit is love, joy, peace, patience, kindness, goodness, faithfulness, gentleness and self-control. Against such things there is no law. Those who belong to Christ Jesus have crucified the sinful nature with its passions and desires. Since we live by the Spirit, let us keep in step with the Spirit. Let us not become conceited, provoking and envying each other. (Gal. 5:16-26)

If we love God as Jesus told us to, this sets in motion, through our lives and all its channels and streambeds of relationship, the life-giving love of God, which "never fails."

> Love is patient, love is kind. It does not envy, it does not boast, it is not proud. It is not rude, it is not self-seeking, it is not easily

---

*See *A Garden Enclosed* (1988, 2003), *Loved into Loving* (1977, 1988, 2007) and *An Introduction to the Temple and Its Foundation* (1983, 1988), all by Blair Adams (Elm Mott, Tex.: Colloquium Press).

angered, it keeps no record of wrongs. Love does not delight in evil but rejoices with the truth. It always protects, always trusts, always hopes, always perseveres.
Love never fails. (1 Cor. 13:4-8)

When our lives pulse with the character of this love, we are not far from the oneness with God that is our salvation, our at-one-ment.

The First Principle of God's First Great Law: Oneness, Wholeness, Integrity

The very word *at-onement* suggests, as so many have shown, that salvation *is* oneness with the God who Himself is One.*[1] So oneness becomes the hallmark of the saved: oneness *with God* and oneness within *ourselves* (not letting our minds, hearts or bodies conflict with each other and not letting them conflict with God); oneness with our *family* (both natural and spiritual); oneness *with creation* and our environment (this includes oneness between, on the one hand, our daily vocation, work and home life and, on the other hand, the principles and vision of the God whom we profess with our mouths to serve—cleanliness, holiness, orderliness, good stewardship of resources, caring for our animals or our tools and so on would all fall under this category). All this in turn suggests that the oneness we always seek rests on *relationship*: we become one with others through our relationships. So we must *guard* our relationships from influences disruptive or polluting to our oneness with God. We must also guard against all that would destroy the harmony of the various elements of our own individual being—our emotions, our intellects, our wills. If this harmony is lost, we feel pulled apart inside, stretched in conflicting directions. So we must guard our minds, hearts, bodies or spirits against anything that would destroy the balance between these different spheres of life—for example, allowing our intellects to arrogantly take inordinate priority over the concerns of our hearts, or the emotional desires of our hearts to take precedence over the guidance of God's Spirit and Truth.

Through his concept of "emotional intelligence," psychologist, bestselling author and two-time Pulitzer Prize nominee Daniel Goleman focuses upon the critical necessity of maintaining this inner harmony, and specifically, upon the integral balance between our emotions and intellect. Goleman has formulated a way to evaluate the level of such balance and maturity by looking at a specific "key set of . . . characteristics" that express

---

* See also *The Quest for Salvation* (1974, 1988), *The Nature and Transformation of God* (1975, 1989, 2002) and The Minister's Dialectical Handbook of Theology and Doctrine *On Atonement, Justification and the Law, Book Two: Justification* (1996, 2005), all by Blair Adams (Elm Mott, Tex.: Colloquium Press).

emotional intelligence.[2] These include the ability to learn to empathize with others, to control oneself in relationship to others and to motivate oneself to endure in these qualities in the face of pressure, opposition and crisis.[3] Goleman added, "There is an old-fashioned word for this body of skills: character."[4] Goleman found that "the root of altruism" lies in these characteristics. Since self-sacrificing generosity requires "empathy," the lack of it short-circuits "the ability to read emotions in others." As Goleman explained, "Where there is no sense of another's need or despair, there is no caring."[5] In short, without "fundamental ethical stances in life" that "stem from underlying *emotional* capacities," we lose our humanity,[6] just as did the highly educated German intellectual elite that supported the Nazis. Then nothing any longer really matters that much, not even the killing of other human beings. It is no extravagance, then, to say that without a mature balance between caring emotions and the ability to assess a situation as it truly is, our lives can lose their direction and meaning— for example, through reliance on the disembodied and detached intellect alone.*

In short, we must not allow an inordinate place for anything within us that would destroy oneness between us and God, between us and our family, between us and our spiritual brothers and sisters, between us and our proper relationship with our environment. (All of these points must be explained in detail to children and disciples so that they can see how such problems could arise. For example, they must see that preoccupation with acquiring some type of knowledge *about* something—even if it is for God's purpose—must never displace the prior importance of our direct and personal relationship with God.)

None of this is to imply, however, that we should ever do anything less than seek to *fulfill* the highest level of potential oneness in each of these areas of relationship. Otherwise, our lives will be distorted and imbalanced. We will be "overemotional" or "overintellectual" or cultivate a stubbornness of will against God's will when He would lead us by His Spirit. If we cultivate only our emotions and seek oneness merely on this level with God, with our fellow man or with our environment, while neglecting our minds and bodies, then we cannot help but fall short of the highest possible oneness within ourselves. Our minds and bodies will fail to develop to our full God-given potential. This means we must also fall short to the same degree in our oneness of relationship with God, our

---

* Goleman also notes that repeatedly confirmed research has demonstrated that such "emotional intelligence" "determines life success"—and does so much more than any measure of mere intelligence, such as that gauged by the IQ and other similar tests.[7] The evidence is so compelling that even Charles Murray, who co-authored *The Bell Curve*, which emphasized the correlation between IQ and achievement, now concedes that IQ is "dwarfed" by "other characteristics that [each person] brings to life," the kinds of characteristics that Goleman's research emphasizes.[8]

fellow man and our environment. Then the witness to the world of God's wholeness and completeness falls short, and our salvation fails to fully express its efficacy to address the whole of human life. This becomes all too evident when believers fall into stereotypes easily dismissed by the world.

The same would be true if our minds or bodies stood in the place of our hearts in the above example. So each part of our being must fulfill its highest potential of oneness in proper God-ordained relationships with everything around us given to us by God; for we know that nature abhors a *vacuum*, and whatever in our lives remains *unfulfilled* through these divine and living patterns of oneness, then the flesh, the world or the devil will move to fill (Luke 11:23-26). If we do not find the meaning for our minds or emotions in the purpose of God, we will look for it in the world and its *zeitgeist*. So we cannot really hope to *guard* ourselves in the *negative* sense without also fulfilling ourselves in the *positive* sense.

God has a gift for us in every area of life. To our bodies—to that part of our being which relates to the material realm, to the earth that sustains us—God has provided a land-centered culture depicted so pervasively in Scripture and functioning consistently with the patterns of life itself. Such a culture provides the proper context in which our physical being can sustain itself for its allotted time on earth. God has further given our souls—that part of our being which relates to animated, conscious being (whether our fellow humans or other creatures)—primarily the community of believers, the *ecclesia* (but even the animated life of the creatures of the earth as well). All this suggests that the church as Christ's own Body on earth must become the full-orbed culture of love that fulfills all the needs of the human mind and heart. Yet above all, God has given our human spirit nothing less than Himself, the Father of all spirits. If we do not find fulfillment in this most comprehensive of all contexts, then we will seek satisfaction in the substitutes manufactured by fallen humanity and the spiritual powers of darkness (Eph. 4:14; 6:12).

That which guards us from the flesh, the world and the devil and at the same time causes us to cling to our relationship with the creation, the church and God—thus enabling us to fulfill our full potential for oneness, harmony and wholeness—is the *covenant*. The covenant surrounds us, holds us together, like the protective walls of Jerusalem; it shuts out that which would destroy our love and wholeness (or purity and integrity) while it binds together that with which we are to be one. A breach in covenant means a breach in the wall of our salvation: what should have been excluded will enter to pollute, and what should have been included, what should have been constrained into ever-greater integrity and oneness, will seep out and dissipate.

If the covenant represents the living form that both separates and contains, the form to be fulfilled, then the *content* that *does the filling* and that actually *binds together* in oneness all that is included within the walls of covenant is redemptive, self-sacrificing *love* (Col. 3:14). *Covenant* is the living *channel* of relationship, but love is the vital content of the relationship that flows through the channel, making those connected by the channel one with each other in the river of God's life.* And this brings us to the second principle of the first great commandment, both the *end and the means* of oneness and integrity.

The Second Principle of the First Great Law: Self-Sacrificing Love

Love the Lord your God with all your heart and with all your soul and with all your mind and with all your strength. (Mark 12:30; Deut. 6:5)

When we "love" God with "all" our "heart" through the vital channels and patterns of His covenant, we make ourselves one with God in our inner being, in the faculties of mind, will and heart, all of which we now direct toward God. When we love Him with "all" our "soul"—the seat of our heart, mind and will as these are directed toward self-consciousness, toward consciousness of the world and toward other conscious creatures— we become one with God through the patterns and channels of covenant that He has established for the soul, that is, the patterns of covenant for the church and family. Then we make ourselves one with God in our souls as the soul comes under the power of the regenerated spirit. When we love God with "all" our "mind," we become one with God in our mind and therefore in everything we do through and with our mind (in our study of His Word, of history, of English, in our taking of dominion over all areas of responsibility in our lives and so on). When we love Him with "all" our "strength," we make ourselves one with God by loving Him with the totality of our physical being, the "all" of that part of our being; and we are enabled to give an all-out effort—not merely a half-baked effort—in every endeavor of every part of our being, the "all" strength of our *minds*, our *hearts*, our *spirits*, our *bodies*, our *souls*. The "all" in each of these areas of love necessitates oneness and wholeness: if we give "all," then nothing is withheld from God. We hold back nothing to give to the flesh, to the world or to the devil because we have already given "all" to God.

---

* See *Loved into Loving* for a full discussion of these points.

The Elements of Christian Character

A. HONOR/DISHONOR

1. Honor

Dishonor stands as one of the straightest roads to perdition and apostasy. But its opposite, honor, is the foundation from which all other elements of Christian character arise. It refers primarily to a condition of the heart and mind, an inner attitude that inevitably manifests itself in outer words, actions and demeanor. Honor expresses the genuine and deep veneration within the child's (or anyone's) heart toward those to whom honor is due. It recognizes an indebtedness, an obligation, to those whom we honor. It expresses the value we place upon them, since if we *value* them, we will *pay* attention to them and *spend* time for them. Because it expresses the sincere and true feeling of our hearts, it will inevitably cause us to act in a way that brings honor toward those for whom we have this feeling. If the child holds honor in his heart toward God, his parents and others to whom it is due, he will seriously strive to submit his life to the processes that bring into that life all the godly character traits discussed in this book. He will not, in other words, simply try to *appear* to have these character traits, but he will genuinely reach to incorporate them into his life. When Paul calls the commandment to honor our parents "the *first* commandment with promise," he states plainly the *foundational* importance of honor. If we *begin* by truly honoring those to whom honor is due, then all other elements of Christian character can come forth in our lives.

We can understand the place of primacy that honor holds in the development of character in a number of ways, all of which overlap. As seen, since honor expresses a condition of the heart, it opens the way to all the other godly character traits. But we can also see honor as a kind of relationship, a relationship that expresses a particular content through a particular form. The type of relationship that characterizes honor is foundational to the relationship of oneness with God, a oneness of relationship that constitutes our very salvation (John 17:1-3; Deut. 6:4-5; Mark 12:29-30). As said in the introduction, salvation or at-one-ment means oneness (John 17),* first oneness with God and then, through Him, oneness within ourselves, oneness with our fellow man and oneness with creation. Herein lies the meaning of our great atonement. So a relationship of oneness with God unfolds into the fullness of our salvation. We become

---

* See *The Quest for Salvation.*

one with Him by submitting to His will, by allowing Him to conform our lives to His image: if we confess Him as Lord—not only by words but by our conduct, our thoughts and our attitudes—then we will be saved (Rom. 10:8-10). We look to Him as our Sovereign and King, and so we must honor Him with our whole lives. That is, we must esteem Him, recognize His true value and worth in every aspect of our lives. Even though His authority is noncoercive and constitutes the unique rule of love, which the kingdom of God counterposes to the rule of brute force in the kingdoms of the world (John 18:33-37), nonetheless, the love that *is* God (1 John 4:8, 16) must have absolute authority in our lives. And our honor of Him forms the basis upon which that authority will effectively work in our lives. Only if we truly honor an authority will we submit to it from the heart, and only such submission is profitable for either our character or our salvation. Grudging or resentful submission only shows that we *know* what is right, but that we don't *love* what is right—we don't *truly* honor it. Some perhaps deeply hidden sin in our heart—often pride—tells us that, really, *we* are far more worthy of honor than those God calls upon us to honor; such pride cannot help but eventually cut us off from God.

Scripture tells us that when Jesus returned to Nazareth after performing many miracles in other places, the people of His "hometown" looked on Him with familiarity and so took offense at Him (Matt. 13:54-57). They refused to submit to the grace or authority of God as it flowed through Him; that is, they refused to honor Him: "But Jesus said to them, 'Only in his *hometown* and in his *own house* is a prophet without *honor*.' And He did not do many miracles there because of their *lack of faith*" (Matt. 13:57-58). So here Jesus explicitly links faith for miracles and healing with a submission that arises from true honor and trust in the authority that is "sent" to us. Because of that link, both honor and humility are tied to our ability to receive the power and grace of God. So here a lack of humility in the people's relationship to someone who is one of their own results in a lack of honor. Instead of humbling themselves, they lift themselves up in pride against Him, comparing themselves with Him. One could imagine them saying, "I could teach just as well as He does. I could tell Him how to do this *better*. I've done as much as He has. Even if He's sacrificed in the past, I'm the one pouring myself out now—*He* should be honoring *me*." This contempt-breeding familiarity really manifests only an envy rooted in pride and therefore a delusory but exalted image of oneself. So the Nazarenes lacked honor toward Jesus because they lacked *humility*. Their lack of honor then, in turn, resulted in a lack of faith. And their lack of faith finally resulted in their loss of God's power and grace to protect, heal, restore or save them. So both honor and faith depend on humbly recognizing our proper relationship to God as well as to those through whom He manifests His authority and power, through whom He has brought us life. (Because the people of Nazareth failed to honor Jesus in the flesh, God could not do His works at Nazareth through Jesus.) Surely, then, as both Paul and Peter instruct (1 Thess. 5:12-13; 1 Tim. 5:17; 1 Pet. 5:5, Ampl.), we, too, must honor those human vessels God sends to us if we would see the power of His love. God commands it for our own good (1 Tim. 5:17; Phil. 2:25-30; 1 Thess. 5:12-13; 1 Pet. 5:5-7).

Luke 7, for instance, shows Jesus standing amazed at "the *faith*" of the centurion, a citizen of high standing in the then most powerful empire on earth. This influential and powerful man publicly declares his unworthiness to have Jesus even come into his home. The centurion indeed expresses an uncommon humility. For a Roman military officer of such high rank in the ruling world culture of the time to tell someone of "no reputation" (Phil. 2:5-7) in a *subject* nation, especially one whose religion was generally despised by those in power in Rome, that this powerful Roman official did not feel worthy for that person to come into his home is extraordinary.

Yet beyond this, the centurion also recognizes the spiritual authority that Jesus possesses, for the centurion says that he, "too," is a man not *with* authority but "*under* authority" (Luke 7:6-9). This, too, is a strange way for a centurion in the Roman Empire to speak. He didn't boast in his own power, but, again, humbled himself; and Jesus called this humility an expression of great faith.

As an officer in the Roman army, this centurion had to have noteworthy gifts, including intelligence, leadership abilities and so on. But the centurion's gifts are not what impress Jesus. What proves decisive to both Jesus and the centurion is submission. Yet it is not submission to some charismatic figure that assumes such centrality. Rather, what the passage emphasizes is submission to a *form* and *order* of authority. As a man *under* authority, the centurion recognizes the basis of Jesus' own authority, and this insight seems to be what amazes Jesus.

So the centurion's "faith" showed itself in both his humble recognition of his own unworthiness and in his honoring of the spiritual authority he perceives in Jesus. In other words, he recognizes Jesus not because He has such "social presence," such "personal bearing"; rather, he recognizes Jesus' spiritual authority because it is analogous to his own condition *under* a larger form and order of authority. This brings a meeting of two hitherto totally separate worlds, as well as amazement at the precise way God manifests Himself in human flesh. This sense of amazement marks not only the centurion but also Jesus when He recognizes the centurion's insight into what is actually involved and at issue.

Yet, in contrast, the people of Nazareth, as seen, exalted themselves above Jesus (by seeing Him in merely the fleshly terms of their own human relationship with Him—"Isn't this Mary's son? Isn't this the carpenter? Don't we know His brothers? So how can He possibly express an authority we should honor or submit to?"). They could not see the kingdom that stood behind His authority, nor could they recognize and honor the form that would define their proper relationship to Him. All they could see was an isolated fleshly entity they had grown up with and, in their opinion, already knew all too well. Therefore they failed to honor their Messiah, as Jesus explicitly declared. So while the Roman centurion's *servant* received his miraculous healing (and how fitting that this centurion's motivation lies in his concern and love for someone *under* him), the people of Nazareth to whom the promise had been originally extended never even glimpsed God's wonders. As far as the latter were concerned, Jesus did not perform miracles in Nazareth simply because He was not sent of God and *could not* perform them. His presence was simply a familiar and therefore minor and insignificant occurrence to them. (We, too, should ask of ourselves— "What familiar person in my life, whom I take so for granted, has actually been sent to me from God, someone worthy of great honor?") Another perspective, in contrast to that of the Nazarenes, would have shown them that miraculous power can flow only through a relationship that truly honors God and the authority He would manifest in the lives of all those who call Him Lord, even as He expresses this authority through (or rather, *especially* as He expresses it through) human beings—in this particular case, through the "Son of Man" Himself. But a self-exalting people or generation will never see the power of God, yet they will always blame it on others—even on God Himself—instead of on the lack of humility and honor they have for those sent to them.

In addition to the centurion, Jesus also praises a Syrophoenician woman for her "great faith." Yet how has she revealed this faith? When Jesus dismisses her as a "dog," she does not bristle. She does not demand or assert her equality or her self-worth in order to elicit better treatment in keeping with her own high self-regard. She does not hint of a complaint that Jesus has slighted her personhood or her dignity as a woman. Rather, she simply submits to His remark. She therefore honors Him and His transcendent spiritual authority above her own slighted image, recognizing her own total dependence on God's gracious sustenance. Political, social or economic empowerment is *not* what this woman is seeking but rather the empowerment and healing of numinous love, of God. Therefore, from out of her mouth comes this extraordinary statement: "Even the dogs eat the crumbs that fall from their master's table" (Matt. 15:27). And in those words resides a power sufficient to capture the heart and attention of God manifest in the flesh, bringing forth the even greater power of a miracle. Thus does Jesus declare to her: "Woman, you have *great faith*! Your request is granted." Again, in response to this *faith*, that is, in response to her humble recognition of her true status in relationship to God, a faith inseparable from honor and humility toward God's authority, the stunningly miraculous power of deliverance flows to the woman's daughter (Matt. 15:28).

We can therefore easily conclude, without stretching the point at all, that Jesus did not do many works in His "hometown" simply because the proper attitude toward and relationship to God and to those He sends was not present in the hearts of the people there—they neither humbled themselves to receive His grace nor honored the representative God sent in human flesh to express divine authority and power to them. They exalted themselves and therefore saw their Messiah only with eyes of flesh—"Isn't this Mary's son . . . ? Aren't His sisters here with us?" In other words, in their view He wasn't sent by God. Rather, He merely came the way we all arrive on the scene, and therefore in their view they insisted that He should have had to enter the political-theological fray for "empowerment" and do so on equal footing with all the rest of them. In short, He wasn't, in their eyes, a supernatural manifestation of God's grace for them. In their pride, they magnified their own importance and, by so doing, could not help but belittle His. They wanted all the honor that should have gone to Him. They thereby cut themselves off from God and His provision for them. And many, of course, still do the same today.

Yet only when we humble ourselves before God's authority can His power flow tangibly into our lives, not only to meet our needs but also to make us instruments through whom He can meet the needs of others as well. This explains why James, quoting Proverbs, wrote, "God resists the proud, but gives grace to the humble" (James 4:6). But if we will humble ourselves before God in all the crucibles of our lives, and if we will then allow the fire of His numinous love to melt all the self-images we have hammered out to exalt ourselves, instead honoring those through whom God would express His authority into our lives, then we will find grace for every circumstance. Then the meltdown of our pride in life's crucible can be transmuted into the pure gold of faith refined in the fire; and, in the end, we can come out of the craft shop of this life as vessels of honor fit for God's glory.

To honor God means both to submit to His authority and to exert His authority in the limited places in which He would use us. Scripture says that a man dishonors God when he prays or prophesies with his head covered (1 Cor. 11:4)—that is, when he refuses to stand in his place of uncovered authority and instead hides it under a covering of *false* humility and submission. True humility and submission prove absolutely essential, but false humility and submission only hurt and destroy. We can know when these are false because they always appear outside the order of God, misplaced, misdirected and usually trying to impress those enslaved to current social trends or whatever is currently politically correct. So we can, in short, master the appearance of humility without the substance.

Passivity also usually marks false humility and submission. Passivity dishonors God because it cuts off the provision of God's power from those who depend on us for their own covering. The pride in the heart of such a tattered covering prevents him from seeing the essential gift of God to him through those in authority sent by God; and so neither does such a person see the necessity of serving this gift of love to those to whom God would send *him*, even in his own family.

Only authentic humility and honor, then, are the channels through which God's power flows into our lives as we acknowledge our true relationship toward, and our total dependence upon, Him. When we recognize our true relationship to God, we will properly *value* God's authority in our lives. This means that we will honor those through whom God exerts His authority by seeking out their guidance (whether directly or otherwise) and following it in good conscience when it comes. Of course, it is possible to seek guidance as a false show of humility and then simply ignore it. But how can this profit anyone?

Peter said that to those who "believe," "the stone is *precious*," the same stone that to the disobedient became "the stone of stumbling, the rock of offense" (1 Pet. 2:7-8; Isa. 8:14; Rom. 9:33). God has laid in Zion a foundation stone, and they that put their *trust in Him*, rather than in themselves, shall not be put to shame. The New Testament clearly identifies this stone of stumbling, this Rock of offense, as Jesus Christ, God manifest in *human form*, the man who made God's abstract authority concrete and immediate (a less than welcome thought to the Pharisees). He therefore made all authority, though "unbacked by force," nonetheless inescapably present to us, thereby forcing us to either accept or reject it (Matt. 16:15-18; 1 Cor. 10:4).

Paul wrote that our relationship to God depends upon our relationship to this stone of stumbling, for how our lives line up to Jesus as the corner*stone* will determine whether we will stand as part of God's people: "Consequently, you're no longer foreigners and aliens but fellow citizens with God's people, members of God's household, built on the *foundation of the apostles and prophets*, with Jesus Christ Himself as the chief cornerstone" (Eph. 2:19-20). To be built up as part of God's household, we must plumb our lives to this cornerstone, to live our lives in line with the life of Jesus Christ; and this will occur by lining ourselves up with the authority of His Body, specifically "apostles and prophets" who are lined up to the cornerstone (see also 1 Cor. 12:28).

When Peter describes the stone as *precious* to those who believe, he uses the Greek word *timē* here translated as *precious*, which also means *honor*. It is the very word Jesus had used when declaring that a prophet is without honor in his hometown. This stone *is* precious. It *is* honored. But unbelief stops the power of God because without honor, without holding His Word as something valuable and "precious" but rather treating it as the common word that might come from anyone, no faith can unfold. Jesus could not do many miracles because they did not honor Him; His sacred Word was reduced in their hearts to something common. They "had no room for His Word" because they would not humble their own self-confident image and empty themselves of their own words and thoughts and ideas about how things should be. Because they were unwilling to honor Jesus, which would have required them to humble themselves before a mere "carpenter's son," who had no certification from the school of Hillel or Gamaliel, the miraculous power of God's grace could not move in their lives. For, again, "God resists the proud, but gives grace to the humble" (James 4:6).

To humble ourselves means to turn away from the self-confident arrogance in our hearts that would resist God's will. So instead of resisting His authority, we must count it as precious, as valuable beyond all measure. When we humble ourselves, we abase ourselves in the flesh so that He can exalt us in the Spirit. The familiarity and pride of the people of Nazareth prevented them from opening their hearts to the power of God's Word. They refused to humble themselves in order to honor Jesus' Word, to count it as "precious," as something of essential *value* to their lives. In contrast, grace could flow to the Syrophoenician woman because she counted His Word as more precious than her own image (Mark 7:24-30). Anyone humble enough to bow the knee to a carpenter and honor Him as precious, more precious than their own image, would receive the faith, and therefore the grace, that comes "from hearing, and hearing by the *word of God*," the Word, Paul said, "*we* preach" (Rom. 10:6-9, 14-17, NASV, KJV). As honor flows from us to God, as we fully value His sovereign authority over us, grace flows from God to us. Then His power and protection will meet all our needs, as well as those under our own authority and covering.

Honoring of Parents

Scripture shows that God's claims to sovereignty over our lives, as well as His worthiness to receive honor, rest upon His Creatorship (Ps. 24:1-2; 100:3; Rev. 4:11). He made us, and so we are His possession (Ps. 100:3; Mal. 3:17). He is our Father, our Origin. Therefore we honor Him (Mal. 1:6). When a child comes into this world, he obviously receives his physical life through his parents. They are the agents of God's authorship of the child's life. As authors, parents therefore rightly have the greatest earthly authority (within limits defined by God's Word) over children.

This authority, however, differs radically from the authority of compulsion based on brute force. We face, in other words, a choice between two authorities—one rooted in love and one rooted in force. So, on the basis of this distinction, Scripture admonishes children to honor their parents and obey them in everything (Eph. 6:1-3; Col. 3:20). By honoring their parents as the immediate source of their physical existence, children honor the God of love, the ultimate Source of their lives. By honoring their parents, children set the pattern for that proper relationship with God through which He can transform them into His image. Only if children truly honor their parents will they allow their parents to disciple them to God's ways. The children can then hope to enter into that proper relationship with God through faith in Christ, a relationship that constitutes salvation. The nature and form of Christ will be infused into their souls, and so all the aspects of Christian character can come forth in their lives. Because authority makes possible training and teaching, and because only honor avails us of *benevolent* authority, only when children truly honor their parents can they be trained up and educated in the way they should go. Only when children honestly venerate and revere their parents can parental discipline prove fully effective. Otherwise, it will merely seem to the children to come as an external imposition. So without honor in the children's hearts, godly character will never be imparted to them. Unless real honor resides in their hearts and souls, when children reach maturity they will merely flee parental (and all other godly) authority. In general, unless people submit in honor for those in authority, God's purpose for authority cannot be fulfilled. The devil's chief business is therefore to preclude or destroy honor, which he has been overtly or covertly at work doing since he tempted Adam and Eve in the garden by slandering God as a hypocrite (Gen. 3:1-5).

If, then, true honor is instilled in the child's heart, all else that pertains to good character will flow forth also. If children really hold honor in their hearts, they will seek and desire to please God, their parents and others worthy of honor. If parents fail to instill genuine honor by first humbling themselves in their own conceits and then exemplifying their honor for those God has sent to them, then all of their efforts will prove fruitless. As already stated, the foundational importance of honor can be seen in Paul's discussion of the fifth commandment: "Honor your father and your mother, as Yahweh your God has commanded you, *so that you may live long and that it may go well with you in the land Yahweh your God is giving you*" (Deut. 5:16; Exod. 20:12; Eph. 6:2). To repeat, Paul calls this "the *first* commandment with a promise" (Eph. 6:2), clearly establishing the primacy of honor as foundational in our relationship with God. To even quote this scripture is to discover the promise: our parents (whether natural or spiritual) are God's most basic form of authority in our lives;

and if we honor them, we will receive life. To receive life is to receive God. To receive God is to receive salvation. Life speaks of wholeness, consistency, cohesiveness and oneness, in contrast to death, which speaks of fragmentation, division, disintegration and decomposition. The promise is that the child who honors his parents will receive "long *life*" and that he will enter into and enjoy the fullness of his inheritance. Spiritually, this means that the child will grow into maturity in the exercise of all of his spiritual gifts and talents and also in the fruit of God's Spirit. So here we see how foundational honor truly is—through it, we enter into all the fullness of our salvation, into the complete fulfillment of our spiritual inheritance of our place in God's kingdom.

We can now look into how honor brings these spiritual riches. How exactly do wholeness and life flow forth from honor? We have repeatedly seen salvation as wholeness.* Only when we honor can we enter into the wholeness of salvation, for only when we honor can we obey from the heart, can we serve God and His authorities with our whole being. Obedience without honor can never be wholehearted. This is why, to repeat, honor avails us of benevolent authority, which in turn brings us into training or discipleship. So if we honor our parents, we will have respect for their authority and submit ourselves to that authority—not only outwardly but also in our hearts. And from this heartfelt submission, parental discipline becomes effectual in molding character. Merely raw, external control does not have the power to bring lasting change, but if the child honors his parents, then he knows that disobedience will elicit not only punishment but also his parents' displeasure and grief. And because he is spurred from his heart by his honor of his parents, he seeks to please them. Because of the honor the child holds for them, their discipline brings a true change of heart in the child.

How Love Comes Down to Us

William Gouge, in a book that served as the principle child-rearing manual for the early colonial settlers in America, said that "love is weighty, and, as weighty things, it descendeth."[9] How does love *descend*, how does it come *down* to us? One way it does so is through discipline: "Those whom the Lord loves He disciplines" (Heb. 12:6). So love brings discipline, and because we *honor* our parents, we thankfully receive their discipline. Indeed, *honor* in Hebrew is the word *kavod*, "weightiness," which derives from the verb *kaved*, meaning "to be heavy," that is, something of weighty importance or even something negative and burdensome. To honor someone is to highly esteem their discipline of love. We honor them by recognizing in our hearts the tremendous importance that their

---

* See *The Quest for Salvation*.

correction and guidance have for us. We value and desire it, even though it may temporarily bring us pain (Heb. 12:11). But we know this pain is the pain of cleansing so that we may experience God's life rather than merely strutting as whited sepulchers, appearing clean on the outside but inwardly full of dead men's bones, destined only for eternal death.

Because weighty things move *down* rather than merely float on the surface, we can receive them only by *lowering* ourselves. Self-confidence and conceit lift us above every good and perfect gift, including love. In fact, they so blind us to the good God would give us from others that we don't even see what we might be missing. But if we abase ourselves, we can look up from that lowly position to suddenly see and receive the descending grace of God. We can recognize it, then, as more important, of greater weight and substance, than ourselves, our own ambitions, plans, thoughts, ideas, hopes, desires. By recognizing it as more important than ourselves, we truly honor it and can hope to receive it. Precisely because God's authority manifests itself into our lives through human flesh, we can always find excuses to *not* honor His authority, just as Korah rejected the authority of Moses (Jude 8-11). Korah stood against Moses and Aaron and said, "You take too much upon yourselves, for all the congregation is holy, every one of them, and Yahweh is among them. Why then do you exalt yourselves above the congregation of Yahweh?" (Num. 16:3). Even though it was God who had "exalted" Moses and manifested His authority through this imperfect man, Korah thought in his own heart he could claim equality. Rather than honoring Moses as the vessel of God's authority, Korah instead looked at and found occasion to judge Moses as a mere man, while he secretly envied Moses' gifts and authority. Although the whole congregation was to indeed be holy, as Korah claimed, nonetheless, God had established a special form and order of authority within the congregation, beginning with Moses. By honoring this authority, Korah would have honored not merely human flesh but God. Therefore, when he rebelled against and judged the man Moses, God judged Korah as a rebel against God's own purposes. Because God manifested His authority through the familiarity of human flesh, Korah allowed that familiarity to breed contempt. Yet how else *would* the God who is love manifest Himself *to human beings* made in His own image and with whom He desires to enter into personal relationship *except through the human form*? While He desires to have a direct relationship with each of us through His Spirit, it is only through His indwelling love abiding in other people that He can *fully* extend His authority tangibly and abidingly into our lives in an orderly way that touches us with His discipling love and brings us into a kingdom larger than ourselves, teaching *us* to learn to love. The love of the Father thus unites us into the *corporate* Body of Christ, the *community* of the kingdom built by the Father's own love.

Jesus similarly admonished us not to allow ourselves to find a cause of offense in Him (Matt. 11:6). Jesus, the prophet like unto Moses (Deut. 18:18), became an offense to those who rejected Him for the same reason Korah found Moses offensive: because Jesus expressed *in human flesh* the authority of the Father, and they resented or envied Him for it (Mark 15:9-11). And just as Korah held Moses' God-ordained authority in contempt, insisting that Moses stood as a mere man to whom all other men were equal, so the people of Nazareth dismissed Jesus because of His familiarity to them: "Isn't this the carpenter's son? Don't we know His sisters and brothers?" Isn't He, in other words, just a mere man like us? They took His humanity as an occasion to find offense, seizing upon this fleshly familiarity as an excuse to fail to render the honor due Him. Jesus seemed to possess such wisdom and supernatural power, they admitted, but they still refused to receive Him because of the familiarity of human flesh (Matt. 13:54-58).

Moreover, God did absolutely nothing to make it easier for their flesh to receive His authority. God didn't manifest Himself as a great political ruler, as a learned scholar, as an amazing athlete, as a prestigious religious figure, but as a carpenter and the son of a carpenter. He didn't want to leave any room for people to exalt themselves by taking pride in the human nature or carnal accomplishments of the man they followed. There was *nothing* desirable or attractive about Jesus' flesh to them (Isa. 53:2). God did this because He wanted them to abase their flesh, to humble themselves completely, to crush their own pride; and they could only do this by abasing themselves through the honor and love they bestowed upon a plain man through whom God had manifested the fullness of His authority.

This is the stone that causes men to stumble, the stone the builders rejected, the Rock of offense (Ps. 118:22-23; Isa. 8:14-15; 1 Pet. 2:4-8). The offense lies in that the Rock, the eternal Spirit, has chosen to be laid as a baby in a manger, to work as a carpenter from Nazareth, to scandalously die as a man falsely condemned for criminal activity and hung in abject humiliation on a cross. The offense is that God lived, suffered and died as not merely a man but a despised and rejected man. Yet this man was offensive precisely because the authority that He manifested did not exalt human flesh but rather only exalted the Spirit. Those who rejected Him did so because He did not come in His own name, that is, He did not come with an image that would puff up the flesh of His followers and enable them to boast in themselves and their religion. Instead, He came in the name of another, in the name of the Father, manifesting the fullness of the Father's authority, an authority that even while *in* the flesh was not *of* flesh but of the Spirit.

People today still stumble at this Rock of offense. Just as did Korah in

Moses' time and the Pharisees of Jesus' day, so do most today come face to face with their own pride when the authority "from above" expresses itself through lowly human flesh. Although Jesus has ascended on high, His authority still resides *in His people* (Eph. 4:7-16). God "reconciled" man "to Himself through Christ," but now He has given believers "the ministry of reconciliation," "making His appeal through" His people (2 Cor. 5:18-20). So He has commissioned and ordained a Body through which to manifest His very Being, and His Being remains inseparable from His spiritual authority. He has sent forth His people, a people in whom He dwells by His Spirit, embodying Himself within them. The word *sent*, *apostello* in the New Testament Greek, used frequently to refer to those delegated to carry God's authority (1 Cor. 4:17; Acts 15:27), is the same word used to refer to Jesus Himself, who was *sent*, *apostello*, by the Father (John 5:36). This word means not merely one sent as a messenger but one *commissioned* with and hence embodying in his own person a *directly* delegated authority. Jesus said to believers, "He who receives you receives Me, and he who receives Me receives the one who *sent* Me" (Matt. 10:40); and to the Father He prayed, "Just as You *sent* Me into the world, I also have *sent* them into the world" (John 17:18, Ampl.). Jesus sends His Body with the authority to bind and to loose, the power that He held to set the captives free (Matt. 16:19; Luke 4:18; Eph. 4:8-13). We can only believe the Word of God by hearing the word of one sent (*apostello*) by God, one directly sent and commissioned to speak God's Word to us (Rom. 10:15). Those so commissioned constitute the members of His Body.

As seen above, to submit to such an authority invested in common human flesh demands an abasement of self that offers no fleshly rewards. On the contrary, it demands nullifying the "things that are," of which Paul spoke. It demands, in short, a humbling of self that negates all the pride of the flesh. To truly honor another man as being sent from God, as not having achieved his influence and position from any human strivings and achievements or institutions but only from the will and anointing of God, ends all the competitive strivings through which the flesh seeks to exalt itself and ascend to a usurped place of authority. It necessitates the recognition that this authority comes through the abasement of flesh and therefore that those who submit must themselves follow this same course. This explains why true godly authority invested in common human flesh remains a stumbling stone to most, for to *truly* honor another man as being sent from God demands such total self-abasement. The fallen nature, then, submits to authority only when it somehow finds the origin and source of that authority, the ultimate author of the authority, in the fallen nature itself. This is why it ultimately will only submit to the coercive authority of brute force that always ends up as a malevolent authority. In the light of this understanding, honoring God's order of authority "sent from above" becomes not oppressive but the gateway of escape from bondage to the sinful nature and the entranceway to eternal life.

The universal rebellion against any noncoercive authority that comes "from above" has always intermittently spent its fury against parental and church authority, continually attempting to demolish the order of the family and the church. Yet this demolition has never led to the liberation of either the child or the believer from all externally imposed structure and order. Rather, such a demolition must lead to the substitution of an alternative structure and order that defines and shapes both the child's and the adult's life. For, as shown extensively elsewhere,* no culture can avoid some social order or another. And, ultimately, the social and even economic order greatly determine how people in any given community will live and work with one another, what their attitudes toward one another and toward truth and deity will be, how authority will be exercised in that society, how decisions will be made and so on. The central question concerning authority in any culture or society, then, isn't whether or not there will be an order, but which order?† In the Biblical view, the

---

* See *Loved into Loving*.

† For believers, but also for many others, this becomes a question of whether the order is generated and created by human beings or by God. The culture's answer to this central question touches every aspect of social life. For the kind of social or political or economic order that exists in a particular community or culture—and therefore the underlying values that order is rooted in—will shape all the relationships (and values) within that community or culture. For example, the answer to this question will determine whether the elderly will have a venerable position in society, with their judgments widely respected and followed, or whether their children will shunt them aside in ritual death (as with some "native" peoples) or into separated compounds (such as in today's old-age 'homes'), where most in their economically and socially busy lives will take scarcely any substantive notice of them at all. The answer will further determine whether youth will be considered a time for learning, or if the young will set the basic trends and patterns for society as a whole.

For instance, a technologically progressive culture—one that depends on the mastery of ever new techniques and gadgets—will tend toward dependency on youth, even exalting youth, since such a culture depends on the energy of youth to master all those ever new techniques and technologies, all of which must constantly ensue if economic (or even, for some, military) survival for the whole culture is to be achieved. Or, finally, we may ask if age will simply be ignored and all individuals reduced to a more or less static equality before some all-powerful "equalizer" in the form of a total State, regardless of those differences among individuals in experience, knowledge and wisdom, which, among some peoples, have been identified with differences in age (at least previous to the generation that insisted on worshiping youth and abdicating adulthood). Regardless of which alternative is chosen, some order of social relationships must mark any community, at least unless the whole society is collapsing (or has already collapsed) into anarchy and chaos.

A community's view of age is, of course, only one way it may at least partially arrange the social order that shapes it into a certain configuration or image. Other examples arise from its attitudes toward work, economy, authority, property, sex, violence, physical abilities, mental aptitudes and so on (as well as other aspects or qualities of human life). Yet what forms the basis by which a community will evaluate and order these characteristics and others? And how will the relationships between its members consequently arrange themselves? Will it merely be an accident, or will some cultural motif insinuate itself into the arrangement or actually be chosen? The answers to such questions will not only affect

family is presented as the most basic unit of this order of authority.* This family order, to the extent that it is not confused and adulterated by surrounding expressions of a desacralized culture, expresses an authority given from above, an authority the legitimacy of which lies in the nature of parenthood itself: the child comes into an order that he does nothing to ordain, establish or even select (although as he matures, he must decide whether he'll remain within it). Everything has been given to him from above, and so he cannot exalt himself within the family order insofar as he submits to it. The submission of a child to a parent has thus, since at least the time of ancient Ur and, later, of Plato's Republic on down to Nazi Germany and Stalinist Russia, embodied the rock of offense to all those authorities who seek to exalt themselves above any authority transcendent to themselves. This explains why children in increasingly dysfunctional cultures today are taught in government schools to "question authority," particularly parental and church authority, and even to report (as was also the case in both Nazi Germany and Stalin's Russia) any parental discipline of children and to assert their rights as children against their father and mother. Such cultures have demeaned the name of fatherhood in every respect, for fatherhood represents an authority above and beyond those subject to it. Fatherhood places the origins of the child, and therefore the ultimate basis for authority, outside the child (Eph. 3:14-15, Ampl.).

Yet what does this rejection of parental authority "free" children to achieve? Children who reject any order that *they* did not choose, such as a submitted relationship to the parents who begot them, are the very ones who continually fall under the peer influence of fads, fashions, heroes and stars that promise to exalt their adherents but in the end merely strip them of all true integrity and identity in God and devastate their bodies, minds and souls. A child, or an adult, who can honor nothing but that which derives from himself in the end never stands exalted but always dissipated, deflated and desolate. Yet he who abases himself with true

---

but also finally determine such ultimately important matters as the exercise of authority and freedom of conscience. It is readily apparent that the way in which any community evaluates these characteristics and then arranges itself will transmit essential, if often unconscious and therefore unarticulated, information to shape its members' views of how they should regard themselves. It will also determine how they regard all the relationships that they form—even how they regard truth and God.

Obviously, for a people who dare to identify themselves as Christ's own Body, the community's attitudes towards all of these matters should ideally be shaped by the Head, who is Christ. And consequently, the relationships concomitant with these attitudes must also be set by Him—not by the ever-shifting fashions of a desacralized world, or even by merely humanly rooted traditions and institutions that have taken God's place as the guiding force in human lives. It is therefore assumed that in Christian community these attitudes and relationships should all be arranged in Christ's Body in such a way as to express God's sovereignty, nature and authority.

* Gen. 2:24; 3:16; 12:3; Exod. 20:12, 14; Mal. 2:14-16; Mark 7:10; 1 Cor. 11:3; Eph. 5:22-33; 6:1-3.

honor before those whom God has sent, those who come in the name of the Lord, will find that authority from above lifting him up above those illusions and deceptions that trap all who find offense in any and every expression of noncoercive authority from above. Anyone coming in the name of the Father, deriving his authority from a lineage *above*, and anyone who submits to and honors such a person stands diametrically opposed to the spirit of an age that will receive only authority certified by "democratic" power, literally, power of the "rule of the people," a rule from below.

The basis of the true honor of God's authority must then extend beyond an assessment of the *perfection* of God's vessel and move on to an acute awareness of God's *ordination* of that vessel. God has established an order of relationships, and respect for that order must ultimately rest on our honor of God. Yet even though God has established this order of love's rule, those who exercise authority are also themselves still *being* perfected. This means that even though they should be more spiritually mature than those who submit to them, those in authority won't be perfect. A child, then, must honor his parents not because of their perfection but because this divine order has set the parents' place as the covering for their child through the vested authority of God. A young child will rarely question the givens of this order, but as he grows (and especially if he has been subjected to propaganda and indoctrination from sources of information opposed to parental authority, such as have flowed through the media and public education systems of increasingly secular but dysfunctional modern nations) the temptation can arise to question the very basis of parental authority. Yet if a parent should fail in some particular action, the child still has no grounds for dishonor, for his honor should remain grounded in the parents' *place* in God's order. A submission on this basis will perfect the child even if the parents' obedience to God might be lacking. God will honor the child's submission, and He will also deal with the parents. The child should not rebel, for divine order is not of his choosing but God's. So only God can change it. Therefore, in submitting to God's order, the child truly honors God by honoring his parents.

Such a radical honor has grown virtually extinct in today's postmodern culture with its radical and indiscriminate egalitarianism, which so often has amounted to little more than leveling all human beings to the lowest common denominator of dust before an apotheosized State. Few in today's generation can even conceive of an honor such as that exhibited by Naaman's servants toward him when he struggled with humbling himself before God. Naaman was a man of high position in the Syrian army. When the prophet ordered him to dip seven times in the Jordan, he lost control to a rage witnessed by all his soldiers and servants. They could have secretly laughed and murmured to themselves, "It's about time someone put that big shot in his place." Yet because they remained loyal to him in his shame, humiliation and confusion, because they kept *chesed** in good conscience before God and truly honored him in their hearts, they could speak a humble word of encouragement and faith to him. They thus became instruments through whom God redeemed him, instruments as essential as the prophet of Israel who spoke the words for healing. Through their faithful honoring, Naaman not only found healing but also the God of his salvation as well (2 Kings 5:15).

Never more than in our own day, then, has it been so vital for all who would serve God to recognize that a genuine confession of Jesus as Lord necessitates looking up to expressions of tangible authority *above* ourselves that come to us in diverse ways. Jesus said, "No one has ever gone up to heaven; but there is *One Who has come down* from heaven, the Son of man" (John 3:13, Ampl.). The One who came from *above* has been sent *down*, has condescended, to robe Himself in human flesh. He manifested His "grace" in that "though He was rich," for our "sakes He became poor, so that . . . through His poverty" we "might become rich" (2 Cor. 8:9). He condescended, *descended* from His heavenly position, to come together *with* man that we might be lifted up to dwell in heavenly places with Him.

> Since the children have flesh and blood, He too shared in their humanity so that by His death He might destroy him who holds the power of death—that is, the devil—and free those who all their lives were held in slavery by their fear of death . . . . For this reason He had to be made like His brothers in every way. (Heb. 2:14-15, 17)

Jesus took this lowly place so that He might become "the firstborn among many brothers" (Rom. 8:29). These brothers, filled with His Spirit and made to sit in heavenly places (Eph. 2:5-6), themselves become the embodiment of that authority "from *above*" which now resides and manifests itself through them. In John 6, Jesus said, "I am the bread that came down from heaven," and "unless you eat the flesh of the Son of man and drink His blood, you have no life in you . . . . Just as the living Father sent Me and I live because of the Father, so the one who feeds on Me will live because of Me. This is the bread that *came down* from heaven" (John 6:41, 53, 57-58). In response to these deeply spiritual words, the multitude of disciples grumbled. To this grumbling, Jesus responded, "Does this offend you? What if you see the Son of Man ascend to where He was before?" (John 6:61-62). Yet how could it possibly offend the disciples that the Son of Man would "ascend to where He was before"? Because when "He ascended on high, He . . . gave gifts to men," the gifts of

---

*The Hebrew word *chesed* means that they kept their covenant obligations (to their master) with loving faithfulness. See also pp. 107-108, 253-254 and the section "Merciful" under "Kindness and Generosity/Meanness and Greed."

"apostles, . . . prophets, . . . evangelists, . . . pastors and teachers . . . for the perfecting of the saints" (Eph. 4:8, 11-12, NIV, KJV). In other words, the offense of Jesus' ascent to His position of supreme authority lay in His delegation of divine authority to those commissioned by His Spirit to manifest that authority on earth. Once this delegation has been made, to receive the One who sent Jesus, we must receive those flesh-and-blood vessels whom He has in turn sent to us. We can only look up to Him by humbling ourselves and looking up through mere human flesh into the divine visage that peers down to us through our brothers coming in God's own benevolent authority. To do this, we must lower ourselves in order to honor the human flesh that carries the *anointing* of God's direct and personal authority, the fleshly vessels through which the Spirit from above comes down to manifest Himself. Because the authority residing in such fleshly vessels is not the authority of the flesh but of the Spirit, to follow such people necessitates that we humble our own flesh before God. It means that we can no longer "love God" as a mere abstraction, a distant entity conformed to our own ideas. We must rather now submit to the human authority through which God manifests His own authority and conform ourselves to that noncoercive authority which expresses the authority of the Spirit. It means that we can no longer take the blessings of God without giving the honor that compels us to acknowledge something weightier than ourselves, that we must lower ourselves and look up to an authority coming from a God more important than ourselves, than our images, than our ideals, than our philosophies and beliefs.

To truly honor God, then, means to give up our authority over our own lives. It means breaking the Adamic nature of rebellion against an authority that would assert itself over us not for the purpose of exalting human flesh but to truly exalt God. There is nothing desirable to our flesh in this stone because the stone opposes pride, the great enemy of God that resides in each of us. We will find nothing in Him for our flesh and pride to glory in because He came to conquer pride. This is why He opposes the proud but gives grace to the humble (James 4:6), to those who abase themselves in order to honor Him, as the Syrophoenician woman did.

When we abase ourselves to honor Jesus as Lord, we lower ourselves, acknowledging the true extent of our need before God. By thus lowering ourselves, we place ourselves in a position to receive the weightiness of His descending love from heaven. Then we recognize the words that He speaks to us through others as being not mere human words but, as they are, the very words of God (1 Thess. 2:13). Then when someone whom God has sent speaks to us, we will honor his words, we will esteem those words as themselves weighty, as valuable, as of life-giving importance. Paul wrote that we should not say that we will "ascend into heaven" "to bring Christ down," nor that we will "descend into the abyss" "to bring Christ up from the dead" (Rom. 10:6-7). Jesus has already risen from the abyss and "ascended far above all the heavens, that He might fill all things" and so give "gifts to men," namely the gifts of "apostles," "prophets," "evangelists," "pastors and teachers" (Eph. 4:8-11). In the very passage in Romans 10 where Paul dismisses trying to descend or ascend to find *Christ*, he immediately reminds us that "the *word* is near you, even in your mouth and in your heart (that is, the word of faith which *we* preach)" (Rom. 10:8, NKJV, KJV). So our salvation comes neither through the Christ in the heavens, nor through the Christ in the abyss, but from the Christ whose will must be done *on earth* as it is in heaven, the Christ speaking through the "word of faith which *we* preach," that is, the words preached by those whom God has "sent" as gifts for the "perfecting of the saints" (Eph. 4:12; Rom. 10:15). True belief comes, then, only when we receive the preaching of those *whom He has sent* (Rom. 10:14-15). When we recognize Him in the authority coming to us through human flesh, we will value His Word, honor it, esteem it, cherish it and conform our lives to it. But when self fills our lives, no room remains for His Word, and so we cannot receive it. If, however, we open our hearts and abase ourselves, acknowledging our need's fullest depth and extent, then we will honor and value His Word and receive in faith not only but even also especially the "weighty word" (Jer. 23:29) that descends as the discipline of the Lord.

Reverential Fear: The Beginning of Wisdom

As said, discipline brings forth reverential restraint.* In regard to our parents, this includes reverential fear of eliciting their displeasure. This reverence instilled in our children must be mixed with, and can only be produced by, great love. Children should in all things *desire* to please and loathe to offend. The true fear of God in turn helps to strengthen (and even forms the basis of) honor; it differs from the fear of a slave, for a child's fear is mixed with love and awe toward his parents. It therefore has respect to the *offense* to the parent, while a slave's fear, ordinarily mixed with resentment or even hatred, has respect only for the punishment. The former corresponds to the fear of a saint for God. Gouge expressed the necessary interrelation of love and fear:

> So entire and so ardent is parents' *affection* towards their children, as it would make children too bold and insolent if there were not *authority* mixed therewith to work fear: and so supreme and absolute is their *authority* . . . it would make children . . . dread their parents, if a fatherly *affection* were not tempered therewith to breed *love*. But both these joined together make a very good composition:

---

* See *Forming Christ's Body, Book Three* by Blair Adams (Elm Mott, Tex.: Colloquium Press, 1977, 1993).

love like [honey] sweeteneth fear, and fear like salt seasoneth love [preserving it] . . . . This *fear* keeps love in compass and *restrains* [the] child from over much *sauciness*, and [*boldness*].[10]

Such a "fear" keeps love from breaking out of the bounds of its proper form and thus from seeping out, dissipating and evaporating. This is why Scripture speaks of such fear as "the beginning of wisdom." But fear can only serve as wisdom's *beginning*, not its end. Love is the end. So without redemptive love, all relationships must fail.

In any case, to sow and cultivate this reverential fear requires both informing children of the place and authority of their parents (that is, that parents stand in God's stead as God's ministers) and discipling them to stand in their place before God. As said, children must understand how they have received the very substance of their lives from the substance of their parents. So again, honor of parents honors God Himself, the ultimate Source and Origin, the ultimate "Parent" (Prov. 23:22; 1 Pet. 1:23, TEV; see also John 1:12-13; 1 John 5:1). Because parents stand in submission to God in a place of authority over children ("in the Lord")—because, that is, children see parental authority resting on God's authority—the loathing to incur parental displeasure becomes a fear of God's displeasure.

So a child's honor cannot end with parents; ultimate honor rests on God. This is the meaning of Ephesians 6:1—"Children, obey your parents *in the Lord*." Why must they obey parents? Because of the parents' *place*—"in the Lord." God forbids all obedience that causes disobedience to Him (Acts 4:19-20). Parents who counter this no longer themselves stand "in the Lord." Yet in Mark 7:11, Jesus rebukes the Pharisees' precepts that render void God's commandment for children to honor and obey their parents. (Here we also see that honor involves meeting a material and physical need as well as maintaining a reverent attitude—see also Prov. 3:9; 1 Tim. 5:4, 8, 16. The Scriptures also tell that we should express such honor towards the elders of the church: 1 Tim. 5:17-18; 1 Cor. 9:11-12; Gal. 6:6.) So no child can forsake a parent apart from an unbending opposition that demands choosing either Christ or the parent. If clinging to parents would draw them from Christ, then children must choose Christ. When children see their obedience to parents as expressing obedience to God and that reverential fear of parental displeasure becomes reverence for God, then they are well on their way to becoming true disciples of Christ. To see this connection between the fear instilled by parental discipline and the fear of the Lord means seeing (although yet more remains to be seen) why the Scriptures tie honor of parents to long life. For the scripture declares "the *fear* of Yahweh [as] a fountain of *life*, turning a man from the snares of *death*" (Prov. 14:27). So, since honoring parents provides the channel of impartation for the fear of the Lord, and the fear of the Lord springs up into a fountain of life, honoring parents brings long life, as the fifth commandment promises. But *how* exactly does the fear of the Lord give rise to life?

What does such a fear cause a child to do? A child's fear of parental displeasure can cause him to hesitate at the thought of conduct incurring that displeasure. Fear will cause the child "to look again," to think twice. *Respect* means literally "to look again." We cannot truly honor someone without respect. The child must have enough consideration to "look again" to his parents by looking beyond the immediacy of his own thoughts, distractions and self-interests. A sensitivity to his parents' attitudes, needs, wants, commands and so on must develop in him. Respect, then, proves impossible without reverential fear. The primary meaning of the Hebrew word *yare*, which is translated "respect" in Leviticus 19:3, is "to fear."

The child only learns "the fear of the Lord" by learning to fear doing evil because he knows it results in discipline. The fear of the Lord is to "depart from evil" (Prov. 3:7, KJV). Therefore, to punish a child for wrongdoing not only teaches but *trains* him to "depart from evil" and thereby establishes the child in the fear of the Lord, that is, "in the way he should go" (Prov. 22:6). Parents cannot simply pray for this and then sit back, passively hoping that God will somehow make their children revere Him, counting on others to step in and do what they've failed to do. The Bible speaks much of the supernatural and miraculous but speaks nothing positive about the realm of magic. Rather, God works "*in us* to *will* and to *do*." Yes, God works "*in us*," but *we* still must "*will* and *do*" according to the work of His Spirit and grace. According to the Bible, we have an active role in seeing "the fear of the Lord" rooted in our children's lives (Prov. 22:6).

Scripture further describes the fear of Yahweh as the beginning also of *knowledge* (Prov. 1:7). So you cannot hope to teach your child to *know* right and wrong (or anything else) if no fear of God takes root in him through discipline. A child remains unteachable in the ways of right and wrong without a fear to do wrong. The Bible describes the fear of the Lord as "to depart from evil" because a child departs from evil when he fears the discipline of love that will come to him if he succumbs to evil.

The Bible declares the fear of Yahweh as "the *beginning* of wisdom" (Ps. 111:10) because fear of discipline motivates a child to *begin* to hear his father's instructions. But the *end* of wisdom resides in the fullness of Christ's love, and "there is no fear in love. But perfect love drives out fear, because fear has to do with punishment" (1 John 4:18). This same passage of Scripture goes on to say that "this is love for God: to obey His commands" (1 John 5:3). In other words, perfect love eludes us if we do not keep His commandments. Therefore, the fear of Yahweh, which "has to do with punishment" for wrongdoing, gives us the hearing ear of a "wise son" (Prov. 13:1), a hearing that brings us into perfect obedience and perfect love. This love stands as the *end* of wisdom. But where we fall short, we must "begin" again to both hear and obey by loving God's discipline and the "fear of the Lord" it brings.

The foundation of discipline doesn't lie in teaching masses of isolated rules and regulations, although children need a clear pattern of conduct. Rather, we can lay such a foundation by teaching children to respect godly authority and to promptly obey their parents as well as all those who express God's noncoercive authority. That is, they must come into proper *relationship* to God-given authority expressing the lordship of love.

To impart this knowledge—that obedience to and honor of godly authority constitutes the most basic ethical imperative of their lives— becomes the first stage in discipleship. So this also constitutes the *primary* goal of child-rearing; and the Bible straightforwardly admonishes not only the use of corporal discipline to drive folly away from a child but also its use to instill the first step in developing wisdom, that is, knowledge (Prov. 10:13; 26:3; 22:15).

Once the necessity of obedience to God's authority takes root, the child can learn greater sensitivity in hearing paternal instruction, and then real understanding of the reasons for and the nature of the patterns of God will begin to grow. But to attempt to instill this understanding prior to a foundation of honor and obedience will prove futile, exhausting, self-defeating and faith-destroying. Only when the individual develops understanding can he then move on to the level of true wisdom to become a living proclamation of the truth of God's Word.*

The foregoing discussion shows that the *fountain* of all duty only profitably springs up from a deep inward disposition of heart compounded of both *love and reverence*. Of course, anyone can fear without loving, but can we love without fearing? The recognition of love surely must precede the ability to love (1 John 4:19). And to recognize love, must we not respect it, standing ready "to look again" at it? The Song of Solomon describes love as a young deer on a hillside: we must walk with due respect and sensitivity or love will flee. Fear of evoking love's displeasure and consequent flight accomplishes this. And whereas love and favor descend ultimately from God to us, fear and honor and submission ascend ultimately from us to God. So for love to descend, honor must first ascend.

If the child has respect for his parents in this sense, he will learn silence at appropriate times. Of course, at other times it is certainly appropriate for

---

*See *Wisdom's Children, Book Two* by Blair Adams (Elm Mott, Tex.: Colloquium Press, 1982, 1989).

children to speak, but a general pattern of quietness and deference should prevail. Silence will augment the child's opportunity to listen for the voice of his parents; and listening is the obvious prerequisite to hearing: you cannot consistently hear unless you listen. Hearing is in turn the obvious prerequisite of obeying: you must hear to obey. Indeed, the word in the Greek New Testament, *hupakouo*, generally translated as "obey," means literally "to come under the hearing of." By instilling all of the characteristics thus far described, parents can teach the child sensitivity to the parental voice and will, with the ultimate goal being the child's sensitivity to the voice and will of God. Of course, the parents' own sensitivity to God encourages the child's sensitivity—as Jesus said, the student can only rise to the level of his teacher (Luke 6:40). But if the parental example teaches the child reverence, respect, silence, attentiveness and obedience to God's will, the child will have an easier time being sensitive to his parent's will and, in turn, to God's will. Thus does the child's discipleship to his parents teach him to listen for, to hear and to obey God's voice. To hear our natural father's voice (Prov. 13:1) teaches us to hear our heavenly Father's, since the one fatherhood derives from the other (Eph. 3:14-15).

So hearing and obeying brings us to wisdom, since only a "wise" son "hears" (Prov. 13:1). Wisdom shows how all things consist or hold together.* This wisdom from God opposes the detached, fragmented knowledge of the Fall, which leads only to death. Scripture makes plain this counterposition between wisdom and death when personified wisdom proclaims in Proverbs 8:36, KJV, "They that hate me love death." So wisdom counterposes death, but it also constitutes the very means to life. Life comes through coherence and wholeness, which only God's wisdom can bring. But, again, only he who *hears* his father's instruction attains to wisdom (Prov. 13:1).

So we can see exactly how a child's honoring of his father and mother can bring him long life: honor lies at the base of God's effective exercise of authority in our lives; authority stands at the foundation of discipline; and discipline in turn becomes the basis of the life that love brings. So, *when authority is motivated by love, it brings a discipline to bear upon the child to mold him into God's image. This discipline then brings reverential fear, fear respect, respect silence, silence listening, listening hearing, hearing obedience, obedience wisdom and wisdom life.* Thus does the fountain of life spring forth from reverential fear and wisdom (Prov. 14:27). These characteristics constitute, as later pages show, the qualities of honor. If our child fails in any of these aspects, he fails to honor his parents, or whatever other authority has been set over him by God.

We can also see here why Solomon could conclude:

---

* See *Wisdom's Children, Book Two.*

> Now all has been heard; *here is the conclusion of the matter: Fear God and keep His commandments, for this is the whole duty of man.* For God will bring every deed into judgment, including every hidden thing, whether it is good or evil. (Eccles. 12:13-14)

If we truly teach our children—in the love of God—to reverence Him, then they will fulfill their whole duty to God. Truly, "the fear of Yahweh is the *beginning* of *wisdom*" (Prov. 9:10). When children honor parents, any parental discipline will only serve to impart to children those characteristics that in turn allow the impartation of God's life to them and make them vessels through whom that life can be imparted to others.

a. Respecting, Reverencing and Honoring Parents

We have described honor as the foundation of character for our children to build upon: "the *first* commandment with promise." Their training begins with respect, reverence and honor shown towards their parents.

> Each of you *must respect his mother and father*, and you must observe My Sabbaths. I am Yahweh your God. (Lev. 19:3)

> For God said, "*Honor your father and mother.*" (Matt. 15:4)

> "*Honor your father and mother*"—which is the first commandment with a promise—"that it may go well with you and that you may enjoy long life on the earth." (Eph. 6:2-3)

The Greek word translated as "honor" is *timao*, which means "to value." To honor our parents means to recognize their true value in our lives, measuring that value according to all we've discussed in previous pages. The following scriptures describe honor largely in terms of the child's direct relationship with his parents. In many respects, however, a child most honors his parents by his witness to others of his relationship with his parents; he truly honors his parents even when they are not present, when the reality of what he is actually becoming in his character, work habits and so on shows in his life apart from any outward appearances he may assume in order to avoid detection of his true but hidden character. How does the child behave in the absence of parental supervision? This truly tests the honor in his heart, for this reveals whether he has allowed their discipline and love to change him inwardly rather than merely superficially.

Clearly, then, in obedience to God's command, our children must honor their parents.

> Noah, a man of the soil, proceeded to plant a vineyard. When he drank some of its wine, he became drunk and lay uncovered inside his tent. Ham, the father of Canaan, saw his father's nakedness and told his two brothers outside. But Shem and Japheth took a garment and laid it across their shoulders; then they walked in backward and covered their father's nakedness. Their faces were

turned the other way so that they would not see their father's nakedness.

When Noah awoke from his wine and found out what his youngest son had done to him, he said, "Cursed be Canaan! The lowest of slaves will he be to his brothers." He also said, "Blessed be Yahweh, the God of Shem! May Canaan be the slave of Shem. May God extend the territory of Japheth; may Japheth live in the tents of Shem, and may Canaan be his slave." (Gen. 9:20-27)

When Bathsheba went to King Solomon to speak to him . . . , the king stood up to meet her, *bowed down to her* and sat down on his throne. He had a throne brought for the king's mother, and she sat down at his right hand. "I have one small request to make of you," she said. "Do not refuse me." The king replied, "Make it, my mother; I will not refuse you." (1 Kings 2:19-20)

As it turned out, Bathsheba's request of King Solomon countered God's will, so Solomon did refuse it. But this passage shows his *attitude* and *intention*, which was to fully honor his mother, even to the point of bowing down before her, though he reigned as king. This form of honoring his mother, his natural origin, pointed to his honor for his ultimate origins in God, and God accepted it. In contrast, when Cornelius knelt before Peter, this did not honor God but Peter in and of himself—even in the place of God:

As Peter entered the house, Cornelius met him and fell at his feet in reverence. But Peter made him get up. "Stand up," he said, "I am only a man myself." (Acts 10:25-26)

On the other hand, when the Philippian jailer fell down before Paul and Silas, he did so acknowledging an eminency in them that came from God and pulled the jailer toward God. The jailer bowed to *God's* expression of authority as he had witnessed it—not to Paul and Silas's authority in and of itself.* He honored God in the men through whom God revealed Himself to the jailer. Solomon honored his natural parents; the jailer honored those who would serve as his spiritual parents; but in so doing, both men honored their ultimate origin in God.

Then Joseph removed [his children] from Israel's knees and bowed down with his face to the ground. (Gen. 48:12)

Joseph had his chariot made ready and went to Goshen to meet his father Israel. As soon as Joseph appeared before him, he threw his arms around his father and wept for a long time. (Gen. 46:29)

---

* Bowing is not the only outward gesture through which one honors and shows submission to someone. A kiss could also serve "as a sign of submission"[11]: "Kiss the Son, lest He be angry and you be destroyed in your way, for His wrath can flare up in a moment. Blessed are all who take refuge in Him." When Pharaoh made Joseph ruler over Egypt (Gen. 41:40), the phrase "all my people are to submit to your orders" means more literally "at your command all my people are to kiss (you)," that is, according to the *NIV Study Bible*, "kiss your hands or feet in an act of homage and submission."[12] (See also 1 Kings 19:18; Hos. 13:2.)

> Sarah . . . obeyed Abraham and called him her master. You are
> her daughters if you do what is right and do not give way to fear.
> (1 Pet. 3:6)

This same Sarah, the mother of the faithful, called her husband "lord"
(1 Pet. 3:6), so how much more should children reverence their fathers
and mothers?

The child's honor for his parents will express itself in his actions toward
his parents, in his attitude toward them, in his demeanor, bearing and
speech while in their presence. Because he honors them in his heart,
he will yield the upper hand or "best place" in love and respect for his
parents' authority and comfort and as tokens of his subordination, or even
as tokens of his present inferiority, not as a person but in experience,
knowledge, understanding and wisdom. Inexperience, of course, never
betokens any inferiority in worth. But in any case, what makes people
strive in competition for the upper hand or for the winning place except
that they might be accounted better than those with whom they strive?
It is not seemly for a child to compete with even his brothers (Phil. 2:3),
much less with his parents, to prove himself better in anything. If he is
better at something, it is only so that he can serve others as they serve
him in that which they better perform. Granted that a child may by some
office or gift or function be so advanced above his father in the eyes of
others that those others may honor and reverence the child more than
they do the father, giving the child the upper place above his father. And
though the child accepts this upper place for the sake of divine order
within the kingdom, nevertheless, since no honor is comparable to the
dignity of fatherhood, such honor always gives greater eminency in the
one-on-one relationship to the parent over the child. So even the child
publicly honored and reverenced by others should honor and reverence
his father not only in private but even also in public as the occasion of
God calls for it (as with Solomon and his mother).

Honor in the heart produces honor in conduct as well. One of the
most distinctive ways a child honors his parents is by seeking his father's
blessing. As said before, a child's physical origins—his parents—tie him to
his ultimate origin in God. To seek the father's blessing ensures that the
long continuing lineage of a godly inheritance comes into the child's life.
In Bible days, even the profane, like Esau, valued the importance of the
father's blessing. And while Jacob's lie greatly dishonored his father, we
see through his actions how greatly he prized the father's blessing:

> Jacob said to his father, "I am Esau your firstborn. I have done as
> you told me. Please sit up and eat some of my game so that you
> may give me your blessing." (Gen. 27:19)

> When Esau heard his father's words, he burst out with a loud and
> bitter cry and said to his father, "Bless me—me too, my father!"

> But he said, "Your brother came deceitfully and took your blessing."
>
> Esau said, "Isn't he rightly named Jacob? He has deceived me these two times: He took my birthright, and now he's taken my blessing!" Then he asked, "Haven't you reserved any blessing for me?"
>
> Isaac answered Esau, "I have made him lord over you and have made all his relatives his servants, and I have sustained him with grain and new wine. So what can I possibly do for you, my son?"
>
> Esau said to his father, "Do you have only one blessing, my father? Bless me too, my father!" Then Esau wept aloud. (Gen. 27:34-38)

> Some time later Joseph was told, "Your father is ill." So he took his two sons Manasseh and Ephraim along with him. When Jacob was told, "Your son Joseph has come to you," Israel rallied his strength and sat up on the bed . . . .
>
> When Israel saw the sons of Joseph, he asked, "Who are these?"
>
> "They are the sons God has given me here," Joseph said to his father. Then Israel said, "Bring them to me so I may bless them." (Gen. 48:1-2, 8-9)

It seems Joseph brought his sons to see his ailing father in order to receive the blessing that Jacob gave.

The Patriarchs as prophets foretold the future of their children; as fathers they obtained the blessings pronounced by faith and prayer. Children should seek ways to do good to their parents, to honor them and to bless them, in order to be reciprocally blessed by their parents.

> Yahweh detests the sacrifice of the wicked, but the prayer of the upright pleases Him. (Prov. 15:8)

But though God may not regard the petitions of wicked parents for their own sakes, He may yet hear them for the love and good of their children. To ask for a blessing does not mark a believer as merely selfish but acknowledges the giver of the blessing as superior in gifts and authority, as Hebrews 7:7 (NASV) so declares: "The lesser is blessed by the greater." And so to seek our parents' blessing is another way of honoring them, of placing the greater value on their life.

Older children honored their parents by providing for their parents materially.

> Now hurry back to my father and say to him, "This is what your son Joseph says: God has made me lord of all Egypt. Come down to me; don't delay. You shall live in the region of Goshen and be near me—you, your children and grandchildren, your flocks and herds, and all you have. *I will provide for you there*, because five years of famine are still to come. Otherwise you and your household and all who belong to you will become destitute." (Gen. 45:9-11)

> *So Joseph settled his father and his brothers in Egypt and gave them property in the best part of the land*, the district of Rameses, as

Pharaoh directed. Joseph also *provided his father and his brothers and all his father's household with food*, according to the number of their children. (Gen. 47:11-12)

And He said to them: "You have a fine way of setting aside the commands of God in order to observe your own traditions! For Moses said, '*Honor your father and your mother*,' and, 'Anyone who curses his father or mother must be put to death.' But you say that if a man says to his father or mother: 'Whatever help you might otherwise have received from me is Corban' (that is, a gift devoted to God), then you no longer let him do anything for his father or mother. Thus you nullify the word of God by your tradition that you have handed down. And you do many things like that." (Mark 7:9-13)

Clearly, then, for children to honor their parents meant for them to provide for their material support. Paul shows this link between honor and material support in regard to the elders of the church:

The elders who direct the affairs of the church well are worthy of *double honor*, especially those whose work is preaching and teaching. For the Scripture says, "Do not muzzle the ox while it is treading out the grain," and "The worker deserves his *wages*." (1 Tim. 5:17-18)

So the "double honor" of the elders "whose work is preaching and teaching" refers directly to material benefits—that is, their "wages."

If we have sown spiritual seed among you, *is it too much if we reap a material harvest from you*? If others have this *right of support* from you, shouldn't we have it all the more? (1 Cor. 9:11-12)

Anyone who receives instruction in the word *must share all good things with his instructor*. (Gal. 6:6)

When Jesus saw His mother there, and the disciple whom He loved standing nearby, *He said to His mother, "Dear woman, here is your son," and to the disciple, "Here is your mother." From that time on, this disciple took her into his home*. (John 19:26-27)

But if a widow has children or grandchildren, these should learn first of all to put their religion into practice by *caring for their own family and so repaying their parents and grandparents, for this is pleasing to God*. (1 Tim. 5:4)

We have said children's honor of their parents leads to their honor of God:

"*A son honors his father*, and a servant his master. If I am a father, where is the *honor due Me*? If I am a master, where is the *respect due Me*?" says Yahweh Almighty. (Mal. 1:6)

Honor Yahweh with your *wealth*, with the firstfruits of all your crops. (Prov. 3:9)

God spoke all the above partly in terms of bringing money, material gifts or offerings.

The following scripture directly connects a father's discipline of his children with their honor of him:

> Moreover, we have all had human fathers who disciplined us and we *respected* them for it. How much more should we submit to the Father of our spirits and live! (Heb. 12:9)

b. Honoring Other Adults

As seen, the ultimate reason for honoring our parents is God. We honor them because of their place—"in the Lord." We honor them as the linear channels through whom God transmits His life, wisdom and love to us. If children learn to recognize the true meaning and importance of honoring their parents, this will naturally lead them to honor other adults also. For these adults also stand as members of their parents' generation through whom God's love and wisdom—and, spiritually, His life—have come to the children.

> Likewise, you who are younger and of lesser rank, *be subject to the elders* (the ministers and spiritual guides of the church)—[*giving them due respect and yielding to their counsel*]. Clothe (apron) yourselves, all of you, with humility [as the garb of a servant, so that its covering cannot possibly be stripped from you, with freedom from pride and arrogance] toward one another. For God sets Himself against the proud (the insolent, the overbearing, the disdainful, the presumptuous, the boastful)—[and He opposes, frustrates, and defeats them], but gives grace (favor, blessing) to the humble. (1 Pet. 5:5, Ampl.)

James quotes the same proverb and ties it to submission to God (James 4:5-7). So to submit to God is to submit to our elders, those who are our origins in God, our linear authority.

> Or do you think Scripture says without reason that the spirit He caused to live in us envies intensely? But He gives us more grace. That is why Scripture says: "God opposes the proud but gives grace to the humble." *Submit yourselves, then, to God.* Resist the devil, and he will flee from you. (James 4:5-7)

> *Rise in the presence of the aged, show respect for the elderly* and *revere your God.* I am Yahweh. (Lev. 19:32)

> Then Esau looked up and saw the women and children. "Who are these with you?" he asked. Jacob answered, "They are the children God has graciously given your servant." Then *the maidservants and their children approached and bowed down.* (Gen. 33:5-6)

Though Esau never became such a channel as described above, Jacob's children still honored him because of his position and age.

c. Silence: Being Quiet around Adults

As seen, respect prompts silence at appropriate times, a quietness of spirit and word in the presence of adults. This silence forms the necessary basis of sensitivity, of having a hearing ear ultimately for God's voice, whether He speaks directly through His Spirit or through people. Of course, the silence of sullenness is a character flaw that must be overcome, but a respectful attitude expressed in a disposition of silence while in the presence of older people can be an expression of honor toward them.

> *Now Elihu had waited before speaking to Job because they were older than he. . . .*
> So Elihu son of Barakel the Buzite said:
> "I am young in years, and you are old; that is why I was fearful, not daring to tell you what I know.
> "I thought, 'Age should speak; advanced years should teach wisdom.'" (Job 32:4, 6-7)

> The young men saw me and hid, and the aged arose and stood; the princes *stopped talking*, and put their hands on their mouths; *the voice of the nobles was hushed*, and their tongue stuck to their palate. (Job 29:8-10, NKJV, NASV)

> *Men listened to me expectantly, waiting in silence* for my counsel. After I had spoken, they spoke no more; my words fell gently on their ears. They waited for me as for showers and drank in my words as the spring rain. (Job 29:21-23)

If adults, even adults with authority (as those mentioned in some of the above scriptures), held their peace in order to hear the wisdom of the mature, how much more should children do so? By their silence, children cease to interfere with or interrupt the flow of adult thought and conversation. Their presence can then bless adults. Not only do they bless and honor adults by their quietness, but they also have the opportunity to learn and grow as they hear adult conversation (when appropriate) and watch adult examples. Of course, at times children can and should speak around adults, but they must learn when to do so. (The topic of "Dishonor" will cover this.)

> My dear brothers, take note of this: Everyone should be *quick to listen, slow to speak* . . . . (James 1:19)

> We all stumble in many ways. If anyone is never at fault *in what he says*, he is a perfect man, able to keep his whole body in check. (James 3:2)

Written examples of children's *silence* in the presence of adults would for obvious reasons be scarce; but numerous scriptures record the presence of children when adults gather to speak; and these show children as saying nothing. In this way, their silence is loud and clear. See, for example, Matthew 19:13-15 and Genesis 31:22-55.

d. Hearing Ear

Wisdom brings us life (Eccles. 7:12). It comes to children primarily through parents and other adults. As shown, children who honor adults will hear adults and thus open the door to wisdom. To hear, requires silence. No one can obey unless they hear; and no one can hear unless they listen; and without listening, they cannot consistently speak what God would have them to speak. To have a hearing ear doesn't mean children merely sit quietly in the presence of adults. It means they attend to, pay attention to, what is said. A hearing ear is not passive but active. Children don't maintain an appropriate measure of silence because they're "supposed to be silent" but because they want to hear and learn from what adults say (that occurs, of course, only when their situation makes listening to adult conversation appropriate). They want to listen so they can learn and grow. And they should listen especially closely when they're spoken to directly.

> But when He, the Spirit of truth, comes, He will guide you into all truth. He will not speak on His own; *He will speak only what He hears*, and He will tell you what is yet to come. (John 16:13)

> I have much to say in judgment of you. But He who sent Me is reliable, and *what I have heard from Him I tell the world.* (John 8:26)

> *Pay attention and listen* to the sayings of the wise; apply your heart to what I teach, for it is pleasing when you keep them in your heart and have all of them ready on your lips. (Prov. 22:17-18)

> No one lights a lamp and hides it in a jar or puts it under a bed. Instead, he puts it on a stand, so that those who come in can see the light. For there is nothing hidden that will not be disclosed, and nothing concealed that will not be known or brought out into the open. Therefore *consider carefully how you listen.* Whoever has will be given more; whoever does not have, even what he thinks he has will be taken from him. (Luke 8:16-18)

> *See to it that you do not refuse Him who speaks.* If they did not escape when they refused him who warned them on earth, how much less will we, if we turn away from Him who warns us from heaven? At that time His voice shook the earth, but now He has promised, "Once more I will shake not only the earth but also the heavens." The words "once more" indicate the removing of what can be shaken—that is, created things—so that what cannot be shaken may remain.
>
> Therefore, since we are receiving a kingdom that cannot be shaken, let us be thankful, and so worship God acceptably with reverence and awe, for our "God is a consuming fire." (Heb. 12:25-29)

We are not, however, simply to hear God's Word with our ears but to be transformed by it, becoming *doers* of His Word (Matt. 7:24-27; James 1:22-25). The Word will never change anyone who pays no attention to it, who will not participate in it and receives it, if at all, only passively, as a spectator, as an "objective observer" (Luke 17:20; Gal. 3:2). Objective, analytical knowledge has always characterized pagan thought, not Biblical belief.* People who detach themselves from direct and experiential involvement, who analyze His Word as an object, never become the positive subject of God's personal attention. So they must instead press into living and loving relationship with both Him and His Word. Jesus and others spoke repeatedly of those who "hear" without understanding: they hear, yet they do not hear.† Such people actually think God's Word can be divorced from God Himself and the experience of Him through His Spirit. They instead seek to know God merely intellectually, analytically, from their own detached, self-centered perspective, as if their fallen minds were superior to God Himself. Rather than submit to God's Word, they try to bring that Word under the sovereign authority of their own lapsed, partial, biased, finite thinking. But only entering the presence of the God who speaks the Word can change us. If we don't *belong* to that Word as a living Word of a living Presence until it also belongs to us, we may hear the sounds and attach our own meaning to them, but we won't hear God (John 8:43).

> "This is why I speak to them in parables:
> 'Though seeing, they do not see; though hearing, they do not hear or understand. In them is fulfilled the prophecy of Isaiah: "You will be ever hearing but never understanding; you will be ever seeing but never perceiving. For this people's heart has become calloused; they hardly hear with their ears, and they have closed their eyes. Otherwise they might see with their eyes, hear with their ears, understand with their hearts and turn, and I would heal them."'" (Matt. 13:13-15)

> Hear this, you foolish and senseless people, who have eyes but do not see, who have ears but do not hear. (Jer. 5:21)

> Again therefore Jesus spoke to them, saying, "I am the light of the world; he who follows Me shall not walk in the darkness . . . ."
> "Why do you not understand what I am saying? It is because you cannot hear My word . . . . He who *belongs to God hears* what God says. The reason you do not hear is that you do not belong to God." (John 8:12, 43, 47, NASV, NIV)

Those Jesus describes here could not escape from darkness and into light because they did not give themselves to God. How could they "belong" to God when they refused to let Him wholly possess them? He wanted all of

---

* See *The Quest for Salvation.*

† Acts 28:26-27; Matt. 13:13-15; Isa. 6:9-10; Jer. 5:21; John 8:43-47.

them—their thoughts, words, attitudes, deeds, ambitions, values, ideas, cherished habits and images of mind and life. But they refused to seek Him or break their will to His. They withheld part or all of themselves from God. And because they did, they couldn't escape the darkness and futility of their own thinking by fleeing completely into His thoughts. These "deaf" men of course heard the sounds of Jesus' words, but they couldn't "understand" what *He* said without "belonging" to God as a bride "belongs" to her husband. They despised such a *covenantal relationship* either with Him or with those He sent. So they remained penned in the arena of indecision. Their lives remained unstained by God's blood or their own. Such self-sacrificing love was foreign to them. So He did not *possess* them, and therefore they could not possess Him. Void of God's Spirit, unpossessed by Christ, they were "none of His" (Rom. 8:9, KJV). At best, they visited back and forth between two opposing kingdoms with their two opposing masters, perhaps functioning in certain "gifts" while remaining in heart, mind and soul unpossessed by redemptive love. They may have technically understood God's language and even perhaps shared it with others, but His words had no *compelling* meaning or force in their own lives because nothing connected the words together in a covenantal bond between Speaker and hearer. So they felt no absolute necessity to obey His Word; they even protected themselves from it and from those who spoke it.

Meaning comes through relationship: we understand a message's meaning because of our relationship with the speaker and because we see how the spoken elements relate to one another and to the one from whom the message comes. Those who heard but could not understand the meaning of Jesus' words refused to become one with Him. They never knew the total given-overness necessary to experience the depth of feeling from which God's words came forth. They could never, therefore, even hope to see how the authority of God's Word could be both noncompulsory and yet absolute. That such a truth might come to them through human flesh just like their own flesh insulted what they saw as their godlike intelligence (John 12:49-50; 1 Thess. 2:13). So Jesus' words remained mere meaningless sounds to them.

Unlike the Thessalonians, those Jesus spoke to did not find faith from the words they heard. The Thessalonians also heard a word preached to them, but they honored Paul as someone sent from God—in other words, their own relationship with God enabled them to accept and enter into the relationship God planned for them with others He had sent.

This whole New Testament picture of relational knowledge resembles an incident where two natives of the Far East happened upon an American traveling through their land. This American spoke their language fluently in several dialects and asked them directions in their own tongue. Yet they simply stared at him in disbelief and strode away laughing. As they sauntered off, the American heard them ask each other if it didn't sound as if that silly American had requested directions in their own tongue (and perfectly at that). These two men even repeated verbatim what the American had in fact just inquired of them.[13] They heard the sounds he spoke; they even understood that those sounds had meaning; but they refused to *consent* to the meaning of the words as *he* spoke them.

But why? Because they refused to trust that his words meant exactly what they seemed to mean. They refused, in short, to participate in his speech. And they did so simply because they were too arrogant and full of their own ideas and assumptions about the inferiority of others to believe that any American could actually speak their language. They had too little honor for the man to even believe he was speaking something intelligible and important to them, though in fact he was, and they even heard the actual words. But they didn't believe the sounds coming to them had any compelling meaning for them. Their arrogance had displaced the possibility of such faith. Similarly, many fail to hear God or those He sends to them, and the cost to them is unfathomable.

The Pharisees, too, heard Jesus' words. That is, technically, they understood what He said. Yet because of an arrogance rooted in their religious standing, because, in short, pride had smothered their faith, they refused to consent to the meaning of His Words, or even to believe His words might exceed the present limits of their own knowledge. They refused because they had separated God's Word from the living authority that spoke that Word. They instead exerted their own authority over God's Word and thus stood in God's place. So God's Word no longer spoke to them with any authority that might enlarge their hearts and minds because they had become their own authority and could get no better or bigger than what they already saw themselves as: their own little gods. They therefore tried to flatten out Jesus' numinous words by minutely analyzing them with their fallen, self-rationalizing understanding. They tried to subordinate God's speech to their objective dissection, to stand back as detached observers to see whether He measured up to their miserly and miserable criteria. Yet they could only have known and understood the truth by bowing before the powerful Spirit that stood behind and actually propelled those words, by subordinating their limited but inflated minds to His infinite spiritual reality. For this very reason Paul had declared, "My message and my preaching were not with persuasive words of human wisdom, but in demonstration of the Spirit and of power" (1 Cor. 2:4, NKJV, NASV). If they had actively poured themselves out seeking the deepest meaning of His words in a direct relationship with the same Spirit that filled the man and therefore that had truly uttered those words, they could have understood Jesus and seen who He was for the first time. Yet only the immersion of their total being into His own anointing, which came to them in His anointed Words, could have revealed the fullness of His truth to them. Yet to do this would have been to surrender themselves, to be carried in their finite minds into the flow of God's eternal Spirit, to "belong to God" rather than to merely themselves. But they couldn't humble themselves and their own high estimation of their opinions and knowledge before the God coming to them in the human flesh that God Himself had sent.

They were too busy being gods themselves and defending themselves against God's presence to do this. So they pretended to misunderstand the words spoken to them, as well as what they were feeling or why they were feeling it. They pretended to be merely puzzled and confused by His words. Jesus therefore characterized them as hypocrites, as of their father, the devil, a liar (John 8:44). After all, the serpent had been the first to talk people into reaching for this godhood by establishing a human-centered criterion of good and evil (Gen. 3:4), of right and wrong, of true and false.

In truth, only through active participation can we understand anything. For example, a musician can read a musical score with technical understanding but never actually "hear" what the piece sounds like. Every musical composition, whether worthy or not, is nonetheless an invocation to full participation. So to hear it as a whole person wholly affected by it demands more than even an active effort on his part: he must consent to its call for full participation. Similarly, people have read operating manuals for machines and studied the manuals' illustrations. They've even made perfect scores on the tests on the material, but they never understood how the machine worked because they refused to put themselves into the instructions. They didn't read for participatory knowledge—knowledge to perform a function for a purpose—but only for abstract knowledge that merely built images and status by passing tests. New workers in businesses have daily studied the operating manuals on machines, passed the written tests on the manual and then begun their jobs only to ruin machines whose operation they had no actual understanding of, in spite of all their study. Though they read words and passed tests, they didn't enter into an understanding of the machines' actual operation *through the words*. They failed to mentally put the words and their meanings together to effectually see how the machines worked. Neither what they read nor what it pertained to nor the one who had given them the material could have been of much importance to them. Thus the words had no relevant meaning for the actions of their workaday lives, or else they couldn't have cared less whether they did or not because they lacked all respect for those who gave it to them.

A working understanding comes only by trusting those whose words you read or hear, even to the point of giving yourself to the person and so to his words, participating in them until they become part of your own experience. To know anyone requires entering their life and works and words. An award-winning author once compared reading a book to entering a covenant between reader and author.[14]

Similarly, you can stare at a painting—and perhaps you even have some impression of a vague structure in the painting. Yet you for some reason then look away with no real experience of what you've just seen. Maybe you are disturbed and distracted by other concerns—perhaps you're simply mentally lazy. Whatever the case, whether legitimate or not, something keeps you from fully participating. And unless you finally look with the vision of the artist and actively seek to reconstruct what he saw, felt and portrayed on the canvas, you can never experience the painting as it conveys the artist's own experience. The painting is more than of some vague structure. If the artist painted a particular building, then it's his visual felt-thought—more even than a farmhouse in a field that the painting may depict, more even than the shake shingles and homespun cotton curtains blowing in the windows of the dog trot. It even goes beyond the cedar logs of the farmhouse, where the girl washing dishes is visible through the window, beyond even the lone figure in a straw hat standing off to the side of the cabin scything in the field, even beyond the girl's distracted and hurt eyes or the man's set jaw. Beyond all these, you must open yourself to the very tone and texture, the mood and atmosphere, the metarealism created by technique and composition. Without active, even vulnerable, participation, you miss everything. But with these, you recognize a nuanced interplay of all the elements. Before, a framed object hung on a wall, suspended in space. Now you see not merely a second-rate reproduction of a way, or sense, of life but a re-creation of an experience in that life, and not merely in obvious facial gestures but in a sense that comes only through how many elements come together in a single whole—a complete design composed of color, form, technique, value patterns and so on, all of which also convey mood and feeling. By attending, you re-create within yourself the painter's own experience. The painting hasn't changed; you've changed because you've poured part of your own life into viewing it. For that moment, you gave yourself to viewing it. You "belonged" to it. So it takes on value for you. It is worth something to you. And all that happens only because it had a cost and you paid the price—you paid attention.

Our experience of anything depends upon just such participation. We can be physically present at an event or a place but remain oblivious to our surroundings and everything else. Whether as an employee on a job, a student in school or a member of a church, the more you give yourself to something, the more you pour yourself into seeing what life shows you, hearing what it says to you, doing what it tells you, the more completely you conform yourself to the image held out to you, whether good or bad.

To participate in the words someone speaks, even the Words carried by the Holy Spirit, means even trusting the reasons of those who speak them. This is why honesty in relationships becomes absolute: it becomes the first essential to a true communication that brings authentic oneness in relationships. When you're dishonest in word, gesture, emotion or deed, you confess that life doesn't really matter to you. And this is why so many don't *pay* attention to anyone—because so few have proven themselves worthy of the effort. This is also why Jesus said, "Will there be any faith when the Son of Man comes?" All the more reason, then, to enter the words and life of those who prove trustworthy, beginning with God Himself. Otherwise, no matter who's speaking, what they say bounces off your eardrums or reflects hollowly off the page. The words will never penetrate your soul or change or help you. The experience offered will wither away for you, and you'll never know the other person in love. This is true even with God and His Word. To refuse to participate confesses our distrust and arrogance. Then the words He speaks have no importance or meaning for our lives. We'll find reasons to resent and reject His Word, as well as those who bring it to us. We'll soon hold truth, especially as it pertains to us, in contempt, despising it. Then, in place of transformation comes condemnation.

Just as we can stand unseeing in front of a painting, so can we stand in the presence of God's Spirit, yet our experience of it will remain relatively untransforming because the depth of our participation falls short. Of course, just as many claim to know the instructions for running certain types of machinery but destroy that machinery when it actually comes to hands-on experience, so many also claim to know God by the instructions given in His Word but fall short of experiencing or knowing God in His actual presence.

Many, for instance, claim to have received, to have been filled with or born of the Holy Spirit—over half a billion in the twentieth century alone have claimed Pentecostal status. But in fact, far more than that— *all* Evangelicals—claim to have been "born again." Twenty percent of all Roman Catholics claim this and more than a third of all adult Americans in general! Yet the experience of many of these groups frequently fails to persuade most others that they have even come close to what seems the norm in the New Testament. Moreover, their lives, unlike those in the book of Acts, often seem to remain untransformed or only temporarily transformed, and many Evangelicals often themselves express disappointment that their encounter with God seems far less than they expected—merely a mental acknowledgment of some verbal representation of God, where someone besides God does the talking and informing, shaping everyone's faith (contrary to Scripture) with human wisdom (1 Cor. 2:13-14). As Miguel de Unamuno once wrote: "Those who say that they believe in God and yet neither love nor fear Him, do not in fact believe in Him but in those who have taught them that God exists . . . . Those who believe that they believe in God, but without any passion in their heart . . . , believe only in the God-Idea, not in God Himself."[15] In other words, many people who vehemently claim and extol their faith seem at times to believe more in their beliefs than they do God, more in the "Christ idea" than in Christ Himself.

Often what seems to block a direct encounter with God is that people approach Him in the wrong mental frame to receive and participate in what God is saying in the way He is saying it. I use the word "frame" here to refer to any given worldview that becomes so embedded in people's thinking that they simply take its assumptions for granted without examining the foundations of their own thinking. Their frame of thought then becomes part of an unconscious way of perceiving and understanding reality. And, with virtually everyone, it is so habitual that it becomes, according to neurologists, encoded in the very functioning of their brains. So the frames within our brains become like labyrinths or mazes that only allow those thoughts to pass through that will follow the course which the labyrinth or maze lays out.

But such a course can only end in personal disaster for a faith that "comes by hearing and hearing by the Word of God" (Rom. 10:17). Such a maze in our thinking, in other words, is calamitous to faith because, as one influential cognitive scientist says: "Frames are mental structures that *shape* the way we see the world. As a result, they *shape* the goals we seek," they *shape* "the plans we make," they *shape* "the way we act, and what counts as . . . good or bad" in the "outcome" of all of our actions. So "in politics our frames shape our social policies."[16]

Even in the everyday life of a community, frames still shape our vision of what a community should be "and the institutions" that "we form" to ensure that those configurations maintain. Therefore, "to change our frames is to change all of this. Reframing *is* social change."[17] Reframing is also individual change. Reframing is cultural change. Reframing is total change.

Perhaps even more significantly, this linguist goes on to say: "You can't see or hear" such "frames. They are part of a cognitive *unconscious*— structures in our brains that we cannot consciously access . . . . Reframing is changing the way" people see "the world. It is changing what counts as common sense." And perhaps most suggestively for the issue at hand, "because language activates frames, new language," he says, "is required for new frames."[18]

Here, then, is a real key for learning to hear and participate in the life-changing words that someone speaks to us, especially when that someone is God. If we have the wrong frame, we simply won't hear, understand or experience God in the way He intended. Part of a genuine rebirth would, then, involve a complete change in frames. Again, I think of Paul's words: "Be not conformed to the patterns [might we not say, "the frames"?] of this world." In other words, "Don't be polluted by idols." But "be transformed [reframed] in the renewing of your mind." Paul, in short, calls us to "total change." So, for instance, a change of frames, say, from an individualistic perspective to one of intentional community, promises to change our very perspective and understanding of Christian truth and life. This is the case even when those truths remain ostensibly the same ones we thought we always knew and understood. If this is true for changing merely *human* cultures, societies and individuals in their relationships with one another, how much greater and more supernatural would the "new language" have to be to usher us into the changes commensurate with being reborn into the kingdom of God!

Of course, to put all this—particularly the requirement of a "new language" for a "new frame"—in a New Testament context, and especially in view of that strain of Christianity that *Life* magazine named "the religion of the century," many of us have had what seems like more than their share of problems and difficulties with the more egregious forms of the Pentecostal or Charismatic movements—it indeed seems that at times either the "frame" that defined these movements was wrong, or else that of those repelled by them is wrong. Most of us, for instance, have at one time or another looked upon "speaking in tongues" as at best unsavory and crude, if not downright bizarre and alarming. Many, even as believers, have seen it as simply, if not alarmingly, imbalanced. But when this linguistics professor says that "a new *language* is required for a new frame," that in itself might well seem sufficient incentive for us to try to reframe everything about glossolalia and then to reexamine it. And in such a new context, it can seem very plausible that in order for an alternative reality from God to emerge, for an alternative to the kingdoms of this world to come into being, a new and *unique language*—as is repeatedly described in the book of Acts, which also describes the birth of the church (Acts 2:1-18; 10:44-46; 11:15-18; 19:1-7)—would mark the birth of the Spirit into that new kingdom, into that entirely new "frame" of existence that Jesus said we must be reborn into (John 3:3, 5-8). This new "frame" would put both the Biblical description and the current experience of glossolalia into a new context.

The problem with "speaking in tongues," at least as dogma, could conceivably, then, be understood as having arisen because it isolated and removed the Biblical experience from the very *context* of a new and larger community life, a community life called "the kingdom of God." Yet only such a larger community life context can make glossolalia meaningful, revealing it to be part of the frame-changing, transformative encounter with God that gives entrance into an alternative reality, culture, community and way of life called "the kingdom of God" (John 3:3, 5).

But many Pentecostals and Charismatics, instead of seeing it as the sign of a new life, a new beginning in a new reality with a new frame "requiring a new language," have merely reduced the experience to something that often seems merely pasted onto old lives, lives that only continue to essentially be lived out in the old frameworks and realities of the kingdoms of this world. In short, no real exodus occurred. Therefore, the experience itself soon became for many people simply representational "doctrine" rather than a presentational supernatural reality based on the believer's own direct experience of the presence of God. It became a mere (and sometimes bizarre and imbalanced) caricature and therefore a *mis*representation. The glossolalic experience was no longer a sacred rite of passage into an entirely new life lived in an utterly different order of reality within an entirely new and life-sustaining mind-frame.

But only in such a new world, new culture and new frame would it even seem conceivable that the life of the Spirit of God could possibly continue to unfold according to God's purpose. God wants to initiate such an exodus into a new order of reality through the coming of His power from heaven, a power that enables us to *think* differently, to *act* differently, to *behave* differently, to *live* differently—all situated in this utterly different cultural order of relationships called the "kingdom of God."

So outside that new *context* of an alternative reality, "speaking in tongues" can (and has) often become merely a parody of new life, trapped and stunted as the experience has been in the context of the old culture. In that old context, glossolalia then becomes analogous to a foreign tongue spoken in a very provincial and backwoods place, a locale where no one has ever seriously spoken in any language but what was native to the place. Then, suddenly, people in that provincial locale begin to hear a growing handful of their old and long-standing citizens speak this different language while carrying on their lives just as they've always done before. As Paul said, such incongruities can seem like a frightening form of "madness" to many people (1 Cor. 14:23, KJV).

Nonetheless, *living* differently, *thinking* differently, in the context of a different culture and order of relationships does indeed first require *speaking* differently, and, according to Jesus and Luke, this in turn requires the initiating experience of a direct *presentational* reality of the Spirit in our lives if we would even first "*enter* the kingdom of God" (John 3:3, 5-8; Acts 2:1-4; 10:46-48; 19:1-7). This entrance into a new kingdom requires, then, a *total* transformation of our lives, not merely the crucial initiation accompanied by the phenomenon of an authentic glossolalia. Surely glossolalia is the legitimate, Biblical sign of the "new language" that necessarily accompanies the entrance into the new order of reality. And for this to occur, we must "offer ourselves as a living sacrifice," *totally* surrendering to God (Rom. 12:1). That's when we will make a complete exodus from the "frames" of the world, being no longer "conformed to this world," but instead becoming "transformed by the renewing of [our] minds" (Rom. 12:2). The ability to offer ourselves in such total surrender, which brings effective transformation, requires not just "hearing" but an active participation—that is, we truly do "*offer* ourselves." And we will not do this unless we value, honor and respect the God we serve as of greater worth than our own desires and inclinations, inclinations that, prior to rebirth, are usually directed toward the all-consuming covetousness of the surrounding world.

In conclusion, godly silence and godly words don't come without first seeing those to whom we offer such silence and words; and we cannot see unless we respect; and we cannot respect unless we reverence; and we cannot reverence unless we fear; and we cannot fear unless we are disciplined. Discipline teaches us to wait upon the Lord and to open our hearts to hear His voice, the voice of the Spirit. The Hebrew word translated "listen" in Deuteronomy 27:9 is *sh'ma*, which means to "hear intelligently," implying "obedience." It means to "give undivided listening attention." We must listen cognizant of our responsibility for what we hear. To hear accurately must precede performing exactly what we've been told to do. Discipline teaches us to hear the way God requires because it teaches us the consequences of failing to do so.

> Then Moses and the priests, who are Levites, said to all Israel, "Be *silent*, O Israel, and *listen*! You have now become the people of Yahweh your God." (Deut. 27:9)

> My dear brothers, take note of this: Everyone should be *quick to listen, slow to speak* and slow to become angry. (James 1:19)

> Sacrifice and meal offering Thou hast not desired; *my ears Thou hast opened*; burnt offering and sin offering Thou hast not required. (Ps. 40:6, NASV)

> Nicodemus, who had gone to Jesus earlier and who was one of their own number, asked, "Does our law condemn anyone *without first hearing him* to find out what he is doing?" (John 7:50-51)

> "Now then, my sons, *listen to me*; blessed are those who keep my ways. *Listen to my instruction and be wise*; do not ignore it. Blessed

is the man who *listens to me*, watching daily at my doors, waiting at my doorway." (Prov. 8:32-34)

Listen to your father, who gave you life, and do not despise your mother when she is old. (Prov. 23:22)

My son, if you accept my words and store up my commands within you, *turning your ear to wisdom* and applying your heart to understanding, and if you call out for insight and cry aloud for understanding, and if you look for it as for silver and search for it as for hidden treasure, then you will understand the fear of Yahweh and find the knowledge of God. (Prov. 2:1-5)

The way of a fool seems right to him, but *a wise man listens to advice*. (Prov. 12:15)

The heart of the discerning acquires knowledge; *the ears of the wise seek it out*. (Prov. 18:15)

The Queen of the South will rise at the judgment with this generation and condemn it; for *she came from the ends of the earth to listen* to Solomon's wisdom, and now one greater than Solomon is here. (Matt. 12:42)

Like an earring of gold or an ornament of fine gold is a wise man's rebuke to *a listening ear*. (Prov. 25:12)

He who has ears, let him *hear*. (Matt. 11:15)

"He who has an ear, let him *hear* what the Spirit says to the churches." (Rev. 2:7, 11, 17, 29; 3:6, 13, 22)

By learning silence and attentiveness to parents, a child discovers the prerequisites to hearing God.

e. Seasonable Speech/Appropriate and Ready Response

When a child truly honors his parents and other adults, when he has a hearing ear and bridles his tongue and keeps his ears open to hear, he will also appropriately respond to his parents. He will relate to them respectfully. Because he attends to them, he knows the appropriate response to their questions or statements. His demeanor and bearing will express respect, meekness and submissiveness, which does not mean servility, cowering and cringing. He will frame his words well. He will speak to the point and clearly, not mumbling or muttering, aware of the importance of the adult's time. Humility and seasonableness will mark his speech. When adults call, the child will have an immediate, ready, willing and proper response. The Hebrew word *kun*, which English translates as "ready" in Proverbs 22:18, literally means a response that is "firm, steadfast, faithful, sure, reliable, fixed, certain."

Pay attention and listen to the sayings of the wise; apply your heart to what I teach, for it is pleasing when you keep them in your heart and have all of them *ready* on your lips. (Prov. 22:17-18)

> Then Yahweh called Samuel. Samuel answered, "Here I am." And he ran to Eli and said, "Here I am; you called me."
>
> But Eli said, "I did not call; go back and lie down." So he went and lay down.
>
> Again Yahweh called, "Samuel!" And Samuel got up and went to Eli and said, "Here I am; you called me."
>
> "My son," Eli said, "I did not call; go back and lie down."
>
> Now Samuel did not yet know Yahweh: The word of Yahweh had not yet been revealed to him.
>
> Yahweh called Samuel a third time, and Samuel got up and went to Eli and said, "Here I am; you called me."
>
> Then Eli realized that Yahweh was calling the boy. So Eli told Samuel, "Go and lie down, and if He calls you, say, 'Speak, Yahweh, for Your servant is listening.'" So Samuel went and lay down in his place . . . .
>
> Samuel lay down until morning and then opened the doors of the house of Yahweh. He was afraid to tell Eli the vision, but Eli called him and said, "Samuel, my son."
>
> Samuel answered, "Here I am."
>
> "What was it He said to you?" Eli asked. "Do not hide it from me. May God deal with you, be it ever so severely, if you hide from me anything He told you." So *Samuel told him everything, hiding nothing from him.* Then Eli said, "He is Yahweh; let Him do what is good in His eyes." (1 Sam. 3:4-9, 15-18)

Samuel's obedient ear to his earthly covering actually allowed him to hear the voice of God.

> When the queen of Sheba heard of Solomon's fame, she came to Jerusalem to test him with hard questions. Arriving with a very great caravan—with camels carrying spices, large quantities of gold, and precious stones—she came to Solomon and talked with him about all she had on her mind. *Solomon answered all her questions; nothing was too hard for him to explain to her.* (2 Chron. 9:1-2)

> "As for Me, this is My covenant with them," says Yahweh. "My Spirit, who is on you, and *My words that I have put in your mouth will not depart from your mouth, or from the mouths of your children, or from the mouths of their descendants* from this time on and forever," says Yahweh. (Isa. 59:21)

> The *mouth of the righteous brings forth wisdom,* but a perverse tongue will be cut out. The *lips of the righteous know what is fitting,* but the mouth of the wicked only what is perverse. (Prov. 10:31-32)

> "No weapon forged against you will prevail, and *you will refute every tongue that accuses you.* This is the heritage of the servants of Yahweh, and this is their vindication from Me," declares Yahweh. (Isa. 54:17)

> *From the fruit of his lips a man is filled with good things* as surely as the work of his hands rewards him. (Prov. 12:14)

A man finds joy in giving *an apt reply*—and *how good is a timely word!* (Prov. 15:23)

A *word aptly spoken* is like apples of gold in settings of silver. (Prov. 25:11)

My son, if your heart is wise, then my heart will be glad; my inmost being will rejoice when *your lips speak what is right.* (Prov. 23:15-16)

Be wise in the way you act toward outsiders; make the most of every opportunity. *Let your conversation be always full of grace, seasoned with salt, so that you may know how to answer everyone.* (Col. 4:5-6)

But in your hearts set apart Christ as Lord. *Always be prepared to give an answer* to everyone who asks you to give the reason for the hope that you have. But *do this with gentleness and respect,* keeping a clear conscience, so that those who speak maliciously against your good behavior in Christ may be ashamed of their slander. (1 Pet. 3:15-16)

f. Saying "Please" and "Thank You," Asking Permission

Proper discipline of children brings proper honor of adults. Saying *please* and *thank you* and asking permission will not burden them; it will become a normal and customary expression of their respect. The Hebrew word translated "bowed" is *shachah*, which means to "humbly beseech." Thus the act of bowing down, of showing honor and submission, often corresponded to saying, "If it pleases you." Saying "please" and "thank you," asking permission, humbles us before others, and humility brings God's grace (James 4:6-10). So we acknowledge an authority over our lives higher than ourselves and submit ourselves to the will of that authority, whether our request is granted or denied. We recognize that we are not the source of permission for ourselves but that we depend upon the graciousness and giving of others. We do not assert our rights and make demands, but we humbly solicit what we want or need—be it for ourselves or others—from a source outside of and beyond ourselves, acknowledging our dependence and need. To take without asking permission is to steal, to be a thief and a robber, whether we take material things or simply take our leave. It says that Jesus has not purchased us (Acts 20:28; 1 Cor. 6:20), that we do not *belong* to Him. It is God's good pleasure to give us our legitimate desires when they conform to His own will and purposes and to bless us accordingly, but if we take without asking, we are covetous, grasping, selfish and even devious. We are also presumptuous, thinking in our pride that we mistakenly deserve and have a right to, or can accomplish, something and that we have no need to ask permission for anything before doing it. We presume it is ours to take and do rather than Jesus', that we need not ask Him as He expresses His authority through our parents or other members of His Body who might express God's authority to us.

> So Ruth the Moabitess said to Naomi, "Please let me go to the field, and glean heads of grain after him in whose sight I may find favor." And she said to her, "Go, my daughter." (Ruth 2:2)

Here Ruth, a grown woman, actually asks permission to *serve* Naomi.

> When Abigail saw David, she quickly got off her donkey and *bowed down before David with her face to the ground. She fell at his feet and said*: "My lord, let the blame be on me alone. *Please let your servant speak to you; hear what your servant has to say.*" (1 Sam. 25:23-24)

> In fact, as soon as she heard about Him, a woman whose little daughter was possessed by an evil spirit came and *fell at His feet.* The woman was a Greek, born in Syrian Phoenicia. She *begged Jesus* to drive the demon out of her daughter.
> "First let the children eat all they want," He told her, "for it is not right to take the children's bread and toss it to their dogs."
> "*Yes, Lord," she replied, "but even the dogs under the table eat the children's crumbs.*"
> Then He told her, "For such a reply you may go; the demon has left your daughter."
> She went home and found her child lying on the bed, and the demon gone. (Mark 7:25-30)

> When he saw Queen Esther standing in the court, he was pleased with her and held out to her the gold scepter that was in his hand. So Esther approached and touched the tip of his scepter.
> Then the king asked, "What is it, Queen Esther? What is your request? Even up to half the kingdom, it will be given you."
> "If it pleases the king," replied Esther, "let the king, together with Haman, come today to a banquet I have prepared for him."
> "Bring Haman at once," the king said, "so that we may do what Esther asks."
> So the king and Haman went to the banquet Esther had prepared. (Esther 5:2-5)

> Therefore, the kingdom of heaven is like a king who wanted to settle accounts with his servants. As he began the settlement, a man who owed him ten thousand talents was brought to him. Since he was not able to pay, the master ordered that he and his wife and his children and all that he had be sold to repay the debt.
> The servant *fell on his knees before him.* "Be patient with me," he begged, "and I will pay back everything." *The servant's master took pity on him, canceled the debt and let him go.* (Matt. 18:23-27)

> So Boaz said to Ruth, "My daughter, listen to me. Don't go and glean in another field and don't go away from here. Stay here with my servant girls. Watch the field where the men are harvesting, and follow along after the girls. I have told the men not to touch you. And whenever you are thirsty, go and get a drink from the water jars the men have filled."
> At this, *she bowed down with her face to the ground.* She exclaimed,

"Why have I found such favor in your eyes that you notice me—a foreigner?" (Ruth 2:8-10)

Then the king said to Ziba, "All that belonged to Mephibosheth is now yours."

"*I humbly bow,*" *Ziba said.* "*May I find favor in your eyes, my lord the king.*" (2 Sam. 16:4)

Yahweh appeared to Abraham near the great trees of Mamre while he was sitting at the entrance to his tent in the heat of the day. Abraham looked up and saw three men standing nearby. When he saw them, *he hurried from the entrance of his tent to meet them and bowed low to the ground.*

He said, "If I have found favor in your eyes, my lord, do not pass your servant by." (Gen. 18:1-3)

The two angels arrived at Sodom in the evening, and Lot was sitting in the gateway of the city. When he saw them, he got up to meet them and *bowed down with his face to the ground.* "My lords," he said, "*please turn aside to your servant's house. You can wash your feet and spend the night and then go on your way early in the morning.*" (Gen. 19:1-2)

So the king asked me, "Why does your face look so sad when you are not ill? This can be nothing but sadness of heart."

I was very much afraid, but I said to the king, "May the king live forever! Why should my face not look sad when the city where my fathers are buried lies in ruins, and its gates have been destroyed by fire?"

The king said to me, "What is it you want?"

Then I prayed to the God of heaven, and I answered the king, "*If it pleases the king and if your servant has found favor in his sight, let him send me to the city in Judah where my fathers are buried so that I can rebuild it.*"

Then the king, with the queen sitting beside him, asked me, "How long will your journey take, and when will you get back?" It pleased the king to send me; so I set a time. (Neh. 2:2-6)

"My father," she replied, "you have given your word to Yahweh. Do to me just as you promised, now that Yahweh has avenged you of your enemies, the Ammonites. But *grant me this one request,*" she said. "Give me two months to roam the hills and weep with my friends, because I will never marry."

"You may go," he said. And he let her go for two months . . . . After the two months, she returned to her father, and he did to her as he had vowed. And she was a virgin. (Judg. 11:36-38)

Since God is the Source of every good gift, all of our thanksgiving should always be ultimately directed to Him.

Don't be deceived, my dear brothers. *Every good and perfect gift is from above, coming down from the Father of the heavenly lights,* who does not change like shifting shadows. (James 1:16-17)

Speak to one another with psalms, hymns and spiritual songs. Sing and make music in your heart to the Lord, *always giving thanks to God the Father for everything*, in the name of our Lord Jesus Christ. (Eph. 5:19-20)

Be joyful always; pray continually; *give thanks in all circumstances*, for this is God's will for you in Christ Jesus. (1 Thess. 5:16-18)

When we take without asking, the Word of God condemns this just as severely as if we were stealing.

Here a dinner was given in Jesus' honor. Martha served, while Lazarus was among those reclining at the table with Him. Then Mary took about a pint of pure nard, an expensive perfume; she poured it on Jesus' feet and wiped His feet with her hair. And the house was filled with the fragrance of the perfume.

But one of His disciples, Judas Iscariot, who was later to betray Him, objected, "Why wasn't this perfume sold and the money given to the poor? It was worth a year's wages." He did not say this because he cared about the poor but because *he was a thief*; as keeper of the money bag, *he used to help himself to what was put into it*. (John 12:2-6)

Then Naaman and all his attendants went back to the man of God. He stood before him and said, "Now I know that there is no God in all the world except in Israel. Please accept now a gift from your servant."

The prophet answered, "As surely as Yahweh lives, whom I serve, I will not accept a thing." And even though Naaman urged him, he refused.

"If you will not," said Naaman, "please let me, your servant, be given as much earth as a pair of mules can carry, for your servant will never again make burnt offerings and sacrifices to any other god but Yahweh. But may Yahweh forgive your servant for this one thing: When my master enters the temple of Rimmon to bow down and he is leaning on my arm and I bow there also—when I bow down in the temple of Rimmon, may Yahweh forgive your servant for this."

"Go in peace," Elisha said.

After Naaman had traveled some distance, Gehazi, the servant of Elisha the man of God, said to himself, "My master was too easy on Naaman, this Aramean, by not accepting from him what he brought. As surely as Yahweh lives, I will run after him and get something from him."

So Gehazi hurried after Naaman. When Naaman saw him running toward him, he got down from the chariot to meet him. "Is everything all right?" he asked.

"Everything is all right," Gehazi answered. "My master sent me to say, 'Two young men from the company of the prophets have just come to me from the hill country of Ephraim. Please give them a talent of silver and two sets of clothing.'"

"By all means, take two talents," said Naaman. He urged Gehazi to accept them, and then tied up the two talents of silver in two bags, with two sets of clothing. He gave them to two of his servants, and they carried them ahead of Gehazi. When Gehazi came to the hill, he took the things from the servants and put them away in the house. He sent the men away and they left. Then he went in and stood before his master Elisha.

"Where have you been, Gehazi?" Elisha asked.

"Your servant didn't go anywhere," Gehazi answered. But Elisha said to him, "Was not my spirit with you when the man got down from his chariot to meet you? Is this the time to take money, or to accept clothes, olive groves, vineyards, flocks, herds, or menservants and maidservants? Naaman's leprosy will cling to you and to your descendants forever." Then Gehazi went from Elisha's presence and he was leprous, as white as snow. (2 Kings 5:15-27)

(Of course, Gehazi not only took the gifts from Naaman without asking his master Elisha's permission, but he even took those gifts in direct disobedience to Elisha, while also lying to both Naaman and Elisha.)

Parents should also teach their children about taking leave without asking permission. A child who ventures off without asking leave dishonors God and his parents. He doesn't stand in his place of responsibility. Moreover, by going off without asking, he may also endanger himself or others. To *take* leave rather than *asking* leave shows that we take for granted that we belong only to ourselves and not to the One who bought us with His blood and entrusted children to their parents' care. A respectful child will not desert, abandon or take leave of his place without permission, but the unfaithful person leaves without asking. Scripture identifies such behavior as irresponsible.

> Woe to the worthless shepherd who *deserts* the flock! (Zech. 11:17)

> I am the good shepherd. The good shepherd lays down his life for the sheep. The hired hand is not the shepherd who owns the sheep. So when he sees the wolf coming, he *abandons* the sheep and runs away. Then the wolf attacks the flock and scatters it. The man runs away because he is a hired hand and cares nothing for the sheep. (John 10:11-13)

> I also learned that the portions assigned to the Levites had not been given to them, and that all the Levites and singers responsible *for the service had gone back to their own fields.* So I rebuked the officials and asked them, "Why is the house of God neglected?" Then I called them together and stationed them at their posts. (Neh. 13:10-11)

> In those days Israel had no king; everyone did *as he saw fit.* (Judg. 21:25)

Taking our leave without permission causes distrust and breaks down relationships.

> From Paphos, Paul and his companions sailed to Perga in Pamphylia, where John left them to return to Jerusalem . . . . Some time later Paul said to Barnabas, "Let us go back and visit the brothers in all the towns where we preached the word of the Lord

and see how they are doing." Barnabas wanted to take John, also called Mark, with them, but Paul did not think it wise to take him, because *he had deserted them* in Pamphylia and had not continued with them in the work. (Acts 13:13 with Acts 15:36-38)

In contrast, Moses honored his father-in-law by asking permission even when *God* sent Moses back to Egypt. Moses didn't *take* his leave just because he felt God had told him to go; he *asked* for it and thereby honored both his father-in-law *and* God.

> Then Moses went back to Jethro his father-in-law and said to him, "Let me go back to my own people in Egypt to see if any of them are still alive."
> Jethro said, "Go, and I wish you well." (Exod. 4:18)

g. Positive Socialization

Often, when children do leave their homes without permission, they are seeking their peers. This exalts horizontal relationships over the vertical relationships through which God most directly relates to children and through which He teaches them to walk in honor, honesty and love. So Moses, Jesus, Paul and the book of Proverbs all direct children to look primarily to their vertical relationships with their parents for guidance and growth.

> *Honor your father and your mother*, that your days may be long upon the land which Yahweh your God is giving you. (Exod. 20:12)

> Train up a child in the way he should go, and when he is old he will not depart from it. (Prov. 22:6)

> The rod and rebuke give wisdom, but *a child left to himself brings shame to his mother.* (Prov. 29:15)

> He said to them, "All too well you reject the commandment of God, that you may keep your tradition. For Moses said, 'Honor your father and your mother'; and, 'He who curses father or mother, let him be put to death.' But you say, 'If a man says to his father or mother, "Whatever profit you might have received from me is Corban"—'(that is, a gift to God), then you no longer let him do anything for his father or his mother, making the word of God of no effect through your tradition which you have handed down. And many such things you do." (Mark 7:9-13)

> *Children, obey your parents in all things*, for this is well pleasing to the Lord. (Col. 3:20)

> *Children, obey your parents in the Lord*, for this is right. "*Honor your father and mother*," which is the first commandment with promise: "that it may be well with you and you may live long on the earth." (Eph. 6:1-3)

> Then He went down with them and came to Nazareth, and *was*

subject to them, but His mother kept all these things in her heart. And Jesus increased in wisdom and stature, and in favor with God and men. (Luke 2:51-52)

In contrast, children who look primarily to their horizontal relationships with their peers for guidance and direction will tend to disdain the authority that comes "from above," and so they'll displace it with the authority of their peers.* These peer relations of unconverted children and youth can be unimaginably debilitating and destructive, ruining a person's entire life. Even in a Christian community, such relationships, because they occur among the yet-to-be converted, are actually taking place outside the God-given order that constitutes the Body of Christ, which in turn, according to Paul, represents the fullness of God on earth.

> And He put all things under His feet, and gave Him to be head over all things to the church, which is His body, the fullness of Him who fills all in all. (Eph. 1:22-23)

So by definition, such horizontal peer relationships can't help but distance those who form them from God, since they occur outside the patterns designated and the close care provided by Christ's Body. Only there, in that Body, can children become an extension of the Body's sanctifying power. Apart from that covering, peer interaction among unconverted children generates toxins that can break down and destroy the spiritual health and life of the Body, not only in the individual children, but potentially in the entire corporate local body as well. This is crucial knowledge for the healthy life and growth of the Body. The honor of these and all other God-given and -designed relationships encourages God's love and power to flow through His Body.

God has made human beings incomplete within themselves because the effort to overcome this incompleteness can teach us to enter into divinely ordered relationships of love with other people and ultimately with God. A young child is a totally dependent being. So as he grows, he looks toward relationships with others to meet his needs. He has not only physical needs, but also spiritual, emotional and intellectual as well. The child often gropes to find the meaning of his life, his direction, his sense of purpose and of identity, often even before he is old enough to be fully aware of these needs. The proper relationship between parents and children provides a vertical relationship to meet all of these needs in God. The child learns to look toward such vertical relationships where adults in authority, and particularly parents, stand as the primary source of meaning and fulfillment in his life. The context of these vertical relationships molds the child's attitudes from above, and so his attention is directed above. Christian

---

* See "Peer Pressure and Socialization," p. 78.

child rearing always teaches and trains children to love the Lord above all and to find the fulfillment of all their needs and desires in Him. But God has incarnated Himself in human flesh to express His love; so He has also established the precise and specific channels of human relationship through which we can learn to truly love Him, relationships that take place through human beings who form the habitation, the intricately designed temple, of God's Holy Spirit (Eph. 2:19-22; 4:11-16; 1 Pet. 2:5). Therefore, we must first learn to love those whom we can see before we can learn to love the One we cannot see (1 John 4:20).

When parents love and guide their children and children learn to submit—not passively but wholeheartedly, with enthusiasm—to these relationships, the children will find their identity and security in the Lord of love. The relationships with siblings in the family will be nurtured properly only in this ordering of love. The deepest needs of children will never be met by their association with and imitation of their similarly searching peers, who also grope for meaning and identity in their own lives. No relationships will be established in their proper order outside a child's proper place in his family. The proper order of relationships in all the families in a community makes it possible for children to love and encourage one another. These relationships can never just be left to themselves. They always require positive oversight and direction from those with an authority that directs the children's attention and yearning above, ultimately toward God.

In his second letter to the Corinthians, Paul emphatically stressed the positive role of authority for the building up of the Body:

> For even if I boast somewhat freely about *the authority the Lord gave us for building you up rather than pulling you down*, I will not be ashamed of it. (2 Cor. 10:8)

> This is why I write these things when I am absent, that when I come I may not have to be harsh in my use of authority—*the authority the Lord gave me for building you up, not for tearing you down.* (2 Cor. 13:10)

The word translated here as "edification" or "building up" is the Greek word *oikodome*, which, according to *The New International Dictionary of New Testament Theology*, "describes the growth and expansion of the community through the Spirit." Edification or "building up" is so central for the purpose of the Body that "there is one rule which applies to everything which happens within the community: it must serve to build up the community."* Children must also see that the primary parental authority in their lives is to build them up. They can grow up, mature, only under the oversight of God's "building up" authority. Jesus said that a

---

* 1 Cor. 14:26; Rom. 14:19; 2 Cor. 12:19; Eph. 2:19-22; 4:11-16, 29; 1 Thess. 5:11.

student cannot rise above the level of his teacher (Luke 6:40). So if children make their peers their primary teachers, they never mature in character, emotions, intellect or spirit. Parents must actively and firmly establish this transcendent order of relationships that builds up and doesn't tear down, an order of relationships that always reaches *up above*, toward God as the ultimate teacher. This should hold even in times of relaxation and recreation. One of the surest paths to hell for a child is peer socialization undirected toward God.

When all adults cooperate to ensure God's covering authority in all relationships, life within the broader context of Christian community will consistently assist the fullest development of each child. But *no one* should *ever* stand in the parents' place except a specifically designated parental substitute for a special or extreme situation. The community, however, does provide the essential context of relationship for the family and so provides a crucial part of the framework in which the child grows. In this context, the child enjoys a wide diversity of relationships with other members of the community, including children outside his own family. He relates, works and plays with them as they grow together *in God.* Children can come together under adult supervision to work in gardens, in farm chores such as milking, in small-scale construction jobs, like making chicken coops; or they can get together with their friends and families to work on common interests, such as sewing, spinning, weaving, leatherworking, harness making, cornhusking or shelling and other similar activities. They can learn to play musical instruments and participate in youth orchestras and smaller instrumental groups as well as choirs and other singing groups. They can also come together in family recreational gatherings, such as in pitching horseshoes, volleyball, swimming, fishing, archery, horseback riding, hiking, camping and so on.

The child who feels needed, wanted and depended on first at home and then in the broader context of community is much more likely to develop a sense of purpose and a stable value system, which is indispensable for positive social interaction. This sense of personal purpose and value develops not only as the child participates in responsibilities and chores that contribute to the welfare of both the family and community but also as he sees that his demeanor, attitude, conduct and character are essential to the true Christian witness of the body of believers with which he is by birth associated and of which he will hopefully aspire to someday become a spiritual member. All those family and community relationships through which he learns to fulfill his practical and spiritual responsibilities provide vital help for full development in the context of a sacralized culture and community. So all of these relationships must, at all times, be covered by parents or responsible adults who have laid hold of the vision for bringing forth Christian character in children. This kind of community life promotes the close bonds and consecrated affection that constitutes a positive "socialization."

> Hear, my children, the instruction *of a father*, and give attention to know understanding . . . . My son, *give attention to my words*; Incline your ear to *my* sayings. Do not let them depart from your eyes; keep them in the midst of your heart; for they are life to those who find them, and health to all their flesh. Keep your heart with all diligence, for out of it spring the issues of life. (Prov. 4:1, 20-23)

> My son, if your heart is wise, my heart will rejoice—indeed, I myself; yes, my inmost being will rejoice when your lips speak right things. *Do not let your heart envy sinners*, but be zealous for the fear of Yahweh all the day; for surely there is a hereafter, and your hope will not be cut off. Hear, my son, and be wise; and guide your heart in the way . . . . *Listen to your father who begot you*, and *do not despise your mother* when she is old. (Prov. 23:15-19, 22)

> *My son*, do not forget my law, but let your heart *keep my commands*; for length of days and long life and peace they will add to you. Let not mercy and truth forsake you; bind them around your neck, write them on the tablet of your heart, and so *find favor and high esteem in the sight of God and man.* (Prov. 3:1-4)

> Then He went down with them and came to Nazareth, and *was subject to [His parents]* . . . . And Jesus *increased in wisdom and stature, and in favor with God and men.* (Luke 2:51-52)

> Now I say that the heir, as long as he is a child, does not differ at all from a slave, though he is master of all, but is under guardians and stewards until *the time appointed by the father.* Even so we, *when we were children, were in bondage* under the elements of the world. But when the fullness of the time had come, God sent forth His Son, born of a woman, born under the law, to redeem those who were under the law, that we might receive the adoption as sons. And because you are sons, God has sent forth the Spirit of His Son into your hearts, crying out, "Abba, Father!" Therefore you are no longer a slave but a son, and if a son, then an heir of God through Christ.(Gal. 4:1-7)

> Therefore, brethren, we are debtors—not to the flesh, to live according to the flesh. For if you live according to the flesh you will die; but if by the Spirit you put to death the deeds of the body, you will live. For as many as are led by the Spirit of God, these are sons of God. For you did not receive the spirit of bondage again to fear, but you received the Spirit of adoption by whom we cry out, "Abba, Father." The Spirit Himself bears witness with our spirit that we are children of God, and if children, then heirs—heirs of God and joint heirs with Christ, if indeed we suffer with Him, that we may also be glorified together. (Rom. 8:12-17)

> Blessed is the man who *walks not in the counsel of the ungodly*, nor stands in the path of sinners, nor sits in the seat of the scornful; but his delight is in the law of Yahweh, and in His law he meditates day and night. He shall be like a tree planted by the rivers of water, that

brings forth its fruit in its season, whose leaf also shall not wither; and whatever he does shall prosper. (Ps. 1:1-3)

I am a companion of all who fear You, and of those who keep Your precepts. (Ps. 119:63)

Then those who feared Yahweh spoke to one another, and Yahweh listened and heard them; so a book of remembrance was written before Him for those who fear Yahweh and who meditate on His name. (Mal. 3:16)

And let us consider one another in order to stir up love and good works. (Heb. 10:24)

He who walks with wise men will be wise, but the *companion of fools will be destroyed.* (Prov. 13:20)

My son, *hear the instruction of your father*, and do not forsake the law of your mother; for they will be a graceful ornament on your head, and chains about your neck. (Prov. 1:8-9)

2. Dishonor

Our discussion of honor shows plainly that if children dishonor their parents (and by doing so dishonor God), then no other godly aspect of an unpolluted and pure character can possibly come forth in their lives. The Hebrew word *qalal*, translated "curse" in the scriptures below, literally means "to make light." The child does not esteem his parents' words as *weighty* (the literal meaning of the Hebrew word for "honor") but "small, easy, trifling." The word in the Old Testament translated "mock" is *laag*, which literally means "to deride, as if imitating a foreigner." The mocker refuses to participate in the word spoken to him—he hears the sounds, but without true understanding. Mockery neglects the Word God speaks to us, refuses to incorporate that Word into our lives, attitudes and actions. The mocking child cannot be trained in godly ways because the godly authority that would do the training depends on honor. The fear of Yahweh finds no place in such a child's heart, and therefore he cannot even begin to walk in the wisdom that comes through the fear of the Lord.

"Cursed is the man who *dishonors* his father or his mother." Then all the people shall say, "Amen!" (Deut. 27:16)

The godly have been swept from the land; not one upright man remains . . . . For a son *dishonors* his father, a daughter *rises up against* her mother. (Micah 7:2, 6)

"Anyone who *curses* his father or mother must be put to death." (Matt. 15:4)

There are those who *curse* their fathers and *do not bless* their mothers; those who are pure in their own eyes and yet are not cleansed of their filth; those whose eyes are ever so *haughty*, whose glances are so *disdainful*; those whose teeth are swords and whose jaws are set with knives to devour the poor from the earth, the needy from among mankind. (Prov. 30:11-14)

If a man *curses* ["*makes light of*"] his father or mother, his lamp will be snuffed out in pitch darkness. (Prov. 20:20)

The eye that *mocks* a father, that *scorns obedience* to a mother, will be pecked out by the ravens of the valley, will be eaten by the vultures. (Prov. 30:17)

"How long will you simple ones love your simple ways? How long will *mockers* delight in *mockery* and fools hate knowledge? If you had responded to my rebuke, I would have poured out my heart to you and made my thoughts known to you. But since you rejected me when I called and no one gave heed when I stretched out my hand, since you ignored all my advice and would not accept my rebuke, I in turn will laugh at your disaster; I will mock when calamity overtakes you—when calamity overtakes you like a storm, when disaster sweeps over you like a whirlwind, when distress and trouble overwhelm you." (Prov. 1:22-27)

Noah, a man of the soil, proceeded to plant a vineyard. When he drank some of its wine, he became drunk and lay uncovered inside his tent. Ham, the father of Canaan, saw his father's nakedness and told his two brothers outside . . . .
  When Noah awoke from his wine and found out what his youngest son had done to him, he said, "Cursed be Canaan! The lowest of slaves will he be to his brothers." (Gen. 9:20-22, 24-25)

Another Hebrew word, *lets*, is translated by the KJV as "scorner" or "mocker," by the NKJV as "scoffer" and the NIV as "mocker." The word carries the connotation of one who derides wholesome reproofs, the one who is contemptuous of correction. The Scripture indicates that the scorner (the fool, the simple) must be punished if he would ever find any wisdom, whereas the wise can receive knowledge by instruction (Prov. 21:11). The scorner does not love the one who corrects him and disdains the correction; so he may turn upon his instructor with resentment and hatred. At the very least, he will try to make him feel embarrassed or guilty or unsure that the correction is really necessary or that—because the scorner brings such strife, contention and reproach to relationship—it is merely a waste of effort to try to correct him (Prov. 9:7; 15:12). The scorner is an abomination to man (Prov. 24:9), and God says judgment and beatings are prepared for him (Prov. 19:29).

Hear instruction and be wise, and do not *disdain* it. (Prov. 8:33)

He who corrects a *scoffer* (scorner) gets shame for himself, and he who rebukes a wicked man only harms himself. Do not correct a *scoffer* (scorner), lest he hate you; rebuke a wise man, and he will love you. (Prov. 9:7-8)

A wise son heeds his father's instruction, but a *scoffer* (scorner) does not listen to rebuke. (Prov. 13:1)

A *scoffer* (scorner) does not love one who corrects him, nor will he go to the wise. (Prov. 15:12)

Judgments are prepared for *scoffers* (scorners), and beatings for the backs of fools. (Prov. 19:29)

When the *scoffer* is *punished*, the simple is made wise; but when the wise is *instructed*, he receives knowledge. (Prov. 21:11)

Cast out the *scoffer* (scorner), and contention will leave; yes, strife and reproach will cease. (Prov. 22:10)

The devising of foolishness is sin, and the *scoffer* (scorner) is an abomination to men. (Prov. 24:9)

a. Ignoring Presence of Adults

Children who do not honor their parents, other adults or God will simply ignore or override the presence of everyone in their lives. To such children, adults neither deserve nor receive any recognition at all. At best, these children regard adults as equals. The ears of such children close to the voice of man and God. Only time's providential crowbar of events can dismantle their arrogant edifice and save them from calamity. If their ears remain closed to all adult wisdom, their fate will be to follow the path of death all the way to the bitter end.

> *Cursed is the one who treats his father or his mother with contempt.* And all the people shall say, Amen! (Deut. 27:16)

> But now *they that are younger than I have me in derision.* (Job 30:1, KJV)

b. Not Discerning Busyness or Mood of Adults

A child void of honor will ignore adult presence, with no awareness of their circumstance or disposition. Such a child lacks a hearing ear to receive adult instructions. He sees nothing of what occupies adults around him and so entirely misses the focus of any purpose and will transcendent to his own. Because of his insensitivity, he moves at cross-purposes to God's purpose. He focuses so entirely upon himself that he cannot even recognize, let alone enter into, any larger meaning, vision or purpose within which God would enfold him. He becomes a hindrance to parents and to God's will because he's too insensitive to discern the busyness or mood of adults engaged in that larger will. He therefore becomes disruptive. Insensitive to man, he must also turn a deaf ear and blind eye to God as well. He wreaks havoc in the lives of his parents and everyone else. Brown,

Driver and Briggs give the literal meaning of *havvah*, which is "calamity" as translated in Proverbs 19:13, as "engulfing ruin, destruction." So the disruptive child can do untold damage to his parents' work or ministry. His self-centeredness makes impossible the oneness of purpose God desires for families, since that oneness can only come when the lives of all cohere around a center transcendent to each and all, namely Christ. So the child's disruptive foolishness fragments the family and destroys its witness of oneness to the world.

> A *foolish son is the calamity* [the engulfing ruin] *of his father.* (Prov. 19:13, KJV)

> So Lot went out and spoke to his sons-in-law, who were pledged to marry his daughters. He said, "Hurry and get out of this place, because Yahweh is about to destroy the city!" But *his sons-in-law thought he was joking.* (Gen. 19:14)

> Now Esau learned that Isaac had blessed Jacob and had sent him to Paddan Aram to take a wife from there, and that when he blessed him he commanded him, "Do not marry a Canaanite woman," and that Jacob had obeyed his father and mother and had gone to Paddan Aram. Esau then realized *how displeasing* the Canaanite women were to his father Isaac; so he went to Ishmael and married Mahalath, the sister of Nebaioth and daughter of Ishmael son of Abraham, in addition to the wives he already had. (Gen. 28:6-9)

Esau saw his father's displeasure with him, but he lacked the spiritual insight to see why. So his efforts at a solution only made matters worse.

c. Overfamiliarity

The child who ignores adults, their situation and their needs will also be overfamiliar and rude with them. He will impudently treat them as equals or even inferiors, dull objects to merely satisfy his needs or extraneous obstacles full of the afflictions of old age and who need to be removed from the adult child's self-centered life. His unrestrained and always self-congratulating flesh, ever seeking to exalt itself, will break through the limitations of any forms of courtesy, quietness and respect. Often such a child will remain totally oblivious to what he has done. The word *familiarity* comes, of course, from the word *family*; the definition of *familiarity* is a "close association" without "formality and ceremony."[19] Children should, of course, move in freedom and ease in the family as long as they recognize the limits of God's order that give the family the only form that can hold it together. True submission to the rule of love that God brings through those He has placed over us also brings a wonderful fellowship to the family. But when someone becomes "overly familiar," a pride enters his heart that disrupts and destroys family unity, order and fellowship. He has lost the fear of God, of God's authority and God's limits.

He has, in short, broken God's form for the family. Perverted relationship then displaces spiritual relationship; the child recklessly disregards all limits, speaking and acting any way he sees fit. He not only disrespects and dishonors his parents in speech and conduct, but he will dishonor and disrespect his siblings in word or deed, even in violence or incest; for all sense of limits to his own will and desires has fallen. Such a child reduces everything to the level of his own desires and impulses; and so he can never rise above that level. He sees nothing above himself, so he sees neither anything to aspire to nor anything to restrain him. Instead, often in a rage of frustration at his meaningless plight, he tears all things down to his own level of meaninglessness as he himself descends to lower depths of misconduct. His at first counterfeit affection for those in authority soon turns to contempt when any reproof or word would come to reveal his sin or self-love and change him. In his blindness, he boldly opposes all purposes transcendent to his own purposeless drives because those higher purposes do not fit into the meaningless and shriveled world of self he has made. He tries to conform God to his image rather than conforming himself to God's image and so becomes godlike in his own eyes.

Some measure of this overfamiliarity even marked Peter's response to Jesus' prediction of His impending death. Peter tried to take Jesus' words out of the realm of the Spirit and bring them into the realm of the flesh. He wanted Jesus to put survival and self-preservation above redemptive, self-sacrificing love. Peter didn't respect his proper relationship with Jesus but tried to bring that relationship onto a carnal, backslapping level. Jesus' response revealed the gravity of such sin.

> From that time on Jesus began to explain to His disciples that He must go to Jerusalem and suffer many things at the hands of the elders, chief priests and teachers of the law, and that He must be killed and on the third day be raised to life.
> Peter took Him aside and *began to rebuke Him.* "Never, Lord!" he said. "This shall never happen to You!"
> Jesus turned and said to Peter, "Get behind Me, Satan! You are a stumbling block to Me; you do not have in mind the things of God, but the things of men." (Matt. 16:21-23)

> *Coming to His hometown,* He began teaching the people in their synagogue, and they were amazed. "Where did this man get this wisdom and these miraculous powers?" they asked.
> *"Isn't this the carpenter's son? Isn't His mother's name Mary, and aren't His brothers James, Joseph, Simon and Judas? Aren't all His sisters with us? Where then did this man get all these things?"* And they took offense at Him.
> But Jesus said to them, *"Only in his hometown and in his own house is a prophet without honor."*
> And He did not do many miracles there because of their lack of faith. (Matt. 13:54-58)

d. Rudeness

Rude children, as seen below, "throw off restraint." In Hebrew this is *shalach resen*, which literally means they "push away the bridle." Scripture discourages the attitude of a horse or mule, which must be handled by a strong bit and bridle (Ps. 32:9); but the rude child refuses the control even a mule accepts. He exalts himself in his heart and refuses any restraint but the severest measures against his arrogant presumptuousness. Many a child of this sort has even ended up in prison. Since nothing inwardly restrains his flesh from even ridiculing or mocking the least rule of love as he dishonors both his parents and other adults, only the severest judgment from the world's agents of wrath has the minutest chance of jerking him back onto the path of reality.

> From there Elisha went up to Bethel. As he was walking along the road, *some youths came out of the town and jeered at him.* "Go on up, you baldhead!" they said. "Go on up, you baldhead!" He turned around, looked at them and called down a curse on them in the name of Yahweh. *Then two bears came out of the woods and mauled forty-two of the youths.* (2 Kings 2:23-24)

> And now their sons *mock me* in song; I have become a *byword* among them. They *detest* me and *keep their distance*; they *do not hesitate to spit in my face.* Now that God has unstrung my bow and afflicted me, *they throw off restraint in my presence.* (Job 30:9-11)

e. Loquacity: Not Knowing When to Stop Talking When Given Leave to Speak by Adults

A disrespectful child is often a loquacious child, not sensing when to stop talking after given leave to speak. His words will run on without regard to the value of the adult's time he is mindlessly consuming. Scripture describes such a child as a fool. The "chattering" of a fool is the translation of the Hebrew *saphah*, which literally means "collecting something into a heap and then sweeping it away." This child simply wastes time, undoing with his many words whatever good may be hidden in the heap of his speech. If he does manage to contribute anything positive or useful, he himself will surely undo it and even proceed to do much damage as his unbridled chattering sweeps the good away. His talk is at best a wasted effort because it crashes through all limits and order.

> As a dream comes when there are many cares, so the speech of a fool *when there are many words.* (Eccles. 5:3)

> The fool *multiplies words.* (Eccles. 10:14)

When *words are many, sin is not absent, but he who holds his tongue is wise.* (Prov. 10:19)

The wise in heart accept commands, but a *chattering* fool comes to ruin. (Prov. 10:8)

Do not let your *mouth lead you into sin.* And do not protest to the temple messenger, "My vow was a mistake." Why should God be angry at what you say and destroy the work of your hands? Much dreaming and *many words are meaningless.* Therefore stand in awe of God. (Eccles. 5:6-7)

An evil man is trapped by his *sinful talk,* but a righteous man escapes trouble. (Prov. 12:13)

f. Unseasonable in Importunity

With no fear of God to restrain him, this child, ignorant of his own place, will be importunate and unseasonable in crowding into the place of others. He refuses to wait for the proper time to speak but instead intrudes himself into any conversation at any time and in any way he so pleases. Insensitivity and total unawareness of the times and seasons of the Lord mark his life. The Hebrew Old Testament word that is translated as "haste" in Proverbs 29:20 is *uts*, literally meaning "to press." The Hebrew word translated "hasty" in Ecclesiastes 5:2 is *mahar*, which literally means "to be liquid, or flow easily." Thus the child who speaks unseasonably feels he must "press" his words into any conversation he chooses, no matter what the occasion. His words "flow easily" because of his insensitivity to any form that would check their easy flow and gather them into a coherence and fullness that might impart something meaningful, perhaps one day even a little wisdom and knowledge that could impact the lives of others and meet the need of someone in trouble. His flow of words, however, is not the flow of the Spirit but of the unrestrained flesh. It respects no boundaries or limitations, and therefore his words create only sloughs that bog down conversations and relationships in the mire of mere carnality.

He who *answers before listening*—that is his folly and his shame. (Prov. 18:13)

Do not be quick with your mouth, do not be hasty in your heart to utter anything before God. God is in heaven and you are on earth, so *let your words be few.* (Eccles. 5:2)

Scripture refers to people as fools when they cannot yield control of their tongues to God's Spirit, when they simply speak whatever comes into their heads without discerning times or seasons. As Scripture shows, the fool's importunity of speech goes together with foolishness of deed, and both stem from a pride that makes the fool as slow to hear as he is quick to speak. He is so full of self that his carnal nature gushes out of him in word and deed; and that flow of self pollutes or even pushes away the words of life God would bring.

> Do you see a man who *speaks in haste*? There is more hope for a fool than for him. (Prov. 29:20)

> The wise in heart accept commands, but a *chattering* fool comes to ruin . . . . He who winks maliciously causes grief, and a *chattering* fool comes to ruin. (Prov. 10:8, 10)

> He who brings trouble on his family will inherit only wind, and the fool will be servant to the wise. (Prov. 11:29)

> The way of a fool seems right to him, but *a wise man listens* to advice . . . . A prudent man keeps his knowledge to himself, but the heart of fools *blurts out* folly. (Prov. 12:15, 23)

> Every prudent man acts out of knowledge, but a fool *exposes* his folly. (Prov. 13:16)

> A wise man fears Yahweh and shuns evil, but a fool is *hotheaded and reckless*. (Prov. 14:16)

> The tongue of the wise commends knowledge, but the mouth of the fool *gushes folly* . . . . A fool spurns his father's discipline, but whoever heeds correction shows prudence . . . . A fool finds no pleasure in understanding but delights in *airing his own opinions*. (Prov. 15:2, 5; 18:2)

> *Arrogant lips* are unsuited to a fool—how much worse *lying lips* to a ruler! . . . Even a fool is thought wise *if he keeps silent*, and discerning *if he holds his tongue*. (Prov. 17:7, 28)

> Better a poor man whose walk is blameless than a fool whose *lips are perverse* . . . . It is not fitting for a fool to live in luxury—how much worse for a slave to rule over princes! (Prov. 19:1, 10)

> It is to a man's honor to avoid strife, but every fool is *quick to quarrel*. (Prov. 20:3)

> Do not speak to a fool, for he will scorn the wisdom of your words. (Prov. 23:9)

> Wisdom is too high for a fool; in the assembly at the gate he has *nothing to say*. (Prov. 24:7)

> Like snow in summer or rain in harvest, honor is not fitting for a fool. (Prov. 26:1)

> He who trusts in himself is a fool, but he who walks in wisdom is kept safe. (Prov. 28:26)

> A fool *gives full vent* to his anger, but a wise man keeps himself under control. (Prov. 29:11)

> Even as he walks along the road, the fool *lacks sense* and *shows everyone* how stupid he is. (Eccles. 10:3)

> My dear brothers, take note of this: Everyone should be *quick to listen, slow to speak and slow to become angry*. (James 1:19)

While the fool speaks when he should be silent, the flip side of this sin shows itself in the failure when called upon to have a response in the Spirit. Scripture admonishes us to

> always *be prepared to give an answer* to everyone who asks you to give the reason for the hope that you have. (1 Pet. 3:15)

The child who is unseasonable in importunity, ready to give a fleshly answer when none is wanted, will also fail to have the seasonable response of the Spirit.

> But when the king came in to see the guests, he noticed a man there who was not wearing wedding clothes. "Friend," he asked, "how did you get in here without wedding clothes?" The man was *speechless*. Then the king told the attendants, "Tie him hand and foot, and throw him outside, into the darkness, where there will be weeping and gnashing of teeth." For many are invited, but few are chosen. (Matt. 22:11-14)

> After Yahweh had said these things to Job, He said to Eliphaz the Temanite, "I am angry with you and your two friends, because you *have not spoken of Me what is right*, as My servant Job has." (Job 42:7)

> I pondered them in my mind and then accused the nobles and officials. I told them, "You are exacting usury from your own countrymen!" So I called together a large meeting to deal with them and said: "As far as possible, we have bought back our Jewish brothers who were sold to the Gentiles. Now you are selling your brothers, only for them to be sold back to us!" They *kept quiet, because they could find nothing to say*. (Neh. 5:7-8)

g. Must Be Told More Than Once

The self-willed child will not readily and promptly obey his parents; he must be told more than once to do anything. His unwillingness to obey necessitates constant prodding and goading. The Hebrew word *qashah*, translated "stiff-necked" in Proverbs 29:1, literally means "to be dense." The child's insensitivity to God and his parents makes any attentiveness on his part merely fleshly. The hallmarks of good character will never be internalized in him. Instead, they will always seem like external impositions. The external law will never become the internal Word that *is* Christ (John 1:14). The vision of God has no part in his inner life, but he moves only when impelled by others. If he *ever* does do what is good, it must be through the external compulsion that comes from some authority of brute force such as rules in the kingdoms of the world, for the noncoercive authority of self-giving love that rules in the kingdom of God will never be allowed entrance into his heart. In short, he has the mentality of a slave rather than a son, for he is blind to the vision and purpose of God and therefore does not know the will of his Father (John 15:15). Even though he technically "hears" what he is told, he does not have a *hearing ear* for the Word of God that would enable that Word to penetrate his heart and lead him to press into a living relationship with God. His parents usually remain his only conscience; and when they are absent, he follows his flesh wherever it leads.

> If your brother sins against you, go and show him his fault, just between the two of you. If he listens to you, you have won your brother over. But *if he will not listen*, take one or two others along, so that every matter may be established by the testimony of two or three witnesses. *If he refuses to listen* to them, tell it to the church; and *if he refuses to listen* even to the church, treat him as you would a pagan or a tax collector. (Matt. 18:15-17)

> A man *who remains stiff-necked after many rebukes* will suddenly be destroyed—without remedy. (Prov. 29:1)

> So, as the Holy Spirit says: *"Today, if you hear His voice, do not harden your hearts as you did in the rebellion*, during the time of testing in the desert, where your fathers tested and tried Me and for forty years saw what I did. That is why I was angry with that generation, and I said, 'Their hearts are always going astray, and they have not known My ways.' So I declared on oath in My anger, 'They shall never enter My rest.'" (Heb. 3:7-11)

> Even the stork in the sky knows her appointed seasons, and the dove, the swift and the thrush observe the time of their migration. But My people *do not know the requirements of Yahweh.* (Jer. 8:7)

> *You have neither heard nor understood; from of old your ear has not been open.* Well do I know how treacherous you are; you were called a rebel from birth. (Isa. 48:8)

> Go to this people and say, "You will be *ever hearing but never understanding*; you will be *ever seeing but never perceiving.*" For this people's *heart has become calloused*; they *hardly hear with their ears*, and they have *closed their eyes.* Otherwise they might see with their eyes, hear with their ears, understand with their hearts and turn, and I would heal them. (Acts 28:26-27)

> This is why I speak to them in parables: "Though seeing, they do not see; though *hearing, they do not hear or understand.* In them is fulfilled the prophecy of Isaiah: 'You will be ever hearing but never understanding; you will be ever seeing but never perceiving. For this people's heart has become calloused; *they hardly hear with their ears*, and they have closed their eyes. Otherwise they might see with their eyes, *hear with their ears, understand with their hearts and turn*, and I would heal them.'" (Matt. 13:13-15)

> He said, "Go and tell this people: 'Be *ever hearing, but never understanding*; be ever seeing, but never perceiving.' Make the heart of this people calloused; make their ears dull and close their eyes. Otherwise they might see with their eyes, *hear with their ears*, understand with their hearts, and turn and be healed." (Isa. 6:9-10)

> Hear this, you foolish and senseless people, who have eyes but do not see, who *have ears but do not hear*. (Jer. 5:21)

> You stiff-necked people, with uncircumcised hearts and ears! You are just like your fathers: You always resist the Holy Spirit! (Acts 7:51)

> Then the word of Yahweh came to Jonah a second time: "Go to the great city of Nineveh and proclaim to it the message I give you." (Jon. 3:1-2)

> Jonadab son of Recab ordered his sons not to drink wine and this command has been kept. To this day they do not drink wine, because they obey their forefather's command. But *I have spoken to you again and again, yet you have not obeyed Me.* Again and again I sent all My servants the prophets to you. They said, "Each of you must turn from your wicked ways and reform your actions; do not follow other gods to serve them. Then you will live in the land I have given to you and your fathers." *But you have not paid attention or listened to Me.* (Jer. 35:14-15)

A child who must be told repeatedly to do something has not yet entered into his inheritance of sonship.

> What I am saying is that as long as the heir is a child, he is no different from a slave, although he owns the whole estate. He is subject to guardians and trustees until the time set by his father. So also, when we were children, we were in slavery under the basic principles of the world. (Gal. 4:1-3)

> Jesus replied, "I tell you the truth, everyone who sins is a slave to sin. Now a slave has no permanent place in the family, but a son belongs to it forever." (John 8:34-35)

> Listen to another parable: There was a landowner who planted a vineyard. He put a wall around it, dug a winepress in it and built a watchtower. Then he rented the vineyard to some farmers and went away on a journey. When the harvest time approached, he sent his servants to the tenants to collect his fruit.
> The tenants seized his servants; they beat one, killed another, and stoned a third. Then he sent other servants to them, more than the first time, and the tenants treated them the same way. Last of all, he sent his son to them. "They will respect my son," he said.
> But when the tenants saw the son, they said to each other, "This is the heir. Come, let's kill him and take his inheritance." So they took him and threw him out of the vineyard and killed him. (Matt. 21:33-39)

h. Unthankful

The child who does not feel and show honor to adults sees everything that comes to him as owed to him. Far from being thankful, nothing he gets ever seems enough. His ingratitude grows in his inability to turn outward in appreciation to the Source of all his blessings or to simply thank whomever God would use to bless him. He even forgets completely all the good done for him, as well as those who did it. In the New Testament, the Greek word translated "unthankful" is *acharistos*, which literally means to be "without grace"; a person without gratitude is without grace.

> Now on His way to Jerusalem, Jesus traveled along the border between Samaria and Galilee. As He was going into a village, ten men who had leprosy met Him. They stood at a distance and called out in a loud voice, "Jesus, Master, have pity on us!"
> When He saw them, He said, "Go, show yourselves to the priests." And as they went, they were cleansed.
> One of them, when he saw he was healed, came back, praising God in a loud voice. He threw himself at Jesus' feet and thanked Him—and he was a Samaritan.
> Jesus asked, *"Were not all ten cleansed? Where are the other nine? Was no one found to return and give praise to God except this foreigner?"* Then He said to him, "Rise and go; your faith has made you well." (Luke 17:11-19)

> No sooner had Gideon died than the Israelites again prostituted themselves to the Baals. They set up Baal-Berith as their god and *did not remember Yahweh their God, who had rescued them* from the hands of all their enemies on every side. They also failed to show kindness to the family of Jerub-Baal (that is, Gideon) for all the good things he had done for them. (Judg. 8:33-35)

> King Joash *did not remember the kindness* Zechariah's father Jehoiada had shown him but killed his son, who said as he lay dying, "May Yahweh see this and call you to account." (2 Chron. 24:22)

> People will be lovers of themselves, lovers of money, boastful, proud, abusive, disobedient to their parents, *ungrateful*, unholy . . . . (2 Tim. 3:2)

> For if you possess these qualities in increasing measure, they will keep you from being ineffective and unproductive in your knowledge of our Lord Jesus Christ. But if anyone does not have them, he is nearsighted and blind, and *has forgotten* that he has been cleansed from his past sins. (2 Pet. 1:8-9)

> They did not keep God's covenant and refused to live by His law. *They forgot* what He had done, the wonders He had shown them. (Ps. 78:10-11)

> Jesus continued: "There was a man who had two sons. The younger one said to his father, 'Father, give me my share of the estate.' So he divided his property between them.
> "Not long after that, the younger son got together all he had, set off for a distant country and there squandered his wealth in wild living." (Luke 15:11-13)

> Then they believed His promises and sang His praise. But *they soon forgot* what He had done and did not wait for His counsel . . . . *They forgot* the God who saved them, who had done great things in Egypt. (Ps. 106:12-13, 21)

I cared for you in the desert, in the land of burning heat. When I fed them, they were satisfied; when they were satisfied, they became proud; then *they forgot Me*. (Hos. 13:5-6)

i. Talking Back

Unable to receive discipline and unsubmissive to authority, a disrespectful child always talks back, always attempts to justify his sin, always makes excuses for his behavior, always tells others they are wrong and he is right. Rather than respectfully listening for God's Word, he will actually reject the Word, which will then rebound to his condemnation. The Hebrew word translated as "arrogance" in 1 Samuel 2:3, *athaq*, literally means "license." In other words, to talk back means to reject all restrictions and controls, to "take license" in coming out from under God's covering and authority. Such a child feels he has the right and freedom to talk back to his parents because he assumes his authority should be as great as theirs. So he "takes license." Such a child has actually put himself in a place of authority above God; he has set himself up as "antichrist," which literally means to put one's self in the place of Christ. He has done this by putting himself in the place of someone else in Christ's own Body, someone who has authority in Christ over him.

> *Do not keep talking so proudly or let your mouth speak such arrogance*, for Yahweh is a God who knows, and by Him deeds are weighed. (1 Sam. 2:3)

> To fear Yahweh is to hate evil; *I hate pride and arrogance, evil behavior and perverse speech*. (Prov. 8:13)

> They close up their callous hearts, and *their mouths speak with arrogance*. (Ps. 17:10)

> *They pour out arrogant words*; all the evildoers are *full of boasting*. (Ps. 94:4)

Then the commander stood and called out in Hebrew: "Hear the word of the great king, the king of Assyria! This is what the king says: Do not let Hezekiah deceive you. He cannot deliver you from my hand. Do not let Hezekiah persuade you to trust in Yahweh when he says, 'Yahweh will surely deliver us; this city will not be given into the hand of the king of Assyria.'

"Do not listen to Hezekiah. This is what the king of Assyria says: Make peace with me and come out to me. Then every one of you will eat from his own vine and fig tree and drink water from his own cistern, until I come and take you to a land like your own, a land of grain and new wine, a land of bread and vineyards, a land of olive trees and honey. Choose life and not death!

"Do not listen to Hezekiah, for he is misleading you when he says, 'Yahweh will deliver us.' Has the god of any nation ever delivered his land from the hand of the king of Assyria? Where are the gods of Hamath and Arpad? Where are the gods of Sepharvaim, Hena and Ivvah? Have they rescued Samaria from my hand? Who of all the gods of these countries has been able to save his land from me? How then can Yahweh deliver Jerusalem from my hand?" (2 Kings 18:28-35)

Woe to him who quarrels with his Maker, to him who is but a potsherd among the potsherds on the ground. *Does the clay say to the potter, "What are you making?"* Does your work say, "He has no hands"? Woe to him who says to his father, "What have you begotten?" or to his mother, "What have you brought to birth?" (Isa. 45:9-10)

j. Peer Pressure and Socialization

We've already stated that for children, the surest path to hell lies in improper socialization. As also stated, children who reject parental authority, the authority given and sent from above, fall under another overcoming power, one that issues from below. In their desire for autonomy, to be as gods in the way the serpent promised, to be a law unto themselves and therefore deciding for themselves what's good and evil, such children reject the relational order of fatherhood just as Adam and Eve did in the garden. They instead hand over their freedom to the one who through the "power of death" brings them into "bondage" through the "fear of death" (Heb. 2:13-14). Rejecting the explicit, personal authority found in the society of family and church, and then thinking themselves to be free, they either personally choose or are unconsciously drawn under the dominion of peer pressure and impersonal, institutionalized authority, all the while professing their own independence.

Numerous studies confirm that peer pressure will exert its influence whenever clearly defined, relational and personal authority is depreciated in any way.[20] Children who spend most of their time with their peers "become dependent on those peers."[21] So they never nurture a sense of personal, moral agency. Likewise, children raised in the collective, group situation of mass education "grow up more and more dependent upon their peers in all social and emotional respects,"[22] being transferred at adulthood to a dependency on a media priesthood to make most of their assessments for them. In short, they seldom become capable of authentically "independent decisions."[23] This is not to say such decisions will be independent from dialogue with legitimate relational authority; but, by definition, they should be free from peer-pressure conformity, which becomes conformity to a media-generated "public opinion," as well as from the illusion of autonomy. But it is not surprising that, in experimental research, it is these very peer- and media-dependent individuals who cling most tenaciously to this very illusion.[24]

To give an example that once might have been (but no longer can be) considered too extreme, a purple and green hairdo or full body tattooing and piercing would seem to express rebellion against all explicit order, all natural "givens," all relational authority. (In fact, a 2003 Harris Poll showed that tattooing made its practitioner "feel more rebellious," 29 percent, yet also more acceptable to their peers and "more attractive" to the opposite sex, 60 percent.[25]) But such fads also increasingly show that behind these expressions of apparent radical "individualism" actually resides a subservience to herd instincts. This can be categorically stated because purple and green, or skinhead, hairdos or tattoos or earrings or nose or tongue studs, or baggy pants and backward baseball caps or stocking caps in summer or all-black outfits, or whatever the latest "rage," actually simultaneously appear on masses of rugged "individuals," perhaps the majority of a certain age group, all across the globe. Of course, all these youths imagine themselves as part of a new rising brotherhood or sisterhood, a collective in revolt against the "meaningless," "dead," "empty," "stupid," "greedy," "selfish," "unenlightened," generation of their parents. Yet they never seem to realize that both their parents and their grandparents participated, or might have participated, in similar revolts, but, in spite of their own revolt, the parents and grandparents nonetheless only ended up further fueling the same dynamic their children or grand-children now claimed to hate. But these adolescents seldom ever stop to ask themselves what exactly is transpiring—what makes each and every generation follow almost precisely the *same* pattern of revolt and assimi-lation. They never seem to see that the individual or group who fancies himself, or itself, autonomous has not been freed, then, from the influence of authorities that shapes his values, tastes and behavior. Rather, he has simply severed all strong ties to *open, apparent* and *personal* authority. He has, in short, cut himself off from the traditional, from the "given" moral community and then submitted totally to peer pressure and other forms of impersonal authority that allow him the *illusion* of individual autonomy, while it all along enslaves him to every latest trend that in turn feeds the "greedy" consumerist economy and makes it necessary to annually buy new clothes, along with all the other accompanying appurtenances, in order to keep in step with all the latest trends of the youth's peers. So the "free" individual is first severed from the traditional and natural order of personal authority, from his family and church and so on, then totally engulfed, drenched, baptized, in a deluge of immorality and conformism within an antireligious, secular culture, and only then told "to make up his own mind." This is called "freedom" and "independence," but it is only freedom from love, virtue and anything spiritually transcendent.

To break free from this tyranny of peer pressure requires recognizing that, as Paul said, freedom from God is bondage to sin: "Do you not know that to whom you present yourselves slaves to obey, you are that one's slaves whom you obey, whether of sin leading to death, or of obedience leading to righteousness? But God be thanked that though you were slaves of sin, yet you obeyed from the heart that form of doctrine to which you were delivered. And having been set free from sin, you became slaves of righteousness" (Rom. 6:16-18). Freedom can only come by voluntarily yielding our hearts and lives to the loving, relational fatherhood that God places in our lives, by "bow[ing our] knees to the Father of our Lord Jesus Christ, from whom the whole fatherhood in heaven and on earth is named" (Eph. 3:14-15). This in turn requires rejecting the "secret power of lawlessness" that works through peer pressure and all authority that issues from below—"that hidden principle of rebellion against constituted authority" (2 Thess. 2:7, NIV, Ampl.). Rather, freedom comes from yielding ourselves to "the Lord" who "is the Spirit; and where the Spirit of the Lord is, there is liberty"; and then, by His grace, we can, day by day, be "transformed into the same image from glory to glory, which comes from the Lord, who is the Spirit" (2 Cor. 3:17-18). We should remember, however, that "by one *Spirit* we are all baptized into one Body" (1 Cor. 12:13); so the Lord who "is the Spirit" is Lord of our lives only within the context of the order of relationships He has placed us within, including the family (1 Cor. 11:1-3). So when we allow entrance into our lives of God's "Spirit of adoption by whom we cry, 'Abba, Father'" (Rom. 8:15), it will necessarily work in us "to turn the hearts of the fathers to the children, and the hearts of the children to the fathers" (Mal. 4:5).

> *Do not follow the mob to do evil;* . . . do not *pervert justice by siding with the mob.* (Exod. 23:2)

> *The fear of man brings a snare,* but whoever trusts in Yahweh shall be safe. (Prov. 29:25)

> Then Saul said to Samuel, "I have sinned, for I have transgressed the commandment of Yahweh and your words, because *I feared the people and obeyed their voice.*" (1 Sam. 15:24)

> Nevertheless even among the rulers many believed in Him, but *because of the Pharisees they did not confess Him,* lest they should be put out of the synagogue. (John 12:42)

> So Pilate, *wanting to gratify the crowd,* released Barabbas to them; and he delivered Jesus, after he had scourged Him, to be crucified. (Mark 15:15-16)

> Now when Peter had come to Antioch, I withstood him to his face, because he was to be blamed; for before certain men came from James, he would eat with the Gentiles; but when they came, he withdrew and separated himself, *fearing those who were of the circumcision.* And the rest of the Jews also played the hypocrite with him, so that even Barnabas was carried away with their hypocrisy. (Gal. 2:11-13)

> And Moses said to Aaron, "What did this people do to you that you

have brought so great a sin upon them?" So Aaron said, "Do not let the anger of my lord become hot. You know the people, that they are set on evil. For they said to me, 'Make us gods that shall go before us; as for this Moses, the man who brought us out of the land of Egypt, we do not know what has become of him.' And I said to them, 'Whoever has any gold, let them break it off.' So they gave it to me, and I cast it into the fire, and this calf came out." (Exod. 32:21-24)

And *do not be conformed to this world, but be transformed by the renewing of your mind*, that you may prove what is that good and acceptable and perfect will of God. (Rom. 12:2)

The *only* relationship for children that God repeatedly emphasizes, and therefore has emphatically arranged, from the beginning of the Bible to the end, is that with their parents:

For I have known him, in order that he may command his children and his household after him, that they keep the way of Yahweh, to do righteousness and justice, that Yahweh may bring to Abraham what He has spoken to him. (Gen. 18:19)

Every one of you shall *revere his mother and his father*, and keep My Sabbaths: I am Yahweh your God. (Lev. 19:3)

"Cursed is the one who treats his father or his mother with contempt." And all the people shall say, "Amen!" (Deut. 27:16)

Children's children are the crown of old men, and *the glory of children is their father*. (Prov. 17:6)

Listen to your father who begot you, and *do not despise your mother when she is old*. (Prov. 23:22)

He answered and said to them, "Why do you also transgress the commandment of God because of your tradition? For God commanded, saying, '*Honor your father and your mother*'; and, '*He who curses father or mother, let him be put to death*.' But you say, 'Whoever says to his father or mother, "Whatever profit you might have received from me is a gift to God"—then he need not honor his father or mother.' Thus you have made the commandment of God of no effect by your tradition. Hypocrites! Well did Isaiah prophesy about you, saying: 'These people draw near to Me with their mouth, and honor Me with their lips, but their heart is far from Me. And in vain they worship Me, teaching as doctrines the commandments of men.'" (Matt. 15:3-9)

For Moses said, *"Honor your father and your mother"*; and, *"He who curses father or mother, let him be put to death."* (Mark 7:10)

Children, obey your parents in the Lord, for this is right. "Honor your father and mother," *which is the first commandment with promise:* "that it may be well with you and you may live long on the earth." (Eph. 6:1-3)

Children, obey your parents in all things, for this is well pleasing to the Lord. Fathers, do not provoke your children, lest they become discouraged. (Col. 3:20-21)

God even makes submission to parents one of ten points for the government and well-being of human life and society on earth:

> *Honor your father and your mother, as Yahweh your God has commanded you*, that your days may be long, and that it may be well with you in the land which Yahweh your God is giving you. (Deut. 5:16; Eph. 6:1-3)

On the other hand, God never mentions the children's "need" for a public or peer "socialization." In fact, whenever He does mention socialization, He does not refer to it positively nearly so often as He points out its dangers and the need for separation from its corrupting influences.

> Joseph is a fruitful bough, a fruitful bough by a well; his branches run over the wall. The archers have bitterly grieved him, shot at him and hated him. But his bow remained in strength, and the arms of his hands were made strong by the hands of the Mighty God of Jacob (from there is the Shepherd, the Stone of Israel), by the God of your father who will help you, and by the Almighty who will bless you with blessings of heaven above, blessings of the deep that lies beneath, blessings of the breasts and of the womb. The blessings of your father have excelled the blessings of my ancestors, up to the utmost bound of the everlasting hills. They shall be on the head of Joseph, and on the crown of the head of him *who was separate from his brothers*. (Gen. 49:22-26)

> Blessed is the man who *walks not in the counsel of the ungodly, nor stands in the path of sinners, nor sits in the seat of the scornful*; but his delight is in the law of Yahweh, and in His law he meditates day and night. He shall be like a tree planted by the rivers of water, that brings forth its fruit in its season, whose leaf also shall not wither; and whatever he does shall prosper. (Ps. 1:1-3)

> My son, hear the instruction of your father, and do not forsake the law of your mother; for they will be a graceful ornament on your head, and chains about your neck. *My son, if sinners entice you, do not consent. If they say, "Come with us, let us lie in wait to shed blood; let us lurk secretly for the innocent without cause; let us swallow them alive like Sheol, and whole, like those who go down to the pit; we shall find all kinds of precious possessions, we shall fill our houses with spoil; cast in your lot among us, let us all have one purse"—my son, do not walk in the way with them, keep your foot from their path*; for their feet run to evil, and they make haste to shed blood. Surely, in vain the net is spread in the sight of any bird; but they lie in wait for their own blood, they lurk secretly for their own lives. So are the ways of everyone who is greedy for gain; it takes away the life of its owners. (Prov. 1:8-19)

> *Do not enter the path of the wicked, and do not walk in the way of evil. Avoid it, do not travel on it; turn away from it and pass on*. For they do not sleep unless they have done evil; and their sleep is taken away unless they make someone fall. For they eat the bread of wickedness, and drink the wine of violence. (Prov. 4:14-17)

He who walks with wise men will be wise, but the companion of fools will be destroyed. (Prov. 13:20)

Do not be envious of evil men, nor desire to be with them; for their heart devises violence, and their lips talk of troublemaking. Through wisdom a house is built, and by understanding it is established. (Prov. 24:1-3)

Do not fret because of evildoers, nor be envious of the wicked. (Prov. 24:19)

Fear Yahweh and the king, my son, and *do not join with the rebellious,* for those two will send sudden destruction upon them, and who knows what calamities they can bring? (Prov. 24:21-22)

Whoever keeps the law is a discerning son, but *a companion of gluttons shames his father.* (Prov. 28:7)

Whoever loves wisdom makes his father rejoice, but *a companion of harlots wastes his wealth.* (Prov. 29:3)

Your princes are rebellious, and *companions of thieves;* everyone loves bribes, and follows after rewards. They do not defend the fatherless, nor does the cause of the widow come before them. (Isa. 1:23)

I did not sit in the assembly of the mockers, nor did I rejoice; I sat alone because of Your hand, for You have filled me with indignation. (Jer. 15:17)

"Now therefore, please pardon my sin, and return with me, that I may worship Yahweh." But Samuel said to Saul, "*I will not return with you, for you have rejected the word of Yahweh,* and Yahweh has rejected you from being king over Israel." . . . Then he said, "I have sinned; yet *honor me now, please, before the elders of my people and before Israel,* and return with me, that I may worship Yahweh your God." (1 Sam. 15:25-26, 30)

Do not be misled: "*Bad company corrupts good character.*" (1 Cor. 15:33)

B. Honesty/Dishonesty

1. Honesty

Our first element of Christian character showed that basic to our relationship with God and with those through whom God expresses His authority to us is the attitude of honor. Now we want to turn to perhaps the greatest means of honoring or respecting someone: honesty and openness with them. When we are honest, in other words, we stand open and exposed before others because we trust them. We throw aside subtleties, evasiveness, manipulations, ambiguities, affectations, maneuverings and half-truths and make ourselves vulnerable to one another, and especially to those who express God's noncoercive authority in our lives. We surrender all evasiveness and subtlety to embrace that transparency necessary for the fullest possible love to flow between us. Neither does this honor stand or fall on the perfection of those in authority over us (any more than we demand our own perfection before requiring our children or those under us on the job to submit to us). If we truly honor someone, we value their importance to our lives, our need for them and for their ministry to us. Yet we recognize that they can only help us if we open ourselves to them in truth. Any attempt to hide the truth from them denies the importance of their function in our lives and so dishonors and disrespects them. If we want guidance in working on our house or car, it makes no sense to hide the problem from the carpenter or mechanic. How much more in our spiritual relationships must we stand open about our needs, our failures, our problems and so on? If we truly recognize our need and appreciate the help of those we honor, then we will open our hearts in trust to them. When we honor someone, we value him or her as a subject with whom we desire to—aspire to—come into oneness; evasion and deception do the opposite of this, treating a person only as an object for maneuvering and manipulating. To truly desire to come into oneness with someone, to honor him, requires honesty and trust, for upon such trust rests all true relationship. Because relationship requires openness, to the extent we close ourselves to one another in distrust and duplicity, the channels of relationship begin to clog up and finally close down. Barriers then arise that shut each off in their own isolated world, and the one who closes himself or herself has started down the dark path of distrust, suspicion and ultimately betrayal. Trust tears down these barriers and heads us down a different path, one of light, so that we can come to know each other as we are known.

In this light, then, to show how detached and *unemotional* we can remain at witnessing someone's dishonesty with us does not express love: it merely reveals the total lack of value we place on the relationship. Conversely, expressed displeasure at dishonesty may even show that we truly value the relationship, that it means enough to us to emotionally engage us. Perhaps Paul refers to this when he says, "Be angry and sin not" (Eph. 4:26, KJV). As James said, the wrath or anger of man does not work the righteousness of God, but, as Jesus Himself showed (Mark 3:4-6), anger can express our altogether normal displeasure with those barriers that prevent God's righteousness from reaching people. Of course, anger can erupt merely because of our offended pride, but this will usually become clear in the context of relationship. Nonetheless, to rebuke someone for dishonesty does not show that we don't love them. It shows just the opposite: that we value the relationship and hate the lies that would destroy it.

So because trust is prerequisite to all relationship, only honesty can uphold all real relationship. Our English word *honest* actually derives from the Latin word *honos*, "honor." Indeed, without honesty, relationship proves impossible. Relationship takes place through communication—by the transfer of words, thoughts, feelings, ideas, hopes, needs and so on. The word "communicate" means to "join" or "unite" in making something "common," by sharing it as one with each other. For two parties to truly communicate in this sense, the one receiving a message must know *exactly* what the one sending the message means to say. So when someone deliberately conceals or distorts his true meaning, he necessarily destroys both communication and relationship and shows his disrespect and contempt for whomever he claims to relate to. To truly seek to enter into a relationship that would honor someone else requires a special diligence in maintaining honesty. It means earnestly seeking the transparency and openness that allow others to see *openly* and *clearly* our intent and meaning. Then we must stand vulnerable, open and ready to receive an equally honest answer in return.

To fully know someone, to open ourselves to the fullest possible relationship with them, means allowing them full access to our hearts and minds, to our inner beings, even when it is painful. And even to open ourselves to someone in any way at all necessitates trusting the God who formed this relationship. We trust someone when we believe them to be true and honest with us. We trust them if we don't suspect them of trying to take advantage of us. But, of course, the serpent induced Adam and Eve to doubt even God. So mistrust can arise simply because of the evil in our own hearts (Col. 1:21).

Radomír Hubálek believed that even a lie testifies to the importance of trust in building a true relationship. He pointed out that a lie not only opposes truth but counterfeits truth. A lie deliberately seeks to imitate the truth and manipulate the trust that makes relationship possible. Yet it destroys the basis of both truth and all relationship, as well as any possibility of virtuous character in the liar. In his letter to the then Communist rulers of what was once Czechoslovakia, written at the risk of his life and liberty, Hubálek said:

> I consider a lie, every lie, every deceitful communication, to be a contribution to an effort of a total destruction of values. A human being who lies, does so in the conviction that it is, for some reason, advantageous for him to deceive intentionally the recipient of his communication. He fails to realize that he himself, the author of the lie, becomes the first and foremost victim of his own deception. In order to be effective, his lie needs one basic precondition—the addressee of the lie must be convinced that the liar is telling the truth [that is, the addressee must trust the liar because of either love for or honor toward the liar]. Thus, a liar bases his lie, tacitly and dishonestly, on the authority enjoyed by the truth. A lie is therefore vitally dependent on truth, but at the same time undermines truth, subverts it, and thus destroys the very value on which it has the effrontery to depend. Therefore, each and every deceitful communication contains automatically its own fundamental contradiction, and therefore can never result in anything good. When a "clever" lie is found out to have used a counterfeited passport of truth, it loses its support and dies because it is nothing but a parasite living off the truth. Truth does not need a lie, but a lie cannot live without the very truth it seeks to deny. Truth is life; lie is nothing but an effort to kill it.[26]

The one who tells the lie (the addresser), then, must hold the one to whom he addresses his lie (the addressee) in dishonor (the same root as *dishonesty*). The addresser sees the addressee as a lower object for manipulation rather than a valued subject with whom the addresser desires to enter into any relationship of oneness. The addresser closes himself to true relationship—indeed destroys the basis for and possibility of true relationship by his dishonesty, subtlety, partial truths, equivocations and manipulations. Honesty, on the other hand, steps into the light because it places such a high value on relationship and knows true relationship cannot exist apart from honesty; but liars hide in darkness because nothing matters more to them than protecting themselves and their image. John declares that only as "we walk in the light as He is in the light" can "we have fellowship with one another" (1 John 1:7). So honesty and openness invite relationship, oneness, trust and love; dishonesty destroys relationship and love as it embraces fragmentation, distrust and hatred.

> To lie one's way to the truth is therefore impossible because a lie is not a direct opposite of the truth but its more or less foul-smelling substitute. The bad smell will not diminish even if I meet it with a smile and pretend not to notice it. The relationship between truth and lie could be best compared to the relationship between

> light and darkness. Light penetrates darkness; never has darkness
> penetrated light. Equally, the darkness of a lie can never overcome
> the light of the truth.
>
> A liar can be best compared to a man who tries intentionally to
> pay with counterfeit money which, too, only appears to be genu-
> ine. And the results are the same—deterioration of the currency
> and also of mutual trust—even though the truthful word remains
> true and the genuine coin remains genuine.[27]

The counterfeit only succeeds because of the addressee's trust in the real. He believes that the addresser truly honors him, truly desires to enter into an open relationship with him. When he finally sees that what he believed to be truth was merely a facade of lies, he recognizes that the edifice of relationship in which he trusted is now an abandoned shack, abused and neglected, undermined and ruined by the very one he loved but who merely manipulated him for selfish ends. Far from being honored, he was being held in contempt and mocked; far from moving forward in relationship, the very basis of true relationship was being eroded. Dishonesty destroys honor, while honesty protects and edifies it. Honesty opens the channels of love that build and refine character into God's image through the truth coming to us from God and through those we love who also love us. Dishonesty perforates that channel till no communication can flow back and forth between individuals to establish any substantive relationship. When, as Paul instructed, we truly give honor to whom it is due (Rom. 13:7, Ampl.), a transparency before others marks our lives— love opens hearts and we step with trembling toward the light of perfect honesty. If we sin, we anxiously repent and openly confess our sin. We do this even apart from anyone else's knowing because of our certainty that hiding sin ultimately severs relationship, whether with our spiritual brothers and sisters, our natural family or with God.

a. Confession without External Constraint or Coercion

Honor for those who bear God's rule of redeeming love over us cannot help but build up their trust in us. One of the most certain and power-ful ways to confirm the trust in us or of those over us is to confess our sin *without external constraint or coercion*. For a child to confess his sin in this way builds up parental confidence in the child's trustworthiness—the parents know the child is walking in a way to please not merely people but God, in short, that their child has a conscience.

The New Testament Greek word translated "confess" is *homologeo*, which according to one lexicon means "to confess by way of admitting one-self guilty of what one is accused of, the result of *inward conviction*, . . . to declare openly by way of speaking out freely, such confession being the effect of deep conviction of facts." Only when the child (or anyone) walks in the light can he be convicted of his sin. The uncoerced confession that comes forth from his heart declares his desire to walk in true fellowship with his parents, for only as we walk in the light as He is in the light can we have fellowship with one another (1 John 1:7). *Homologeo* also means "to speak the same thing" or the "same word." To freely confess one's sin is, then, to speak a word that conforms to the truth not only of some particular circumstance but also of Scripture as it applies to the circumstances we live in. If children speak the same thing, in this sense, that parents do, the children will live harmoniously with their parents and with God.

Some "confess" their sins only out of fear of punishment and in hopes of avoiding that punishment and receiving mercy. They have no respect toward the offense and how it hurts God and others but only toward the punishment and how they might be hurt by it. This is normal for the very young who have no conscience outside their relationship with their parents; but when older children or even adults still think this way, the development of their character has somehow terribly short-circuited. Confession is, with such children or people, not the fruit of a sincere conscience before God but the result of a mechanical process, where to achieve the desired goal—escape from punishment or hell—they suppose they must merely first go through the required motions. They really care nothing about overcoming sin but only about protecting themselves. No real love motivates these confessions. Such a "confession" comes from purely selfish impulses and is no confession at all, since it fails to truly "speak the same thing" that God is speaking, fails to possess the strength of conviction not only of the sinfulness of the sin but also of how sin must and will be overcome by faith working through love (Gal. 5:6). Children or adults with such an attitude and perspective never seem to realize in their lovelessness and self-centeredness that they carry their own growing punishment and hell around with them and that these will only continue to metastasize in the sinner's increasingly sophisticated selfishness and self-interest. All this can only eventually destroy real love, relationship and trust. Such false confessions can therefore never fully liberate anyone.

The Hebrew word in the Old Testament translated "confess" is *yadah*. It literally means "to hold out the hand." To extend the open hand signals openness and defenselessness, a sign of complete surrender and trust. By "extending his hand" in this way, by confessing his sin without external constraint, the child takes initiative to honor and to build up the trust those in authority have toward him. Whenever a child must be prodded and prompted to confess sin, it shows a love-destroying self-defensiveness, that the child does not see himself as standing *with* his parents on the same side of truth. The importance of truth does not transcend his own image or even his defense of that image.

Therefore *confess your sins to each other* and pray for each other so that you may be healed. The prayer of a righteous man is powerful and effective. (James 5:16)

If we confess our sins, He is faithful and just and will forgive us our sins and *purify us from all unrighteousness.* (1 John 1:9)

If you have been trapped by what you said, ensnared by the words of your mouth, then do this, my son, to free yourself, since you have fallen into your neighbor's hands: *Go and humble yourself; press your plea with your neighbor! Allow no sleep to your eyes, no slumber to your eyelids.* Free yourself, like a gazelle from the hand of the hunter, like a bird from the snare of the fowler. (Prov. 6:2-5)

David was conscience-stricken after he had counted the fighting men, and he said to Yahweh, "I have sinned greatly in what I have done. *Now, O Yahweh, I beg You, take away the guilt of Your servant.* I have done a very foolish thing." (2 Sam. 24:10)

He who conceals his sins does not prosper, but whoever *confesses and renounces* them finds mercy. (Prov. 28:13)

Then the man who had the evil spirit jumped on them and overpowered them all. He gave them such a beating that they ran out of the house naked and bleeding.
  When this became known to the Jews and Greeks living in Ephesus, they were all seized with fear, and the name of the Lord Jesus was held in high honor. *Many of those who believed now came and openly confessed their evil deeds.* (Acts 19:16-18)

Go, proclaim this message toward the north: "'Return, faithless Israel,' declares Yahweh, 'I will frown on you no longer, for I am merciful,' declares Yahweh, 'I will not be angry forever. Only *acknowledge your guilt*—you have rebelled against Yahweh your God, you have scattered your favors to foreign gods under every spreading tree, and have not obeyed Me,'" declares Yahweh. (Jer. 3:12-13)

On the twenty-fourth day of the same month, the Israelites gathered together, fasting and wearing sackcloth and having dust on their heads. Those of Israelite descent had separated themselves from all foreigners. *They stood in their places and confessed their sins and the wickedness of their fathers.* They stood where they were and read from the Book of the Law of Yahweh their God for a quarter of the day, and spent another quarter in *confession* and in worshiping Yahweh their God. (Neh. 9:1-3)

Return, O Israel, to Yahweh your God. Your sins have been your downfall! Take words with you and return to Yahweh. Say to Him: "*Forgive all our sins and receive us graciously*, that we may offer the fruit of our lips. Assyria cannot save us; we will not mount warhorses. We will never again say 'Our gods' to what our own hands have made, for in You the fatherless find compassion." (Hos. 14:1-3)

"Even now," declares Yahweh, "*return to Me with all your heart,* with fasting and weeping and mourning." Rend your heart and not your garments. Return to Yahweh your God, for He is gracious and compassionate, slow to anger and abounding in love, and He relents from sending calamity. Who knows? He may turn and have pity and leave behind a blessing—grain offerings and drink offerings for Yahweh your God. Blow the trumpet in Zion, declare a holy fast, call a sacred assembly. Gather the people, consecrate the assembly; bring together the elders, gather the children, those nursing at the breast. Let the bridegroom leave his room and the bride her chamber. Let the priests, who minister before Yahweh, weep between the temple porch and the altar. Let them say, "Spare Your people, O Yahweh. Do not make Your inheritance an object of scorn, a byword among the nations. Why should they say among the peoples, 'Where is their God?'" (Joel 2:12-17)

b. Love of Truth

As said, only continuing in the truth can preserve a relationship of love with parents, with God and with all of God's people. So to love God, to love our parents in the Lord and to love the people of God means loving the truth. Only a love of truth can motivate the diligent search necessary to find it, which means that God leads us to truth, since "God *is* love" (1 John 4:8, 16). So those without an all-consuming love for the truth will ultimately be deceived and lost, as their relationship with Jesus, who is the truth (John 14:6), must ultimately die, setting them adrift in their own self-deceptions.

> The coming of the lawless one is according to the working of Satan, with all power, signs, and lying wonders, and with all unrighteous deception among those who perish, *because they did not receive the love of the truth*, that they might be saved. And for this reason God will send them strong delusion, that they should believe the lie, that they all may be condemned who did not believe the truth but had pleasure in unrighteousness. (2 Thess. 2:9-12)

> Do not follow the crowd in doing wrong. When you give testimony in a lawsuit, do not pervert justice by siding with the crowd. (Exod. 23:2)

> *Guide me in Your truth* and teach me, for You are God my Savior, and my hope is in You all day long. (Ps. 25:5)

> Do not withhold Your mercy from me, O Yahweh; *may Your* love and Your *truth always protect me.* (Ps. 40:11)

> Surely *You desire truth in the inner parts*; You teach me wisdom in the inmost place. (Ps. 51:6)

> Teach me Your way, O Yahweh, and *I will walk in Your truth*; give me an undivided heart, that I may fear Your Name. (Ps. 86:11)

> Yahweh, who may dwell in Your sanctuary? Who may live on Your holy hill? He whose walk is blameless and who does what is righteous, *who speaks the truth from his heart.* (Ps. 15:1-2)

> You who are far away, hear what I have done; you who are near, ac-

knowledge My power! The sinners in Zion are terrified; trembling grips the godless: "Who of us can dwell with the consuming fire? Who of us can dwell with everlasting burning?" He who walks righteously and *speaks what is right*, who rejects gain from extortion and keeps his hand from accepting bribes, who stops his ears against plots of murder and shuts his eyes against contemplating evil—this is the man who will dwell on the heights, whose refuge will be the mountain fortress. His bread will be supplied, and water will not fail him. (Isa. 33:13-16)

For Your love is ever before me, and *I walk continually in Your truth*. (Ps. 26:3)

Send forth Your light and Your truth, let them guide me; let them bring me to Your holy mountain, to the place where You dwell. (Ps. 43:3)

I have chosen *the way of truth*; I have set my heart on Your laws. (Ps. 119:30)

Do not snatch *the word of truth* from my mouth, for I have put my hope in Your laws. (Ps. 119:43)

From Your precepts I get understanding; Therefore *I hate every false way*. (Ps. 119:104, NASU)

Therefore I esteem right all *Your* precepts concerning everything. I hate every false way. (Ps. 119:128, NASU)

"These are the things you are to do: *Speak the truth* to each other, and *render true and sound judgment* in your courts; do not plot evil against your neighbor, and do not love to swear falsely. I hate all this," declares Yahweh. (Zech. 8:16-17)

Then we will no longer be infants, tossed back and forth by the waves, and blown here and there by every wind of teaching and by the cunning and craftiness of men in their deceitful scheming. Instead, *speaking the truth in love*, we will in all things grow up into Him who is the Head, that is, Christ. (Eph. 4:14-15)

I speak the truth in Christ—I am not lying, my conscience confirms it in the Holy Spirit. (Rom. 9:1)

"You are a king, then!" said Pilate. Jesus answered, "You are right in saying I am a king. In fact, for this reason I was born, and for this I came into the world, to testify to the truth. *Everyone on the side of truth listens to Me*." (John 18:37)

It gave me great joy to have some brothers come and tell about *your faithfulness to the truth* and how you *continue to walk in the truth. I have no greater joy than to hear that my children are walking in the truth*. (3 John 3-4)

A truthful witness gives honest testimony, but a false witness tells lies. (Prov. 12:17)

Truthful lips endure forever, but a lying tongue lasts only a moment. (Prov. 12:19)

Yahweh detests lying lips, but He *delights in men who are truthful*. (Prov. 12:22)

A truthful witness saves lives, but a false witness is deceitful. (Prov. 14:25)

Kings take pleasure in honest lips; they *value a man who speaks the truth*. (Prov. 16:13)

What a man desires is unfailing love; *better to be poor than a liar*. (Prov. 19:22)

An honest answer is like a kiss on the lips. (Prov. 24:26)

Two things I ask of You, O Yahweh; do not refuse me before I die: *Keep falsehood and lies far from me*; give me neither poverty nor riches, but give me only my daily bread. Otherwise, I may have too much and disown You and say, "Who is Yahweh?" Or I may become poor and steal, and so dishonor the name of my God. (Prov. 30:7-9)

c. Walking into the Light

Love of the truth and a desire to have fellowship with God and His people will lead us in continuous pilgrimage into the light, a pilgrimage that ever exposes us to God's Word (Eph. 5:8-15; 1 John 1:5-7). Our relationship with God will become an unfolding walk of ever-greater truth and light. Each step in our walk of faith requires a voluntary choice to step into the light:

> Every moment of our lives is a moment of truth because it is given to us only once, and it is up to us to decide to what we will freely consecrate this moment; whether to the truth of our conscience— or if we waste it irrevocably by deceit and lie.[28]

Every choice for truth, on however small a scale, brings some victory over darkness and deceit that then encourages us on into ever-greater truth. But every choice for darkness makes more difficult any walk in the path of truth until finally the path turns into an overgrown trail coming to a dead end in the dark jungle of our deceit with all its briars, brambles and predators. So each of our daily decisions will add its weight, no matter how small or great, to the final outcome of our lives, determining whether our lives will ultimately be testimonies for truth or for the lie.

The Hebrew word translated as "choose" in Joshua 24:15 is *bachar*; it literally means "to prove, try, distinguish." It refers to something that "is judged to be excellent." It is the word in Proverbs 10:20 translated as "*choice*" silver. Scripture encourages us to "taste and see that Yahweh is good" (Ps. 34:8) and to *choose* to walk in His light and truth—to come into a real relationship with Him. The Psalmist wrote, "I have *chosen* (*bachar*) rather to be a doorkeeper in the house of my God, than to dwell in tents of wickedness (Ps. 84:10, YLT). God sets a choice before us between the eternal riches of His kingdom or the pottage of this world. Yet we must have spiritual eyes, eyes opened to discern this choice, in order to decide rightly and take the "excellent" way. Again, life is a perpetual chain of choices between truth and falsehood, between light and darkness, and each choice can carry ultimate consequences.

> But if serving the Lord seems undesirable to you, then *choose for yourselves this day whom you will serve*, whether the gods your forefathers served beyond the River, or the gods of the Amorites, in whose land you are living. But as for me and my household, we will serve Yahweh. (Josh. 24:15)

> So, as the Holy Spirit says: "Today, *if you hear His voice, do not harden your hearts* as you did in the rebellion, during the time of testing in the desert, where your fathers tested and tried Me and for forty years saw what I did. That is why I was angry with that generation, and I said, 'Their hearts are always going astray, and they have not known My ways.' So I declared on oath in My anger, 'They shall never enter My rest.'" (Heb. 3:7-11)

> This day I call heaven and earth as witnesses against you that I have set before you life and death, blessings and curses. Now choose life, so that you and your children may live and that you may love Yahweh your God, listen to His voice, and hold fast to Him. For Yahweh is your life, and He will give you many years in the land He swore to give to your fathers, Abraham, Isaac and Jacob. (Deut. 30:19-20)

> If we claim to have fellowship with Him yet walk in the darkness, we lie and do not live by the truth. But *if we walk in the light, as He is in the light, we have fellowship with one another*, and the blood of Jesus, His Son, purifies us from every sin. (1 John 1:6-7)

> In Him was life, and that life was *the light of men*. The light shines in the darkness, but the darkness has not understood it. (John 1:4-5)

> And we have the word of the prophets made more certain, and you will do well to pay attention to it, as to *a light shining in a dark place, until the day dawns and the morning star rises in your hearts*. (2 Pet. 1:19)

> If they speak not according to this word, it is because there is no *light* in them. (Isa. 8:20, KJV)

> This is the verdict: Light has come into the world, but men loved darkness instead of light because their deeds were evil. Everyone who does evil hates the light, and will not come into the light for fear that his deeds will be exposed. But *whoever lives by the truth comes into the light*, so that it may be seen plainly that what he has done has been done through God. (John 3:19-21)

> When Jesus spoke again to the people, He said, "*I am the light of the world*. Whoever follows Me will never walk in darkness, but will have the light of life." (John 8:12)

> Then Jesus told them, "You are going to have the light just a

little while longer. *Walk while you have the light*, before darkness overtakes you. The man who walks in the dark does not know where he is going." (John 12:35)

Jesus answered, "Are there not twelve hours of daylight? A man who walks by day will not stumble, for he sees by this world's light. It is when he walks by night that he stumbles, for he has no light." (John 11:9-10)

Your word is *a lamp to my feet* and *a light for my path*. (Ps. 119:105)

The path of the righteous is like *the first gleam of dawn, shining ever brighter till the full light of day*. (Prov. 4:18)

Come, O house of Jacob, *let us walk in the light* of Yahweh. (Isa. 2:5)

For you were once darkness, but now *you are light in the Lord. Live as children of light*. (Eph. 5:8)

d. Integrity

To walk in the light, to be honest and open before God and our brothers and sisters in the Lord, expresses the true meaning of integrity. Integrity suggests an unbrokenness of relationship with God and in the whole intricately designed order through which He moves, the order of the Body of Christ. Such "unbrokenness" brings wholeness within ourselves and oneness to our relationship with God and God's people.* In Hebrew, the words we translate as "integrity" are *tamim* and *tam*, which also can be translated as "plain," "perfect" or "blameless." Two related Hebrew nouns for "integrity" are *tom*, which also can be translated as "perfection" or "uprightness," and *tummah* which means "integrity" or "completeness with regard to one's relationship with God" which "manifests itself in concrete actions." So people with integrity strive for the grace to serve God wholeheartedly, in both the integrity of their hearts and in their concrete actions, as they open their whole being to God and to the covenant people of God. This sacrifice to God will also be unbroken and unblemished and whole—that is, offered to God not only wholeheartedly but also without ever turning back to self as the center.

Scripture shows us that integrity cannot originate within human flesh but only in God. It repeatedly reveals that the *character attributes* of true integrity are found only in Him (Prov. 11:3; 20:7; Ps. 25:21; Job 2:3; Titus 2:7). This means that we can only walk in integrity by the grace of God and by dying to the carnal nature that rejects that grace.† Integrity comes through the real change that takes place in those who truly believe in

---

* See the Introduction above and *Wisdom's Children, Book One.*

† Rom. 6:1-7, 11-14; 8:4-11; 1 Pet. 2:24; Gal. 2:20; 5:24; Col. 2:11-13, 20; 3:3.

God and who thus enter into God's own nature.* They have received a grace to live lives of integrity in the power of God's righteous Spirit (Gen. 17:1; Prov. 20:7, NKJV; 11:3), and without this grace and supernatural transformation, no one can have true integrity.

Scripture also shows that integrity depends upon God by consistently identifying integrity with righteousness, which can also come *only* from the Lord. Our own righteousness, Isaiah says, is as filthy rags, and Paul quotes the Psalmist to tell us emphatically, "There is none righteous, no not one" (Rom. 3:10). Not only can righteousness not be separated from integrity: we can go so far as to claim that Scripture sets forth integrity *as* righteousness. For instance, Proverbs 20:7 tells us that "the *righteous* man walks in his *integrity*." Job proclaims this truth in the following parallelism: "I will not put away my *integrity* from me. My *righteousness* I hold fast" (Job 27:5-6). Psalm 7 reads, "Judge me . . . according to my *righteousness*, and according to my *integrity* within me" (Ps. 7:8). Proverbs 11:3 (NKJV) says that "the *integrity* of the *upright*," that is, of the righteous, "will guide them." In Genesis 17:1 (KJV), God tells Abraham to "walk before" Him and to be "perfect." This is the above-mentioned Hebrew word *tamim*, which is, as noted, often translated as "integrity."[29] In the next chapter of Genesis, the nineteenth verse, God says that He has raised up this man of integrity (Abraham) to train his children "to *do righteousness and justice, that*" God "*may bring to Abraham what He has spoken to Him.*" Note that here Abraham's faith, the faith we are to emulate, produces deeds of righteousness.

Nor does this confluence of integrity and righteousness suddenly end with the Old Testament. Jesus similarly said that, with the coming of the New Covenant, the believer's "righteousness" had to "exceed" that of those who followed Mosaic Law, and He then went on to immediately show that what He was referring to was the righteousness not *merely* of deed but also of all those attitudes and motives that constitute an integrity of character, a character that lay behind, and even prior to, the deeds. So the New Testament took the integrity of the Old Testament and made it apply not only to deeds but to attitudes and motives. In short, righteousness as integrity would now permeate our *whole* being. Thus Jesus finally concluded with the command for us to be as "perfect" as our Father in heaven (Matt. 5:48). The word used here for "perfect," *teleios*, means "complete" or "wanting nothing necessary to completeness" and can connote "consummate human *integrity* and virtue." Mounce says this word "can refer to something of the highest standard (i.e., 'perfect' Jas. 1:4a, 17, 25) or fully developed, 'perfect' or 'complete' in a moral sense (Mt. 5:48; Jas. 1:4b; 3:2)."[30] This indicates our need to continually press

---

* 2 Pet. 1:1-4; Col. 3:9-10; Eph. 4:22-24; Rom. 8:29; 2 Cor. 3:18.

toward the perfect standard of integrity in every area of life by having a perfect *will* toward the necessity of our obedience to God. So again and again righteousness and integrity are identified and carried to ever-greater levels in human lives.

In the Old Testament, the Hebrew word *tamim* meant not only "integrity" but also "singleness" and, as noted, "plainness," which are also attributes of integrity. In the New Testament, Paul carries forward this idea when he writes, "For our boasting is this: the testimony of our *conscience* that we *conducted* ourselves in the world in *simplicity* [*haplotes*]" (2 Cor. 1:12, NKJV). This Greek word *haplotes*, like the Hebrew *tamim*, is translated "singleness," "plain," as well as by other words that indicate the characteristics of integrity. This same word appears in 2 Corinthians 11:3 (NKJV): "But I fear, lest somehow, as the serpent deceived Eve by his [cunning] craftiness, so your minds may be corrupted from the *simplicity* that is in Christ." Here, by "simplicity" Paul means undivided, wholehearted devotion, without duplicity. Again, he's talking about *integrity*. The English definition of this word stays close to the meaning of the Greek and the Hebrew: "the quality or state of being complete; unbroken condition; wholeness . . . perfect condition . . . uprightness, honesty and sincerity"; also, "the quality or condition of being whole or undivided."

Therefore we can understand why Jesus' words in Matthew 5:48 echo God's injunction to Abraham earlier in Genesis 17:1: "Therefore you shall be perfect, just as your Father in heaven is perfect." We've seen how in the twentieth verse of Matthew 5, Jesus had already specified what this perfection entailed: "For I say to you, that unless your *righteousness* exceeds the righteousness of the scribes and Pharisees, *you will by no means* enter the kingdom of heaven." According to Jesus, then, without this commitment of a perfect will toward God in deed, thought and attitude to integrity, to righteousness, we deceive ourselves if we think we can enter into heaven.

Paul prayed, "Now may the God of peace Himself sanctify you *completely*; and may your *whole spirit*, *soul*, and *body* be preserved *blameless* at the coming of our Lord Jesus Christ" (1 Thess. 5:23). Then Romans 6 reads that "to whom you offer yourselves slaves to obey, you are that one's slaves . . . , whether of sin leading to death, or of *obedience leading to righteousness*," indicating that there are commands and words that we must obey and that this obedience will bring us to a place of righteousness. Jesus, of course, made all this possible with His death on the cross when He offered the sinless sacrifice that we ourselves could never offer. But now our task is to die to sin (Rom. 6:1-7, 11-17) and be united with Him in the likeness of His sacrificial life and death (Rom. 6:5, NKJV) so that in our resurrected life we might also be united with Him in His righteousness as

He imparts His grace, His Spirit, His power to us to become new creations in Christ (2 Cor. 5:17), conformed to the image of God's Son (Rom. 8:29). It is this commitment to walk in this path of obedience, to deny ourselves, to pray as Jesus did, "Nevertheless, not My will, but *Thine*, be done," that enables us to partake of *His* righteousness. We become partakers of this righteousness, then, as we maintain our commitment to Jesus in integrity. Integrity, then, both depends completely upon God and is a necessary expression of our identification with the righteousness of God. All this shows the absolute necessity of living lives completely dependent on God's grace, and pressing forward in the sanctification that conforms us to the image of the One who perfectly embodies integrity.

> And when Abram was ninety years old and nine, Yahweh appeared to Abram, and said unto him, I am the Almighty God; walk before me, and be thou perfect [*tamim*]. (Gen. 17:1, KJV)

> For I say to you, that unless your righteousness exceeds the righteousness of the scribes and Pharisees, you will by no means enter the kingdom of heaven. (Matt. 5:20)

> Therefore you shall be perfect, just as your Father in heaven is perfect. (Matt. 5:48)

> The *integrity of the upright* will guide them, but the perversity of the unfaithful will destroy them. (Prov. 11:3)

> The *righteous man walks in his integrity*; his children are blessed after him. (Prov. 20:7)

> Let *integrity and uprightness* preserve me, for I wait for You. (Ps. 25:21)

> Then Yahweh said to Satan, "Have you considered My servant Job? No one else on earth is like him, a *man of perfect integrity* [*tam*], who fears God and turns away from evil. He still retains his *integrity* [*tummah*], even though you incited Me against him, to destroy him without just cause." (Job 2:3, HCSB)

> . . . in all things showing yourself to be *a pattern of good works*; in doctrine *showing integrity*, reverence, incorruptibility. (Titus 2:7)

> I know, my God, that You test the heart and are *pleased with integrity*. All these things have I given willingly and with honest intent. And now I have seen with joy how willingly Your people who are here have given to You. (1 Chron. 29:17)

> Let Yahweh judge the peoples. Judge me, O Yahweh, according to my righteousness, *according to my integrity*, O Most High. (Ps. 7:8)

> *In my integrity You uphold me* and set me in Your presence forever. (Ps. 41:12)

> And David shepherded them *with integrity of heart*; with skillful hands he led them. (Ps. 78:72)

> *The man of integrity walks securely*, but he who takes crooked paths will be found out. (Prov. 10:9)

Righteousness guards the man of integrity, but wickedness overthrows the sinner. (Prov. 13:6)

And the boys grew: and Esau was a cunning hunter, a man of the field; and *Jacob was a plain [tam] man*, dwelling in tents. (Gen. 25:27, KJV)

His wife said to him, "Are you still holding on to your *integrity [tummah]*? Curse God and die!"
He replied, "You are talking like a foolish woman. Shall we accept good from God, and not trouble?"
In all this, Job did not sin in what he said. (Job 2:9-10)

After the wall had been rebuilt and I had set the doors in place, the gatekeepers and the singers and the Levites were appointed. I put in charge of Jerusalem my brother Hanani, along with Hananiah the commander of the citadel, because he was a *man of integrity* and feared God more than most men do. (Neh. 7:1-2)

They did not require an accounting from those to whom they gave the money to pay the workers, because they acted with complete honesty. (2 Kings 12:15)

Be perfect, therefore, as your heavenly Father is perfect. (Matt. 5:48)

For the upright will live in the land, and *the blameless will remain in it*. (Prov. 2:21)

The righteousness of the blameless [tamim] makes a straight way for them, but the wicked are brought down by their own wickedness. (Prov. 11:5)

When you enter the land Yahweh your God is giving you, do not learn to imitate the detestable ways of the nations there . . . . Anyone who does these things is detestable to Yahweh, and because of these detestable practices the Lord your God will drive out those nations before you. You must be *blameless [tamim]* before Yahweh your God. (Deut. 18:9, 12-13)

I will sing of Your love and justice; to You, O Lord, I will sing praise. *I will be careful to lead a blameless [tamim] life*—when will You come to me? *I will walk in my house with blameless [tom] heart* . . . . My eyes will be on the faithful in the land, that they may dwell with me; *he whose walk is blameless [tamim] will minister to me*. (Ps. 101:1-2, 6)

Yahweh, who may dwell in Your sanctuary? Who may live on Your holy hill? *He whose walk is blameless [tamim]* and who does what is righteous, who speaks the truth from his heart. (Ps. 15:1-2)

This is the account of Noah. Noah was a righteous man, *blameless [tamim]* among the people of his time, and he walked with God. (Gen. 6:9)

Till we all come to the unity of the faith and the knowledge of the Son of God, to *a perfect man*, to the measure of the stature of the fullness of Christ. (Eph. 4:13)

Not that I have already attained, or am already perfected; but I press on, that I may lay hold of that for which Christ Jesus has also laid hold of me.

Brethren, I do not count myself to have apprehended; but one thing I do, forgetting those things which are behind and reaching forward to those things which are ahead, *I press toward the goal for the prize of the upward call of God in Christ Jesus.*

Therefore let us, as many as are mature, have this mind; and if in anything you think otherwise, God will reveal even this to you. (Phil. 3:12-15)

Him we preach, warning every man and teaching every man in all wisdom, that we may present every man *perfect in Christ Jesus.* (Col. 1:28)

Epaphras, who is one of you, a servant of Christ, greets you, always laboring fervently for you in prayers, *that you may stand perfect and complete in all the will of God.* (Col. 4:12)

But let patience have its perfect work, that you may be *perfect and complete, lacking nothing.* (James 1:4)

For we all stumble in many things. If anyone does not stumble in word, he is *a perfect man*, able also to bridle the whole body. (James 3:2)

Finally, brothers, good-by. *Aim for perfection*, listen to my appeal, be of one mind, live in peace. And the God of love and peace will be with you. (2 Cor. 13:11)

Examples of Integrity:

The king of Sodom said to Abram, "Give me the people and keep the goods for yourself."

But Abram said to the king of Sodom, "I have raised my hand to Yahweh, God Most High, Creator of heaven and earth, and have taken an oath that I will accept nothing belonging to you, not even a thread or the thong of a sandal, so that you will never be able to say, 'I made Abram rich.' I will accept nothing but what my men have eaten and the share that belongs to the men who went with me—to Aner, Eshcol and Mamre. Let them have their share." (Gen. 14:21-24)

"Here I stand. Testify against me in the presence of Yahweh and His anointed. Whose ox have I taken? Whose donkey have I taken? Whom have I cheated? Whom have I oppressed? From whose hand have I accepted a bribe to make me shut my eyes? If I have done any of these, I will make it right."

"You have not cheated or oppressed us," they replied. "You have not taken anything from anyone's hand." (1 Sam. 12:3-4)

When they arrived, he said to them: "You know how I lived the whole time I was with you, from the first day I came into the province of Asia. I served the Lord with great humility and with tears, although I was severely tested by the plots of the Jews. You know that I have not hesitated to preach anything that would be helpful to you but have taught you publicly and from house to house. I have declared to both Jews and Greeks that they must turn to God in repentance and have faith in our Lord Jesus . . . .

Now I know that none of you among whom I have gone about preaching the kingdom will ever see me again. Therefore, I declare to you today that I am innocent of the blood of all men. For I have not hesitated to proclaim to you the whole will of God." (Acts 20:18-21, 25-27)

But Daniel resolved not to defile himself with the royal food and wine, and he asked the chief official for permission not to defile himself this way. (Dan. 1:8)

A Perfect Sacrifice:

When anyone brings from the herd or flock a fellowship offering to Yahweh to fulfill a special vow or as a freewill offering, it must be *without defect or blemish [tamim]* to be acceptable. Do not offer to Yahweh the blind, the injured or the maimed, or anything with warts or festering or running sores. Do not place any of these on the altar as an offering made to Yahweh by fire. (Lev. 22:21-22)

Yahweh called to Moses and spoke to him from the Tent of Meeting. He said, "Speak to the Israelites and say to them: 'When any of you brings an offering to Yahweh, bring as your offering an animal from either the herd or the flock.

"'If the offering is a burnt offering from the herd, he is to offer a male *without defect*. He must present it at the entrance to the Tent of Meeting so that it will be acceptable to Yahweh . . . .

"'If the offering is a burnt offering from the flock, from either the sheep or the goats, he is to offer a male *without defect*.'" (Lev. 1:1-3, 10)

Therefore, I urge you, brothers, in view of God's mercy, to offer your bodies as *living sacrifices, holy and pleasing to God*—which is your spiritual worship. (Rom. 12:1)

e. Sincerity

Unbroken relationship with God and His people requires genuineness and authenticity; our *actual* character must correspond to what we *appear* to be. We must speak with our "real voice." We must first discover and then think, feel, speak and act in conformity to the unique and intricate image of God that He has made us to be in Christ. We cannot pretend to be what we are not or live according to some image that has come to us from other sources besides God; to do so is to live out our entire existence as a lie. We must struggle to get through all the clutter and debris of counterfeit images of ourselves to find what we are in Christ as we conform to His image for our own particular life within the context of His corporate life in the church. Only the deepest and most prayerful relationship with God can bring this liberation into our identity revealed as the sons of God, but if we maintain this relationship in integrity and sincerity, we can be confident that "He who began a good work in us" will bring it to completion.

> For as many as are led by the Spirit of God, these are sons of God. For you did not receive the spirit of bondage again to fear, but you received the Spirit of adoption by whom we cry out, "Abba, Father." The Spirit Himself bears witness with our spirit that we are children of God, and if children, then heirs—heirs of God and joint heirs with Christ, if indeed we suffer with Him, that we may also be glorified together. For I consider that the sufferings of this present time are not worthy to be compared with the glory which shall be revealed in us. For the earnest expectation of the creation eagerly waits for the *revealing of the sons of God.* For the creation was subjected to futility, not willingly, but because of Him who subjected it in hope; because the creation itself also will be delivered from the bondage of corruption into the glorious liberty of the children of God. (Rom. 8:14-21)

> Now the Lord is the Spirit; and where the Spirit of the Lord is, there is liberty. But we all, with unveiled face, beholding as in a mirror the glory of the Lord, are being transformed into the same image from glory to glory, just as by the Spirit of the Lord. (2 Cor. 3:17-18)

> For you, brethren, have been called to liberty; only do not use liberty as an occasion for the flesh, but through love serve one another. (Gal. 5:13)

> Behold what manner of love the Father has bestowed on us, that we should be called children of God! Therefore the world does not know us, because it did not know Him. Beloved, now we are children of God; and it has not yet been revealed what we shall be, but we know that when He is revealed, we shall be like Him, for we shall see Him as He is. (1 John 3:1-2)

> Now this is our boast: Our conscience testifies that we have conducted ourselves in the world, and especially in our relations with you, *in the holiness and sincerity that are from God.* We have done so not according to worldly wisdom but according to God's grace. (2 Cor. 1:12)

> Unlike so many, we do not peddle the word of God for profit. On the contrary, in Christ *we speak before God with sincerity*, like men sent from God. (2 Cor. 2:17)

> I am not commanding you, but I want to test the sincerity of your love by comparing it with the earnestness of others. For you know the grace of our Lord Jesus Christ, that though He was rich, yet for your sakes He became poor, so that you through His poverty might become rich.
>
>   And here is my advice about what is best for you in this matter: Last year you were the first not only to give but also to have the desire to do so. (2 Cor. 8:8-10)

> Slaves, obey your earthly masters with respect and fear, and with *sincerity of heart*, just as you would obey Christ. (Eph. 6:5)

Every day they continued to meet together in the temple courts. They broke bread in their homes and ate together with *glad and sincere hearts*, praising God and enjoying the favor of all the people. And the Lord added to their number daily those who were being saved. (Acts 2:46-47)

Love must be sincere. Hate what is evil; cling to what is good. (Rom. 12:9)

Rather, as servants of God we commend ourselves in every way: in great endurance; in troubles, hardships and distresses; . . . in purity, understanding, patience and kindness; in the Holy Spirit and in *sincere* love . . . . (2 Cor. 6:4, 6)

But I am afraid that just as Eve was deceived by the serpent's cunning, your minds may somehow be led astray from your *sincere and pure devotion to Christ.* (2 Cor. 11:3)

The goal of this command is love, which comes from a pure heart and a good conscience and a *sincere faith.* (1 Tim. 1:5)

. . . and since we have a great priest over the house of God, *let us draw near to God with a sincere heart in full assurance of faith*, having our hearts sprinkled to cleanse us from a guilty conscience and having our bodies washed with pure water. (Heb. 10:21-22)

But the wisdom that comes from heaven is first of all pure; then peace-loving, considerate, submissive, full of mercy and good fruit, impartial and *sincere*. (James 3:17)

Now that you have purified yourselves by obeying the truth so that *you have sincere love for your brothers*, love one another deeply, from the heart. (1 Pet. 1:22)

Therefore let us keep the Festival, not with the old yeast, the yeast of malice and wickedness, but with bread without yeast, the bread of *sincerity* and truth. (1 Cor. 5:8)

Better to be a nobody and yet have a servant than pretend to be somebody and have no food. (Prov. 12:9)

f. Openness, Transparency, Vulnerability

Openness characterizes honest and sincere people, people standing wholly in the light. The Greek word in the New Testament translated "sincere" is *eilikrines*, which literally means "clearness," "judged by the sunlight." Honest people don't hide in darkness or try to escape the light. They open their hearts to God's Word. They don't try to appear to be something they're not. They walk transparently without pretense. The "sunlight" of God's Word shines right through them. Many times we can hardly bring ourselves to look directly into the face of someone for fear of what we might see: a lie, a lust, an arrogance, a greediness, a selfishness, a cruelty. But if you yourself walk in the light, you can look into the face of any honest person with joy and anticipation. And when you do, you can *see* the *real* person; you can look into him and know with certainty what he actually is. His life is an open book. And because he trusts God, he trusts those with whom God has brought him into covenant relationship. He unveils his face. He casts away all masks and pretenses. He can then with equal candor look into the unveiled faces of all his spiritual brothers and sisters who "all reflect the Lord's glory" (2 Cor. 3:18). So his very transparency and vulnerability make him part of that Body of overcomers who "are being transformed into" the Lord's "likeness with ever-increasing glory, which comes from the Lord, who is the Spirit" (2 Cor. 3:18).

Paul describes the Spirit of the Lord as the Spirit of liberty (2 Cor. 3:17); and James admonishes us to look intently "into the perfect law of liberty" (1:25), never forgetting what we have seen in this mirror of the Spirit. In this mirror, this "perfect law of liberty," we gaze into the "unveiled faces" of those who "*reflect* the Lord's glory"—they *are* this mirror. So to veil and mask our faces, to refuse to make ourselves vulnerable in the presence of the Lord and His people, means to cease being transformed into the Lord's image. It means we refuse to come into the oneness that marks true love. Only when we tear off the masks, always the false refuge of the thief or hypocrite (which means literally a "mask wearer"), do our vulnerability and transparency carry us into that love and oneness Jesus described as marking His disciples and showing the world that the Messiah has truly come (John 13:35; 17:20-23).

Outside of the bounds of covenant love and oneness in Jesus, nakedness becomes indecency. Yet those inside the walls need feel no shame for their inner nakedness, the exposure before their heavenly Husband of their sins, failures and weaknesses. If they walk in His light, His blood will cleanse them of these (1 John 1:7). So Christians make their inner self vulnerable within the covenant because redemptive love—in their covenant oneness with God—"*covers* a multitude of sins" (1 Pet. 4:8, NASV).

The walls of the city *are* our salvation (Isa. 26:1-3; 60:18): only those who come within God's covenant walls can become one with Him in a redemptive love defined by God Himself. And only this covenantal openness, this complete vulnerability to God, brings true oneness with Him. No one but the "faithful" who "keep . . . their troth" can enter into the gates of this city (Isa. 26:2). These gates mark the contours of the covenant by which all those within the walls have given their solemn pledge to live under the sacred rule of a love unbacked by force (Isa. 26:2). Moreover, only those who "plight their troth" (Isa. 26:2; Ezek. 16:8, Ampl.) to hold fast to the covenant can sustain the relationship of love that brings oneness—that oneness which *is* our salvation.*

---

* See *The Quest for Salvation.*

Mutual love given in covenant commitment becomes a great source of courage. The knowledge of such a love's sure and unfailing steadfastness brings the courage to open our hearts and make known our own deepest needs, even as we take responsibility for serving the needs of others. Such a life dedicated to love really offers no alternative to vulnerability. After all, life is full of *unknowns*, and to open ourselves up to what we do *not* know in others defines the very essence of vulnerability, of faith in God to lead us on our pilgrimage of love to a place of relationship we also do not yet know, a land of uncertainties that constitutes our entire future life, and all in Him (our life both on earth and, as we believe, in heaven). Again, a sacralized covenant is precisely what gives us the courage to become vulnerable in this way—the enduring terms of the covenant, with its commitment and faithfulness to a given form of relationship, cover us in our inner exposure and vulnerability. And since all life faces unknowns that make everyone vulnerable, covenant alone can cover the totality of life, even its unknowns. To enter covenant, then, means somehow finding the faith to totally trust not ultimately people but the God who puts people together to endure and prevail in love. And so this trust must also prevail, no matter how appearances may seem to dictate otherwise. This, in turn, means opening ourselves and exposing ourselves—becoming vulnerable to the vicissitudes of life and all its unknowns, which all must face anyway.

To commit to God and stand vulnerable in this way constitutes the very meaning of Christianity—that God will work through Christ's own corporate Body to daily conform our attitudes and lives to Christ's image (Matt. 28:19-20; Phil. 2:5, 14, NIV; Rom. 8:29). These details must include even our attitudes, since Jesus is concerned first with the heart, the internal, and only then with the external expression that flows from it (Matt. 5:20-48; 6:1-34; 15:7-11, 15-20; Luke 6:43-45). This explains why Paul declared, "Your *attitude* should be the same as that of Christ Jesus" and then enumerates what that includes (Phil. 2:5). God may, then, speak to us from His Word about our *attitudes* toward washing dishes, cleaning our homes, working on our jobs, the clothes we wear, getting along with our family and neighbors, submitting to governing authorities, as well as overcoming specific temptations to sins of the flesh. He will also deal with our *attitudes* about our relationships with our brothers and sisters (Rom. 13:9) or with teaching our children at home (Eph. 6:4) or with submitting to parents or to the laws and government of the State (Eph. 6:1-3; Col. 3:20; Rom. 13:1-7; 1 Pet. 2:13-17).

God works in such areas of human life, some of which we may even have classified as our private domain, because these everyday affairs and matters are, in the end, all that *can* express our true identity and relationship in God. The way we daily act and relate, our attitudes and behavior, a deed and a word, in all our different everyday circumstances reveal our true selves. It is only as we *willingly* make ourselves vulnerable to God in the context of His people that He begins to conform us to His own image (Rom. 8:29), for He will never coercively impose His love and guidance upon us. If we actually seek to make ourselves known to Him, in our covenant relationships, He will transform our identity until "who we truly are" ever more completely identifies with who He truly is (1 John 2:5-6). He wants us, in short, as Paul says, to "be like Him" (Rom. 8:29; 2 Cor. 3:18; Eph. 4:24; 1 John 3:2; 4:17).

So God cares about the details of our lives. He concerns Himself even with what seem like small matters because they make up real life, the little foxes that spoil the vine (Song of Sol. 2:15). Finally, Jesus said that those faithful in the least will be faithful in much (Luke 16:10). So we should not "despise the day of *small* things," the day when God's "master builders" (Zech. 4:10; 1 Cor. 3:9-11) use God's "plumb line" to ensure the temple (that is, the church and our individual temples that constitute it) measures up to God's Word (Zech. 2:1). God wants to draw us ever upward and increasingly into His perfection, with our entire lives more and more perfectly expressing His love and power, which with God are always one and the same (Matt. 5:48; Eph. 4:11-16).

In all this, God sets people free from whatever conforms them to any image other than His own. After all, most "personal" characteristics that people so tenaciously cling to did not originate within themselves. They come from the first Adam, or they were implanted by the culture of that first nature, or else people merely imitate others and then cling to that imitation until it becomes part of "their" identity. Again, God wants to free people from conformity to any image other than His own (Rom. 8:29). And what greater freedom could anyone find than that?

> When Jesus saw Nathanael approaching, He said of him, "Here is a true Israelite, *in whom there is nothing false*." (John 1:47)

> One day Elisha went to Shunem. And a well-to-do woman was there, who urged him to stay for a meal. So whenever he came by, he stopped there to eat. She said to her husband, "I know that this man who often comes our way is a holy man of God." (2 Kings 4:8-9)

> Rather, we have renounced secret and shameful ways; we do not use deception, nor do we distort the word of God. On the contrary, by setting forth the truth plainly we commend ourselves to every man's conscience in the sight of God. (2 Cor. 4:2)

> You yourselves are our letter, written on our hearts, known and read by everybody. (2 Cor. 3:2)

> With this fear of the Lord before our eyes we address our appeal to men. *To God our lives lie open, as I hope they also lie open to you* in your heart of hearts. (2 Cor. 5:11, NEB)

> As water reflects a face, so a man's heart reflects the man. (Prov. 27:19)

When we are in Jesus, our unveiled transparency, which alone can hope to reflect *His* glory, corresponds to the "white linen" symbolizing the righteousness of God's people (Rev. 19:8). To overcome all sin separates us from any darkness marring the transparency of God's light in our lives. The more the transparency, the more His light suffuses our whole being and His victory prevails.

> Yet you have a few people in Sardis who have not soiled their clothes. They will walk with Me, dressed in white, for they are worthy. *He who overcomes will, like them, be dressed in white.* I will never blot out his name from the book of life, but will acknowledge his name before My Father and His angels. (Rev. 3:4-5)

> I counsel you to buy from Me gold refined in the fire, so you can become rich; and *white clothes* to wear, so you can cover your shameful nakedness; and salve to put on your eyes, so you can see. (Rev. 3:18)

> Surrounding the throne were twenty-four other thrones, and seated on them were twenty-four elders. They were *dressed in white* and had crowns of gold on their heads. (Rev. 4:4)

> After this I looked and there before me was a great multitude that no one could count, from every nation, tribe, people and language, standing before the throne and in front of the Lamb. They were *wearing white robes* and were holding palm branches in their hands. (Rev. 7:9)

> I answered, "Sir, you know." And he said, "These are they who have come out of the great tribulation; they have *washed their robes and made them white in the blood of the Lamb.*" (Rev. 7:14)

> "*Fine linen, bright and clean*, was given her to wear." (*Fine linen stands for the righteous acts of the saints.*) (Rev. 19:8)

> I am jealous for you with a godly jealousy. I promised you to one husband, to Christ, so that I might present you as a *pure* virgin to Him. (2 Cor. 11:2)

> *Pure and undefiled religion* before God and the Father is this: to visit orphans and widows in their trouble, and to *keep oneself unspotted from the world.* (James 1:27)

> . . . that He might present it to Himself a glorious church, *not having spot or wrinkle or any such thing*, but that it should be *holy and without blemish.* (Eph. 5:27)

> And others save with fear, pulling them out of the fire, *hating even the garment defiled by the flesh.* (Jude 23)

> You are all fair, my love, and there is *no spot in you.* (Song of Sol. 4:7)

> Therefore, beloved, looking forward to these things, be diligent to be found by Him in peace, *without spot and blameless.* (2 Pet. 3:14)

. . . that you keep this commandment *without spot, blameless* until our Lord Jesus Christ's appearing. (1 Tim. 6:14)

g. Receiving Correction

True character comes to light in crises. Pressure pushes the truth, whether good or bad, out of all its hiding places. The fire drives out the serpents (Acts 28:3) and brings up the dross (Zech. 13:9). When God's Word comes to us like a fire (Jer. 23:29), our hearts burn within us (Jer. 20:9; Luke 24:32). What we then do in response reveals whether we're truly honest or not. So the true test of honesty comes with direct confrontation from God's truth against our sin. Honesty will receive further truth or correction *actively*, as distinct from passively. The honest know that correction maintains, restores and deepens our relationship with God. So Scripture distinguishes the legitimate son of God from the illegitimate by the former's ability to receive correction (Heb. 12:7-8). A true son is defined by his willingness to receive God's correction, rebuke and chastisement actively so that it conforms that son to God's image. To refuse to actively participate in that correction is to despise God and His Word. When we reject that Word, we exalt ourselves above our Creator. We become the clay mixed with thorns that time and again wounds the potter's hands until those bloodied hands finally must scrape us into the potter's field. According to Rienecker, the Greek word *nothos*, translated "illegitimate," "not only indicates that the father is not sufficiently interested in them to inflict on them the discipline that fits his legitimate children, but it is also to be taken in the legal sense in which an illegitimate child does not enjoy the inheritance rights and the rights to participate in family worship." Of course, the Father God desires to discipline all His children in love, but the illegitimate son acts as though he were disinterested; he spurns the Father's discipline and chooses instead the path of self-will and lies.

David prayed for Yahweh to allow the "righteous" to "strike" and "rebuke" him (Ps. 141:5). He called it a "kindness." He said that if a righteous man struck him on the head, struck at the very source of his own life's authority, his head would not refuse it (Ps. 141:5). The Hebrew word translated as "kindness" is the word *chesed*. *Chesed* is the fulfillment in love of our covenant obligation. The word translated "strike" is *halam*, meaning to "strike, hammer, stamp, beat to pieces, be dissolved, break up, be scattered." In the context of the covenant, our old nature must be "scattered," "dissolved" and broken up as God reshapes and forms us both individually and corporately into His image. David valued, above all, his relationship with God, and so he prayed that Yahweh would bring discipline into his life to deliver him from sin. He knew sin would separate him from God. David therefore said that whoever administered that discipline would be showing him *chesed*, showing faithfulness to their covenant obligations. This is the attitude children should have towards parentaldiscipline. To refuse this discipline is to reject the covenant and to exalt ourselves above God and His divine order. When the child refuses to submit to parental discipline, he exalts himself to the place of primacy above God and parent, setting himself in the place of Christ—that is, again, he flirts with the spirit of antichrist, who may then decide to take him for a ride in his "car" and will be "hard-pressed to stop him from going too far"[31] (2 Thess. 2:4). Such a child has broken out of the restraints of God's Spirit, and God's judgment becomes the only form through which His mercy, albeit a severe mercy, can reach this child.

> In your struggle against sin, you have not yet resisted to the point of shedding your blood. And you have forgotten that word of encouragement that addresses you as sons: "My son, do not make light of the Lord's discipline, and do not lose heart when He rebukes you, because the Lord disciplines those He loves, and He punishes everyone He accepts as a son."
> Endure hardship as discipline; God is treating you as sons. For what son is not disciplined (and everyone undergoes discipline), then you are illegitimate children and not true sons. Moreover, we have all had human fathers who disciplined us and we respected them for it. How much more should we submit to the Father of our spirits and live! Our fathers disciplined us for a little while as they thought best; but God disciplines us for our good, that we may share in His holiness. No discipline seems pleasant at the time, but painful. *Later on, however, it produces a harvest of righteousness and peace for those who have been trained by it.* (Heb. 12:4-11)

> Though He slay me, yet will I hope in Him. (Job 13:15)

> My son, do not despise Yahweh's discipline and do not resent His rebuke, because *Yahweh disciplines those He loves*, as a father the son He delights in. (Prov. 3:11-12)

> For these commands are a lamp, this teaching is a light, and *the corrections of discipline are the way to life.* (Prov. 6:23)

> *He who heeds discipline shows the way to life*, but whoever ignores correction leads others astray. (Prov. 10:17)

> Do not rebuke a mocker or he will hate you; *rebuke a wise man and he will love you.* (Prov. 9:8)

> *Whoever loves discipline loves knowledge*, but he who hates correction is stupid. (Prov. 12:1)

> *Let a righteous man strike me—it is a kindness; let him rebuke me— it is oil on my head.* My head will not refuse it. Yet my prayer is ever against the deeds of evildoers. (Ps. 141:5)

> *A wise son heeds his father's instruction*, but a mocker does not listen to rebuke. (Prov. 13:1)

He who ignores discipline comes to poverty and shame, but *whoever heeds correction is honored.* (Prov. 13:18)

A fool spurns his father's discipline, but *whoever heeds correction shows prudence.* (Prov. 15:5)

He who listens to a life-giving rebuke will be at home among the wise. He who ignores discipline despises himself, but *whoever heeds correction gains understanding.* (Prov. 15:31-32)

A rebuke impresses a man of discernment more than a hundred lashes a fool. (Prov. 17:10)

Flog a mocker, and the simple will learn prudence; rebuke a discerning man, and he will gain knowledge. (Prov. 19:25)

Like an earring of gold or an ornament of fine gold is a wise man's rebuke to a listening ear. (Prov. 25:12)

He who rebukes a man will in the end gain more favor than he who has a flattering tongue. (Prov. 28:23)

Whoever gives heed to instruction prospers, and blessed is he who trusts in Yahweh. (Prov. 16:20)

Then David said to Nathan, "I have sinned against Yahweh." Nathan replied, "Yahweh has taken away your sin. You are not going to die. But because by doing this you have made the enemies of Yahweh show utter contempt, the son born to you will die." (2 Sam. 12:13-14)

2. Dishonesty

Again, dishonesty is the most iniquitous form of dishonoring. *Dishonesty* transmutes all that we should be doing from a heart of service into a means of manipulation (Matt. 6:1-4), an act of hypocrisy. *Hypocrite* means mask-wearer, actor. A hypocrite puts on a false facade, tries to appear to be something other than what he really is inside. He cares only about appearances. Substance means nothing to him (although as a hypocrite he may well pretend to care *only* about substance and *nothing* about appearances). True relationship only comes through finding real connections, real points of contact, points at which lives touch, intertwine and merge. The hypocrite severs all these true connections. Again, dishonesty, as in our initial discussion of honesty, severs relationship with both man and God. Dishonesty prevents conformity to the image of God, since such flawed character can never be infused with the Spirit of the Christ who never lied. Rather than reflecting God's light and truth, our character collapses into the pit of self-centeredness and carnality. Thorns and thistles come forth and dominate our lives, choking out the fruit of the Spirit.

a. Lying

Just as honoring parents establishes a relationship to help tie children to God, so lying to and deceiving parents severs a child's relationship with the God worthy of all honor. The Hebrew word *shaqar*, which is translated "lie," means "to cheat," "to deceive . . . , i.e., to break a covenant, to act falsely, to be false to one's faith." It means "to paint a falsehood." To lie is to destroy all covenant, as Ananias and Sapphira did at the church's beginning (Acts 5:1-11). When we cut ourselves off from those channels through whom God's authority comes to our lives, we cut ourselves off from the ultimate Source of the authority that redeems us. God has established the rule of parents over children (Eph. 6:1-3; Col. 3:20). He has made parents instruments through whom He not only reveals His general patterns of life but also for addressing the details and specifics that conform children to those patterns day by day. When children lie to their parents, they reject the provision of God's guidance in their lives. They refuse to permit Him to lead and conform them to His image. But only when they welcome His guidance do children advance on their journey to heaven.

Children who lie to parents and are then, through one way or another, separated from the relationship often end up becoming inveterate liars whose whole life becomes marked by constant lying. Even if they one day feel a deep revulsion for themselves and their constant lying, they will seldom find the means to break the habit unless they come back into a covenanted relationship with an authority loving enough to bring them into accountability for their lies, a relationship that takes the place, in other words, of that with their parents which they rejected. People given over in this way to ubiquitous and unceasing lying soon can't even remember the truth of the incidents and memories of their own lives. Their identity is so shattered and fractured by constant lying that their life *becomes* a lie and they live a lie.

> They perish because they *refused to love the truth* and so be saved. For this reason God sends them a powerful delusion so that they will believe the lie and so that all will be condemned who have not believed the truth but have delighted in wickedness. (2 Thess. 2:10-12)
>
> No one *who practices deceit* will dwell in My house; no one who speaks falsely will stand in My presence. (Ps. 101:7)
>
> There are six things Yahweh hates, seven that are detestable to Him: haughty eyes, *a lying tongue*, hands that shed innocent blood . . . *a false witness* who pours out lies and a man who stirs up dissension among brothers. (Prov. 6:16-17, 19)
>
> But the cowardly, the unbelieving, the vile, the murderers, the

sexually immoral, those who practice magic arts, the idolaters and *all liars*—their place will be in the fiery lake of burning sulfur. This is the second death. (Rev. 21:8)

We also know that *law* is made *not for the righteous* but for lawbreakers and rebels, the ungodly and sinful, the unholy and irreligious; for those who kill their fathers or mothers, for murderers, for adulterers and perverts, for slave traders and *liars and perjurers*—and for whatever else is contrary to the sound doctrine that conforms to the glorious gospel of the blessed God. (1 Tim. 1:9-11)

(Note that in the above passage Paul places liars and perjurers in the same category as slave traders and those who kill their mothers and fathers.)

Then Yahweh said to Cain, "Where is your brother Abel?"
"I don't know," he replied. "Am I my brother's keeper?" (Gen. 4:9)

Truthful lips endure forever, but *a lying tongue lasts only a moment.* (Prov. 12:19)

Yahweh detests lying lips, but He delights in men who are truthful. (Prov. 12:22)

A truthful witness does not deceive, but *a false witness pours out lies.* (Prov. 14:5)

The tongue that brings healing is a tree of life, but *a deceitful tongue* crushes the spirit. (Prov. 15:4)

A wicked man listens to evil lips; *a liar pays attention to a malicious tongue.* (Prov. 17:4)

A man of perverse heart does not prosper; *he whose tongue is deceitful falls into trouble.* (Prov. 17:20)

A false witness will not go unpunished, and *he who pours out lies will perish.* (Prov. 19:9)

A corrupt witness mocks at justice, and the *mouth of the wicked gulps down evil.* (Prov. 19:28)

A fortune made by a *lying tongue* is a fleeting vapor and a deadly snare. (Prov. 21:6)

As a north wind brings rain, so a *sly tongue* brings angry looks. (Prov. 25:23)

A false witness will perish, and whoever listens to him will be destroyed forever. (Prov. 21:28)

A truthful witness gives honest testimony, but *a false witness tells lies.* (Prov. 12:17)

Not a word from their mouth can be trusted; their heart is filled with destruction. Their throat is an open grave; *with their tongue they speak deceit.* (Ps. 5:9)

You shall not give false testimony against your neighbor. (Exod. 20:16)

Do not spread false reports. Do not help a wicked man by being a *malicious witness.* (Exod. 23:1)

Yahweh said to Moses: "If anyone sins and is unfaithful to Yahweh by *deceiving his neighbor* about something entrusted to him or left in his care or stolen, or if he cheats him, or if he finds lost property and lies about it, or if he *swears falsely,* or if he commits any such sin that people may do—when he thus sins and becomes guilty, he must return what he has stolen or taken by extortion, or what was entrusted to him, or the lost property he found, or whatever it was he *swore falsely* about. He must make restitution in full, add a fifth of the value to it and give it all to the owner on the day he presents his guilt offering." (Lev. 6:1-5)

Do not lie. Do not deceive one another. *Do not swear falsely* by My name and so profane the name of your God. I am Yahweh. Do not defraud your neighbor or rob him. Do not hold back the wages of a hired man overnight. Do not curse the deaf or put a stumbling block in front of the blind, but fear your God. I am Yahweh. *Do not pervert justice;* do not show partiality to the poor or favoritism to the great, but judge your neighbor fairly. *Do not go about spreading slander* among your people. Do not do anything that endangers your neighbor's life. I am Yahweh. (Lev. 19:11-16)

If a *malicious witness* takes the stand to accuse a man of a crime, the two men involved in the dispute must stand in the presence of Yahweh before the priests and the judges who are in office at the time. The judges must make a thorough investigation, and if the *witness proves to be a liar, giving false testimony against his brother,* then do to him as he intended to do to his brother. You must purge the evil from among you. The rest of the people will hear of this and be afraid, and never again will such an evil thing be done among you. (Deut. 19:16-20)

You, however, *smear me with lies;* you are worthless physicians, all of you! (Job 13:4)

"So how can you console me with your nonsense? Nothing is left of your answers but *falsehood!*" (Job 21:34)

My lips will not speak wickedness, and *my tongue will utter no deceit.* (Job 27:4)

Does He not see my ways and count my every step? If I have *walked in falsehood* or my foot has *hurried after deceit*—let God weigh me in honest scales and He will know that I am blameless. (Job 31:4-6)

You destroy *those who tell lies;* bloodthirsty and *deceitful* men Yahweh abhors. (Ps. 5:6)

Everyone *lies* to his neighbor; their *flattering lips* speak with *deception.* (Ps. 12:2)

Who may ascend the hill of Yahweh? Who may stand in His holy place? He who has clean hands and a pure heart, who does not lift up his soul to an idol or *swear by what is false.* (Ps. 24:3-4)

Keep your tongue from evil and your *lips from speaking lies*. (Ps. 34:13)

For, "Whoever would love life and see good days must *keep his tongue from evil* and his *lips from deceitful speech*." (1 Pet. 3:10)

Ruthless witnesses come forward; they question me on things I know nothing about. (Ps. 35:11)

The *words of his mouth are wicked and deceitful*; he has ceased to be wise and to do good. (Ps. 36:3)

You *use your mouth for evil and harness your tongue to deceit*. (Ps. 50:19)

Your *tongue plots destruction*; it is like a sharpened razor, you who *practice deceit*. (Ps. 52:2)

Even from birth the wicked go astray; from the womb they are wayward and *speak lies*. (Ps. 58:3)

They fully intend to topple him from his lofty place; *they take delight in lies*. With their mouths they bless, but in their hearts they curse. (Ps. 62:4)

But the king will rejoice in God; all who swear by God's name will praise Him, while *the mouths of liars will be silenced*. (Ps. 63:11)

Whoever *slanders his neighbor* in secret, him will I put to silence; whoever has haughty eyes and a proud heart, him will I not endure. (Ps. 101:5)

For wicked and *deceitful men have opened their mouths* against me; they have *spoken against me with lying tongues*. (Ps. 109:2)

Though the arrogant have *smeared me with lies*, I keep Your precepts with all my heart. (Ps. 119:69)

I *hate and abhor falsehood* but I love Your law. (Ps. 119:163)

A scoundrel and villain, who goes about with a *corrupt mouth*, who winks with his eye, signals with his feet and motions with his fingers, who plots evil with *deceit* in his heart—he always stirs up dissension. Therefore disaster will overtake him in an instant; he will suddenly be destroyed—without remedy. (Prov. 6:12-15)

The man of integrity walks securely, but he who takes *crooked paths* will be found out. He who winks maliciously causes grief, and a chattering fool comes to ruin. (Prov. 10:9-10)

He who conceals his hatred has *lying lips*, and *whoever spreads slander* is a fool. (Prov. 10:18)

The mouth of the righteous brings forth wisdom, but *a perverse tongue will be cut out*. (Prov. 10:31)

With his mouth the godless destroys his neighbor, but through knowledge the righteous escape. (Prov. 11:9)

The righteous hate what is false, but *the wicked bring shame and disgrace*. (Prov. 13:5)

A truthful witness does not deceive, but *a false witness pours out lies*. (Prov. 14:5)

Food gained by *falsehood* tastes sweet to a man, but he ends up with a mouth full of gravel. (Prov. 20:17)

Do not testify against your neighbor without cause, or *use your lips to deceive.* (Prov. 24:28)

Like a club or a sword or a sharp arrow is the man who *gives false testimony against his neighbor.* (Prov. 25:18)

Like a madman shooting firebrands or deadly arrows is a man who *deceives* his neighbor and says, "I was only joking!" Without wood a fire goes out; *without gossip a quarrel dies down.* As charcoal to embers and as wood to fire, so is a *quarrelsome man for kindling strife.* The *words of a gossip* are like choice morsels; they go down to a man's inmost parts. Like a coating of glaze over earthenware are *fervent lips with an evil heart. A malicious man disguises himself with his lips, but in his heart he harbors deceit.* Though his speech is charming, do not believe him, for seven abominations fill his heart. His malice may be *concealed by deception,* but his wickedness will be exposed in the assembly. If a man digs a pit, he will fall into it; if a man rolls a stone, it will roll back on him. *A lying tongue hates those it hurts, and a flattering mouth works ruin.* (Prov. 26:18-28)

Whom have you so dreaded and feared that you *have been false to Me,* and have neither remembered Me nor pondered this in your hearts? Is it not because I have long been silent that you do not fear Me? (Isa. 57:11)

For your hands are stained with blood, your fingers with guilt. *Your lips have spoken lies, and your tongue mutters wicked things.* (Isa. 59:3)

He said, "Surely they are My people, sons who *will not be false* to Me"; and so He became their Savior. (Isa. 63:8)

Therefore say to them, "This is the nation that has not obeyed Yahweh its God or responded to correction. *Truth has perished; it has vanished from their lips.*" (Jer. 7:28)

Your brothers, your own family—even they have betrayed you; they have raised a loud cry against you. *Do not trust them, though they speak well of you.* (Jer. 12:6)

Hear the word of Yahweh, you Israelites, because Yahweh has a charge to bring against you who live in the land: "There is no faithfulness, no love, *no acknowledgment of God* in the land." (Hos. 4:1)

All your allies will force you to the border; your friends will *deceive* and overpower you; those who eat your bread will set a trap for you, but you will not detect it. (Obad. 1:7)

Yahweh Almighty declares, "I will send it out, and it will enter the house of the thief and the house of him who *swears falsely* by My name. It will remain in his house and destroy it, both its timbers and its stones." (Zech. 5:4)

For out of the heart come evil thoughts, murder, adultery, sexual immorality, theft, *false testimony, slander.* (Matt. 15:19)

You belong to your father, the devil, and you want to carry out your father's desire. He was a murderer from the beginning, *not holding to the truth, for there is no truth in him. When he lies, he speaks his native language, for he is a liar and the father of lies.* (John 8:44)

Though you do not know Him, I know Him. If I said I did not, I would be *a liar like you*, but I do know Him and keep His word. (John 8:55)

Therefore each of you must *put off falsehood and speak truthfully* to his neighbor, for we are all members of one body. (Eph. 4:25)

Do not lie to each other, since you have taken off your old self with its practices. (Col. 3:9)

Such teachings come through *hypocritical liars*, whose consciences have been seared as with a hot iron. (1 Tim. 4:2)

Outside are the dogs, those who practice magic arts, the sexually immoral, the murderers, the idolaters and *everyone who loves and practices falsehood.* (Rev. 22:15)

Say it to yourself again and again: lies destroy relationship, for all relationship must be founded on trust. Only trust opens us to what others communicate to us. It alone brings consent to what they share with us. But who can trust a liar? As shown, a lie only works insofar as someone believes it—insofar as he trusts what is said, opens himself up to it, participates in it and becomes one with it. But after all this, when someone discovers he's been lied to, he feels violated, betrayed. So the lie desolates, decomposes and destroys human relationships. Joseph Conrad wrote:

There is a taint of death . . . in lies . . . . It makes me miserable and sick, like biting something rotten would do.[32]

That's *just* the way it is—we bite because we expect nourishment and health, but we get only sickness and rot; so we become reluctant to bite again. Relationship then dissolves in the corrosion of falsehood.

An offended brother is more unyielding than a fortified city, and disputes are like the barred gates of a citadel. (Prov. 18:19)

"They make ready their tongue like a bow, to shoot lies; it is not by truth that they triumph in the land. They go from one sin to another; they do not acknowledge Me," declares Yahweh. "Beware of your friends; do not trust your brothers. For every brother is a deceiver, and every friend a slanderer. Friend deceives friend, and no one speaks the truth. They have taught their tongues to lie; they weary themselves with sinning. You live in the midst of deception; in their deceit they refuse to acknowledge Me," declares Yahweh. Therefore this is what Yahweh Almighty says: "See, I will refine and test them, for what else can I do because of the sin of My people? Their tongue is a deadly arrow; it speaks with deceit. With his mouth each speaks cordially to his neighbor, but in his heart he sets a trap for him." (Jer. 9:3-8)

Do not drag me away with the wicked, with those who do evil, who speak cordially with their neighbors *but harbor malice in their hearts.* (Ps. 28:3)

What if some did not have faith? Will their lack of faith nullify God's faithfulness? Not at all! *Let God be true, and every man a liar.* As it is written: "So that You may be proved right when You speak and prevail when You judge." (Rom. 3:3-4)

b. Hypocrisy

Every liar is a hypocrite, hiding his lie behind a pretense of truth. The hypocrite is the greatest enemy of truth just because he hides his lies behind such a facade of truth. He tries to impress us with a show of right-eousness that becomes a mockery of righteousness, making righteousness itself appear to be a lie, a mere performance. Consequently, the real person behind the mask is never seen. The hypocrite cannot enter into a real relationship with God or man because no one can truly know him. The Old Testament Hebrew word translated "hypocrite" is *chaneph*, which literally means "to soil, corrupt, defile, pollute, profane." Thus the hypocrite can only "soil" the truth he pretends to stand for.

Romans 2 (see whole chapter)

If we *claim to have fellowship with Him yet walk in the darkness, we lie* and *do not live by the truth.* (1 John 1:6)

If we *claim to be without sin,* we *deceive* ourselves and *the truth is not in us.* (1 John 1:8)

The *man who says, "I know Him,"* but *does not do what He commands is a liar, and the truth is not in him.* (1 John 2:4)

A truthful witness does not deceive, but a *false witness pours out lies.* (Prov. 14:5)

A truthful witness saves lives, but a *false witness is deceitful.* (Prov. 14:25)

Someone might argue, "If my falsehood enhances God's truthful-ness and so increases His glory, why am I still condemned as a sinner?" Why not say—as we are being slanderously reported as saying and as some claim that we say—"Let us do evil that good may result"? Their condemnation is deserved. (Rom. 3:7-8)

Your tongue plots destruction; it is like a sharpened razor, you who *practice deceit.* You *love evil* rather than good, *falsehood* rather than speaking the truth. You *love every harmful word, O you deceitful tongue!* (Ps. 52:2-4)

Woe to you, teachers of the law and Pharisees, you *hypocrites!* You are *like whitewashed tombs, which look beautiful on the outside but on the inside are full of dead men's bones and everything unclean.* In the same way, on the outside you *appear to people as righteous* but on the inside you are *full of hypocrisy and wickedness.* (Matt. 23:27-28)

Listen to this, O house of Jacob, you who are called by the name of Israel and come from the line of Judah, you who *take oaths in the name of Yahweh and invoke the God of Israel—but not in truth or righteousness*—you who call yourselves citizens of the holy city and rely on the God of Israel—Yahweh Almighty is His name. (Isa. 48:1-2)

"The multitude of your sacrifices—what are they to Me?" says Yahweh. "I have more than enough of burnt offerings, of rams and the fat of fattened animals; I have no pleasure in the blood of bulls and lambs and goats. When you come to appear before Me, who has asked this of you, this trampling of My courts? Stop bringing *meaningless offerings!* Your *incense is detestable* to Me. New Moons, Sabbaths and convocations—I cannot bear your evil assemblies. Your New Moon festivals and your appointed feasts My soul hates. They have become a burden to Me; I am weary of bearing them. When you spread out your hands in prayer, I will hide My eyes from you; even if you offer many prayers, I will not listen. Your hands are full of blood; wash and make yourselves clean. *Take your evil deeds out of My sight! Stop doing wrong, learn to do right!* Seek justice, encourage the oppressed. Defend the cause of the fatherless, plead the case of the widow." (Isa. 1:11-17)

His speech is smooth as butter, yet war is in his heart; his words are more soothing than oil, yet they are drawn swords. (Ps. 55:21)

They fully intend to topple him from his lofty place; they take delight in lies. *With their mouths they bless, but in their hearts they curse.* (Ps. 62:4)

Do not drag me away with the wicked, with those who do evil, who *speak cordially with their neighbors but harbor malice in their hearts.* (Ps. 28:3)

One man *pretends* to be rich, yet has nothing; another *pretends* to be poor, yet has great wealth. (Prov. 13:7)

So, because you are lukewarm—neither hot nor cold—I am about to spit you out of My mouth. You say, "I am rich; I have acquired wealth and do not need a thing." But you do not realize that you are wretched, pitiful, poor, blind and naked. (Rev. 3:16-17)

From the least to the greatest, all are greedy for gain; prophets and priests alike, all *practice deceit.* They dress the wound of My people as though it were not serious. "Peace, peace," they say, when there is no peace. (Jer. 6:13-14)

Like a *coating of glaze over earthenware are fervent lips with an evil heart.* A malicious man *disguises himself with his lips, but in his heart he harbors deceit.* Though his *speech is charming, do not believe him,* for seven abominations fill his heart. His malice may be *concealed by deception,* but his wickedness will be exposed in the assembly. (Prov. 26:23-26)

How can you say, "We are wise, for we have the law of Yahweh," when actually the *lying pen of the scribes has handled it falsely?* The wise will be put to shame; they will be dismayed and trapped. Since they have rejected the word of Yahweh, what kind of wisdom do they have? (Jer. 8:8-9)

But you must not mention "the oracle of Yahweh" again, because every man's own word becomes his oracle and so you *distort the words of the living God*, Yahweh Almighty, our God. (Jer. 23:36)

c. Affected Love, Insincerity and Disobedience

The hypocrite hides lovelessness behind feigned love, manipulative care, ingratiating kindness, insincere sincerity and a mockery of obedience. He even deceives himself into believing that his relationship with others rests on his false image in their eyes. He tries to manufacture the fruit of God's Spirit, but his plastic fruit can only turn away in bitter disappointment those hungry for the sweet reality of God's tender love. Can there be any greater enemy of God and destroyer of souls than the hypocrite, the sham Christian?

The Greek word in the New Testament translated "hypocrisy" is *hupokrisis*. Rienecker states that "the basic meaning of the word is 'to answer from under' and refers to actors who spoke under a mask in playing a part. The actors hid their true selves behind the role they were playing. The word indicates the concealing of wrong feelings, character, etc. under the pretense of better ones." The hypocrite affects or strikes a pose; he puts on false feelings and engages in false actions to mask and disguise what is truly taking place inside of himself. He isn't an open book but speaks from under a false cover.

> Yahweh says: "These people come near to Me *with their mouth and honor Me with their lips, but their hearts are far from Me.* Their worship of Me is made up only of rules taught by men." (Isa. 29:13)

> You have planted them, and they have taken root; they grow and bear fruit. *You are always on their lips but far from their hearts.* (Jer. 12:2)

> While He was still speaking a crowd came up, and the man who was called Judas, one of the Twelve, was leading them. He approached Jesus to kiss Him, but Jesus asked Him, "Judas, are you *betraying the Son of Man with a kiss*?" (Luke 22:47-48)

> What good is it, my brothers, if a man *claims to have faith but has no deeds*? Can such faith save him? Suppose a brother or sister is without clothes and daily food. If one of you says to him, "Go, I wish you well; keep warm and well fed," but *does nothing about his physical needs*, what good is it? (James 2:14-16)

> When Peter came to Antioch, I opposed him to his face, because

he was clearly in the wrong. Before certain men came from James, he used to eat with the Gentiles. But when they arrived, he began to draw back and separate himself from the Gentiles because he was afraid of those who belonged to the circumcision group. The other Jews joined him in his *hypocrisy*, so that by their *hypocrisy* even Barnabas was led astray. (Gal. 2:11-13)

Also, whenever anyone approached him to bow down before him, Absalom would reach out his hand, take hold of him and kiss him. Absalom behaved in this way toward all the Israelites who came to the king asking for justice, and so he *stole the hearts* of the men of Israel. (2 Sam. 15:5-6)

But one of His disciples, Judas Iscariot, who was later to betray Him, objected, "Why wasn't this perfume sold and the money given to the poor? It was worth a year's wages." *He did not say this because he cared about the poor but because he was a thief;* as keeper of the money bag, he used to help himself to what was put into it. (John 12:4-6)

d. Hardness of Heart

The deceiver's heart hardens against truth. *Poroo* is the Greek word in the New Testament translated "harden" and is used to describe the hardening heart. One lexicon gives the literal meaning of the noun form of this word, *porosis*, as "a hardening, a covering with a *poros*, a kind of stone." According to Thayer, *poroo* also means "to cover with a thick skin, to harden by covering with a callus." A callus forms when skin is continually irritated. Rather than allowing his heart to be pierced, penetrated, convicted, the dishonest child resists God's Word. He merely becomes irritated at it, until at last, through the constant friction of his resistance, a thick callus forms over his heart. Only God can give us a heart of flesh, a heart open and circumcised to love. If we allow self-deceit to sever our relationship with God, the callousness of sin immediately hardens our hearts.

But they refused to pay attention; stubbornly they turned their backs and stopped up their ears. *They made their hearts as hard as flint and would not listen to the law or to the words that Yahweh Almighty had sent* by His Spirit through the earlier prophets. So Yahweh Almighty was very angry. (Zech. 7:11-12)

A man who remains stiff-necked after many rebukes will suddenly be destroyed—without remedy. (Prov. 29:1)

Blessed is the man who always fears Yahweh, but *he who hardens his heart falls into trouble.* (Prov. 28:14)

Then Yahweh said to Cain, "Where is your brother Abel?"
  "I don't know," he replied. *"Am I my brother's keeper?"* (Gen. 4:9)

This is what Yahweh said to me: "Go and buy a linen belt and put it around your waist, but do not let it touch water." So I bought a belt, as Yahweh directed, and put it around my waist.

Then the word of Yahweh came to me a second time: "Take the belt you bought and are wearing around your waist, and go now to Perath and hide it there in a crevice in the rocks." So I went and hid it at Perath, as Yahweh told me.

Many days later Yahweh said to me, "Go now to Perath and get the belt I told you to hide there." So I went to Perath and dug up the belt and took it from the place where I had hidden it, but now it was ruined and completely useless.

Then the word of Yahweh came to me: "This is what Yahweh says: In the same way I will ruin the pride of Judah and the great pride of Jerusalem. These wicked people, who refuse to listen to My words, *who follow the stubbornness of their hearts* and go after other gods to serve and worship them, will be like this belt—completely useless!" (Jer. 13:1-10)

But these people have stubborn and rebellious hearts; they have turned aside and gone away. (Jer. 5:23)

But you have behaved more wickedly than your fathers. See how each of you is *following the stubbornness of his evil heart* instead of obeying Me. (Jer. 16:12)

They keep saying to those who despise me, "Yahweh says: You will have peace." And to all *who follow the stubbornness of their hearts* they say, "No harm will come to you." But which of them has stood in the council of Yahweh to see or to hear His word? Who has listened and heard His word? (Jer. 23:17-18)

Listen to Me, *you stubborn-hearted*, you who are far from righteousness. (Isa. 46:12)

"But My people would not listen to Me; Israel would not submit to Me. So *I gave them over to their stubborn hearts* to follow their own devices." (Ps. 81:11-12)

He looked around at them in anger and, *deeply distressed at their stubborn hearts*, said to the man, "Stretch out your hand." He stretched it out, and his hand was completely restored. (Mark 3:5)

You stiff-necked people, with uncircumcised hearts and ears! You are just like your fathers: You always resist the Holy Spirit! Was there ever a prophet your fathers did not persecute? They even killed those who predicted the coming of the Righteous One. And now you have betrayed and murdered Him—you who have received the law that was put into effect through angels but have not obeyed it. (Acts 7:51-53)

e. Failure to Confess a Given Sin before Exposed

The liar hardens his heart and so closes himself off from the experience of grace and mercy. Like Achan, his sin is "covered over," the literal meaning of the Hebrew word *taman*, translated "hidden." Rather than willingly and voluntarily confessing his sin, he waits until his sin is exposed before he will even acknowledge it, much less confess it. This is also a lie, since he hides the real behind the false. So he compounds and deepens the distrust his parents and others feel toward him.

> Yahweh sent Nathan to David. When he came to him, he said, "There were two men in a certain town, one rich and the other poor. The rich man had a very large number of sheep and cattle, but the poor man had nothing except one little ewe lamb he had bought. He raised it, and it grew up with him and his children. It shared his food, drank from his cup and even slept in his arms. It was like a daughter to him.
>
> "Now a traveler came to the rich man, but the rich man refrained from taking one of his own sheep or cattle to prepare a meal for the traveler who had come to him. Instead, he took the ewe lamb that belonged to the poor man and prepared it for the one who had come to him."
>
> David burned with anger against the man and said to Nathan, "As surely as Yahweh lives, the man who did this deserves to die! He must pay for that lamb four times over, because he did such a thing and had no pity."
>
> Then Nathan said to David, "*You are the man*! This is what Yahweh, the God of Israel, says: 'I anointed you king over Israel, and I delivered you from the hand of Saul. I gave your master's house to you, and your master's wives into your arms. I gave you the house of Israel and Judah. And if all this had been too little, I would have given you even more. Why did you despise the word of Yahweh by doing what is evil in His eyes? You struck down Uriah the Hittite with the sword and took his wife to be your own. You killed him with the sword of the Ammonites. Now, therefore, the sword will never depart from your house, because you despised Me and took the wife of Uriah the Hittite to be your own.'" (2 Sam. 12:1-10)

> Now a man named Ananias, together with his wife Sapphira, also sold a piece of property. With his wife's full knowledge he kept back part of the money for himself, but brought the rest and put it at the apostles' feet.
>
> Then Peter said, "Ananias, how is it that Satan has so filled your heart that *you have lied to the Holy Spirit and have kept for yourself some of the money you received for the land*? Didn't it belong to you before it was sold? And after it was sold, wasn't the money at your disposal? What made you think of doing such a thing? *You have not lied to men but to God*."
>
> When Ananias heard this, he fell down and died. And great fear seized all who heard what had happened. Then the young men came forward, wrapped up his body, and carried him out and buried him.
>
> About three hours later his wife came in, not knowing what had happened. *Peter asked her, "Tell me, is this the price you and Ananias got for the land?"*

"Yes," she said, "that is the price."

Peter said to her, "How could you agree to test the Spirit of the Lord? Look! The feet of the men who buried your husband are at the door, and they will carry you out also."

At that moment she fell down at his feet and died. Then the young men came in and, finding her dead, carried her out and buried her beside her husband. Great fear seized the whole church and all who heard about these events. (Acts 5:1-11)

Early in the morning Samuel got up and went to meet Saul, but he was told, "Saul has gone to Carmel. There he has set up a monument in his own honor and has turned and gone on down to Gilgal."

When Samuel reached him, Saul said, "Yahweh bless you! *I have carried out Yahweh's instructions."*

But *Samuel said, "What then is this bleating of sheep in my ears? What is this lowing of cattle that I hear?"*

Saul answered, "The soldiers brought them from the Amalekites; they spared the best of the sheep and cattle to sacrifice to Yahweh your God, but we totally destroyed the rest."

"Stop!" Samuel said to Saul. "Let me tell you what Yahweh said to me last night."

"Tell me," Saul replied.

Samuel said, "Although you were once small in your own eyes, did you not become the head of the tribes of Israel? Yahweh anointed you king over Israel. And he sent you on a mission, saying, Go and completely destroy those wicked people, the Amalekites; make war on them until you have wiped them out. Why did you not obey Yahweh? Why did you pounce on the plunder and do evil in the eyes of Yahweh?"

"But I did obey Yahweh," Saul said. "I went on the mission Yahweh assigned me. I completely destroyed the Amalekites and brought back Agag their king. The soldiers took sheep and cattle from the plunder, the best of what was devoted to God, in order to sacrifice them to Yahweh your God at Gilgal."

But Samuel replied: *"Does Yahweh delight in burnt offerings and sacrifices as much as in obeying the voice of Yahweh? To obey is better than sacrifice, and to heed is better than the fat of rams.* For rebellion is like the sin of divination, and arrogance like the evil of idolatry. Because you have rejected the word of Yahweh, He has rejected you as king."

Then Saul said to Samuel, *"I have sinned. I violated Yahweh's command and your instructions. I was afraid of the people and so I gave in to them."* (1 Sam. 15:12-24)

"In the morning, present yourselves tribe by tribe. The tribe that Yahweh takes shall come forward clan by clan; the clan that Yahweh takes shall come forward family by family; and the family that Yahweh takes shall come forward man by man. He who is caught with the devoted things shall be destroyed by fire, along with all that belongs to him. He has violated the covenant of Yahweh and has done a disgraceful thing in Israel!"

Early the next morning Joshua had Israel come forward by tribes, and Judah was taken, the clans of Judah came forward, and he took the Zerahites. He had the clan of the Zerahites come forward by families, and Zimri was taken. Joshua had his family come forward man by man, and Achan son of Carmi, the son of Zimri, the son of Zerah, of the tribe of Judah, was taken.

Then Joshua said to Achan, "My son, give glory to Yahweh, the God of Israel, and give Him the praise. *Tell me what you have done; do not hide it from me.*"

Achan replied, "*It is true! I have sinned against Yahweh, the God of Israel.* This is what I have done: When I saw in the plunder a beautiful robe from Babylonia, two hundred shekels of silver and a wedge of gold weighing fifty shekels, I coveted them and took them. They are hidden in the ground inside my tent, with the silver underneath." (Josh. 7:14-21)

Failure to confess sin incapacitates us for virtuous action: covering sin thwarts the ability to do God's will. Pilate knew that Jesus was innocent and should therefore be released; he even wanted to set Him free (Luke 23:16). But when he insisted that Jesus be set free, the ultra-orthodox rabbinical Jews kept shouting, "If you let this man go, you are no friend of Caesar" (John 19:12). Scripture says that, following this cry, Pilate brought Jesus out to the crowd and shortly afterward handed Him over to be crucified. Why would a Roman governor be intimidated by an alien mob's suggestion that he was "no friend of Caesar"? Historians describe Pilate's whole administration as rife with corruption and that the one thing he feared was an inspection by the Roman emperor.[33] To accuse him of being "no friend of Caesar" was to implicitly threaten such an investigation. The crowd well knew about his corrupt and weak character—that he had lied to and cheated those over him and then hidden it from them. Because of his past sins and the corruption of his administration—sins and corruption that he had sought to hide and cover up—he couldn't help Jesus, even though he seemed to want to, knowing as he did that the Nazarene was guiltless. Because Pilate had, time after time, year after year, sought to hide his sin, when the ultimate test came, he could take no stand for truth and instead dipped his hand, in the very act of trying to wash it, into the blood of the crucified Lord. He had lived his life in the darkness of his lies. Board by board, with each lie, with each coverup, he had dismantled the house of any good character he might have once possessed and thrown each board into a fire that gave only a temporary warmth to his naked exposure. This is all that his lies afforded him, until at last no substance was left of his life; and so at the great test, the moment of ultimate decision and destiny in his life, he crumbled to the pressure of the mob and aided and abetted the crucifixion of the Savior of the world. It is said that, like Judas, Pilate died at his own hand.

To cover our sins is death. Judas finally recognized his own sin against innocent blood, but he did not come to any level of repentance that would have brought him deliverance. If he had, he could have broken through the crowds at Pilate's palace. He could have made his way to Jesus and begged forgiveness. But this would have tarred him with the same brush he'd used to tar Jesus. So he found no repentance, only remorse. Instead of turning to God and dying in one moment on the "sword" of repentance, he went and hanged himself and died eternally (Matt. 27:5). True repentance never leads to the death of our souls but to the death of our sins through confession. Judas voiced his sin, but his was not the deep *confession* of someone liberated by God's love from sin. So again, uncoerced confession of sin can only come from true repentance.

f. Evasiveness and Partial Truths

Even when the liar feeds out some nibble of truth, his words are laced with the poison of evasion and partiality. He, too, only has respect for the punishment and not the offense. Since lies counterfeit truth, evasive and partial truths are therefore not truth at all. Rather, they stand as the greatest enemies of truth, for they are its most effective, closest counterfeits. The liar hopes to tell just enough to protect himself from the fullness of the light. He uses *partial* truths in order to destroy the *whole* truth. He does not stand in integrity before God and therefore does not care enough about his relationship with God, with his brothers and sisters or with his parents to be honest and truthful. Because he lacks the integrity and love of truth that holds relationships together, his relationships disintegrate, and he ends up trying to destroy the truth that exposed him and that still holds together the relationships of others, whom the liar secretly envies and openly hates.

Those who hide from the light refuse to speak clearly and completely—refuse to speak the *whole* truth plainly and forthrightly. They either carefully alter or avoid specifics because they don't want their lives and character measured by the words they speak. They don't want their words to form a clear image that their own lives might later be measured against, but only a vague, blurred or distorted image that obscures everyone's clear vision. Instead of speaking plainly, like the serpent, they insinuate their meanings through innuendo and subtlety, the true implications of which they can later deny when confronted with what they said. They speak equivocally, out of both sides of their mouths, so they can never be held responsible for what they say. They also speak ambiguously because they seek to avoid the commitment that truth requires. They don't want to speak words to stand by, precise words of a living faith that will not rest until the Word of truth has become flesh in the believer's own life, character and relationships with others.

Imprecise words reveal the absence of conviction, and the absence of conviction reveals the absence of faith. So imprecise words are words already bending and breaking down under the weight of doubt. In short, the one uttering them will never be able to stand by them and therefore won't do so. Generalities, ambiguities and equivocations do not offer the firm footing for those seeking to stand for truth. Only words of precision offer such solid ground. God Himself does not equivocate when He speaks crucial words to a people (1 Cor. 14:8; Num. 23:19; Ps. 18:30; 2 Cor. 1:17-20). His sovereign freedom is never, as some would like for us to believe, impinged upon because of His own consistency with His own words. Those who would have us believe so usually show more concern about their own sovereign freedom than God's. As Tolstoy said, theology can become exceedingly complicated and convoluted, as well as vague and ambiguous, for those trying to evade God and truth. God, however, has made His Word precise to those who would give themselves to, actually participate in, His voice (John 8:43-47). Although He remains not just a mystery but a *total* mystery to the arrogant and insincere, God makes Himself known, reveals Himself, to the honest because He is sincere and wants to stand by words that His people can understand, believe and trust in.

We said that the insincere speak vaguely, ambiguously and equivocally because they fear to speak words that they *must* then stand by, words that can call them into accountability to what they've spoken. G. K. Chesterton said about morality what we have said here about theology: it becomes extremely complex to the man who has lost his principles and his integrity. Such people must always speak words that no one can quite pin down, mercurial words that can be interpreted and reinterpreted so as to avoid the necessity of standing by anything clearly spoken. Yet their insincerity is evident to all who walk in the light. Only precise words can be stood by. A coward simply cannot live a moral life.

> Forever, O Yahweh, Your word is settled in heaven. (Ps. 119:89)

> For assuredly, I say to you, till heaven and earth pass away, one jot or one tittle will by no means pass from the law till all is fulfilled. (Matt. 5:18)

> Then the man and his wife heard the sound of Yahweh God as He was walking in the garden in the cool of the day, and *they hid from Yahweh God* among the trees of the garden. But Yahweh God called to the man, "Where are you?"
>
> He answered, "I heard You in the garden, and *I was afraid* because I was naked; *so I hid.*"
>
> And He said, "Who told you that you were naked? Have you eaten from the tree that I commanded you not to eat from?"
>
> The man said, "*The woman You put here with me*—she gave me some fruit from the tree, and I ate it."

Then Yahweh God said to the woman, "What is this you have done?"

The woman said, "*The serpent deceived me, and I ate.*" (Gen. 3:8-13)

He said to Aaron, "What did these people do to you, that you led them into such great sin?"

"Do not be angry, my lord," Aaron answered. "*You know how prone these people are to evil.* They said to me, Make us gods who will go before us. As for this fellow Moses who brought us up out of Egypt, we don't know what has happened to him. So I told them, Whoever has any gold jewelry, take it off. Then they gave me the gold, *and I threw it into the fire, and out came this calf!*" (Exod. 32:21-24)

Now a man named Ananias, together with his wife Sapphira, also sold a piece of property. With his wife's full knowledge he kept back part of the money *for himself,* but brought the rest and put it at the apostles' feet.

Then Peter said, "Ananias, how is it that *Satan has so filled* your heart that you have lied to the Holy Spirit and have kept for yourself some of the money you received for the land? Didn't it belong to you before it was sold? And after it was sold, wasn't the money at your disposal? What made you think of doing such a thing? You have not lied to men but to God."

When Ananias heard this, he fell down and died. And great fear seized all who heard what had happened. Then the young men came forward, wrapped up his body, and carried him out and buried him.

About three hours later his wife came in, not knowing what had happened. Peter asked her, "Tell me, is this the price you and Ananias got for the land?"

"Yes," she said, "that is the price."

Peter said to her, "How could you agree to test the Spirit of the Lord? Look! The feet of the men who buried your husband are at the door, and they will carry you out also." (Acts 5:1-9)

Samuel said, "Although you were once small in your own eyes, did you not become the head of the tribes of Israel? Yahweh anointed you king over Israel. And he sent you on a mission, saying, 'Go and completely destroy those wicked people, the Amalekites; make war on them until you have wiped them out.' Why did you not obey Yahweh? Why did you pounce on the plunder and do evil in the eyes of Yahweh?"

"*But I did obey Yahweh,*" Saul said. "I went on the mission Yahweh assigned me. *I completely destroyed the Amalekites and brought back Agag their king.*" (1 Sam. 15:17-20)

But one of his disciples, Judas Iscariot, who was later to betray Him, objected, "Why wasn't this perfume sold and the money given to the poor? It was worth a year's wages." *He did not say this because he cared about the poor but because he was a thief; as keeper of the money bag, he used to help himself to what was put into it.* (John 12:4-6)

The manufacturer of evasiveness and partial truths ceases to be a child of God and soon becomes a child of the father of lies, the devil.

> You belong to your father, the devil, and you want to carry out your father's desire. He was a murderer from the beginning, not holding to the truth, for there is no truth in him. When he lies, he speaks his native language, *for he is a liar and the father of lies.* (John 8:44)

g. Defensiveness, Excuses, Suspicion and Mistrust

Because people fail to obediently respond to God's dealings, whether in simple matters like cleaning house or even in deeper transgressions, their countenance becomes "downcast," like Cain's. They become depressed, perhaps even bitter. They are then sick or tired *because* they haven't cleaned their room or their house or severed themselves from evil relationships or activities or attitudes or behavior patterns or even "little" transgressions of God's Word like constantly interrupting, trying to finish someone else's thought with their own words, speaking too assertively and insensitively and so on. They have instead expended all their energies defensively fighting God's conviction on these matters, justifying themselves, evading responsibility by blame shifting and making excuses, pitying themselves, seeking distractions, running from the light or even bristling at and resenting, or wearing themselves out deceiving and hiding from, anyone who might call them to account. In such cases, the refusal to straighten their room or house—or attitudes or conversation (or life) or to conform to God's Word in any way—represents the first level of disobedience. The struggles against the conviction then become the second-level pattern of misbehavior that causes the emotional effects and also can point to the third level: enslavement to sin, a habituated pattern of behavior that conforms a person not to God's image but to the fallen, downcast and finally hopeless condition of the Adamic nature.

These habits of mind and heart develop over years of conditioning from certain wrong responses to peer influence, to other relationships, to stress, to temptation, to trials and other problems—that is, from the failure to cut off one's sinful attitudes and connections to evil conduct and people whenever they arise. To address only the consequences and fruit of disobedience, such as defensiveness, mistrust, suspicion and excuses, can become like stomping out a brush fire or bailing out a leaking boat— a mere crisis management. Believers must allow ministry to caulk and fill and mend the leaking hole, the broken form, the flawed character— that whole unextirpated strain of the old Adamic nature that has not yet died and that continually leads us to respond in certain negative and destructive ways to problems and temptations and people. If an individual has, from childhood, repeatedly responded to correction with evasiveness and defensiveness, or perhaps even with bristling and sullen resentment or inward anger and rage to others' reluctance to concede that his way and perspective must naturally be right, then a deeply embedded and conditioned response—a habit—will have developed. This conditioned behavior may even endure past any growing desire to overcome it. But otherwise, while ministry must deal with specific instances of outbursts, it should still nonetheless use the specific circumstances to point toward the underlying habitual condition. Its goal is to point to the only solution in the total dismantling of the entire thought pattern and the complete restructuring of this individual's attitudes and perspectives and relationships and life according to God's composition and orchestration. Such a dismantling goes far beyond any minor adjustments. It amounts to a total cutting off—a mortification, a death to the conditioned response and all the attitudes that produced and support it.

If this turning to God and dismantling of the conditioned response of sin—this repentance—is authentic, then hiding from the light will utterly cease. Resistance—whether mental, emotional, verbal or behavioral—will end. A veil of rationalizations, defensiveness or false propriety and self-protective images will no longer cover sin. A new transparency and vulnerability will prompt the offender to snatch off every mask, tear down every facade and topple all proud self-images by crying out to God and standing open before those God has joined him to. He'll even beg God, as Jacob did (Hos. 12:3-5), to allow him to see God face to face so that the light of His countenance (Ps. 90:8) will expose the core sin separating him from God (Isa. 59:2). Then he'll know the mask of his defenses has dropped. Then he'll confess his failures and guilt according to God's Word. Then he'll find the freedom from sin that comes only with obedience to the truth and walking in the light of the Word. Then he'll be able to say with David: "Who can understand his errors? Cleanse me from *secret* faults" (Ps. 19:12).

Excuses and Blame Shifting

Two of the most common defensive postures of the sinful nature when confronted by the light are blame shifting and excuses. A key question, then, confronts each of us: will we take full and complete responsibility for our own life, for the base forces and drives that control us, and for the disastrous results so often following our irresponsibility and delusions? There are two worldviews that come into play when approaching this question. One is that of the therapeutic culture that affords boundless opportunities to excuse ourselves as victims, and often this involves scapegoating; but in the traditional Christian view, any whiff of an excuse merely stifles the full acknowledgment of sin, and this only leads to worse evil. It thus short-circuits any authentic repentance and condemns us to endlessly repeating the same destructive habits of sin as they grow progressively more malevolent. In this day especially, individuals and natural families are encouraged to refuse to take any decisive responsibility for the inconsistencies and failures in their relationships, whether with others or even with God, much less for the condition of their lives. We allow these attitudes to subconsciously seep in and pamper the baser nature, preventing a full acknowledgment of our own full responsibility for our unconscious but nonetheless sinful habits (Ps. 19:12), even often as we scorn or mock those attitudes with our words and conscious thoughts. Christians have traditionally believed that only a radical and undiluted desire to face the full truth about ourselves can wholly uproot such subtle excuses; but this desire is, after all, what moves us toward authentic repentance. And when that radical desire *fully* seizes hold of us in an unreserved acknowledgment, then both the excuse and the need for the excuse die as people then allow the truth to wholly set them free. Only this kind of acknowledgment, without any hint of evasion, can enable people to come to the changes they long for and to an escape from their dilemmas.

So in every circumstance in which sin arises, God wants to lay the ax at the root of sin, to totally demolish the whole old structure and edifice of it. We can only become God's temple by demolishing the entire structure and patterns of both the thought and behavior habits (same root as *habitation*) of sin. Then we turn from the habitual response of the sinful nature that always blames others or circumstances or God or misunderstandings for our own sins and failures (the sinful responses that always ask, "Why are *they* like this?" or, "Why did *God* make me like this?" or, "Why does this *always* have to happen?"). If we want victory, then we must stop excusing, justifying and defending ourselves; we must stop blame shifting like Adam did in the garden.

> Then Yahweh God called to Adam and said to him, "Where are you?" So he said, "I heard Your voice in the garden, and I was afraid because I was naked; and I hid myself." And He said, "Who told you that you were naked? Have you eaten from the tree of which I commanded you that you should not eat?" Then the man said, *"The woman whom You gave to be with me, she gave me of the tree, and I ate."* And Yahweh God said to the woman, "What is this you have done?" *The woman said, "The serpent deceived me, and I ate."* (Gen. 3:9-13)

Both Adam and Eve tried to shift the blame from themselves. Neither wanted to go to the root of their sin—their disobedience to God's clear command. They wanted to convince themselves and God that it wasn't *their* fault, that *they* weren't really responsible. But only by repenting of our sins can we find deliverance from them. Blame shifting and dishonesty represent the worst sort of denial. They can only keep us from facing and overcoming the ravages of sin in our own lives, as well as in the lives of others. No real escape ever lies in such denials. We must, instead, recognize our need for a total restructuring according to God's blueprint and living pattern for His temple. When we *fully* recognize this and commit to utterly change our behavior accordingly, the old habits *will* die. Then God can rebuild us if we'll continue to walk in a transparent consciousness of Him, stepping into His light faithfully and obediently on a day-by-day, moment-by-moment basis, acknowledging and confessing our sins and mistakes each and every time they arise, cutting them off at the first hint of their appearance. If we do this consistently, God will work a change and create His new image in us. Old things will pass away, and all things will be made new (2 Cor. 5:17).

> "But they all with one accord *began to make excuses*. The first said to him, 'I have bought a piece of ground, and I must go and see it. I ask you to have me excused.' And another said, 'I have bought five yoke of oxen, and I am going to test them. I ask you to have me excused.'" (Luke 14:18-19)

> If I had not come and spoken to them, they would not be guilty of sin. Now, however, they have *no excuse* for their sin. (John 15:22)

> For since the creation of the world His invisible attributes are clearly seen, being understood by the things that are made, even His eternal power and Godhead, so that they are *without excuse*. (Rom. 1:20)

> Therefore *you have no excuse or defense or justification*, O man, whoever you are who judges and condemns another. For in posing as judge and passing sentence on another, you condemn yourself, because you who judge are habitually practicing the very same things [that you censure and denounce]. (Rom 2:1, Ampl.)

> Samuel also said to Saul, "Yahweh sent me to anoint you king over His people, over Israel. Now therefore, heed the voice of the words of Yahweh. Thus says Yahweh of hosts: 'I will punish Amalek for what he did to Israel, how he ambushed him on the way when he came up from Egypt. Now *go and attack Amalek, and utterly destroy all that they have, and do not spare them*. But kill both man and woman, infant and nursing child, ox and sheep, camel and donkey.'" . . .
> And Saul attacked the Amalekites, from Havilah all the way to Shur, which is east of Egypt. He also took Agag king of the Amalekites alive, and utterly destroyed all the people with the edge of the sword. But *Saul and the people spared Agag and the best of the sheep, the oxen, the fatlings, the lambs, and all that was good, and were unwilling to utterly destroy them*. But everything despised and worthless, that they utterly destroyed.
> Now the word of Yahweh came to Samuel, saying, "I greatly regret that I have set up Saul as king, for he has turned back from

following Me, and has not performed My commandments." And it grieved Samuel, and he cried out to Yahweh all night . . . .

Then Samuel went to Saul, and *Saul said* to him, "Blessed are you of Yahweh! *I have performed the commandment of Yahweh.*"

But Samuel said, "What then is this bleating of the sheep in my ears, and the lowing of the oxen which I hear?"

And Saul said, "They have brought them from the Amalekites; for *the people spared the best of the sheep and the oxen, to sacrifice to Yahweh your God*; and the rest we have utterly destroyed."

Then Samuel said to Saul, "Be quiet! And I will tell you what Yahweh said to me last night."

And he said to him, "Speak on."

So Samuel said, "When you were little in your own eyes, were you not head of the tribes of Israel? And did not Yahweh anoint you king over Israel? Now Yahweh sent you on a mission, and said, 'Go, and utterly destroy the sinners, the Amalekites, and fight against them until they are consumed.' Why then did you not obey the voice of Yahweh? Why did you swoop down on the spoil, and do evil in the sight of Yahweh?"

And Saul said to Samuel, "*But I have obeyed the voice of Yahweh, and gone on the mission on which Yahweh sent me*, and brought back Agag king of Amalek; I have utterly destroyed the Amalekites. But *the people took of the plunder, sheep and oxen, the best of the things which should have been utterly destroyed*, to sacrifice to Yahweh your God in Gilgal."

So Samuel said: "Has Yahweh as great delight in burnt offerings and sacrifices, as in obeying the voice of Yahweh? Behold, to obey is better than sacrifice, and to heed than the fat of rams. For *rebellion is as the sin of witchcraft, and stubbornness is as iniquity and idolatry*. Because you have rejected the word of Yahweh, He also has rejected you from being king." (1 Sam. 15:1-3, 7-11, 13-23)

Suspicion and Mistrust

Adam and Eve turned their backs on God because satan promised that they themselves would "be as God, knowing good and evil." The devil, in short, took advantage of their gullible pride by casting suspicion on God and God's motives. Belief in the serpent's fateful words suddenly reframed their entire vision of God and their circumstances. God suddenly became little more to them than what people today would call a "control freak." Supposedly, what God had told them wasn't even necessary—rather, God had supposedly lied to them (thus satan's words, "You will *not surely* die"). And since, therefore, it wasn't fully necessary, it must have been a *serious* "deprivation," but ironically, over nothing but a "trivial" matter, like food. Yet God only forbade them *one* thing—just one tree withheld. The tree represented covetousness and pride; it represented earthly cunning passing itself off as wisdom and freedom and the worldly knowledge of evil (now added to the knowledge of good);

and it represented the lust of the eyes and of the flesh—all these were tied to that one tree. Yet the whole rest of paradise had lain before them to enjoy, but they believed they were unfairly "deprived" because God denied them access to that one tree. Therefore they concluded that the only road to "freedom" lay in rebellion against God's commandment— tear down the wall of relationship inherent in that commandment and then eat whatever they wanted, eat from that one forbidden tree. And this they did. They played with the serpent, utterly stunned when he struck them, when his poison surged into their minds and hearts and attitudes, when what God had warned against did in fact happen, exactly what the devil claimed would never happen. In short, they died, first spiritually, as they lost their spiritual life and relationship with God. This was inevitable the moment they had first mistrusted God, instead believing the devil when he insinuated that God was an envious control freak, an authoritarian tyrant who did not love them enough to provide them with everything they wanted. God was a "legalist" with all sorts of "unnecessary" restrictions that were just "add-ons." And these "add-ons" supposedly served no purpose other than inflating His own megalomania, a megalomania defended against the just rights of His pitifully "deprived" children to themselves be as God (Gen. 3:1-6).

So, according to the devil, God deprived people unjustly. And for what reason? Well, God hadn't given them any reason for what He forbade them to do, except that they would die if they broke faith with Him, thereby destroying their relationship with Him as the source of life. No, God gave them the *consequence* of the sin, *not the reason* to avoid it; and they simply didn't believe or trust Him. And if God didn't explain everything to them, didn't put them on the same level as Himself and thus make them gods equal with Himself, pretending their minds could understand as much as His could, well, that only seemed *prima facie* evidence that satan was right—God was simply arbitrarily denying them godhood. So they believed satan when he told them, "You won't surely die." They believed him when he said that what God was asking just wasn't necessary, just wasn't fair. Yet it *was* necessary, but this would not be the last time suspicion, envy and slander triumphed over truth and love in human minds.

The word translated as "suspicion" in the verse "Saul looked at David with *suspicion* from that day on" (1 Sam. 18:9, NASU) is simply the word "eyed." Saul convinced himself that he had to continually and defensively *watch* David, as though if he took his eye off of him for a moment, David might harm him. But Saul looked at David that way because Saul had allowed the spirit of envy and jealousy into his own heart, even though Saul was in reality the one planning to harm, and even kill, David. David had done nothing wrong. In fact, at each step along the way David had faithfully followed the instructions of God, and even of Saul. As a result, he had won great victories for the whole kingdom. But because of the sin that Saul had allowed to come into his own heart, Saul mistrusted David and "eyed" him—looked upon everything he did with suspicion.

So the root of suspicion and mistrust, especially when directed toward parents and others standing over us in a position of loving, caring authority, can simply be the sin that we've allowed into our own heart and that affects everything we see. Jesus said: "If your eye is evil, your whole body will be full of darkness" (Matt. 6:23). And John wrote, "He who says he is in the light and hates his brother is in darkness until now . . . . He who hates his brother . . . does not know where he is going, because *the darkness has blinded his eyes*" (1 John 2:9, 11). Hatred and jealousy bring a darkness that blinds us, and in the darkness we strike out defensively against enemies we see as external but that really lie deep within us. The whole constellation of defensive reactions—excuses, blame shifting, mistrust, fear, suspicion and so on—as with Adam and Eve, arises because our "deeds are evil." Our reactions against truth only show that we "love darkness" and defend ourselves *against* the light.

> The world cannot hate you, but it hates Me because I testify of it that *its works are evil.* (John 7:7)

> And this is the condemnation, that the light has come into the world, and men loved darkness rather than light, *because their deeds were evil. For everyone practicing evil hates the light and does not come to the light, lest his deeds should be exposed.* But he who does the truth comes to the light, that his deeds may be clearly seen, that they have been done in God. (John 3:19-21)

> Once you were alienated from God and were *enemies in your minds because of your evil behavior.* (Col. 1:21)

> And have no fellowship with the *unfruitful works of darkness,* but rather *expose them.* For it is shameful even to speak of those things which are done by them in secret. But all things that are exposed are *made manifest by the light,* for *whatever makes manifest is light.* Therefore He says: "Awake, you who sleep, arise from the dead, and Christ will give you light." See then that you walk circumspectly, not as fools but as wise, redeeming the time, because the days are evil. (Eph. 5:11-16)

h. Resisting Correction

Make it part of the framework of your thinking; repeat it over and over: the dishonest person does anything and everything to evade the light and resist exposure of his sin. He seeks to hide from the dimmest candle, to snuff it out and cover his sin with a tattered quilt patched together from darkness, lies and deceit. But even all of these deceptions ultimately prove ineffective against the light. So if the deceiver would continue in his lie, he must eventually come against the instruments through which the light burns; he must, in other words, not only try to snuff out the flame but also destroy even the candles. First, he will actively resist all correction God holds out to him. Because his lie has been fully exposed, because God's light has shone upon him, he can only continue in the lie by then directly contradicting God's Word, by denying God's truth, by refusing God's direction, by attacking God's minister. So the one who makes this refusal finally closes his ears to not only God's Word but also to God's minister of that Word; if that Word penetrates through this barrier, he wags his head in denial of the truth of this Word, then argues against it. Soon he is muttering and mumbling, whining and complaining, then slandering and accusing any and every instrument of truth. This is the spirit that ended in the stoning of both Stephen and the prophets as well as the crucifixion of the Lord.

> *Woe to those who go to great depths to hide their plans from Yahweh,* who *do their work in darkness and think, "Who sees us? Who will know?"* (Isa. 29:15)

> But *whoever hates his brother is in the darkness and walks around in the darkness*; he *does not know where he is going*, because *the darkness has blinded him.* (1 John 2:11)

> For *although they knew God, they neither glorified Him as God nor gave thanks to Him, but their thinking became futile and their foolish hearts were darkened.* (Rom. 1:21)

> So I tell you this, and insist on it in the Lord, that *you must no longer live as the Gentiles do, in the futility of their thinking. They are darkened in their understanding and separated from the life of God because of the ignorance that is in them due to the hardening of their hearts.* (Eph. 4:17-18)

> *Woe to those who call evil good and good evil, who put darkness for light and light for darkness, who put bitter for sweet and sweet for bitter.* (Isa. 5:20)

> This is the verdict: *Light has come into the world, but men loved darkness instead of light because their deeds were evil. Everyone who does evil hates the light, and will not come into the light for fear that his deeds will be exposed.* (John 3:19-20)

> But to the wicked, God says: "What right have you to recite My laws or take My covenant on your lips? *You hate My instruction and cast My words behind you. When you see a thief, you join with him; you throw in your lot with adulterers. You use your mouth for evil and harness your tongue to deceit. You speak continually against your brother and slander your own mother's son.* These things you have done and I kept silent; you thought I was altogether like you. But I will rebuke you and accuse you to your face." (Ps. 50:16-21)

> This is what Sovereign Yahweh, the Holy One of Israel, says: "In

repentance and rest is your salvation, in quietness and trust is your strength, but *you would have none of it.* You said, 'No, we will flee on horses.' Therefore you will flee! You said, 'We will ride off on swift horses.' Therefore your pursuers will be swift! A thousand will flee at the threat of one; at the threat of five you will all flee away, till you are left like a flagstaff on a mountaintop, like a banner on a hill." Yet Yahweh longs to be gracious to you; He rises to show you compassion. For Yahweh is a God of justice. Blessed are all who wait for Him! (Isa. 30:15-18)

To whom can I speak and give warning? Who will listen to me? *Their ears are closed so they cannot hear. The word of Yahweh is offensive to them; they find no pleasure in it.* (Jer. 6:10)

This is what Yahweh says: "Stand at the crossroads and look; ask for the ancient paths, ask where the good way is, and walk in it, and you will find rest for your souls. But you said, '*We will not walk in it.*' I appointed watchmen over you and said, 'Listen to the sound of the trumpet!' But *you said, 'We will not listen.*'" (Jer. 6:16-17)

Then Jesus began to denounce the cities in which most of His miracles had been performed, because they did not repent. "Woe to you, Korazin! Woe to you, Bethsaida! If the miracles that were performed in you had been performed in Tyre and Sidon, they would have repented long ago in sackcloth and ashes. But I tell you, it will be more bearable for Tyre and Sidon on the day of judgment than for you. And you, Capernaum, will you be lifted up to the skies? No, you will go down to the depths. If the miracles that were performed in you had been performed in Sodom, it would have remained to this day. But I tell you that it will be more bearable for Sodom on the day of judgment than for you." (Matt. 11:20-24)

O Yahweh, do not Your eyes look for truth? You struck them, but they felt no pain; You crushed them, but *they refused correction. They made their faces harder than stone and refused to repent.* (Jer. 5:3)

Therefore say to them, "This is the nation that *has not obeyed Yahweh its God or responded to correction.* Truth has perished; it has vanished from their lips." (Jer. 7:28)

"But if you *will not listen to Me* and carry out all these commands, and if you *reject My decrees and abhor My laws and fail to carry out all My commands and so violate My covenant,* . . . I will set My face against you so that you will be defeated by your enemies; those who hate you will rule over you, and you will flee even when no one is pursuing you.

"If after all this you *will not listen to Me,* I will punish you for your sins seven times over. I will break down your stubborn pride and make the sky above you like iron and the ground beneath you like bronze. Your strength will be spent in vain, because your soil will not yield its crops, nor will the trees of the land yield their fruit.

"If you *remain hostile toward Me and refuse to listen to Me,* I will multiply your afflictions seven times over, as your sins deserve. I will send wild animals against you, and they will rob you of your children, destroy your cattle and make you so few in number that your roads will be deserted.

"If in spite of these things *you do not accept My correction but continue to be hostile toward Me*, I Myself will be hostile toward you and will afflict you for your sins seven times over. And I will bring the sword upon you to avenge the breaking of the covenant. When you withdraw into your cities, I will send a plague among you, and you will be given into enemy hands. When I cut off your supply of bread, ten women will be able to bake your bread in one oven, and they will dole out the bread by weight. You will eat, but you will not be satisfied.

"If in spite of this *you still do not listen to Me but continue to be hostile toward Me*, then in My anger I will be hostile toward you, and I Myself will punish you for your sins seven times over. You will eat the flesh of your sons and the flesh of your daughters. I will destroy your high places, cut down your incense altars and pile your dead bodies on the lifeless forms of your idols, and I will abhor you. I will turn your cities into ruins and lay waste your sanctuaries, and I will take no delight in the pleasing aroma of your offerings. I will lay waste the land, so that your enemies who live there will be appalled. I will scatter you among the nations and will draw out My sword and pursue you. Your land will be laid waste, and your cities will lie in ruins. Then the land will enjoy its sabbath years all the time that it lies desolate and you are in the country of your enemies; then the land will rest and enjoy its sabbaths. All the time that it lies desolate, the land will have the rest it did not have during the sabbaths you lived in it." (Lev. 26:14-15, 17-35)

Now Eli, who was very old, heard about everything his sons were doing to all Israel and how they slept with the women who served at the entrance to the Tent of Meeting. So he said to them, "Why do you do such things? I hear from all the people about these wicked deeds of yours. No, my sons; it is not a good report that I hear spreading among Yahweh's people. If a man sins against another man, God may mediate for him; but if a man sins against Yahweh, who will intercede for him?" *His sons, however, did not listen to their father's rebuke*, for it was Yahweh's will to put them to death. (1 Sam. 2:22-25)

. . . *always learning but never able to acknowledge the truth.* Just as Jannes and Jambres opposed Moses, so also these men *oppose the truth*—men of depraved minds, who, as far as the faith is concerned, are rejected. (2 Tim. 3:7-8)

He *who conceals his sins does not prosper*, but whoever confesses and renounces them finds mercy. (Prov. 28:13)

The fear of Yahweh is the beginning of knowledge, *but fools despise wisdom and discipline.* (Prov. 1:7)

If you had responded to My rebuke, I would have poured out My heart to you and made My thoughts known to you. But since *you rejected Me* when I called and *no one gave heed* when I stretched out My hand, since *you ignored all My advice and would not accept My rebuke*, I in turn will laugh at your disaster; I will mock when calamity overtakes you—when calamity overtakes you like a storm, when disaster sweeps over you like a whirlwind, when distress and trouble overwhelm you. (Prov. 1:23-27)

At the end of your life you will groan, when your flesh and body are spent. You will say, "*How I hated discipline! How my heart spurned correction! I would not obey my teachers or listen to my instructors.* I have come to the brink of utter ruin in the midst of the whole assembly." (Prov. 5:11-14)

He who heeds discipline shows the way to life, *but whoever ignores correction leads others astray.* (Prov. 10:17)

A longing fulfilled is sweet to the soul, but *fools detest turning from evil.* (Prov. 13:19)

Whoever loves discipline loves knowledge, but *he who hates correction is stupid.* (Prov. 12:1)

A wise son heeds his father's instruction, but *a mocker does not listen to rebuke.* (Prov. 13:1)

He who scorns instruction will pay for it, but he who respects a command is rewarded. (Prov. 13:13)

He who ignores discipline comes to poverty and shame, but whoever heeds correction is honored. (Prov. 13:18)

A fool spurns his father's discipline, but whoever heeds correction shows prudence. (Prov. 15:5)

Stern discipline awaits him who leaves the path; *he who hates correction will die.* (Prov. 15:10)

A mocker resents correction; he will not consult the wise. (Prov. 15:12)

He who ignores discipline despises himself, but whoever heeds correction gains understanding. (Prov. 15:32)

Stop listening to instruction, my son, and you will stray from the words of knowledge. (Prov. 19:27)

See Acts 6:8–8:1 about Stephen's works and words. At the close of his message in Acts 7, he said:

"You stiff-necked people, with uncircumcised hearts and ears! You are just like your fathers: *You always resist the Holy Spirit!* Was there ever a prophet your fathers did not persecute? They even killed those who predicted the coming of the Righteous One. And now you have betrayed and murdered Him—you who have received the law that was put into effect through angels but have not obeyed it."

When they heard this, they were furious and gnashed their teeth at him. But Stephen, full of the Holy Spirit, looked up to heaven and saw the glory of God, and Jesus standing at the right hand of God. "Look," he said, "I see heaven open and the Son of Man standing at the right hand of God."

At this they covered their ears and, yelling at the top of their voices, they all rushed at him, dragged him out of the city and began to stone him. Meanwhile, the witnesses laid their clothes at the feet of a young man named Saul.

While they were stoning him, Stephen prayed, "Lord Jesus, receive my spirit." Then he fell on his knees and cried out, "Lord, do not hold this sin against them." When he had said this, he fell asleep.

And Saul was there, giving approval to his death. (Acts 7:51–8:1)

C. ACTIVE OBEDIENCE/DISOBEDIENCE

1. Active Obedience

Honor, with all its transparency and willingness to walk in the light of truth, comes first. Then honesty preserves a child's unbroken relationship not only with his parents but also with God's people and with God Himself. It further lays the indispensable groundwork for submission—to walk in the light means to come into submission to the guidance of God's Spirit. This brings us to our current element of Christian character: submission entails *active*, as opposed to passive, obedience. The child's obedience to his parents testifies to the legitimacy of the authority of his parents and is the surest evidence of the honor a child holds for them. Thus it is a virtue expressly commanded in the New Testament text:

> Children, *obey* your parents in everything, for this pleases the Lord. (Col. 3:20)

> Children, *obey* your parents in the Lord, for this is right. (Eph. 6:1)

> For you were once darkness, but now you are light in the Lord. Live as children of light (for the fruit of the light consists in all goodness, righteousness and truth) and *find out what pleases* the Lord. (Eph. 5:8-10)

What pleases the Lord is *active* obedience to parents, a full *participation* in the word they speak to the child and the duties they assign him or her. The New Testament Greek word translated as "active" is *energes*, from which we get our English word *energy*. It expresses activity that is "energetic," "active, effective, productive, powerful." It is a characteristic of the very "Word of God" that is "living and active" (*energes*) or "powerful" (Heb. 4:12). Paul writes to Philemon of his desire that Philemon's "sharing of his faith" may become "effective" (*energes*). This, then, should characterize the nature of obedience. This active attitude and action is what "pleases the Lord." In this sense, Scripture tells us to "find out what pleases the Lord": we should find it out so we can please Him by *doing* His will, His good, perfect and *pleasing* will (Rom. 12:1-3). Any participation demands the active exertion of our energy, an effort that calls into play every aspect of our being. This is our "reasonable form of service" (Rom. 12:1), and nothing less will reveal God's will. This is the only sacrifice that pleases Him, the *obedience* that comes through faith (Rom. 1:5; Phil. 2:17; Heb. 11:4).

Reverence without obedience is mockery. Of the two, better that the child fail in the former. At least commitment to obedience holds out the hope of shaping character, while reverence without obedience corrodes character in the acid of hypocrisy.

> "What do you think? There was a man who had two sons. He went to the first and said, 'Son, go and work today in the vineyard.'
> "'I will not,' he answered, but later he changed his mind and went.
> "Then the father went to the other son and said the same thing. He answered, 'I will, sir,' but he did not go."
> "Which of the two did what his father wanted?"
> "The first," they answered.
> Jesus said to them, "I tell you the truth, the tax collectors and the prostitutes are entering the kingdom of God ahead of you." (Matt. 21:28-31)

In the absence of obedience, reverence also becomes a self-righteous and self-serving formality used to cultivate only our own image in the eyes of others. Obedience is the content of the form that makes honor real and stands as the surest test of the dutiful child. So proper is obedience to childhood that Peter uses the combination of obedience and children as an example for all believers:

> As *obedient children*, do not conform to the evil desires you had when you lived in ignorance. (1 Pet. 1:14)

So obedience is what saves us from "evil desires." Christ set our highest example in this: "He was subject to His parents" (Luke 2:51).

Whatever lawful commandments parents give their children, the children must to their uttermost readily obey. Children should respond immediately to their parents' call:

> *And he ran to Eli and said, "Here I am; you called me."*
> But Eli said, "I did not call; go back and lie down." So he went and lay down.
> Again Yahweh called, "Samuel!" And Samuel got up and went to Eli and said, "Here I am; you called me."
> "My son," Eli said, "I did not call; go back and lie down."
> Now Samuel did not yet know Yahweh: The Word of Yahweh had not yet been revealed to him.
> Yahweh called Samuel a third time, and Samuel got up and went up to Eli and said, "Here I am; you called me."
> Then Eli realized that Yahweh was calling the boy. So Eli told Samuel, "Go and lie down, and if He calls you, say, 'Speak, Yahweh, for Your servant is listening.'" So Samuel went and lay down in his place. (1 Sam. 3:5-9)

(Though Eli was not Samuel's natural father, he did raise Samuel in the Lord and served as a covering to him.)

> So he [David's father, Jesse] *sent and had him brought in*. He was ruddy, with a fine appearance and handsome features.

Then Yahweh said, "Rise and anoint him; he is the one." (1 Sam. 16:12)

Then *Jacob summoned his sons* and said, "Assemble yourselves that I may tell you what shall befall you in the days to come.

"Gather together and hear, O sons of Jacob; and listen to Israel your father." (Gen. 49:1-2, NASV)

The child must always willingly go when *sent* at his parents' word:

Then *Isaac sent Jacob* on his way, and he went to Paddan Aram, to Laban son of Bethuel the Aramean, the brother of Rebekah, who was the mother of Jacob and Esau. (Gen. 28:5)

Now his brothers had gone to graze their father's flocks near Shechem, and Israel said to Joseph, "As you know, your brothers are grazing the flocks near Shechem. Come, *I am going to send you* to them."

"*Very well*," *he replied.*

So he said to him, "Go and see if all is well with your brothers and with the flocks, and bring word back to me." So *he sent him off* from the Valley of Hebron. (Gen. 37:12-14)

When Jacob learned that there was grain in Egypt, he said to his sons, "Why do you just keep looking at each other?" He continued, "I have heard that there is grain in Egypt. *Go down there* and buy some for us, so that we may live and not die."

Then ten of *Joseph's brothers went down* to buy grain from Egypt. (Gen. 42:1-3)

Now *Jesse said to his son David*, "Take this ephah of roasted grain and these ten loaves of bread for your brothers and *hurry to their camp*." . . .

Early in the morning *David left* the flock with a shepherd, loaded up and set out, *as Jesse had directed.* He reached the camp as the army was going out to its battle positions, shouting the war cry. (1 Sam. 17:17, 20)

Children are required to *attend to and serve their parents*:

Abraham took the wood for the burnt offering and placed it on his son Isaac, and he himself carried the fire and the knife. As the two of them went on together . . . . (Gen. 22:6)

Children should *cheerfully and faithfully perform* any *task or business* their parents request of them. The Greek New Testament word *hilaros*, which is translated "cheerful," also means "prompt or willing." The Hebrew *nadab*, translated as "willingly," literally means "to present spontaneously—offer freely, [to] offer self willingly," and this "has the flavor of an uncompelled, free movement of the will for divine service or sacrifice."

Each man should give what he has decided in his heart to give, not reluctantly or under compulsion, for *God loves a cheerful giver.* (2 Cor. 9:7)

Serve Yahweh with gladness; come before His presence with singing. (Ps. 100:2)

The people rejoiced at the willing response of their leaders, *for they had given freely and wholeheartedly to the Lord.* David the king also rejoiced greatly. (1 Chron. 29:9)

And here is my advice about what is best for you in this matter: Last year you were the first not only to give but also to have the desire to do so. *Now finish the work, so that your eager willingness to do it may be matched by your completion of it,* according to your means. (2 Cor. 8:10-11)

When the princes in Israel take the lead, when the people *willingly offer themselves*—praise the Lord! (Judg. 5:2)

When the days of mourning had passed, Joseph said to Pharaoh's court, "If I have found favor in your eyes, speak to Pharaoh for me. Tell him, 'My father made me swear an oath and said, "I am about to die; bury me in the tomb I dug for myself in the land of Canaan." Now let me go up and bury my father; then I will return.'" (Gen. 50:4-5)

This is the word that came to Jeremiah from Yahweh during the reign of Jehoiakim son of Josiah king of Judah: "Go to the Recabite family and invite them to come to one of the side rooms of the house of Yahweh and give them wine to drink."

So I went to get Jaazaniah son of Jeremiah, the son of Habazziniah, and his brothers and all his sons—the whole family of the Recabites. I brought them into the house of Yahweh, into the room of the sons of Hanan son of Igdaliah the man of God. It was next to the room of the officials, which was over that of Maaseiah son of Shallum the doorkeeper. Then I set bowls full of wine and some cups before the men of the Recabite family and said to them, "Drink some wine."

But they replied, "We do not drink wine, *because our forefather Jonadab son of Recab gave us this command:* 'Neither you nor your descendants must ever drink wine. Also you must never build houses, sow seed or plant vineyards; you must never have any of these things, but must always live in tents. Then you will live a long time in the land where you are nomads.' We have obeyed everything our forefather Jonadab son of Recab commanded us. Neither we nor our wives nor our sons and daughters have ever drunk wine or built houses to live in or had vineyards, fields or crops. We have lived in tents and have fully obeyed everything our forefather Jonadab commanded us. But when Nebuchadnezzar king of Babylon invaded this land, we said, 'Come, we must go to Jerusalem to escape the Babylonian and Aramean armies.' So we have remained in Jerusalem."

Then the word of Yahweh came to Jeremiah, saying; "This is what Yahweh Almighty, the God of Israel, says: Go and tell the men of Judah and the people of Jerusalem, 'Will you not learn a lesson and obey My words?' declares Yahweh. 'Jonadab son of Recab ordered his sons not to drink wine and this command has been kept. To this day they do not drink wine, *because they obey their forefather's command.* But I have spoken to you again and again, yet you have not obeyed Me. Again and again I sent all My servants the prophets to you. They said, "Each of you must turn from your wicked ways and reform your actions; do not follow other gods to serve them. Then you will live in the land I have given to you and your fathers." But you have not paid attention or listened to Me. The descendants of Jonadab son of Recab have carried out the command their forefather gave them, but these people have not obeyed Me.'

"Therefore, this is what Yahweh God Almighty, the God of Israel, says: 'Listen! I am going to bring on Judah and on everyone living in Jerusalem every disaster I pronounced against them. I spoke to them, but they did not listen; I called to them, but they did not answer.'"

Then Jeremiah said to the family of the Recabites, "This is what Yahweh Almighty, the God of Israel, says: *'You have obeyed the command of your forefather Jonadab and have followed all his instructions and have done everything he ordered.'* Therefore, this is what Yahweh Almighty, the God of Israel, says: 'Jonadab son of Recab will never fail to have a man to serve Me.'" (Jer. 35:1-19)

Then David gave his son Solomon the plans for the portico of the temple, its buildings, its storerooms, its upper parts, its inner rooms and the place of atonement. He gave him the plans of all that the Spirit had put in his mind for the courts of the temple of Yahweh and all the surrounding rooms, for the treasuries of the temple of God and for the treasuries for the dedicated things. He gave him instructions for the divisions of the priests and Levites, and for all the work of serving in the Temple of Yahweh, as well as for all the articles to be used in its service . . . .

David also said to Solomon his son, "Be strong and courageous, and do the work. Do not be afraid or discouraged, for Yahweh, my God, is with you. He will not fail you or forsake you until all the work for the service of the temple of Yahweh is finished." (1 Chron. 28:11-13, 20)

Yahweh has kept the promise He made. I have succeeded David my father and now I sit on the throne of Israel, just as Yahweh promised, and I have built the temple for the Name of Yahweh, the God of Israel. (2 Chron. 6:10)

So, too, David took care to leave his father's sheep with keepers (1 Sam. 17:20), and 1 Samuel 17:34 tells of how David risked his very life to perform his father's business:

Saul replied, "You are not able to go out against this Philistine and fight him; you are only a boy, and he has been a fighting man from his youth."

But David said to Saul, "Your servant has been keeping his father's sheep. When a lion or a bear came and carried off a sheep from the flock, I went after it, struck it and rescued the sheep from its mouth. When it turned on me, I seized it by its hair, struck it and killed it." (1 Sam. 17:33-35)

a. Submissiveness

Active obedience, then, means to submit with all our hearts to God and those He places over us (Heb. 13:17). To truly submit requires our active placing of ourselves under God's authority. The Greek word *hupeiko*, translated "submit," literally means "to yield under" authority. Another word translated "submit," *hupotasso*, also carries the definite sense of voluntarily ranking oneself under a hierarchical authority, as in a military organization. Rienecker says, "The word has primarily the idea of giving up one's own right or will, i.e., 'to subordinate one's self.'" Submission is something the child must actively do, placing himself *under* (sub-) the common *mission* that binds him together with his parents and to all others in God's kingdom. (He can only place himself under the common mission, be truly submitted, if his parents impart to him the vision of that mission.)

> *Obey your leaders and submit to their authority.* They keep watch over you as men who must give an account. Obey them so that their work will be a joy, not a burden, for that would be of no advantage to you. (Heb. 13:17)

> Then He went down to Nazareth with them and *was obedient to them.* But his mother treasured all these things in her heart. And Jesus grew in wisdom and stature, and in favor with God and men. (Luke 2:51-52)

> You know that the household of Stephanas were the first converts in Achaia, and they have devoted themselves to the service of the saints. *I urge you, brothers, to submit to such as these and to everyone who joins in the work, and labors at it.* (1 Cor. 16:15-16)

> Moreover, we have all had human fathers who disciplined us and we respected them for it. *How much more should we submit to the Father of our spirits and live!* (Heb. 12:9)

True submission comes only by submitting with all our hearts.

> Then they answered Joshua, "Whatever you have commanded us we will do, and wherever you send us we will go. Just as *we fully obeyed Moses, so we will obey you.* Only may Yahweh your God be with you as He was with Moses." (Josh. 1:16-17)

> All these were fighting men who volunteered to serve in the ranks. They came to Hebron *fully determined* to make David king over all Israel. All the rest of the Israelites were also *of one mind* to make David king. (1 Chron. 12:38)

> Jonathan said to his young armor-bearer, "Come, let's go over to the outpost of those uncircumcised fellows. Perhaps Yahweh will act in our behalf. Nothing can hinder Yahweh from saving, whether by many or by few."
> "Do all that you have in mind," his armor-bearer said. "Go ahead; *I am with you heart and soul.*" (1 Sam. 14:6-7)

b. Attentiveness

The active effort to submit entails another virtue on the part of children. We've earlier encountered the Greek word *hupakoe*. Another lexicon translates this form of the word *obedience* as literally "attentive hearkening."* Submissive children will *attend expectantly to the words and needs* of their parents or others in authority. So consent to such authority comes not passively but actively through energy and effort. They won't merely acquiesce to serving God, His people and His purpose but actively seek opportunities to do so. They listen carefully, paying diligent attention to what parents say and do. Only in this way can they fulfill their duty to God and parents.

> Blessed is the man who listens to me, watching daily at my doors, waiting at my doorway. (Prov. 8:34)

> There Yahweh made a decree and a law for them, and there He tested them. He said, "If *you listen carefully* to the voice of Yahweh your God and do what is right in His eyes, if you *pay attention* to His commands and keep all His decrees, I will not bring on you any of the diseases I brought on the Egyptians, for I am Yahweh, who heals you." (Exod. 15:25-26)

To "listen carefully" to God's voice is to "listen carefully" to the voice of those over us: children with parents (Eph. 6:1-3), wives with husbands (Eph. 5:22), disciples with elders (1 Thess. 2:13; Rom. 10:8, 14-17). It is to "watch daily at that authority's doors," "to pay attention" to all his words.

> *Pay attention to him* and *listen to what he says. Do not rebel* against him; he will not forgive your rebellion, since My Name is in him. If you *listen carefully* to what he says and do all that I say, I will be an enemy to your enemies and will oppose those who oppose you. (Exod. 23:21-22)

To fail to "pay attention" and "listen carefully" is to "rebel."

> We must *pay more careful attention*, therefore, to what we have heard, *so that we do not drift away*. For if the message spoken by angels was binding, and every violation and disobedience received its just punishment, how shall we escape *if we ignore* such a great salvation? This salvation, which was first announced by the Lord, was confirmed to us by those who heard Him. (Heb. 2:1-3)

To be ignorant of—that is, to ignore—God's Word when He speaks condemns us to "drift away" and unravels our relationship with God and those who cover us in Him.

> *Listen*, my sons, to a father's instruction; *pay attention* and gain understanding. (Prov. 4:1)

---

* See the section "Hearing Ear" under "Honor" on p. 42.

Pay attention and *listen* to the sayings of the wise; apply your heart to what I teach. (Prov. 22:17)

If only you had paid attention to My commands, your peace would have been like a river, your righteousness like the waves of the sea. (Isa. 48:18)

Let the wise *listen* and add to their learning, and let the discerning get guidance. (Prov. 1:5)

Listen, my son, to your father's instruction and do not forsake your mother's teaching. (Prov. 1:8)

Listen, my son, accept what I say, and the years of your life will be many. (Prov. 4:10)

My son, *pay attention* to what I say; *listen closely* to my words. *Do not let them out of your sight, keep them within your heart*; for they are life to those who find them and health to a man's whole body. (Prov. 4:20-22)

My son, *pay attention* to my wisdom, *listen well to my words* of insight, that you may maintain discretion and your lips may preserve knowledge. (Prov. 5:1-2)

Now then, my sons, *listen* to me; do not turn aside from what I say. (Prov. 5:7)

Listen to my instruction and be wise; *do not ignore it*. Blessed is the man who *listens to me, watching daily* at my doors, *waiting at* my doorway. For whoever finds me finds life and receives favor from Yahweh. (Prov. 8:33-35)

And we also thank God continually because, when you received the word of God, which you heard from us, you accepted it not as the word of men, but as it actually is, the word of God, which is at work in you who believe. (1 Thess. 2:13)

c. Complete, Consistent and Timely Obedience

Attentiveness makes us responsible, that is, responsive, able to respond consistently to God's authority in our lives. Our hearts can then become fully committed to active obedience. The submitted child who attends to his parents will seek to diligently, quietly and completely fulfill the entire counsel of God at all times and on all occasions. This is not to say he actually *will* do so or should be censured if he doesn't. It only says his *will* and *attitude* are perfect toward God.

The Israelites had done all the work just as Yahweh had commanded Moses. *Moses inspected the work and saw that they had done it just as Yahweh had commanded*. So Moses blessed them. (Exod. 39:42-43)

As Yahweh commanded His servant Moses, so Moses commanded Joshua, and Joshua did it; *he left nothing undone* of all that Yahweh commanded Moses.

So Joshua took this entire land: the hill country, all the Negev, the whole region of Goshen, the western foothills, the Arabah and the mountains of Israel with their foothills, from Mount Halak, which rises toward Seir, to Baal Gad in the Valley of Lebanon below Mount Hermon. He captured all their kings and struck them down, putting them to death. (Josh. 11:15-17)

Yahweh said to Moses and Aaron, "These are the regulations for the Passover:

"No foreigner is to eat of it. Any slave you have bought may eat of it after you have circumcised him, but a temporary resident and a hired worker may not eat of it.

"It must be eaten inside one house; take none of the meat outside the house. Do not break any of the bones. The whole community of Israel must celebrate it.

"An alien living among you who wants to celebrate Yahweh's Passover must have all the males in his household circumcised; then he may take part like one born in the land. No uncircumcised male may eat of it. The same law applies to the native-born and to the alien living among you."

All the Israelites did just what Yahweh had commanded Moses and Aaron. And on that very day Yahweh brought the Israelites out of Egypt by their divisions. (Exod. 12:43-51)

When Moses went and told the people all Yahweh's words and laws, they responded with one voice, *"Everything Yahweh has said we will do." Moses then wrote down everything Yahweh had said.* (Exod. 24:3-4)

Then he took the Book of the Covenant and read it to the people. They responded, *"We will do everything Yahweh has said; we will obey."* (Exod. 24:7)

So Aaron and his sons *did everything Yahweh commanded through Moses.* (Lev. 8:36)

Whenever the tabernacle is to move, the Levites are to take it down, and whenever the tabernacle is to be set up, the Levites shall do it. Anyone else who goes near it shall be put to death. The Israelites are to set up their tents by divisions, each man in his own camp under his own standard. The Levites, however, are to set up their tents around the tabernacle of the Testimony so that wrath will not fall on the Israelite community. The Levites are to be responsible for the care of the tabernacle of the Testimony.

The Israelites did all this just as Yahweh commanded Moses. (Num. 1:51-54)

On the day the tabernacle, the Tent of the Testimony, was set up, the cloud covered it. From evening till morning the cloud above the tabernacle looked like fire. That is how it continued to be; the cloud covered it, and at night it looked like fire. Whenever the cloud lifted from above the Tent, the Israelites set out; wherever the cloud settled, the Israelites encamped. At Yahweh's command the Israelites set out, and at his command they encamped. As long as the cloud stayed over the tabernacle, they remained in camp.

When the cloud remained over the tabernacle a long time, the Israelites obeyed Yahweh's order and did not set out. Sometimes the cloud was over the tabernacle only a few days; *at Yahweh's command* they would encamp, and then *at his command* they would set out. Sometimes the cloud stayed only from evening till morning, and when it lifted in the morning, they set out. Whether by day or by night, whenever the cloud lifted, they set out. Whether the cloud stayed over the tabernacle for two days or a month or a year, the Israelites would remain in camp and not set out; but when it lifted, they would set out. At *Yahweh's command* they encamped, and at *Yahweh's command* they set out. They *obeyed Yahweh's order,* in accordance with *His command through Moses.* (Num. 9:15-23)

Yahweh then said to Noah, "Go into the ark, you and your whole family, because I have found you righteous in this generation. Take with you seven of every kind of clean animal, a male and its mate, and two of every kind of unclean animal, a male and its mate, and also seven of every kind of bird, male and female, to keep their various kinds alive throughout the earth. Seven days from now I will send rain on the earth for forty days and forty nights, and I will wipe from the face of the earth every living creature I have made."
And Noah *did all that Yahweh commanded him.* (Gen. 7:1-5)

For the generations to come every male among you who is eight days old must be circumcised, including those born in your household or bought with money from a foreigner—those who are not your offspring . . . . *On that very day Abraham took his son Ishmael and all those born in his household* or bought with his money, every male in his household, *and circumcised them, as God told him.* (Gen. 17:12, 23)

Yahweh had said to Abram, "Leave your country, your people and your father's household and go to the land I will show you.
 "I will make you into a great nation and I will bless you; I will make your name great, and you will be a blessing. I will bless those who bless you, and whoever curses you I will curse; and all peoples on earth will be blessed through you."
 So Abram left, as Yahweh had told him; and Lot went with him. Abram was seventy-five years old when he set out from Haran. (Gen. 12:1-4)

The king of Egypt said to the Hebrew midwives, whose names were Shiphrah and Puah, "When you help the Hebrew women in childbirth and observe them on the delivery stool, if it is a boy, kill him; but if it is a girl, let her live." *The midwives, however, feared God and did not do what the king of Egypt had told them to do;* they let the boys live. Then the king of Egypt summoned the midwives and asked them, "Why have you done this? Why have you let the boys live?"
 The midwives answered Pharaoh, "Hebrew women are not like Egyptian women; they are vigorous and give birth before the midwives arrive."

So God was kind to the midwives and the people increased and became even more numerous. (Exod. 1:15-20)

So Bezalel, Oholiab and every skilled person to whom Yahweh has given skill and ability to know how to carry out all the work of constructing the sanctuary are to do the work *just as Yahweh has commanded*. (Exod. 36:1)

He held fast to Yahweh and *did not cease to follow Him*; he kept the commands Yahweh had given Moses. (2 Kings 18:6)

When Joseph and Mary had *done everything required by the Law of the Lord*, they returned to Galilee to their own town of Nazareth. (Luke 2:39)

Now if you *obey Me fully* and keep My covenant, then out of all nations you will be My treasured possession. Although the whole earth is Mine . . . . (Exod. 19:5)

Oh, that their hearts would be inclined to fear Me *and keep all My commands always*, so that it might go well with them and their children forever! (Deut. 5:29)

So *be careful to do what Yahweh your God has commanded you*; do not turn aside to the right or to the left. (Deut. 5:32)

And if you *walk in My ways and obey My statutes and commands* as David your father did, I will give you a long life. (1 Kings 3:14)

But the man who looks intently into the perfect law that gives freedom, and continues to do this, not forgetting what he has heard, *but doing it*—he will be blessed in what he does. (James 1:25)

Therefore everyone who hears these words of Mine *and puts them into practice* is like a wise man who built his house on the rock. (Matt. 7:24)

As Jesus was walking beside the Sea of Galilee, He saw two brothers, Simon called Peter and his brother Andrew. They were casting a net into the lake, for they were fishermen. "Come, follow Me," Jesus said, "and I will make you fishers of men." *At once they left their nets and followed Him.*

Going on from there, He saw two other brothers, James son of Zebedee and his brother John. They were in a boat with their father Zebedee, preparing their nets. Jesus called them, *and immediately they left the boat and their father and followed Him.* (Matt. 4:18-22)

As Jesus went on from there, He saw a man named Matthew sitting at the tax collector's booth. "Follow Me," He told him, and Matthew *got up and followed Him*. (Matt. 9:9)

Simon answered, "Master, we've worked hard all night and haven't caught anything. *But because You say so, I will let down the nets.*" (Luke 5:5)

And after she had said this, she went back and called her sister Mary aside. "The Teacher is here," she said, "and is asking for you." When Mary heard this, *she got up quickly and went to Him.* (John 11:28-29)

"Whoever *has My commands and obeys them, he is the one who loves Me.* He who loves Me will be loved by My Father, and I too will love him and show Myself to him." (John 14:21)

So then, King Agrippa, *I was not disobedient to the vision from heaven.* (Acts 26:19)

He who obeys instructions guards his life, but he who is contemptuous of his ways will die. (Prov. 19:16)

To *do what is right and just* is more acceptable to Yahweh than sacrifice. (Prov. 21:3)

If you follow My decrees and are careful to obey My commands, I will send you rain in its season, and the ground will yield its crops and the trees of the field their fruit. Your threshing will continue until grape harvest and the grape harvest will continue until planting, and you will eat all the food you want and live in safety in your land. (Lev. 26:3-5)

This consistent, obedient response to authority marks the faithful. A faithful child respects, attends, submits and responds habitually.

2. Disobedience

So active obedience—the willingness and desire to do what God commands—shows the reality of a child's honor for his parents and for God. Active obedience only comes from a love of the truth, a walk in the light. The place of transparency is the only entryway to a communion with God that allows Him to will and do His deeds through us (Phil. 2:13). Disobedience derives from dishonor like hail does from water: a child's mind and attitude become a cold cloud of dishonor that comes before the hailstones of open disobediences begin to fall. So disobedience usually also accompanies dishonesty and refusal to walk in the light of truth. These both sever godly relationship in the child's life. No channels then lie open through which God's grace can flow to the child. Instead, the child lives in a dark cave of self-will, and the bones and carnage in that cave bring reproach to the way of truth.

One lexicon describes *apeitheia* (disobedience) as literally "the condition of being unpersuadable," being the opposite of "*peitho,* to persuade." The root of disobedience lies in a person's unwillingness to surrender his own will to God's, a refusal to be fully persuaded of the truth or necessity of God's Word. The Greek word further denotes an "obstinate rejection of the will of God; hence, 'disobedience.'" The Old Testament word for "disobedience," *maal,* describes one who "is deliberately defecting from the faith." It is therefore said that "our expression 'break faith' captures the essence of this word."

Disobedience, then, arises from a condition of the heart that moves through various levels and forms before it expresses itself in open rebellion. Someone may in his external actions seem obedient, while the sin of disobedience increasingly festers within his deep-seated feelings of dishonor toward truth or its messengers. Such people may even seem to at first act in conformity to what they are told, but they refuse to become fully persuaded of the truth and necessity of it. They don't believe God has spoken to them, but through their actions they pretend that they do. Because they refuse to be fully persuaded, they become sullen, brooding or even resentful as they only grudgingly and half-heartedly do what they're told. Next they begin to bristle at the authority of God. Resentment grows. Finally, unless they repent of all this and seek to be fully persuaded of the necessity of His truth and authority, they will reject God's Word and embrace open rebellion. If the downward slide does not stop, they'll finally completely reject God.

So disobedience takes many forms, of which open rebellion is perhaps the least common in the Christian home. Much more common is the attempt to hide disobedience under a facade of obedience. But because the child's heart doesn't truly honor his parents and his God, because he doesn't truly walk in honesty, light and truth, his surface obedience becomes merely the most insidious form of disobedience. We'll now describe and explain these hidden forms of disobedience.

a. Passive Obedience

Passive obedience is a form of disobedience, possibly the worst of all because it stems from an unwillingness to come into the light of truth. It refuses any transformation of heart or mind or attitude that would seek and then be consumed with God's purpose and love. It is so much worse in some cases than open disobedience because it is disobedience compounded by a lie. It can therefore only further disdain and profane relationship and love. At most, passive obedience only superficially obeys, masking its spiritually dead soul with a dishonest and counterfeit obedience. It is, in other words, the obedience of the hypocrite, a mask of obedience that hides a careless, resentful, rebellious and nonparticipating heart. Not simply the gesture but the attitude of anyone who does anything, as well as the purpose for which he does it, makes every deed, including every act of obedience, either worthy or unworthy. So Scripture condemns those who "draw near with their mouth" but remain far away in their "hearts" (Isa. 29:13; Matt. 15:7-9). Behind every word and deed lies intention, and this is what God looks at (Heb. 4:12-13). So God does not merely look to see whether we do an act that He told us to; He looks to see whether we "obey from the heart" (1 Sam. 16:7; Rom. 6:17). So parents must pray for genuine insight into even a seemingly obedient child's attitude.

In true, active obedience, the child yields not merely in his body but in his heart, becoming emotionally *pliable* to the parents' will. Passive obedience may arise from mere sullenness and an outward affectation of bending to what this child may mistakenly view as sheer force. Or perhaps a child might forbear doing something without the consent of his parents simply because he hates to even ask his parents: he would rather deny his own desires than to openly humble and subject himself to his parents' will. This only reveals a disdainful and rebellious heart. To forbear from doing an unlawful thing is but to abstain from evil. It is therefore only at best the righteousness of the law. But to *do* what is good, as well as to abstain from evil, distinguishes the New Testament righteousness that comes from the power of God to those in union with Christ.

> For I know that in me (that is, in my flesh) nothing good dwells; for to will is present with me, but how to perform what is good I do not find. (Rom. 7:18)

> There is therefore now no condemnation to those who are in Christ Jesus, who *do not walk according to the flesh, but according to the Spirit.* For the law of the Spirit of life in Christ Jesus has made me free from the law of sin and death. For what *the law could not do* in that *it was weak through the flesh,* God did by sending His own Son in the likeness of sinful flesh, on account of sin: He condemned sin in the flesh, *that the righteous requirement of the law might be fulfilled in us who do not walk according to the flesh but according to the Spirit.* (Rom. 8:1-4)

> *Turn from evil and do good;* seek peace and *pursue* it. (Ps. 34:14)

> Do you not know that to whom you present yourselves slaves to obey, you are that one's slaves whom you obey, whether of sin leading to death, or of *obedience leading to righteousness?* But God be thanked that though you were slaves of sin, yet you obeyed from the heart that form of doctrine to which you were delivered. And having been set free from sin, you became slaves of righteousness. (Rom. 6:16-18)

> Or do you despise the riches of His goodness, forbearance, and longsuffering, not knowing that *the goodness of God leads you to repentance?* But in accordance with your hardness and your impenitent heart you are treasuring up for yourself wrath in the day of wrath and revelation of the righteous judgment of *God,* who *"will render to each one according to his deeds": eternal life to those who* by patient continuance *in doing good* seek for glory, honor, and immortality; but to those who are self-seeking and do not obey the truth, but *obey unrighteousness*—indignation and wrath, tribulation and anguish, on every soul of man who does evil, of the Jew first and also of the Greek; but *glory, honor, and peace to everyone who works what is good,* to the Jew first and also to the Greek. (Rom. 2:4-10)

So we are commanded to *seek* after God and His kingdom.

> Again, the kingdom of heaven is like a merchant looking for fine pearls. When he found one of great value, he went away and *sold everything he had and bought it.* (Matt. 13:45-46)

> There is nothing concealed that will not be disclosed, or hidden that will not be made known. (Luke 12:2) [The Spirit reveals to us the things that pertain to the kingdom.]

> And you, my son Solomon, acknowledge the God of your father, and *serve Him with wholehearted devotion and with a willing mind,* for Yahweh searches every heart and understands every motive behind the thoughts. If *you seek Him, He will be found by you;* but if you forsake Him, He will reject you forever. (1 Chron. 28:9)

> I have not spoken in secret, from somewhere in a land of darkness; I have not said to Jacob's descendants, "*Seek Me* in vain." I, Yahweh, speak the truth; I declare what is right. (Isa. 45:19)

> *Seek Yahweh while He may be found; call on Him while He is near.* (Isa. 55:6)

> God did this so that men would *seek Him and perhaps reach out for Him and find Him, though He is not far from each one of us.* "For in Him we live and move and have our being." As some of your own poets have said, "We are His offspring." (Acts 17:27-28)

> Sow for yourselves righteousness, reap the fruit of unfailing love, and break up your unplowed ground; for *it is time to seek Yahweh, until He comes* and showers righteousness on you. (Hos. 10:12)

> I love those who love Me, and *those who seek Me find Me.* (Prov. 8:17)

> Do you not know that in a race all the runners run, but only one gets the prize? *Run in such a way as to get the prize.* Everyone who competes in the games goes into strict training. They do it to get a crown that will not last; but we do it to get a crown that will last forever. (1 Cor. 9:24-25)

> Although most of the many people who came from Ephraim, Manasseh, Issachar and Zebulun had not purified themselves, yet they ate the Passover, contrary to what was written. But Hezekiah prayed for them, saying, "May Yahweh, who is good, *pardon everyone who sets his heart on seeking God*—Yahweh, the God of his fathers—even if he is not clean according to the rules of the sanctuary." (2 Chron. 30:18-19)

> The Spirit of God came upon Azariah son of Oded. He went out to meet Asa and said to him, "Listen to me, Asa and all Judah and Benjamin. Yahweh is with you when you are with Him. *If you seek Him, He will be found by you, but if you forsake Him, He will forsake you.*" (2 Chron. 15:1-2)

> *They entered into a covenant to seek Yahweh,* the God of their fathers, *with all their heart and soul. All who would not seek Yahweh, the God of Israel, were to be put to death, whether small or great, man or woman.* They took an oath to Yahweh with loud acclamation, with

shouting and with trumpets and horns. All Judah rejoiced about the oath because they had sworn it *wholeheartedly.* They *sought God eagerly, and He was found by them. So Yahweh gave them rest on every side.* (2 Chron. 15:12-15)

Therefore let everyone who is godly pray to You while You may be found; surely when the mighty waters rise, they will not reach him. (Ps. 32:6)

By faith Abraham, when called to go to a place he would later receive as his inheritance, *obeyed and went,* even though he did not know where he was going. By faith he made his home in the promised land like a stranger in a foreign country; he lived in tents, as did Isaac and Jacob, who were heirs with him of the same promise. *For he was looking forward to the city with foundations, whose architect and builder is God.* (Heb. 11:8-10)

All these people were still living by faith when they died. They did not receive the things promised; they only saw them and welcomed them from a distance. And they admitted that they were aliens and strangers on earth. People who say such things show that *they are looking for a country of their own.* If they had been thinking of the country they had left, they would have had opportunity to return. *Instead, they were longing for a better country—a heavenly one. Therefore God is not ashamed to be called their God, for He has prepared a city for them.* (Heb. 11:13-16)

Those who passively obey will never effectively seek after God, and so they will never find Him. We can only find Him if we seek Him with all our hearts (Jer. 29:13), but those who obey passively refuse to do this very thing.

King Rehoboam established himself firmly in Jerusalem and continued as king. He was forty-one years old when he became king, and he reigned seventeen years in Jerusalem, the city Yahweh had chosen out of all the tribes of Israel in which to put His Name. His mother's name was Naamah; she was an Ammonite. He did evil because *he had not set his heart on seeking Yahweh.* (2 Chron. 12:13-14)

In his pride the wicked does not seek Him; in *all his thoughts there is no room for God.* (Ps. 10:4)

You want something but don't get it. You kill and covet, but you cannot have what you want. You quarrel and fight. You do not have, because *you do not ask God. When you ask,* you do not receive, because *you ask with wrong motives,* that you may spend what you get on your pleasures. (James 4:2-3)

And without faith it is impossible to please God, because anyone who comes to Him must believe that He exists and that He rewards those who *earnestly seek Him.* (Heb. 11:6)

But because of your stubbornness and your unrepentant heart, you are storing up wrath against yourself for the day of God's wrath, when His righteous judgment will be revealed. God "will give to each person according to what he has done." To those who by *persistence in doing good seek glory, honor and immortality*, He will give eternal life. But for those who are *self-seeking* and who reject the truth and follow evil, there will be wrath and anger. There will be trouble and distress for every human being who does evil: first for the Jew, then for the Gentile. (Rom. 2:5-9)

Then I will go back to My place until they admit their guilt. And *they will seek My face; in their misery they will earnestly seek Me.* (Hos. 5:15)

Surely the arm of Yahweh is not too short to save, nor His ear too dull to hear. But your iniquities have separated you from your God; your sins have hidden His face from you, so that He will not hear. (Isa. 59:1-2)

Submit yourselves, then, to God. Resist the devil, and he will flee from you. *Come near to God and He will come near to you.* Wash your hands, you sinners, and purify your hearts, you double-minded. Grieve, mourn and wail. Change your laughter to mourning and your joy to gloom. Humble yourselves before the Lord, and He will lift you up. (James 4:7-10)

Passive obedience, a merely surface and superficial show of obedience, will, often in the name of "grace" and "faith," eventually even oppose active obedience and thus often actually tries to cloak a passive resistance to God, which is nonetheless nothing but insidious rebellion and stubbornness.

God came to Balaam and asked, "Who are these men with you?"

Balaam said to God, "Balak son of Zippor, king of Moab, sent me this message: 'A people that has come out of Egypt covers the face of the land. Now come and put a curse on them for me. Perhaps then I will be able to fight them and drive them away.'"

But God said to Balaam, "Do not go with them. You must not put a curse on those people, because they are blessed."

The next morning Balaam got up and said to Balak's princes, "Go back to your own country, for Yahweh has refused to let me go with you."

So the Moabite princes returned to Balak and said, "Balaam refused to come with us."

Then Balak sent other princes, more numerous and more distinguished than the first. They came to Balaam and said: "This is what Balak son of Zippor says: Do not let anything keep you from coming to me, because I will reward you handsomely and do whatever you say. Come and put a curse on these people for me."

But Balaam answered them, "Even if Balak gave me his palace filled with silver and gold, I could not do anything great or small to go beyond the command of Yahweh my God. Now stay here tonight as the others did, and I will find out what else Yahweh will tell me."

That night God came to Balaam and said, "Since these men have come to summon you, go with them, but do only what I tell you."

Balaam got up in the morning, saddled his donkey and went with the princes of Moab. (Num. 22:9-21)

Elisha said, "Get a bow and some arrows," and he did so. "Take the bow in your hands," he said to the king of Israel. When he had taken it, Elisha put his hands on the king's hands.

"Open the east window," he said, and he opened it. "Shoot!" Elisha said, and he shot. "Yahweh's arrow of victory, the arrow of victory over Aram!" Elisha declared. "You will completely destroy the Arameans at Aphek."

Then he said, "Take the arrows," and the king took them. Elisha told him, "Strike the ground." He struck it three times and stopped. *The man of God was angry with him and said, "You should have struck the ground five or six times; then you would have defeated Aram and completely destroyed it. But now you will defeat it only three times."* (2 Kings 13:15-19)

Then a teacher of the law came to Him and said, "Teacher, I will follow You wherever You go."

Jesus replied, "Foxes have holes and birds of the air have nests, but the Son of Man has no place to lay His head."

Another disciple said to Him, "Lord, first let me go and bury my father."

But Jesus told him, "Follow Me, and let the dead bury their own dead." (Matt. 8:19-22)

What shall we say then? *Shall we continue in sin that grace may abound*? *Certainly not!* How shall we who died to sin live any longer in it? (Rom. 6:1-2)

For sin shall not have dominion over you, for you are not under law but under grace. What then? *Shall we sin because we are not under law but under grace? Certainly not!* (Rom. 6:14-15)

For certain men whose condemnation was written about long ago have secretly slipped in among you. They are godless men, who *change the grace of our God into a license for immorality* and deny Jesus Christ our only Sovereign and Lord. (Jude 1:4)

Unless the child repents of the cause of his merely passive obedience, he will bristle more and more against God's authority; a deep-seated resentment against this authority will lodge in his heart, with terrifying consequences for his future.

b. Partial Obedience

Partial obedience, like passive obedience, is unacceptable to God. It, too, hides disobedience, laziness or rebellion behind a facade of obedience. Partial obedience manifests disobedience of the heart, a disobedience all the more evil because it presents itself in the guise of serving God. Partial obedience is incomplete and inconsistent. It cannot be counted upon, for it will fail and fall short; this is why God refuses to accept it. God requires a will set on perfect obedience and abhors a divided heart (1 Kings 11:4-6). Only a will toward perfect obedience can ever hope to express God's grace without admixture of sin.

> When Samuel reached him, Saul said, "Yahweh bless you! I have carried out Yahweh's instructions."
> But Samuel said, "What then is this bleating of sheep in my ears? What is this lowing of cattle that I hear?"
> Saul answered, "The soldiers brought them from the Amalekites; they spared the best of the sheep and cattle to sacrifice to Yahweh your God, but we totally destroyed the rest." . . .
> "Why did you not obey Yahweh? Why did you pounce on the plunder and do evil in the eyes of Yahweh?"
> "But I did obey Yahweh," Saul said. "I went on the mission Yahweh assigned me. I completely destroyed the Amalekites and brought back Agag their king. The soldiers took sheep and cattle from the plunder, the best of what was devoted to God, in order to sacrifice them to Yahweh your God at Gilgal."
> But Samuel replied: *"Does Yahweh delight in burnt offerings and sacrifices as much as in obeying the voice of Yahweh? To obey is better than sacrifice, and to heed is better than the fat of rams.* For rebellion is like the sin of divination, and arrogance like the evil of idolatry. Because you have rejected the word of Yahweh, He has rejected you as king." (1 Sam. 15:13-15, 19-23)

> When they came to the threshing floor of Nacon, Uzzah reached out and took hold of the ark of God, because the oxen stumbled. Yahweh's anger burned against Uzzah because of his irreverent act; therefore God struck him down and he died there beside the ark of God. (2 Sam. 6:6-7)

> Ephraim mixes with the nations; Ephraim is a flat cake not turned over. (Hos. 7:8)

c. Passive Resistance

Passive resistance stands as one of the most effective forms of rebellion and so one of the most evil. Passive resistance *willfully* refuses to do what we know to do. Passive resistance feigns innocence—"See, I'm not doing anything wrong," the child coyly says in his inaction. Yet he knows full well his deep resistance and rebellion. The campus sit-ins of the 1960's and 1970's offered an excellent example of the nature of passive resistance. This form of rebellion was the most effective action taken by the radicals and rebels of those years. It won much public sympathy and gained results for their causes. Rather than using active violence against their opponents (which is, of course, also a great sin), in the sit-ins those in rebellion struck a pose of passivity, simply sitting still and insisting on their "right" to do so: blocking hallways and offices by sitting in public buildings and so on. In order to stop them in their rebellion, the authorities would have to apply some form of force against *them*, and so those in rebellion could appear to be passive and nonviolent while the authorities were forced to appear violent, even though the sit-ins had deliberately provoked this reaction.

Thus passive resistance is one of the greatest forms of rebellion because, instead of acknowledging and confessing its own sins, it exalts itself as more righteous than the authority that it rebels against. A deeply embedded arrogance and superiority serves as its motive force. It sees itself as "holier than thou," and this expresses the greatest contempt for authority. Because of the passive rebellion that confronts him, the one in responsibility is forced to act against someone who seems to be sitting quietly, doing nothing wrong. The passive rebel thus deliberately seeks to create a situation that will embarrass the one in authority, thus expressing his real hatred and contempt for that authority. Though the passive rebel presents a guise of peace, war and destruction lie deep in his heart (Jer. 9:8; Prov. 26:24-26; Ps. 55:21).

> He who hates, disguises it with his lips, and lays up deceit within himself; when he speaks kindly, do not believe him, for there are seven abominations in his heart; though his hatred is covered by deceit, his wickedness will be revealed before the assembly. (Prov. 26:24-26)

> The words of his mouth were smoother than butter, but war was in his heart; his words were softer than oil, yet they were drawn swords. (Ps. 55:21)

> Then another servant came and said, "Sir, here is your mina; I have kept it laid away in a piece of cloth. I was afraid of you, because you are a hard man. You take out what you did not put in and reap what you did not sow."
> His master replied, "I will judge you by your own words, you wicked servant! You knew, did you, that I am a hard man, taking out what I did not put in, and reaping what I did not sow? Why then didn't you put my money on deposit, so that when I came back, I could have collected it with interest?"
> Then he said to those standing by, "Take his mina away from him and give it to the one who has ten minas."
> "Sir," they said, "he already has ten!"
> He replied, "I tell you that to everyone who has, more will be given, but as for the one who has nothing, even what he has will be taken away. But those enemies of mine who did not want me to be king over them—bring them here and kill them in front of me." (Luke 19:20-27)

> Just as he finished making the offering, Samuel arrived, and Saul went out to greet him.
> "What have you done?" asked Samuel.
> Saul replied, "When I saw that the men were scattering, and that you did not come at the set time, and that the Philistines were assembling at Micmash, I thought, 'Now the Philistines will come down against me at Gilgal, and I have not sought Yahweh's favor.' So I felt compelled to offer the burnt offering."

"You acted foolishly," Samuel said. "*You have not kept the command Yahweh your God gave you*; if you had, He would have established your kingdom over Israel for all time." (1 Sam. 13:10-13)

When Samuel reached him, Saul said, "Yahweh bless you! *I have carried out Yahweh's instructions.*"

But Samuel said, "*What then is this bleating of sheep in my ears? What is this lowing of cattle that I hear?*"

Saul answered, "The soldiers brought them from the Amalekites; they spared the best of the sheep and cattle to sacrifice to the Lord your God, but we totally destroyed the rest."

"Stop!" Samuel said to Saul. "Let me tell you what Yahweh said to me last night."

"Tell me," Saul replied.

Samuel said, "Although you were once small in your own eyes, did you not become the head of the tribes of Israel? Yahweh anointed you king over Israel. And He sent you on a mission, saying, 'Go and completely destroy those wicked people, the Amalekites; make war on them until you have wiped them out.' *Why did you not obey Yahweh*? Why did you pounce on the plunder and do evil in the eyes of Yahweh?"

"But I did obey Yahweh," Saul said. "I went on the mission Yahweh assigned me. I completely destroyed the Amalekites and brought back Agag their king. The soldiers took sheep and cattle from the plunder, the best of what was devoted to God, in order to sacrifice them to Yahweh your God at Gilgal." (1 Sam. 15:13-21)

Their tongue is a deadly arrow; it *speaks with deceit*. With his mouth *each speaks cordially to his neighbor, but in his heart he sets a trap for him*. (Jer. 9:8)

"What do you think? There was a man who had two sons. He went to the first and said, 'Son, go and work today in the vineyard.'

"'I will not,' he answered, but later he changed his mind and went.

"Then the father went to the other son and said the same thing. *He answered, 'I will, sir,' but he did not go.*

"Which of the two did what his father wanted?"

"The first," they answered.

Jesus said to them, "I tell you the truth, the tax collectors and the prostitutes are entering the kingdom of God ahead of you." (Matt. 21:28-31)

d. Rebellion

Rebellion is the antipode of obedience and the greatest overt impeachment of parental or any other kind of authority that exists. It is the direct continuation of the original sin in the Garden of Eden—man and woman consciously deciding for themselves, from their own minds, apart from God, what actions to take regardless of and even against what God has spoken. Rebellion in this sense shows an active and deliberate antagonism to, and rejection of, the will of God. The Hebrew word *pesha* is translated "rebellion," a "willful deviation from the path of righteousness," "a premeditated crossing of the line of God's law." It is rooted in the Hebrew word *pasha,* which means to "break away." Another Hebrew word for rebellion is *meri,* which is derived from *marah,* which literally means "bitter." It expresses the bitter attitude of those who despise God's rule in their lives. The other Hebrew word translated "rebellion" is *carah.* This word literally means "to turn off" the path of obedience, indicating a "defection" from God and His covenant.

> Korah son of Izhar, the son of Kohath, the son of Levi, and certain Reubenites—Dathan and Abiram, sons of Eliab, and On son of Peleth—became insolent and *rose up against Moses.* With them were 250 Israelite men, well-known community leaders who had been appointed members of the council. They *came as a group to oppose Moses and Aaron* and said to them, "You have gone too far! The whole community is holy, every one of them, and Yahweh is with them. Why then do you set yourselves above Yahweh's assembly?"
>
> When Moses heard this, he fell facedown. Then he said to Korah and all his followers: "In the morning Yahweh will show who belongs to Him and who is holy, and He will have that person come near Him. The man He chooses He will cause to come near Him. You, Korah, and all your followers are to do this: Take censers and tomorrow put fire and incense in them before Yahweh. The man Yahweh chooses will be the one who is holy. You Levites have gone too far!"
>
> Moses also said to Korah, "Now listen, you Levites! Isn't it enough for you that the God of Israel has separated you from the rest of the Israelite community and brought you near Himself to do the work at Yahweh's tabernacle and to stand before the community and minister to them? He has brought you and all your fellow Levites near Himself, but *now you are trying to get the priesthood too. It is against Yahweh that you and all your followers have banded together.* Who is Aaron that you should grumble against him?"
>
> Then Moses summoned Dathan and Abiram, the sons of Eliab. But they said, "*We will not come!* Isn't it enough that you have brought us up out of a land flowing with milk and honey to kill us in the desert? And now you also want to lord it over us? Moreover, you haven't brought us into a land flowing with milk and honey or given us an inheritance of fields and vineyards. Will you gouge out the eyes of these men? No, *we will not come!*"
>
> Then Moses became very angry and said to Yahweh, "Do not accept their offering. I have not taken so much as a donkey from them, nor have I wronged any of them."
>
> Moses said to Korah, "You and all your followers are to appear before Yahweh tomorrow—you and they and Aaron. Each man is to take his censer and put incense in it—250 censers in all—and present it before Yahweh. You and Aaron are to present your censers also." So each man took his censer, put fire and incense in

it, and stood with Moses and Aaron at the entrance to the Tent of Meeting. When Korah had *gathered all his followers in opposition* to them at the entrance to the Tent of Meeting, the glory of Yahweh appeared to the entire assembly. Yahweh said to Moses and Aaron, "Separate yourselves from this assembly so I can put an end to them at once."

But Moses and Aaron fell facedown and cried out, "O God, God of the spirits of all mankind, will you be angry with the entire assembly when only one man sins?"

Then Yahweh said to Moses, "Say to the assembly, 'Move away from the tents of Korah, Dathan and Abiram.'"

Moses got up and went to Dathan and Abiram, and the elders of Israel followed him. He warned the assembly, "Move back from the tents of these wicked men! Do not touch anything belonging to them, or you will be swept away because of all their sins." So they moved away from the tents of Korah, Dathan and Abiram. Dathan and Abiram had come out and were standing with their wives, children and little ones at the entrances to their tents.

Then Moses said, "This is how you will know that Yahweh has sent me to do all these things and that it was not my idea: If these men die a natural death and experience only what usually happens to men, then Yahweh has not sent me. But if Yahweh brings about something totally new, and the earth opens its mouth and swallows them, with everything that belongs to them, and they go down alive into the grave, then you will know that *these men have treated Yahweh with contempt.*"

As soon as he finished saying all this, the ground under them split apart and the earth opened its mouth and swallowed them, with their households and all Korah's men and all their possessions. They went down alive into the grave, with everything they owned; the earth closed over them, and they perished and were gone from the community. At their cries, all the Israelites around them fled, shouting, "The earth is going to swallow us too!"

And fire came out from Yahweh and consumed the 250 men who were offering the incense. (Num. 16:1-35)

Woe to them! They have taken the way of Cain; they have rushed for profit into Balaam's error; they have been destroyed in Korah's *rebellion*.

These men are blemishes at your love feasts, eating with you without the slightest qualm—shepherds who feed only themselves. They are clouds without rain, blown along by the wind; autumn trees, without fruit and uprooted—twice dead. They are wild waves of the sea, foaming up their shame; wandering stars, for whom blackest darkness has been reserved forever.

Enoch, the seventh from Adam, prophesied about these men: "See, the Lord is coming with thousands upon thousands of His holy ones to judge everyone, and to convict all the ungodly of all the ungodly acts they have done in the ungodly way, and of all the harsh words ungodly sinners have spoken against Him." These men are grumblers and faultfinders; they follow their own evil desires; they boast about themselves and flatter others for their own advantage. (Jude 11-16)

But there were also false prophets among the people, just as there will be false teachers among you. They will *secretly introduce destructive heresies, even denying the sovereign Lord who bought them*—bringing swift destruction on themselves. Many will follow their shameful ways and will bring the way of truth into disrepute. In their greed these teachers will exploit you with stories they have made up. Their condemnation has long been hanging over them, and their destruction has not been sleeping.

For if God did not spare angels when they sinned, but sent them to hell, putting them into gloomy dungeons to be held for judgment; if He did not spare the ancient world when He brought the flood on its ungodly people, but protected Noah, a preacher of righteousness, and seven others; if He condemned the cities of Sodom and Gomorrah by burning them to ashes, and made them an example of what is going to happen to the ungodly; and if He rescued Lot, a righteous man, who was distressed by the filthy lives of lawless men (for that righteous man, living among them day after day, was tormented in his righteous soul by the lawless deeds he saw and heard)—if this is so, then the Lord knows how to rescue godly men from trials and to hold the unrighteous for the day of judgment, while continuing their punishment. This is especially true of those who follow the corrupt desire of the sinful nature and *despise authority*.

Bold and arrogant, these men are not afraid to slander celestial beings; yet even angels, although they are stronger and more powerful, do not bring slanderous accusations against such beings in the presence of the Lord. But these men blaspheme in matters they do not understand. They are like brute beasts, creatures of instinct, born only to be caught and destroyed, and like beasts they too will perish.

They will be paid back with harm for the harm they have done. Their idea of pleasure is to carouse in broad daylight. They are blots and blemishes, reveling in their pleasures while they feast with you. With eyes full of adultery, they never stop sinning; they seduce the unstable; they are experts in greed—an accursed brood! They have left the straight way and wandered off to follow the way of Balaam son of Beor, who loved the wages of wickedness. But he was rebuked for his wrongdoing by a donkey—a beast without speech—who spoke with a man's voice and restrained the prophet's madness.

These men are springs without water and mists driven by a storm. Blackest darkness is reserved for them. For they mouth empty, boastful words and, by appealing to the lustful desires of sinful human nature, they entice people who are just escaping from those who live in error. They promise them freedom, while they themselves are slaves of depravity—for a man is a slave to whatever has mastered him. If they have escaped the corruption of the world by knowing our Lord and Savior Jesus Christ and are again entangled in it and overcome, they are worse off at the end than they were at the beginning. It would have been better for them not to have known the way of righteousness, than to have known it and then to turn their backs on the sacred command that was passed on to them. Of them the proverbs are true: "A dog returns to its vomit," and, "A sow that is washed goes back to her wallowing in the mud." (2 Pet. 2:1-22)

But when they said, "Give us a king to lead us," this displeased Samuel; so he prayed to Yahweh. And Yahweh told him: "Listen to all that the people are saying to you; *it is not you they have rejected, but they have rejected Me as their king.* As they have done from the day I brought them up out of Egypt until this day, forsaking Me and serving other gods, so they are doing to you." (1 Sam. 8:6-8)

An *evil man is bent only on rebellion*; a merciless official will be sent against him. (Prov. 17:11)

Fear Yahweh and the king, my son, and *do not join with the rebellious*, for those two will send sudden destruction upon them, and who knows what calamities they can bring? (Prov. 24:21-22)

From one man He made every nation of men, that they should inhabit the whole earth; and He determined the times set for them and the exact places where they should live. (Acts 17:26)

Now the whole world had one language and a common speech. As men moved eastward, they found a plain in Shinar and settled there.
   They said to each other, "Come, let's make bricks and bake them thoroughly." They used brick instead of stone, and tar for mortar. Then they said, "Come, let us build ourselves a city, with a tower that reaches to the heavens, so that we may *make a name for ourselves* and not be scattered over the face of the whole earth."
   But Yahweh came down to see the city and the tower that the men were building. Yahweh said, "If as one people speaking the same language they have begun to do this, then nothing they plan to do will be impossible for them. Come, let us go down and confuse their language so they will not understand each other."
   So Yahweh scattered them from there over all the earth, and they stopped building the city. That is why it was called Babel—because there Yahweh confused the language of the whole world. From there Yahweh scattered them over the face of the whole earth. (Gen. 11:1-9)

Miriam and Aaron began to *talk against Moses* because of his Cushite wife, for he had married a Cushite. "Has Yahweh spoken only through Moses?" they asked. "Hasn't he also spoken through us?" And Yahweh heard this.
   (Now Moses was a very humble man, more humble than anyone else on the face of the earth.)
   At once Yahweh said to Moses, Aaron and Miriam, "Come out to the Tent of Meeting, all three of you." So the three of them came out. Then Yahweh came down in a pillar of cloud; He stood at the entrance to the Tent and summoned Aaron and Miriam. When both of them stepped forward, He said, "Listen to My words:

"When a prophet of Yahweh is among you, I reveal Myself to Him in visions, I speak to Him in dreams.

But this is not true of My servant Moses; he is faithful in all My house.

With him I speak face to face, clearly and not in riddles; he sees the form of Yahweh. Why then were you not afraid to speak against My servant Moses?"

The anger of Yahweh burned against them, and He left them.

When the cloud lifted from above the Tent, there stood Miriam—leprous, like snow. Aaron turned toward her and saw that she had leprosy. (Num. 12:1-10)

"And I will bring you to the land I swore with uplifted hand to give to Abraham, to Isaac and to Jacob. I will give it to you as a possession. I am Yahweh."

Moses reported this to the Israelites, but *they did not listen to him* because of their discouragement and cruel bondage. (Exod. 6:8-9)

While the Israelites were in the desert, a man was found gathering wood on the Sabbath day. Those who found him gathering wood brought him to Moses and Aaron and the whole assembly, and they kept him in custody, because it was not clear what should be done to him. Then Yahweh said to Moses, "The man must die. The whole assembly must stone him outside the camp." So the assembly took him outside the camp and stoned him to death, as Yahweh commanded Moses. (Num. 15:32-36)

"What have you done?" asked Samuel.

Saul replied, "When I saw that the men were scattering, and that you did not come at the set time, and that the Philistines were assembling at Micmash, I thought, 'Now the Philistines will come down against me at Gilgal, and I have not sought Yahweh's favor.' So I felt compelled to offer the burnt offering."

"You *acted foolishly,*" Samuel said, "*You have not kept the command Yahweh your God gave you*; if you had, He would have established your kingdom over Israel for all time. But now your kingdom will not endure; Yahweh has sought out a man after His own heart and appointed him leader of His people, because you *have not kept Yahweh's command.*" (1 Sam. 13:11-14)

By the word of Yahweh one of the sons of the prophets said to his companion, "Strike me with your weapon," *but the man refused.*

So the prophet said, "Because you have not obeyed Yahweh, as soon as you leave me a lion will kill you." And after the man went away, a lion found him and killed him. (1 Kings 20:35-36)

The king said to the man of God, "Come home with me and have something to eat, and I will give you a gift."

But the man of God answered the king, "Even if you were to give me half your possessions, I would not go with you, nor would I eat bread or drink water here. For *I was commanded by the word of Yahweh*: 'You must not eat bread or drink water or return by the way you came.'" So he took another road and did not return by the way he had come to Bethel . . . .

The old prophet answered, "I too am a prophet, as you are. And an angel said to me by the word of Yahweh: 'Bring him back with you to your house so that he may eat bread and drink water.'" (But he was lying to him.) So the man of God returned with him and ate and drank in his house.

While they were sitting at the table, the word of Yahweh came to the old prophet who had brought him back. He cried out to the man of God who had come from Judah, "This is what Yahweh says: *'You have defied the word of Yahweh and have not kept the command Yahweh your God gave you.* You came back and ate bread and drank water in the place where He told you not to eat or drink. Therefore your body will not be buried in the tomb of your fathers.'" (1 Kings 13:7-10, 18-22)

Aaron's sons Nadab and Abihu took their censers, put fire in them and added incense; and they offered unauthorized fire before Yahweh, *contrary to His command.* So fire came out from the presence of Yahweh and consumed them, and they died before Yahweh. Moses then said to Aaron, "This is what Yahweh spoke of when He said: 'Among those who approach Me I will show Myself holy; in the sight of all the people I will be honored.'" (Lev. 10:1-3)

When the woman saw that the fruit of the tree was good for food and pleasing to the eye, and also desirable for gaining wisdom, she took some and ate it. She also gave some to her husband, who was with her, and he ate it. Then the eyes of both of them were opened, and they realized they were naked; so they sewed fig leaves together and made coverings for themselves.

Then the man and his wife heard the sound of Yahweh God as He was walking in the garden in the cool of the day, and they hid from Yahweh God among the trees of the garden. But Yahweh God called to the man, "Where are you?"

He answered, "I heard You in the garden, and I was afraid because I was naked; so I hid."

And He said, "Who told you that you were naked? Have you eaten from the tree that I commanded you not to eat from?" (Gen. 3:6-11)

As soon as they had brought them out, one of them said, "Flee for your lives! Don't look back, and don't stop anywhere in the plain! Flee to the mountains or you will be swept away!" . . .

But Lot's wife looked back, and she became a pillar of salt. (Gen. 19:17, 26)

On a hill east of Jerusalem, Solomon built a high place for Chemosh the detestable god of Moab, and for Molech the detestable god of the Ammonites. He did the same for all his foreign wives, who burned incense and offered sacrifices to their gods.

Yahweh became angry with Solomon because his heart had turned away from Yahweh, the God of Israel, who had appeared to him twice. Although He had forbidden Solomon to follow other gods, *Solomon did not keep Yahweh's command.* (1 Kings 11:7-10)

But the Israelites acted unfaithfully in regard to the devoted things; Achan son of Carmi, the son of Zimri, the son of Zerah, of the tribe of Judah, took some of them. So Yahweh's anger burned against Israel. (Josh. 7:1)

Though you already know all this, I want to remind you that the Lord delivered His people out of Egypt, but later destroyed those who did not believe. And the angels who did not keep their positions of authority but abandoned their own home—these He has kept in darkness, bound with everlasting chains for judgment on the great Day. In a similar way, Sodom and Gomorrah and the surrounding towns gave themselves up to sexual immorality and perversion. They serve as an example of those who suffer the punishment of eternal fire.

In the very same way, these dreamers pollute their own bodies, *reject authority and slander celestial beings.* But even the archangel Michael, when he was disputing with the devil about the body of Moses, did not dare to bring a slanderous accusation against him, but said, "The Lord rebuke you!" Yet these men *speak abusively* against whatever they do not understand; and what things they do understand by instinct, like unreasoning animals—these are the very things that destroy them.

Woe to them! They have taken the way of Cain; they have rushed for profit into Balaam's error; they have been destroyed in Korah's *rebellion.* (Jude 5-11)

Queen Vashti also gave a banquet for the women in the royal palace of King Xerxes. On the seventh day, when King Xerxes was in high spirits from wine, he commanded the seven eunuchs who served him—Mehuman, Biztha, Harbona, Bigtha, Abagtha, Zethar and Carcas—to bring before him Queen Vashti, wearing her royal crown, in order to display her beauty to the people and nobles, for she was lovely to look at. *But when the attendants delivered the king's command, Queen Vashti refused to come.* Then the king became furious and burned with anger. Since it was customary for the king to consult experts in matters of law and justice, he spoke with the wise men who understood the times and were closest to the king—Carshena, Shethar, Admatha, Tarshish, Meres, Marsena and Memucan, the seven nobles of Persia and Media who had special access to the king and were highest in the kingdom. "According to law, what must be done to Queen Vashti?" he asked. "*She has not obeyed the command of King Xerxes* that the eunuchs have taken to her." Then Memucan replied in the presence of the king and the nobles, "*Queen Vashti has done wrong, not only against the king but also against all the nobles and the peoples of all the provinces of King Xerxes. For the queen's conduct will become known to all the women, and so they will despise their husbands* and say, 'King Xerxes commanded Queen Vashti to be brought before him, but she would not come.' This very day the Persian and Median women of the nobility who have heard about the queen's conduct will respond to all the king's nobles in the same way. *There will be no end of disrespect and discord.* Therefore, if it pleases the king, let him issue a royal decree and let it be written in the laws of Persia and Media, which cannot be repealed, that Vashti is never again to enter the presence of King Xerxes. Also let the king give her royal position to someone else who is better than she. Then when the king's edict is proclaimed throughout all his vast realm, all the women will respect their husbands, from the least to the greatest." The king and his nobles were pleased with this advice, so the king did as Memucan proposed. (Esther 1:9-21)

e. Stubbornness

Paul reckons disobedient children among the most malicious people on earth and says, "Have nothing to do with them" (2 Tim. 3:2, 5). Deuteronomy 13:13 speaks of evil men as the *sons of Belial*, a Hebrew phrase meaning "sons without profit," that is, "sons without yoke," who refuse any subjection to their parents. The Old Testament punishment of such stubborn children under the law of the *elohim* was death. "Stubborn" is the translation of the Hebrew word *sarar*, which pictures "an untamed cow, . . . stubborn animals shaking the yoke off from their shoulders." Stubbornness against God's will marks us as brute animals rather than children of God.

> The Israelites are stubborn, like a stubborn heifer. How then can Yahweh pasture them like lambs in a meadow? (Hos. 4:16)

> Do not be like the horse or the mule, which have no understanding but must be controlled by bit and bridle or they will not come to you. (Ps. 32:9)

> *"Woe to the obstinate children,"* declares Yahweh, "to those who carry out plans that are not Mine, forming an alliance, but not by My Spirit, heaping sin upon sin; who go down to Egypt without consulting Me; who look for help to Pharaoh's protection, to Egypt's shade for refuge." (Isa. 30:1-2)

> What man is wise enough to understand this? Who has been instructed by Yahweh and can explain it? Why has the land been ruined and laid waste like a desert that no one can cross?
> Yahweh said, "It is because they have forsaken My law, which I set before them; they have not obeyed Me or followed My law. *Instead, they have followed the stubbornness of their hearts*; they have followed the Baals, as their fathers taught them." (Jer. 9:12-14)

> *But because of your stubbornness and your unrepentant heart*, you are storing up wrath against yourself for the day of God's wrath, when His righteous judgment will be revealed. (Rom. 2:5)

> *For rebellion is as the sin of witchcraft, and stubbornness is as iniquity and idolatry.* Because you have rejected the word of Yahweh, He also has rejected you from being king. (1 Sam. 15:23)

> If a man has a stubborn and rebellious son who does not obey his father and mother and will not listen to them when they discipline him, his father and mother shall take hold of him and bring him to the elders of his town. They shall say to the elders, "This son of ours is stubborn and rebellious. He will not obey us. He is a

profligate and a drunkard." Then all the men of his town shall stone him to death. You must purge the evil from among you. All Israel will hear of it and be afraid. (Deut. 21:18-21)

Since this law given through angels (Acts 7:53; Gal. 3:19) was first pronounced, nothing has changed in regard to the loathing of the *elohim* toward these sins (Mal. 3:6). These judgments still stand as just. What has changed, and it is a great change, is that Jesus has received the just punishment of those who willfully and irrevocably unite with Him by burying themselves into His sacrificial death and then rising in the power of His resurrected life (Rom. 6:3-8; 8:9-14; 2 Tim. 2:11; Isa. 53:6). So these punishments are no longer to be applied. In other words, we certainly are not supposed to stone to death rebellious children. But if we willfully sin, trample underfoot God's Son (Heb. 10:29), then no more sacrifice remains (Heb: 10:26), but only a fearful expectation of the judgment we deserve (Heb. 10:27). We are removed from the covering of Christ's sacrificial Body, which received our just punishment. We are then exposed to the world and its agency of wrath as it is released against us. We have, in other words, removed ourselves from the lordship of love so that only other lordships of principalities, powers and the rulers of this world can now prevail in our thoughts, attitudes, emotions, plans, deeds, relationships and lives.

> Which of the prophets did your fathers not persecute? And they killed those who foretold the coming of the Just One, of whom you now have become the betrayers and murderers, who have *received the law by the direction of angels* and have not kept it. (Acts 7:52-53)

> What purpose then does the law serve? It was added because of transgressions, till the Seed should come to whom the promise was made; and *it was appointed through angels* by the hand of a mediator. (Gal. 3:19)

> For I am Yahweh, *I do not change*; therefore you are not consumed, O sons of Jacob. (Mal. 3:6)

> Or do you not know that as many of us as were baptized into Christ Jesus were *baptized into His death*? Therefore we were *buried with Him through baptism into death*, that just as Christ was raised from the dead by the glory of the Father, even so *we also* should walk in newness of life. For if we have been *united together in the likeness of His death, certainly we also shall be in the likeness of His resurrection*, knowing this, that our old man was *crucified with Him*, that the body of sin might be done away with, that we should no longer be slaves of sin. For he who has died has been justified from sin. Now *if we died with Christ, we believe that we shall also live with Him*. (Rom. 6:3-8)

> But you are not in the flesh but in the Spirit, if indeed the Spirit of God dwells in you. Now if anyone does not have the Spirit of Christ, he is not His. And if Christ is in you, the body is dead because of sin, but the Spirit is life because of righteousness. But *if*

the Spirit of Him who raised Jesus from the dead dwells in you, He who raised Christ from the dead will also give life to your mortal bodies through His Spirit who dwells in you. Therefore, brethren, we are debtors—not to the flesh, to live according to the flesh. For if you live according to the flesh you will die; but *if by the Spirit you put to death the deeds of the body, you will live.* For as many as are led by the Spirit of God, these are sons of God. (Rom. 8:9-14)

This is a faithful saying: for *if we died with Him, we shall also live with Him.* (2 Tim. 2:11)

All we like sheep have gone astray; we have turned, every one, to his own way; and Yahweh has laid on Him the iniquity of us all. (Isa. 53:6)

For *if we sin willfully* after we have received the knowledge of the truth, there *no longer remains a sacrifice for sins,* but *a certain fearful expectation of judgment, and fiery indignation* which will devour the adversaries. Anyone who has rejected Moses' law dies without mercy on the testimony of two or three witnesses. Of how much worse punishment, do you suppose, will he be thought worthy who has *trampled the Son of God underfoot, counted the blood of the covenant by which he was sanctified a common thing, and insulted the Spirit of grace?* For we know Him who said, "Vengeance is Mine, I will repay," says the Lord. And again, "The LORD will judge His people." (Heb. 10:26-30)

D. Responsibility and Faithfulness/ Irresponsibility and Unfaithfulness

1. Responsibility, Faithfulness

True honor opens children to parents and to God. They walk in God's light, hear His voice and obey it. They *respond*, in other words, to God. To thus respond obviously defines responsibility. So passive obedience can never make anyone responsible. Only active obedience from a heart prompted by reverence leads to responsibility and faithfulness.

> By faith Noah, when warned about things not yet seen, in holy fear built an ark to save his family. By his faith he condemned the world and became heir of the righteousness that comes by faith. (Heb. 11:7)

A responsible person is also a *reliable* person (2 Tim. 2:2), someone *liable* for an answer or an accounting of his or her actions (Heb. 13:17). So such a person *must* prove himself reliable, trustworthy, for fulfilling his responsibilities (Matt. 25:14-30; Luke 19:11-27; 1 Cor. 4:1-3; see also the chapter "Chesed" in *Loved into Loving*). You cannot be truly responsible until you accept liability for giving answer in fulfilling your tasks.

Obviously, different children will be able to become liable on very different levels, according to their degree of maturity. But Paul instructed Timothy to entrust unto *"reliable men"* the things entrusted by Paul to Timothy. These men would in turn share what was given them with others who also accepted liability, men who were prepared, liable and ready to give an account. Only such men could be *relied* upon for the great task and vision of God.

The root of the word *reliable* is *ligare*, meaning "to bind." This is also the root of the word *religion*, which literally means "a binding together." Finally, the word *ligament*, the binding tissue of the body, also derives from the same root. So, Paul declares, from Jesus Christ Himself "the whole body, joined and held together by every supporting *ligament*, grows and builds itself up in love, as each part does its work" (Eph. 4:16). This describes the "ligaments" in terms of God's covenant of holy love that "binds" every member to every other in making each liable and reliable to "do its work." What enables us to actually *be* bound together in that love covenant—as contrasted to merely *saying* that we are bound together—is this reliability, this *willingness* to serve and fulfill our responsibilities as people who give an account for their actions (Heb. 13:17). Jesus touched on this when He asked Peter if he truly loved Him, truly had God's *agape* love for Him (John 21:15-19). Peter could not say that he had that love at that time, for it was before God had filled him with that same Holy Spirit by which "the love of God is shed abroad in our hearts" (Acts 2:1-4; Rom. 5:5, KJV). But Jesus told Peter that a time would come when he would be girded up, "bound," by someone other than himself and led in a way that his flesh would not want to go. So Peter would be made liable, bound together in the covenant of God's love to fulfill his place of service in the Body of Christ. Then he could feed God's sheep (John 21:15-17).

And this is what God seeks to do with each and all: *ligare* us together in the love covenant with Him by making us *reliable* people, people fully aware of the necessity to give an account before Him, fully aware of their liability for everything entrusted into their hands. For the Lord can depend upon only such people to accomplish His purpose. So God wants to bring forth in His Body men and women who constantly carry the concern, the responsibility, the awareness of their liability. We are to train ourselves and our children to be these people.

a. Working unto the Lord

To fulfill all God has given us to do requires working *unto the Lord* faithfully in everything.

> Consider now, for Yahweh has *chosen you to build a temple* as a sanctuary. *Be strong and do the work.* (1 Chron. 28:10)

> And *whatever you do, whether in word or deed, do it all in the name of the Lord Jesus, giving thanks to God the Father* through Him. (Col. 3:17)

> Therefore, I urge you, brothers, in view of God's mercy, to *offer your bodies as living sacrifices, holy and pleasing to God—this is your spiritual act of worship.* Do not conform any longer to the pattern of this world, but be *transformed by the renewing of your mind.* Then you will be able to test and approve what God's will is—His good, pleasing and perfect will. (Rom. 12:1-2)

Our work is our worship toward God. Hebrew, Latin and English show a direct link between the word *worship* and the word indicating the most prevalent form of work throughout human history—the *cultivating* of the soil. The same Hebrew word, *avad*, can be translated as "to worship" or "to cultivate," as in soil cultivation. The etymology of the English word *agriculture* is also revealing. It derives from the Latin *ager*, meaning "field," and the Latin *cultus*, which means "honoring," "religious worship." The Latin root of *cultus*, *colere*, can mean either "to worship" or "to cultivate." In fact, both Hebrew and Latin reveal as interchangeable the words for "cultivate" and "worship." This surprises only those of us too long separated from our roots in the Biblical mandate God placed upon man in the Garden:

> Yahweh God took the man and put him into the garden of Eden to cultivate it and keep it. (Gen. 2:15, NASV)

The word *cultivate* is also directly related to the word *culture*, which covers the whole of a people's way of life.* And our English word *culture*, in the most literal sense of that word, derives from the Latin word *cultus* and means both "a nurturing habitat" and "worship, honouring," "religious worship." Various cultures constitute "nurturing habitats" for all that a people "worship," "honor" and "religiously" devote themselves to.* Those who seek to worship Yahweh see everything they do and say as part of a nurturing habitat to draw them closer to Him. To truly worship Him with *all* our being means to diligently fulfill all He gives us to do in *every* aspect of our lives. Work that pleases God only comes from a heart wholly submitted to God.

> Whatever you do, work at it with all your heart, as working for the Lord, not for men. (Col. 3:23)

To work wholeheartedly unto the Lord means to work fully devoted to Him. It means that the thoughts and meditations of our hearts, our attitudes, our feelings, our words, actions and so on will all work together to offer a positive worship to God in fulfilling His purpose and edifying His Body. An attitude of pouting, resentment, double-mindedness, boredom, procrastination, distracted thoughts and so on all signal a failure to work wholeheartedly unto the Lord.

> So we rebuilt the wall till all of it reached half its height, for the people *worked with all their heart*. (Neh. 4:6)

> This is what Hezekiah did throughout Judah, doing what was good and right and faithful before Yahweh his God. In everything that he undertook in the service of God's temple and in obedience to the law and the commands, *he sought his God and worked wholeheartedly*. And so he prospered. (2 Chron. 31:20-21)

b. Diligence

Diligence suggests perseverance and care in all we do according to the exact specifications and will of God. The literal meanings of the Hebrew words translated "diligence" add insight to our perspective. *Yatab* means "to make well, sound, beautiful, successful, right." The word *mahir* means "skillful." *Shanan* means "to sharpen," as to sharpen a knife on a

---

* See *A Garden Enclosed*.

whetstone. So diligence in work involves exceeding care and responsibility as well as a skill and keenness that truly bring glory to God.

> Whatever the God of heaven has prescribed, let it be done with *diligence* for the temple of the God of heaven. Why should there be wrath against the realm of the king and of his sons? (Ezra 7:23)

> Make this tabernacle and all its furnishings *exactly* like the pattern I will show you. (Exod. 25:9)

> They serve at a sanctuary that is a copy and shadow of what is in heaven. This is why Moses was warned when he was about to build the tabernacle: "See to it that you *make everything according to the pattern* shown you on the mountain." (Heb. 8:5)

> Lazy hands make a man poor, but *diligent* hands bring wealth. (Prov. 10:4)

> . . . not lagging behind in *diligence, fervent in spirit, serving the Lord.* (Rom. 12:11, NASV)

> The plans of the *diligent* lead to profit as surely as *haste leads to poverty.* (Prov. 21:5)

> Do you see a man *diligent and skillful* in his business? He will stand before kings; he will not stand before obscure men. (Prov. 22:29, KJV, NASV)

> *Diligent hands will rule,* but *laziness ends in slave labor.* (Prov. 12:24)

> The lazy man does not roast his game, but the *diligent* man prizes his possessions. (Prov. 12:27)

> The sluggard craves and gets nothing, but the desires of the *diligent* are fully satisfied. (Prov. 13:4)

c. Bringing a Job to Quality Completion

A responsible child won't leave a job partially done, but will strive to complete his work to the best of his abilities and not give up until he has succeeded. When Jesus spoke of "finishing" God's work, the Greek word used is *teleioo.* One lexicon describes it as "akin to the adjective *teleios,* complete, perfect," and it "denotes to bring to an end in the sense of completing or perfecting." *Artios* is another Greek word translated "complete" or "perfect." According to Danker, this word "pertains to being *well* fitted for some function." And Thayer says it refers to "a special aptitude for given uses." So this word can also "signify right ordering and arrangement" and "indicates a close relationship between character and destiny." It is the root of the word *katartismos* used in Ephesians 4:12-13 to show that the process of "perfecting" the individual members (v. 12) leads to the "perfect [complete, *teleios*] man" of the complete Body of Christ (v. 13). This "perfecting" on both individual and corporate levels takes place as the Body is "fitted and held together by what every joint supplies" (v. 16). So, for the Body to function properly, to be complete in the sense of finishing God's work, each "joint" must be fitted "exactly right." Rienecker says *artios* means "fit, complete, capable, sufficient; i.e., able to meet all demands." So a responsible child strives to bring God's work to a quality completion that glorifies the Lord in the child's (or disciple's) ability to meet the need. The child somehow senses that with God only finishing a task brings rest. So the responsible child always presses, whether consciously or not, to find and fulfill his place in that Body being perfected in God's will (Eph. 4:11-16; 1 Cor. 12:4-12; Heb. 10:5-7). The child's very sense of responsibility, of responding to something greater and more important than himself, puts this drive in him.

> Then God saw everything that He had made, and indeed it was very good. So the evening and the morning were the sixth day. Thus the heavens and the earth, and all the host of them, were *finished*. And on the seventh day God ended His work which He had done, and *He rested* on the seventh day from all His work which He had done. Then God blessed the seventh day and sanctified it, because in it *He rested from all His work* which God had created and made. (Gen. 1:31–2:3)

> And He Himself gave some to be apostles, some prophets, some evangelists, and some pastors and teachers, for the *perfecting* of the saints for the work of ministry, for the edifying of the body of Christ, till we all come to the unity of the faith and of the knowledge of the Son of God, to a *perfect man*, to the measure of the stature of the fullness of Christ; that we should no longer be children, tossed to and fro and carried about with every wind of doctrine, by the trickery of men, in the cunning craftiness of deceitful plotting, but, speaking the truth in love, may grow up in all things into Him who is the head—Christ—from whom the whole body, *fitted and held together by what every joint supplies*, according to the effective working by which every part does its share, causes growth of the body for the edifying of itself in love. (Eph. 4:11-16)

> I have *brought You glory* on earth by *completing the work* You gave Me to do. (John 17:4)

> "My food," said Jesus, "is to do the will of Him who sent Me and to *finish His work*." (John 4:34)

> For it was Yahweh Himself who hardened their hearts to wage war against Israel, so that He might destroy them totally, exterminating them without mercy, as Yahweh had commanded Moses.
> At that time Joshua went and destroyed the Anakites from the hill country: from Hebron, Debir and Anab, from all the hill country of Judah, and from all the hill country of Israel. Joshua totally destroyed them and their towns. No Anakites were left in Israelite territory; only in Gaza, Gath and Ashdod did any survive. So Joshua took the entire land, just as Yahweh had directed Moses,

and he gave it as an inheritance to Israel according to their tribal divisions.

Then the land had rest from war. (Josh. 11:20-23)

So *the wall was completed* on the twenty-fifth of Elul, in fifty-two days. When all our enemies heard about this, all the surrounding nations were afraid and lost their self-confidence, because they realized that *this work had been done* with the help of our God. (Neh. 6:15-16)

So all the work on the tabernacle, the Tent of Meeting, was completed. The Israelites did everything just as Yahweh commanded Moses. (Exod. 39:32)

Then Moses set up the courtyard around the tabernacle and altar and put up the curtain at the entrance to the courtyard. *And so Moses finished the work.* Then the cloud covered the Tent of Meeting, and the glory of Yahweh filled the tabernacle. (Exod. 40:33-34)

When *all the work King Solomon had done for the temple of Yahweh was finished*, he brought in the things his father David had dedicated—the silver and gold and the furnishings—and he placed them in the treasuries of Yahweh's temple . . . .

When the priests withdrew from the Holy Place, the cloud filled the temple of Yahweh. And the priests could not perform their service because of the cloud, for *the glory of Yahweh filled His temple.* (1 Kings 7:51; 8:10-11)

And here is my advice about what is best for you in this matter: Last year you were the first not only to give but also to have the desire to do so. Now *finish the work*, so that your eager willingness to do it may be matched by your *completion of it*, according to your means. (2 Cor. 8:10-11)

And now, compelled by the Spirit, I am going to Jerusalem, not knowing what will happen to me there. I only know that in every city the Holy Spirit warns me that prison and hardships are facing me. However, *I consider my life worth nothing to me, if only I may finish the race and complete the task the Lord Jesus has given me*—the task of testifying to the gospel of God's grace. (Acts 20:22-24)

I have fought the good fight, *I have finished the race*, I have kept the faith. (2 Tim. 4:7)

When he had received the drink, Jesus said, *"It is finished."* With that, He bowed His head and gave up His spirit. (John 19:30)

To work in accordance with the Word of God is a reward in itself. The child will recognize the privilege of having the opportunity to serve God and will derive joy from such work.

Give her the reward she has earned, and *let her works bring her praise at the city gate.* (Prov. 31:31)

. . . who gave Himself for us to redeem us from all wickedness and to purify for Himself a people that are His very own, *eager to do what is good.* (Titus 2:14)

Command them to do good, *to be rich in good deeds*, and to be generous and willing to share. (1 Tim. 6:18)

In Joppa there was a disciple named Tabitha (which, when translated, is Dorcas), who was *always doing good and helping* the poor. (Acts 9:36)

Live such good lives among the pagans that, though they accuse you of doing wrong, *they may see your good deeds and glorify God* on the day He visits us. (1 Pet. 2:12)

. . . and is *well known for her good deeds*, such as bringing up children, showing hospitality, washing the feet of the saints, helping those in trouble and *devoting herself to all kinds of good deeds*. (1 Tim. 5:10)

In the same way, let your light shine before men, that they may *see your good deeds* and praise your Father in heaven. (Matt. 5:16)

d. Working in God's Time

God reserves the times and seasons unto Himself (Acts 1:7), and just as there is a time to plant and then to harvest, so there is a time for everything God has given under heaven for us to accomplish. Given this truth, procrastination becomes just another form of laziness and irresponsibility. We must not be ignorant but know the times and the seasons (Eccles. 3:1-8), or else the harvest will come, and we will not yet be saved (Jer. 8:20). To truly submit to God means to conform to His patterns in every respect. We must train our children to complete tasks within time limits set by God. The Hebrew word used in Genesis 1:14, *moed*, which is translated "seasons," also means "festival, assembly, congregation." To complete God's work in His time, in season, is truly to enter into a festival-celebration of His grace and love. Great joy comes with flowing in God's own times and seasons, completing what He gives us to do in the time in which He gives us to do it.

There is *a time for everything, and a season for every activity under heaven: a time* to be born and *a time* to die, *a time* to plant and *a time* to uproot, *a time* to kill and *a time* to heal, *a time* to tear down and *a time* to build, *a time* to weep and *a time* to laugh, *a time* to mourn and *a time* to dance, *a time* to scatter stones and *a time* to gather them, *a time* to embrace and *a time* to refrain, *a time* to search and *a time* to give up, *a time* to keep and *a time* to throw away, *a time* to tear and *a time* to mend, *a time* to be silent and *a time* to speak, *a time* to love and *a time* to hate, *a time* for war and *a time* for peace. (Eccles. 3:1-8)

Six days you shall labor and do all your work . . . . (Exod. 20:9)

"For *six years* you are to *sow* your fields and *harvest* the crops, but during the *seventh year* let the land lie unplowed and unused. Then the poor among your people may get food from it, and the wild animals may eat what they leave. Do the same with your vineyard and your olive grove.

"*Six days do your work, but on the seventh day do not work*, so that your ox and your donkey may rest and the slave born in your household, and the alien as well, may be refreshed." (Exod. 23:10-12)

Six days you shall labor, but on the *seventh day you shall rest*; *even during the plowing season and harvest you must rest*. (Exod. 34:21)

As long as it is day, we must *do the work* of Him who sent Me. Night is coming, when *no one can work*. (John 9:4)

Go to the ant, you sluggard; consider its ways and be wise! It has no commander, no overseer or ruler, yet *it stores its provisions in summer and gathers its food at harvest*. (Prov. 6:6-8)

He who *gathers crops in summer* is a wise son, but he who sleeps during harvest is a disgraceful son. (Prov. 10:5)

Even the stork in the sky knows her *appointed seasons*, and the dove, the swift and the thrush observe *the time* of their migration. But My people do not know the requirements of Yahweh. (Jer. 8:7)

"The *days are coming*," declares Yahweh, "*when the reaper will be overtaken by the plowman and the planter by the one treading grapes*. New wine will drip from the mountains and flow from all the hills." (Amos 9:13)

In other words, it is not the natural children who are God's children, but it is the children of the promise who are regarded as Abraham's offspring. For this was how the promise was stated: "*At the appointed time* I will return, and Sarah will have a son." (Rom. 9:8-9)

Do you *not say, "Four months more and then the harvest"*? I tell you, *open your eyes and look at the fields! They are ripe for harvest*. Even now the reaper draws his wages, even now he harvests the crop for eternal life, so that the sower and the reaper may be glad together. Thus the saying "One sows and another reaps" is true. I sent you to reap what you have not worked for. Others have done the hard work, and you have reaped the benefits of their labor. (John 4:35-38)

You see, *at just the right time*, when we were still powerless, Christ died for the ungodly. (Rom. 5:6)

When a farmer plows for planting, does he plow continually? Does he keep on breaking up and harrowing the soil? When he has leveled the surface, does he not sow caraway and scatter cummin? Does he not plant wheat in its place, barley in its plot, and spelt in its field? His God instructs him and teaches him the right way. Caraway is not threshed with a sledge, nor is a cartwheel rolled over cummin; caraway is beaten out with a rod, and cummin with a stick. Grain must be ground to make bread; so one does not go on threshing it forever. Though he drives the wheels of his threshing cart over it, his horses do not grind it. All this also comes from Yahweh Almighty. (Isa. 28:24-29)

> For the earth which drinks in the rain that often comes upon it, and bears herbs useful for those by whom it is cultivated, receives blessing from God; but if it bears thorns and briers, it is rejected and near to being cursed, whose end is to be burned. (Heb. 6:7-8)

> And He made known to us the mystery of His will according to His good pleasure, which He purposed in Christ, to be *put into effect when the times will have reached their fulfillment*—to bring all things in heaven and on earth together under one head, even Christ. (Eph. 1:9-10)

> Then Yahweh said, "My Spirit *will not contend with man forever*, for he is mortal; *his days will be a hundred and twenty years*." (Gen. 6:3)

> And He said to them, "It is not for you to know *times or seasons* which the Father has put in His own authority." (Acts 1:7)

Yet even if we can't know those "times and seasons" reserved to God's own authority, we can know those He's given into our hands, and we can know and obey the God who knows *all* the times and seasons.

e. Working with Concentration

Children must make "the most of every opportunity, because the days are evil" (Eph. 5:16). This means working with total concentration and singleness of heart and mind, desiring to honor God in everything. The only acceptable sacrifice is to love the Lord with *all* our heart, soul, mind and strength. To hold back part of ourselves, to refuse to fully participate in our labors, is to offer a blemished sacrifice. Nothing can be allowed to distract us from accomplishing God's purposes with singleness of eye, heart and mind, giving God's work all priority and all our undivided attention.

> And they, continuing daily with one accord in the temple, and breaking bread from house to house, did eat their meat with gladness and *singleness of heart*. (Acts 2:46, KJV)

> Servants, be obedient to them that are your masters according to the flesh, with fear and trembling, *in singleness of your heart, as unto Christ*. (Eph. 6:5, KJV)

> Servants, obey in all things your masters according to the flesh; not with eyeservice, as menpleasers; *but in singleness of heart, fearing God*. (Col. 3:22, KJV)

> Be sure you know the condition of your flocks, *give careful attention* to your herds. (Prov. 27:23)

> Now I am ready to visit you for the third time, and I will not be a burden to you, because what I want is not your possessions but you. After all, children should not have to save up for their parents, but parents for their children. So *I will very gladly spend for you*

everything I have and expend myself as well. If I love you more, will you love me less? (2 Cor. 12:14-15)

So we continued the work with half the men holding spears, from the first light of dawn till the stars came out. At that time I also said to the people, "Have every man and his helper stay inside Jerusalem at night, so they can serve us as guards by night and workmen by day." Neither I nor my brothers nor my men nor the guards with me took off our clothes; each had his weapon, even when he went for water. (Neh. 4:21-23)

f. Orderliness and Neatness

Our work should be neat and orderly because God is a God of order, not a God of confusion (1 Cor. 14:33). Neatness and orderliness are inseparable. *Neat* is defined as "orderly and clean,"[34] and Webster's also says, "Neat suggests cleanness and orderliness and, hence, connotes a lack of superfluous or confusing details." This word's roots trace back to the Latin *nitere* meaning "to shine."[35] Neatness, then, is the removal of everything that obscures the essentials or the essence. In our life in Christ, the removal of everything unclean, superfluous and confusing allows His light to shine forth in and through our lives.

Given this understanding of neatness, we can readily see why this word is defined to mean "orderliness," for it is the removal of everything disorderly. Disorder can only be removed through the positive establishment of order. When perfect order is established, all disorder is removed. The word *order* in turn derives from the same Indo-European root as the word *art*. It means "to *fit* together," as in contrast to either an anarchical disorder or a coercive order that *forces* together. Originally, the word *order* began its long and varied life by being used to designate a row of threads on a loom. From the same root of *art* and *order*, the Greek word *harmos*, comes the carpenter's word for *joinery* and also the word for *harmony*. So the concept of order, and thus also of neatness, can presumably take on the connotations of an art; and a life characterized by neatness and order can become like a beautifully designed cabinet made by the carpenter's craft of joinery, an intricate tapestry created through the weaver's craft of warping and wefting, an inspiring symphony produced by the composer's craft of harmonics in music. In other words, not only the product of the craftsman but also the context in which he or she works can express that harmonious song that Jesus came to sing through the lives of His people.

If all this seems to exaggerate the importance of neatness and order, recall the scene of the most significant miracle in the history of the universe. When Peter and John entered the empty tomb, they saw that after conquering death, sin, hell and satan by rising from the dead, Jesus had stopped to neatly fold His grave cloth (John 20:6-7). After winning the greatest triumph in the history of the world, He stopped to make a piece of cloth neat and orderly, then inspired John to record this.

To erase any ambiguity concerning the central part that order should play in our lives, Paul admonished the Corinthians, "*All things* must be done decently and *in order.*" Central to the kingdom that Jesus came to bring, as the angelic announcement to the shepherds made explicit, was the bringing of peace, not like that which the world brings (Luke 1:79; 2:13-14; John 14:27; 16:33; Rom. 10:15). Indeed, the kingdom of God *is* peace, together with joy and love in the Holy Spirit (Rom. 14:17). Yet this peace comes only with order and through order, when we come under the rule of the King (Isa. 9:7). Thus Isaiah prophesied of Jesus that "of the increase of His *government* and *peace* there will be no end, upon the throne of David and over His kingdom, *to order it* and establish it with judgment and justice" (Isa. 9:7).

From the beginning of creation God has been bringing form and order out of chaos. God could obviously have begun creation with perfect form and order rather than an initial chaos, without order and form. Yet He chose instead by His Word and the moving of His Spirit to bring forth all of the world order from an initial chaos through a process of demarcation, distinction and separation—of ordering. The light was separated from darkness, the dry land from the waters and so on. He then set in order day and night, the stars, the seasons, the planets and creatures of land and sea.

At the culmination of this creation, God made man and woman. Humanity, made in the image of God, was brought forth to bring this ordering process to completion—this is why man was given dominion and rule (Gen. 1:26-30). All of God's work had been perfect, but He purposefully left a work for human beings to do. Through participation in the completion of this work of ordering, man and woman would participate in the completion of the expression of God's love and peace, both in creation and in their own lives.

But this process could fulfill God's purpose only if man and woman moved forward in perfect submission to God. Through His work of creation, God established not only that He is sovereign but the nature of His sovereignty—the *Author* is the *authority*. But, to repeat, His is a uniquely noncoercive authority that is exercised through and expresses love. All creation is responsible to God, subject to the self-sacrificing love that *is* God (1 John 4:8, 16). Thus everything is dependent upon God and His love. He is the *Father*, the origin, of all things. Everett Fox notes that the Genesis account of creation stresses "the principle of order," which God brings forth.[36] This natural order comes to completion only with the creation of "humanity," made "in the divine 'image.'"[37] God sets up a definitive social order based upon the fatherhood principle, which expresses His own noncoercive and relational authority and control over life, including the life of humanity.

Just as there is an order between humanity and the rest of creation, over which people are given conservatory dominion to express the sovereignty of the God who is life and love, so is there an order within the human family and community. As the apostle Paul declared, God's is the "fatherhood from whom the whole fatherhood in heaven and earth is named" (Eph. 3:15). The family constitutes the basic unit of that order in the human sphere. The Bible opens with a description of a family (Gen. 1:26-28; 2:18-25), and the Old Testament closes with the need for the hearts of fathers and children to turn to one another (Mal. 4:5-6). Then the New Testament opens with family genealogies and the birth of Messiah, the incarnation of God, into a family (Matt. 1:1-25; Luke 2:1-7). It ends with a description of the familial motif of the church as a bride and Christ as a groom (Rev. 21:1-2, 9-11; 22:17). The whole order of creation is to be realized in the kingdom of God, the noncompulsory familial kingdom ruled by the authority of redemptive love. Entrance into this kingdom is by birth of sons, who, when born of the Father's Spirit, "cry out, 'Abba, Father'" (Rom. 8:14-17; Gal. 4:4-7).

Human beings did not, of course, submit to this ordering process through all of creation and society under the dominion of God. Instead, they chose a path that would exalt themselves as gods as they usurped that dominion. But Jesus Christ, through His atoning blood, has made the way for us to die to the fallen root of rebellion and disorder in our lives and enter, by His grace, into the new, redeemed order of His kingdom. In this context, He establishes the God-designed order of human relationships that have been ruptured and fractured by human rebellion.

By entering into and submitting to the order of God's community of faith, which is the kingdom designed for our perfection, we can be conformed by His Spirit to His glorious image as we bring our lives into submission to His vivifying pattern of human relationships. So He has ordained definite relations for His people in every sphere of their lives: for example, that parents should exercise the rule of loving care over their children (1 Tim. 3:4, 12); that husbands should love and care for and exercise a self-sacrificing authority over their wives (Eph. 5:25-33; 1 Pet. 3:7; Col. 3:19); that wives should willingly submit to and serve their husbands (Eph. 5:22-24; Col. 3:18; Titus 2:4-5; 1 Pet. 3:1-6); that members bearing responsibility and authority should function as leaders in the community of believers;* that the people of God should submit

---

* Eph. 4:11-12; 1 Cor. 12:28; 1 Tim. 3:1-13; Rom. 12:4-8; Heb. 13:7, 17; 1 Pet. 5:5, Ampl.

to and serve one another in accord with the design of God for human relationships (Eph. 6:1-4; Heb. 13:17; Eph. 5:21). He has established a definite relationship between citizens and their governments (Acts 5:29; Rom. 13:1-7; 1 Pet. 2:13-14), between workers and employers (Eph. 6:5-9; 1 Pet. 2:18) and so on. By finding our place in His Body, by entering into our God-given functions and our God-ordained relationships with others in Christ, and by submitting appropriately to the laws of the surrounding kingdom as well, each of us can reflect a facet of that love that comes "from above." Only as we conform ourselves to that order pulsating with God's life, flowing from God's own noncoercive authority "from above," can we see God's animated patterns necessary for relating both to Him and to others in a way that sustains life. And thus do we receive the knowledge of God that brings salvation, that is, that brings oneness with God (John 17:3).

So we can see how God's arrangement for fitting together the members of the Body—how the pattern of God-ordered relationships—constitutes the channel, the vehicle, through which the love of God flows from the Head to every member. Therefore, a believer may have the *experience* of covenant love, and he may even make the *vows* of covenant commitment (as in marriage, or in what Peter called "the pledge" of baptism that constitutes our spiritual marriage to the suffering Servant). Yet unless that commitment is also to and within the living *patterns* of covenant relationship, true covenant love cannot be fully sustained. I say this because only the proper *form* can hold the content and keep that content from dissipating.*
Thus do Spirit and Truth interlock as one (John 4:23-24; 14:17; 16:13).

In other words, the gospel that Paul said is the death, burial and resurrection of Jesus (1 Cor. 15:1-4) (corresponding to repentance, water baptism and the birth of the Spirit) is, again, not a door hung in the emptiness of space—it rather constitutes the barest *entrance* into a kingdom. It is not a one-dimensional wall, but a gateway into a well-developed and intricate order of relationships and life, both of which constitute the kingdom behind the entrance. That kingdom is where the King of love rules in every sphere of life. Thus Jesus called the gospel "the gospel *of the kingdom*" (Matt. 4:23; 9:35; 24:14). It is the "*good* news" because, if we obey and enter the reality of it, we can make an exodus from all the lapsed kingdoms of this world and be "born again" into the kingdom "fitly framed together" by God in Christ (John 3:3, 5; Eph. 4:11-16). The new birth is the entryway into a new realm where Jesus brings maturity to those who have bowed their selfish nature before the rule of the King in the kingdom of love. Thus does He increasingly manifest His lordship, His kingship, over their lives, by bringing them into conformity to His own image (Rom. 8:29;

---

* See *Loved into Loving.*

2 Cor. 3:18). This image comes to us through the unfolding revelation of the knowledge of God that is our salvation (John 17:1-3).

So all of life, animate and inanimate, originally reflected God's created order that truly was "so good, so good." But with the Fall, man and woman introduced death and disorder (and what is death but the breakdown of the order of life?). The fallen human nature now even threatens a final disorder and cataclysmic chaos through his ability to split apart the most foundational order of creation—atomic structure. Through destruction brought about by eroding, and ultimately even destroying, the patterns of family and covenant community, fallen humanity has unleashed social chaos in the vain attempt to establish an autonomy based on each individual's effort to re-create himself in his own self-ordained image. Yet God still hovers over and moves into the chaos of fractured human lives and dismembered relationships by the same Spirit of love and power that first created us. This redemptive love wants to restore us to the order of the fatherhood that would conform us to God's image as, at the beginning, He re-creates our redeemed lives through the process of demarcation, distinction and separation from the forces of chaos and dissolution found in the world, reordering our hearts, minds and lives within His kingdom. His call to us is to "come out of her and be *separate*"* by entering into His alternative kingdom of love, a kingdom of "His government and peace" set in place "to order and establish" us in His loving fatherhood, which shall know no end.

God wants to clear our lives from the superfluities and confusions of the world so that we can shine brightly both individually and as members of a corporate order, a city set on a hill that cannot be hid. He wants neatness and orderliness in this sense to pervade our lives and relationships, as Paul said, in "all things." Our hearts and minds, our relationships, our work, our play, our workshops, offices, homes and bedrooms, can all become expressions of the God who defeated all the forces of evil in the universe, but then stopped to neatly fold His burial cloth before stepping forth to the light of a new day for all creation.

> Then Simon Peter, who was behind him, arrived and went into the tomb. He saw the strips of linen lying there, as well as the burial cloth that had been around Jesus' head. *The cloth was folded up by itself*, separate from the linen. (John 20:6-7)
>
> *The steps of a good man are ordered by Yahweh*, and He delights in his way. (Ps. 37:23)
>
> So God led the people around by way of the wilderness of the Red Sea. And the children of Israel went up *in orderly ranks* out of the land of Egypt. (Exod. 13:18)

---

* 2 Cor. 6:14-18; Rev. 18:4-5; 1 John 2:15-17; James 4:4; 1 John 5:19.

Although my house is not so with God, yet He has made with me an everlasting covenant, *ordered in all things and secure. For this is all my salvation* and all my desire; will He not make it increase? (2 Sam. 23:5)

Whoever offers praise glorifies Me; and *to him who orders his conduct aright I will show the salvation of God.* (Ps. 50:23)

In those days Hezekiah was sick and near death. And Isaiah the prophet, the son of Amoz, went to him and said to him, "Thus says Yahweh: '*Set your house in order*, for you shall die, and not live.'" (2 Kings 20:1)

He said to them, "You are the heads of the fathers' houses of the Levites; sanctify yourselves, you and your brethren, that you may bring up the ark of Yahweh God of Israel to the place I have prepared for it. For because you did not do it the first time, Yahweh our God broke out against us, because *we did not consult Him about the proper order.*" (1 Chron. 15:12-13)

Now all the work of Solomon was *well-ordered* from the day of the foundation of the house of Yahweh until it was finished. So the house of Yahweh was completed. (2 Chron. 8:16)

A land as dark as darkness itself, *as the shadow of death, without any order*, where even the light is like darkness. (Job 10:22)

If you can answer me, *set your words in order before me*; take your stand. (Job 33:5)

When a country is rebellious, it has many rulers, but *a man of understanding and knowledge maintains order.* (Prov. 28:2, NIV)

And moreover, because the Preacher was wise, he still taught the people knowledge; yes, *he pondered and sought out and set in order many proverbs.* (Eccles. 12:9)

Of the increase of His government and peace there will be no end, upon the throne of David and over His kingdom, *to order it and establish it* with judgment and justice from that time forward, even forever. The *zeal of the Lord of hosts will perform this.* (Isa. 9:7)

When an unclean spirit goes out of a man, he goes through dry places, seeking rest, and finds none. Then he says, "I will return to my house from which I came." And when he comes, he finds it empty, swept, *and put in order.* (Matt. 12:43-44)

Inasmuch as many have taken in hand *to set in order a narrative* of those things which have been fulfilled among us, just as those who from the beginning were eyewitnesses and ministers of the word delivered them to us, it seemed good to me also, having had perfect understanding of all things from the very first, to write to you *an orderly account*, most excellent Theophilus. (Luke 1:1-3)

Take them and be purified with them, and pay their expenses so that they may shave their heads, and that all may know that those things of which they were informed concerning you are nothing, but *that you yourself also walk orderly and keep the law.* (Acts 21:24)

Let all things be done decently and in order. (1 Cor. 14:40)

But *each one in his own order*: Christ the firstfruits, afterward those who are Christ's at His coming. (1 Cor. 15:23)

For though I am absent in the flesh, yet I am with you in spirit, *rejoicing to see your good order and the steadfastness of your faith in Christ.* (Col. 2:5)

For this reason I left you in Crete, *that you should set in order the things that are lacking, and appoint elders in every city as I commanded you.* (Titus 1:5)

Therefore, if perfection were through the Levitical priesthood (for under it the people received the law), what further need was there that another priest should rise according to *the order of Melchizedek,* and not be called according to *the order of Aaron?* (Heb. 7:11)

When the queen of Sheba perceived all the wisdom of Solomon, the house that he had built, the food of his table, the way his servants were arranged, the attendance of his waiters and their attire, his cupbearers, his ascent by which he went up to the house of Yahweh, she was overwhelmed. (1 Kings 10:4-5, NASV, NIV, Ampl., Moffat)

Make this tabernacle and all its furnishings *exactly like the pattern I will show you.* (Exod. 25:9)

2. Irresponsibility, Unfaithfulness, Halfheartedness, Procrastination

To work responsibly, then, "as unto the Lord," means submitting to God in our hearts and readily responding to His authority, both as expressed to us directly by His Spirit and through the divine order of His Body. If we refuse to respond to the Lord and to submit to Him with all our hearts, then only perpetual irresponsibility and inconsistency in obeying Him can result. And to serve inconsistently is to serve unfaithfully. In other words, we serve God with a double mind and halfheartedness. Our thoughts are distracted; our desire wavers in serving and pleasing God. Our thoughts wander from the reality of God's purpose to the fantasies of our own or other minds.

If honor and reverence of the Lord do not make us responsive to Him and keep us on the path of wisdom, we will become passive and lazy, content to halfheartedly do half a job, always procrastinating and putting off every task.

a. Passivity

Passivity represents a failure to participate, to consent to the rightness of God's requirements by our active participation in the vision and purpose of God. A passive person refuses to pour himself into God's purpose. He may not be physically lazy, but neither is he consumed with a godly zeal that glorifies a great God. He refuses to serve God with all his heart, soul, mind and strength. Instead, he hangs back from full involvement and participation, keeping at least part of himself for himself. He refuses to give himself enough to God to even find the energy to either understand why he should or to commit himself completely and unreservedly to a course of action that might not have arisen from his own impulses toward self-centered pleasure or greed.

> In the spring, *at the time when kings go off to war*, David sent Joab out with the king's men and the whole Israelite army. They destroyed the Ammonites and besieged Rabbah. But *David tarried in Jerusalem.* (2 Sam. 11:1)

> Woe to you who are *complacent* in Zion, and to you who feel secure on Mount Samaria, you notable men of the foremost nation, to whom the people of Israel come! (Amos 6:1)

> Elisha said, "Get a bow and some arrows," and he did so. "Take the bow in your hands," he said to the king of Israel. When he had taken it, Elisha put his hands on the king's hands.
> "Open the east window," he said, and he opened it. "Shoot!" Elisha said, and he shot. "Yahweh's arrow of victory, the arrow of victory over Aram!" Elisha declared. "You will completely destroy the Arameans at Aphek."
> Then he said, "Take the arrows," and the king took them. Elisha told him, "Strike the ground." *He struck it three times and stopped. The man of God was angry with him and said, "You should have struck the ground five or six times; then you would have defeated Aram and completely destroyed it. But now you will defeat it only three times."* (2 Kings 13:15-19)

b. Laziness

A passive attitude will ultimately express itself in the child's failure to work diligently. He will instead put off every task. Then laziness will immediately appear in the child's sloppy work habits, his failure to work the *way* he should, his lackadaisical attitude and other related character flaws. The Greek word *ataktos*, translated "idle," literally means, according to Rienecker, "to be out of rank, to be out of order, to be disorderly, to be idle, to be a loafer." The lazy child resembles the soldier who refuses to hold his position in the ranks. He not only fails to do his own tasks in the larger interrelated functions of the family but also throws others out of step in doing theirs. He becomes a breach inviting "enemy" penetration into the "ranks" of the family and community, and therewith brings defeat. The lazy child doesn't see the day of small things in fulfilling God's purpose as worth the effort. So self-centered is he that he assumes God owes *him* something, never realizing both his obligation and privilege in giving all to be even the smallest part of God's great vision and purpose. The lazy child cannot work "as unto the Lord" because the love and vision of God don't motivate him. Only what pleases his own flesh can serve to motivate him. His parents never imparted to him the vision of something greater than himself; or, if they did, his own self-importance somewhere along the way trumped it.

> For who has despised the day of *small things*? (Zech. 4:10)

> The next section was repaired by the men of Tekoa, but their nobles *would not put their shoulders to the work* under their supervisors. (Neh. 3:5)

> If a man is *lazy*, the rafters sag; if his hands are *idle*, the house leaks. (Eccles. 10:18)

> The *lazy man* does not roast his game, but the diligent man prizes his possessions. (Prov. 12:27)

> *Lazy hands* make a man poor. (Prov. 10:4)

> The sluggard's craving will be the death of him, because *his hands refuse to work*. (Prov. 21:25)

> As a door turns on its hinges, so a *sluggard* turns on his bed. The *sluggard* buries his hand in the dish; he is *too lazy* to bring it back to his mouth. The sluggard is wiser in his own eyes than seven men who answer discreetly. (Prov. 26:14-16)

> *Laziness* brings on deep sleep, and the *shiftless* man goes hungry. (Prov. 19:15)

> Diligent hands will rule, but *laziness* ends in slave labor. (Prov. 12:24)

> In the name of the Lord Jesus Christ, we command you, brothers, to keep away from every brother *who is idle* and does not live according to the teaching you received from us. For you yourselves know how you ought to follow our example. *We were not idle* when we were with you, nor did we eat anyone's food without paying for it. On the contrary, *we worked night and day, laboring and toiling so that we would not be a burden to any of you*. We did this, not because we do not have the right to such help, but in order to make ourselves *a model for you to follow*. For even when we were with you, we gave you this rule: "If *a man will not work, he shall not eat*." We hear that some among you are *idle*. They are *not busy*; they are busybodies. Such people we command and urge in the Lord Jesus Christ to *settle down and earn the bread they eat*. (2 Thess. 3:6-12)

> *Not slothful* in diligence; fervent in spirit; serving the Lord . . . .
> (Rom. 12:11, NIV, KJV)

Laziness often prompts us to "just get by." The lazy child will try to gauge how much he can get away with, pinching out the most minute measures of his time and labor, trying to sink as far below God's standard as he can without being called to account. He might know how to perfectly complete a job his mother or father requires, but his parents are temporarily absent, and the baby sitter or second in authority doesn't seem so hard to please if he's just nice and respectful to them, helping them in ways that require little responsibility or work from him. So he'll just cut a few corners. No one will ever see it anyway. Such a child never "works as unto the Lord" but deliberately or mindlessly ignores the Lord in hopes that he can get by or even deceive others.

> Then another servant came and said, "Sir, here is your mina (talent); I have kept it laid away in a piece of cloth. I was afraid of you, because you are a hard man. You take out what you did not put in and reap what you did not sow."
> His master replied, "I will judge you by your own words, you wicked servant! You knew, did you, that I am a hard man, taking out what I did not put in, and reaping what I did not sow? Why then didn't you put my money on deposit, so that when I came back, I could have collected it with interest?"
> Then he said to those standing by, "Take his mina away from him and give it to the one who has ten minas." (Luke 19:20-24)

> Jesus told His disciples: "There was a rich man whose manager was accused of wasting his possessions. So he called him in and asked him, 'What is this I hear about you? Give an account of your management, because you cannot be manager any longer.'
> "The manager said to himself, 'What shall I do now? My master is taking away my job. I'm not strong enough to dig, and I'm ashamed to beg—I know what I'll do so that, when I lose my job here, people will welcome me into their houses.'
> "So he called in each one of his master's debtors. He asked the first, 'How much do you owe my master?'
> "'Eight hundred gallons of olive oil,' he replied.
> "The manager told him, 'Take your bill, sit down quickly, and make it four hundred.'
> "Then he asked the second, 'And how much do you owe?'
> "'A thousand bushels of wheat,' he replied.
> "He told him, 'Take your bill and make it eight hundred.'
> "The master commended the dishonest manager because he had *acted shrewdly*. For the people of this world are more *shrewd* in dealing with their own kind than are the people of the light. I tell you, use worldly wealth to gain friends for yourselves, so that when it is gone, you will be welcomed into eternal dwellings.
> "Whoever can be trusted with very little can also be trusted with much, and whoever is dishonest with very little will also be dishonest with much. So if you have not been trustworthy in

handling worldly wealth, who will trust you with true riches? And if you have not been trustworthy with someone else's property, who will give you property of your own?

"*No servant can serve two masters.* Either he will hate the one and love the other, or he will be devoted to the one and despise the other. *You cannot serve both God and money.*" The Pharisees, who loved money, heard all this and were sneering at Jesus. (Luke 16:1-14)

To repeat, our work "as unto the Lord" is our worship; so we must do it with reverence. But the word *worship* is rooted in the word *worthy*; so we must also see how *worthy* God is of our best labors, that He is our *worthship*, worthy of our worship. One major translation of the word *tamim* is "unblemished." Work that isn't wholehearted and unblemished before the Lord is a faulty and blemished sacrifice (Mal. 1:6-8). The lazy child, offering a faulty sacrifice, declares God unworthy and therefore shows contempt for God. He instead ignores God's honor and worthship and attempts to make a lesser sacrifice that will merely appease certain people while hurting those he's called to serve, by just "getting by."

c. Doing Half a Job

The lazy child therefore does everything incompletely. He stops work whenever his prompters are absent, or whenever the work begins to even slightly tire or bore him, or if he might have to stretch himself somewhat and work a little harder than accustomed to. He leaves his work undone because nothing seems of greater worth than his own interests, comfort or convenience. Therefore he is unwilling to pay the price needed to complete any task that might discomfort or inconvenience him. He believes his half-finished job should satisfy anyone who sees just how important he really is, how much he has been put out by the little he does (which he thinks is a great deal, since he has no measure beyond himself). So he believes that anyone who "really loves him" will see that his failure must obviously result from circumstances beyond his control or abilities, from the unfair or excessive demands of some "harsh master" who doesn't see that the child is too important to be pressed in this way. It never seems to occur to him that he should ever stretch himself to grow into an image greater than what he now is. He always has the highest possible view of whatever he sees himself as right now; and so he also has an excellent and ready excuse for his incomplete work, or so he imagines. He does not recognize for what it truly is his own self-centered unwillingness to invest the necessary effort and energy for a cause greater than himself. It's too petty for him to be so much concerned with what should cause him to lay down his life.

So the lazy child's work will never bring glory to God. Instead, he becomes a sloth and sluggard, working, if at all, at his own convenience without the slightest consciousness of God's times and seasons.

> But Manasseh did not drive out the people of Beth Shan or Taanach or Dor or Ibleam or Megiddo and their surrounding settlements, for the Canaanites were determined to live in that land. When Israel became strong, they pressed the Canaanites into forced labor but *never* drove them out *completely*. Nor did Ephraim drive out the Canaanites living in Gezer, but the Canaanites continued to live there among them. Neither did Zebulun drive out the Canaanites living in Kitron or Nahalol, who remained among them; but they did subject them to forced labor. Nor did Asher drive out those living in Acco or Sidon or Ahlab or Aczib or Helbah or Aphek or Rehob, and because of this the people of Asher lived among the Canaanite inhabitants of the land. Neither did Naphtali drive out those living in Beth Shemesh or Beth Anath; but the Naphtalites too lived among the Canaanite inhabitants of the land, and those living in Beth Shemesh and Beth Anath became forced laborers for them. The Amorites confined the Danites to the hill country, not allowing them to come down into the plain. And the Amorites were determined also to hold out in Mount Heres, Aijalon and Shaalbim, but when the power of the house of Joseph increased, they too were pressed into forced labor. The boundary of the Amorites was from Scorpion Pass to Sela and beyond. (Judg. 1:27-36)

> Suppose one of you wants to build a tower. Will he not first sit down and estimate the cost to see if he has enough money to complete it? For if he lays the foundation and is not able to finish it, everyone who sees it will ridicule him, saying, "This fellow began to build and was not able to finish." (Luke 14:28-30)

> Yahweh said to Jehu, "Because you have done well in accomplishing what is right in My eyes and have done to the house of Ahab all I had in mind to do, your descendants will sit on the throne of Israel to the fourth generation." Yet Jehu was *not careful to keep the law of Yahweh*, the God of Israel, *with all his heart*. He did not turn away from the sins of Jeroboam, which he had caused Israel to commit. (2 Kings 10:30-31)

> He did what was right in the eyes of Yahweh, just as his father Uzziah had done. The high places, however, were not removed; the people continued to offer sacrifices and burn incense there. Jotham rebuilt the Upper Gate of the temple of Yahweh. (2 Kings 15:34-35)

> "A son honors his father, and a servant his master. If I am a father, where is the honor due Me? If I am a master, where is the respect due Me?" says Yahweh Almighty. "It is you, O priests, who despise My name.
> "But you ask, 'How have we despised Your name?' You place defiled food on My altar.
> "But you ask, '*How have we defiled You?*'
> "*By saying that Yahweh's table is contemptible. When you bring blind animals for sacrifice, is that not wrong? When you sacrifice crippled*

or diseased animals, is that not wrong? Try offering them to your governor! Would he be pleased with you? Would he accept you?" says Yahweh Almighty. (Mal. 1:6-8, NIV, KJV)

A curse on him who is lax in doing Yahweh's work! A curse on him who keeps his sword from bloodshed! (Jer. 48:10)

He who is *slothful in his work* is a brother to him who is a great destroyer. (Prov. 18:9)

d. Sluggish and Slothful

The sluggish and slothful child crawls along at a snail's pace and must be constantly prodded every step along the way, which he then deeply resents. He lacks all necessary inward incentive, all relationship with God that would inspire him beyond his own self-centered motives and selfish ambitions. The Hebrew word for "sluggard," *atsel*, comes from the verb meaning to "be slothful" or "to lean idly." He cannot himself stand on the Rock but must be supported by already overburdened others who will fill in for him by doing his work as well as their own. He lacks initiative to press ahead in any task that doesn't exalt or please his selfish nature, yet he remains blissfully unconscious of the workings of that nature. So he refuses to pour himself out to move forward in God's empowering grace because such grace will never empower the self-exaltation of the flesh that such a child seeks. So he misses the grace of God and thus fails to participate in God's glory. He always holds himself in reserve, evading both responsibility and accountability, saving his energy and strength for a day that never comes. So all his reserves of energy and strength usually merely atrophy and dissipate in the self-serving life of a spiritual couch potato. This must be the case, since strength grows through exercise and resistance, and the sluggard refuses to expend the effort needed for either. So not only does he fail to accomplish what he should, but he also personally suffers as well. In 1 Peter 4:18, NKJV, the Scripture says, "If the righteous one is scarcely saved, where will the ungodly and the sinner appear?" This suggests that the godly are saved only with the greatest expenditure of sacrifice and just in the nick of time, without a moment to spare and no reserves left over. The word translated as "scarcely" is *molis*, which combined with *ischuo* is translated "had much work." Thus we must expend ourselves completely to completely enter God's work—*we* must "*labor* to enter *His* rest" (Heb. 4:9-11, KJV). So, obviously, *everything* will be required of us in order to find salvation in God's time, which is the *only* time we have.

This doesn't mean that our works *save* us; as Paul says, "It is *by grace* you have been saved, through faith—and this not from yourselves, it is the gift of God—*not by works*, so that no one can boast" (Eph. 2:8-9). But Paul then immediately in the next verse goes on to say, "For we are

God's *workmanship*, created in Christ Jesus *to do good works*, which *God prepared in advance for us to do*." We aren't saved by the dead works of the flesh, which God commands us to renounce and repent from (Heb. 6:1, NKJV), but when God's Spirit fills us, He works in us "both to will and *to work* for His good pleasure" (Phil. 2:13, NASV). Paul says that God's "*grace* to me was not without effect. No, *I worked harder* than all of [the apostles]—yet not I, but *the grace of God working in me*" (1 Cor. 15:10, NKJV, LB). Paul plainly implies here that if he had not "worked"—even worked *hard*—God's grace would have been without effect. So Paul's work proved that God's saving grace was at work within him. James makes this connection between works, grace and saving faith even clearer when he asks,

> What use is it, my brethren, if a man says he has faith, but he has no works? Can that faith save him? (James 2:14, NASV)

James makes unmistakably clear that the answer is *no*—a faith that does not produce the works of God (again, as contrasted to the works of the flesh) can*not* save us. If faith "has no works," James explains, it "is dead" (James 2:17, NASV), "useless" (James 2:20, NASV). He goes on to declare that Abraham's faith worked with "his works," as in the offering of Isaac, and that "as a result of the works, faith was perfected" (James 2:21-22, NASV). So "a man is *justified by works*, and not by faith alone": "Just as the body without the spirit is dead, so also *faith without works is dead*" (James 2:24, 26, NASV). Just as the grace working within us to bring our salvation produces the fruit of the Spirit spoken of in Galatians 5:22-23, so it also brings forth the works "God prepared in advance for us to do." If the works of the Spirit do not come forth, if we resist yielding ourselves to the hard work God calls us to perform for His purpose, then we resist the Spirit and grace of God that works to bring us into our salvation.

Jesus told the disciples that His "food" was "to do the will of Him who sent Me and to *finish His work*" (John 4:34), and at the cross He declared, "It is finished" and "bowed His head and gave up His spirit" (John 19:30). John correspondingly declared that if we "claim to live in Him," we "must walk as Jesus did," which means that we, too, must complete the works He has ordained for us. Paul likewise wrote to Archippus in Colossians, "See to it that you *complete the work* you have received in the Lord" (Col. 4:17). So the Lord admonishes us to press forward and complete His work. To fail to work hard, to be sluggish and slothful, is to miss God's time and purpose and thus the very purpose of our life.

The sluggish and slothful child has no conception of working in God's time, since it demands diligence and perseverance. Scripture often pictures the sluggish and slothful as unwilling to keep pace with the times and seasons ordained by God. Therefore the sluggard misses out on the blessings that accompany working in God and thus in God's time.

> Then He told this parable: "A man had a fig tree, planted in his vineyard, and he went to look for fruit on it, but did not find any. So he said to the man who took care of the vineyard, 'For three years now I've been coming to look for fruit on this fig tree and haven't found any. Cut it down! Why should it use up the soil?' 'Sir,' the man replied, 'leave it alone for one more year, and I'll dig around it and fertilize it. If it bears fruit next year, fine! If not, then cut it down.'" (Luke 13:6-9)

The tree has a set time to bear its fruit; if it fails to do it, the husbandman destroys it (Matt. 21:19).

> Do you not say, "Four months more and then the harvest"? I tell you, open your eyes and look at the fields! They are ripe for harvest. (John 4:35)

The time to labor is now. Sluggishness and sloth keep us from working in God's time and so cause us to miss the harvest.

> *A sluggard does not plow in season*; so at harvest time he looks but finds nothing. (Prov. 20:4)

> I went past the *field of the sluggard*, past the vineyard of the *man who lacks judgment*; *thorns had come up everywhere*, the ground was *covered with weeds*, and *the stone wall was in ruins*. I applied my heart to what I observed and learned a lesson from what I saw: A little sleep, a little slumber, a little folding of the hands to rest— and poverty will come on you like a bandit and scarcity like an armed man. (Prov. 24:30-34)

> One who is *slack in his work* is brother to one who destroys. (Prov. 18:9)

> The way of the *sluggard* is blocked with thorns. (Prov. 15:19)

> Go to the ant, you *sluggard*; consider its ways and be wise! It has no commander, no overseer or ruler, yet it stores its provisions in summer and gathers its food at harvest. (Prov. 6:6-8)

> How long will you lie there, you *sluggard*? When will you get up from your sleep? (Prov. 6:9)

> As vinegar to the teeth and smoke to the eyes, so is a *sluggard* to those who send him. (Prov. 10:26)

> The appetite of the *sluggard* craves and gets nothing. (Prov. 13:4, Ampl.)

> But *he who sleeps during harvest* is a disgraceful son. (Prov. 10:5)

> *Do not love sleep* or you will grow poor; stay awake and you will have food to spare. (Prov. 20:13)

e. Sloppy

Sloppy work signals an unwillingness to offer an acceptable sacrifice to God. What we then do offer is slipshod because we don't pay the price that a truly worthy sacrifice demands. God and His purpose are simply not worth the time and effort to such people. They don't understand why those like David insisted on paying the full price for the sacrifice he made to God (2 Sam. 24:23-25). So they don't even put forth the effort to search the Word of God to find God's acceptable way to do something. They have contempt for God: anything—the most crippled and diseased lamb of the flock—will do for Him; just give Him whatever you yourself don't want or need, whether of time, effort, wealth or material things. As the selfish man said, "Oh, the blessing of giving—especially when it's something I don't want." The sloppy child similarly defiles whatever he places his hand to. This child's life is like the untuned strings on a musical instrument: when played, they only express disorder and dissonance because no care was taken to tune the strings to the proper pitch. Instead of the tension of the tuned string, such a child's life is marked by the laxness and sloppiness of the slug.

> "A son honors his father, and a servant his master. If I am a father, *where is the honor due Me*? If I am a master, *where is the respect due Me*?" says Yahweh Almighty. "It is you, O priests, *who show contempt* for My name.
> "But you ask, '*How have we shown contempt* for Your name?'
> "*You place defiled food on My altar.*
> "But you ask, 'How have we defiled You?'
> "By saying that Yahweh's table is contemptible. When *you bring blind animals for sacrifice*, is that not wrong? When *you sacrifice crippled or diseased animals*, is that not wrong? Try offering them to your governor! Would he be pleased with you? Would he accept you?" says Yahweh Almighty. (Mal. 1:6-8)

> He said to them, "You are the heads of the Levitical families; you and your fellow Levites are to consecrate yourselves and bring up the ark of Yahweh, the God of Israel, to the place I have prepared for it. It was because you, the Levites, *did not bring it up the first time* that Yahweh our God broke out in anger against us. We *did not inquire of Him about how to do it in the prescribed way*." (1 Chron. 15:12-13)

> Araunah said to David, "Let my lord the king take whatever pleases him and offer it up. Here are oxen for the burnt offering, and here are threshing sledges and ox yokes for the wood. O king, Araunah gives all this to the king." Araunah also said to him, "May Yahweh your God accept you."
> But the king replied to Araunah, "*No, I insist on paying you for it. I will not sacrifice to Yahweh my God burnt offerings that cost me nothing.*" (2 Sam. 24:22-24)

For *God is not a God of disorder* but of peace. (1 Cor. 14:33)

But everything should be *done in a fitting and orderly way*. (1 Cor. 14:40)

f. Absent-minded

An irresponsible child has not "girded up the loins" of his mind, pulling in tightly the loose ends of fantasy, daydreaming, vain imagination and laziness. Instead, he gives himself over completely to absent-mindedness and fantasy and daydreaming. In contrast to working with his whole being unto the Lord, a lazy child is easily distracted from the task at hand. He has no single-minded resolve to press through whatever God has assigned him to do. He doesn't fully concentrate, giving himself wholly to a task. Consequently he never experiences the joy of bringing anything important to completion. He ever remains unmindful of God's will and purpose. His thoughts wander from God's purpose into his own fantasies. His thoughts never come into captivity to the mind of Christ, but they stumble about haphazardly without direction or purpose, roaming around everywhere until they fall into some ambush of the arch-predator in some jungle or tangle of carnality, or some fetid slough of filth where his daydreaming curiosity at last brings him down.

> For the *waywardness* of the simple *will kill them*, and the *complacency of fools will destroy them*. (Prov. 1:32)
>
> He who works his land will have abundant food, but *he who chases fantasies* lacks judgment. (Prov. 12:11)
>
> He who works his land will have abundant food, but *the one who chases fantasies* will have his fill of poverty. (Prov. 28:19)
>
> Wherefore *gird up the loins of your mind, be sober*, and hope to the end for the grace that is to be brought unto you at the revelation of Jesus Christ. (1 Pet. 1:13, KJV)
>
> We demolish arguments and *every pretension* that sets itself up against the knowledge of God, and *we take captive every thought to make it obedient to Christ*. (2 Cor. 10:5)

E. Good Stewardship/ Bad Stewardship

1. Good Stewardship

The Greek word translated "stewardship" is *oikonomia*. From it we derive the English word *economy*. According to Arndt and Gingrich, this word also means "arrangement, order, plan." It refers literally to the ordering or law of a household or home. Good stewards arrange and order according to God's plan all that has been entrusted to them. Everyone in God's kingdom has been given some area of dominion and responsibility. So we must all work to conform that area to the perfect will of God. We must use all of the resources placed in our hands so that they, both each taken individually and all taken together, glorify God. These resources include our time. Good stewards won't waste time but will use it wisely for God's purpose. What needs doing is done at the right time, spending neither too much nor too little time on any job. A good steward doesn't squander time. Time is life—it's the course of *becoming* for fallen people that takes them into the *Being* of God and His eternal life; so to squander it is to squander life and risk falling short of our life's eternal purpose.

Therefore the good steward will use all of his resources to the best advantage. In a good steward's garden, all the vegetables will be planted in neat and orderly beds. Weeds will be few or none. The good steward will companion-plant his vegetables, with those that help and protect each other placed close together and those that hurt each other kept far apart. He will double-dig his vegetable beds for optimum use of space and soil nutrients. He will make the paths between the beds neat and orderly and compost the weeds and pulled-up garden plants in well-kept bins. All resources will be used for maximum advantage to maximum effect. This orderly arrangement of things used to their best advantage becomes a song of praise to the Creator of every good and perfect gift.

The good steward enjoys the blessing of doing work that glorifies God. He recognizes, not grudgingly but with joy and excitement, that what he has dominion over is not his own but has been entrusted to him by another to whom it belongs. So his stewardship entails participation in a purpose that draws him beyond the domain of personal ambitions, aims and goals. He's not trying to just make his fortune or a name for himself; so he escapes the vanity and meaninglessness of human labor (Eccles. 1:2-3). As good stewards, our children will be concerned to make sure that their Master's possessions are well cared for and used to His glory and according to His purpose.

a. Constructive and Productive

Everything the good steward puts his hands to contributes to the building up of the kingdom of God, to bringing forth fruit, to the increase of His kingdom rule of love. This includes proper use of resources. So the companion-planted garden of deep beds puts resources to the greatest productive use: the seeds planted in such a prepared soil will give the most, the biggest, the healthiest plants possible.

God has similarly called us to bear fruit that remains. As co-laborers with Him, we work with Him in the construction of His great spiritual temple, the corporate Body of Christ. A failure to labor productively with God means scattering abroad, working against His kingdom. Constructive work builds up, edifies God's kingdom. The Greek word for "edify," *oikodomeo*, literally means "to build a house." The servants of God's kingdom join together to build their corporate, eternal homes in the Body of Christ. Jesus said that in His house were many abodes and that He went before us to prepare places for each one of us (John 14:2). In short, He ascended to the place of headship over His now corporate Body and has given gifts unto men to prepare God's people until they become the full measure of Christ's own perfection in corporate form (Eph. 4:7-16). We must, then, join with Him in actually building up this spiritual temple of which we are the members, the "abodes."

We cannot be constructive and productive, however, if we labor as "mere men" (1 Cor. 3:3). In fact, to labor as mere men means inevitably harming and obstructing God's purpose, for lapsed human-centered knowledge by its very nature proves destructive (Matt. 16:21-23). We can only fulfill God's purpose by putting on the mind of Christ. How can we by our own power know the best and most productive way to use the resources that God gives us? Widely ranging alternatives always present themselves. To be truly constructive and productive, Scripture repeatedly shows that we must have God's wisdom, His perspective; He alone sees the total situation and so is alone competent to make the best choice among alternative possibilities in every situation. Therefore to be constructive and productive requires more than hard work; the work must come from the Spirit, following Jesus as He leads and guides us in the construction of His great building project.

Unless *Yahweh builds the house,* they labor in vain who build it;

unless Yahweh guards the city, the watchman stays awake in vain. (Ps. 127:1)

The wise woman *builds* her house. (Prov. 14:1)

By wisdom a house is built, and *through understanding* it is established; *through knowledge* its rooms are filled with rare and beautiful treasures. (Prov. 24:3-4)

According to the grace of God which was given to me, as *a wise master builder I laid a foundation,* and another is building upon it. But *let each man be careful how he builds upon it.* (1 Cor. 3:10, NASV)

Wisdom has built her house; she has hewn out its seven pillars. She has prepared her meat and mixed her wine; she has also set her table. (Prov. 9:1-2)

No one sews a patch of unshrunk cloth on an old garment, for the patch will pull away from the garment, making the tear worse. Neither do men pour new wine into old wineskins. If they do, the skins will burst, the wine will run out and the wineskins will be ruined. No, they pour new wine into new wineskins, and both are preserved. (Matt. 9:16-17)

Only God Himself can make us constructive and productive for His kingdom. Only His Spirit can propel us toward the edification of His Body, whether in natural gardening or spiritual gardening.

b. Conservation

To use to the best advantage all God has given us means not wasting these resources but conserving them. Adam was the first man to whom God gave stewardship. Adam was to "tend" the Garden of Eden. The Hebrew word translated "tend" is *shamar,* meaning literally "to preserve," "retain," "keep safe," "guard." God entrusted this task to Adam and his descendants.

Yahweh God took the man and put him in the Garden of Eden to work it and *take care* of it. (Gen. 2:15)

When they had all had enough to eat, He said to His disciples, "Gather the pieces that are left over. *Let nothing be wasted.*" (John 6:12)

During the seven years of abundance the land produced plentifully. Joseph collected all the food produced in those seven years of abundance in Egypt and stored it in the cities. In each city he put the food grown in the fields surrounding it. Joseph *stored up* huge quantities of grain, like the sand of the sea; it was so much that he stopped keeping records because it was beyond measure . . . .
   The seven years of abundance in Egypt came to an end, and the seven years of famine began, just as Joseph had said. There was famine in all the other lands, but in the whole land of Egypt there

was food. When all Egypt began to feel the famine, the people cried to Pharaoh for food. Then Pharaoh told all the Egyptians, "Go to Joseph and do what he tells you."

When the famine had spread over the whole country, Joseph opened the storehouses and sold grain to the Egyptians, for the famine was severe throughout Egypt. And all the countries came to Egypt to buy grain from Joseph, because the famine was severe in all the world. (Gen. 41:47-49, 53-57)

So he said to the man who took care of the vineyard, "For three years now I've been coming to look for fruit on this fig tree and haven't found any. Cut it down! Why should it use up the soil?"

"Sir," the man replied, "leave it alone for one more year, and I'll *dig around it and fertilize it*." (Luke 13:7-8)

c. Reliability

Good stewardship entails complete reliability.* One careless mistake can destroy all that was well-preserved and cared for over generations of good stewardship. A beautiful, productive forest, one that has stood for hundreds of years, can be destroyed overnight by one careless match. A book preserved for generations can be badly damaged by one thoughtless person in one careless moment. A good steward is always conscientious to be reliable in caring for and making the best use of what has been entrusted to him. He works as one who is accountable for everything with which he has been entrusted. He knows that, in the end, he will give an account to his Master for what he has done and how he has done it. Not only must he vigilantly care for the resources God has given him, but he must also always make his gifts and resources available where and when they are needed. One of the Hebrew words translated "reliable" is *yashar*, which, according to Brown, Driver and Briggs, literally means "straight, right . . . level." A truly reliable person will take consistent care to try to walk the straight and narrow way of the Spirit.

I put Shelemiah the priest, Zadok the scribe, and a Levite named Pedaiah in charge of the storerooms and made Hanan son of Zaccur, the son of Mattaniah, their assistant, because *these men were considered trustworthy*. They were made responsible for distributing the supplies to their brothers. (Neh. 13:13)

Now Daniel so distinguished himself among the administrators and the satraps by his exceptional qualities that the king planned to set him over the whole kingdom. At this, the administrators and the satraps tried to find grounds for charges against Daniel in his conduct of government affairs, but they were unable to do so. They could find no corruption in him, because he was *trustworthy and neither corrupt nor negligent*. (Dan. 6:3-4)

---

* See pp. 170-171.

Joseph found favor in his eyes and became his attendant. Potiphar put him in charge of his household, and he *entrusted to his care* everything he owned. From the time he put him in charge of his household and of all that he owned, Yahweh blessed the household of the Egyptian because of Joseph. The blessing of Yahweh was on everything Potiphar had, both in the house and in the field. So he left in Joseph's care everything he had; with Joseph in charge, he did not concern himself with anything except the food he ate . . . .

Yahweh was with him; He showed him kindness and granted him favor in the eyes of the prison warden. So *the warden put Joseph in charge* of all those held in the prison, and he was *made responsible* for all that was done there. The warden paid no attention to anything under Joseph's care, because Yahweh was with Joseph and gave him success in whatever he did. (Gen. 39:4-6, 21-23)

And the things you have heard me say in the presence of many witnesses entrust to *reliable men* who will also be qualified to teach others. (2 Tim. 2:2)

d. Faithfulness

In every situation and circumstance, a good steward must faithfully try to carry the burden to fulfill his entrusted responsibilities. Brown, Driver and Briggs state that the literal meaning of the Hebrew word *emunah*, which is translated "faithfulness," is "firmness, steadfastness, fidelity." Reliability and faithfulness closely correspond, the former emphasizing action, the latter emphasizing the condition of the heart. Someone truly faithful can be relied upon to care in the Spirit for his areas of responsibility, to bring them into conformity to God's patterns and purpose.

But there were not made for the house of Yahweh silver cups, snuffers, bowls, trumpets, any vessels of gold, or vessels of silver from the money which was brought into the house of Yahweh; for they gave that to those who did the work, and with it they repaired the house of Yahweh.

Moreover, they did not require an accounting from the men into whose hand they gave the money to pay to those who did the work, for they *dealt faithfully.* (2 Kings 12:13-15, NASV)

The man bowed down his head, and worshiped the Lord, and said, Blessed be Yahweh, the God of my master Abraham, Who has not left my master bereft and destitute of His lovingkindness and steadfastness. I being in the way [*of obedience and faith*] Yahweh led me to the house of my master's kinsmen. (Gen. 24:26-27, Ampl.)

The man who had received the five talents brought the other five. "Master," he said, "you entrusted me with five talents. See, I have gained five more."

His master replied, "Well done, *good and faithful servant!* You have been *faithful* with a few things; I will put you in charge of many things. Come and share your master's happiness!"

The man with the two talents also came. "Master," he said, "you entrusted me with two talents; see, I have gained two more."

His master replied, "Well done, *good and faithful servant!* You have been *faithful* with a few things; I will put you in charge of many things. Come and share your master's happiness!" (Matt. 25:20-23)

He who is *faithful* in a very little thing is *faithful* also in much; and he who is unrighteous in a very little thing is unrighteous also in much. (Luke 16:10, NASV)

2. Bad Stewardship

The bad steward fails to deal with the resources God entrusted him with in the order God has ordained. He wastes time, using it unwisely. He uses his time for his own projects and pleasures instead of for all that has been assigned him to do. His projects, then, often rest only on his own selfish ambitions merely disguised as "God's will" rather than God's will as revealed through the order of the Body "prepared to do His will." If he's not seeking to fulfill his own secret ambitions, then he's either spending too much time on a job because his heart has strayed elsewhere; or, for the same reason, he spends too little time to do it correctly; or else, for the same reason, he squanders his time rather than using it productively. His labors do not work together to fulfill God's purpose. Figuratively, the garden of the bad steward lies in ragged rows of shallow beds crowded with weeds. Different plants are thrown together haphazardly, with incompatibles often growing close together while mutually beneficial plants grow far apart. Disorder and disharmony reign, stultifying all growth. The turkeys die without water. The chickens cease to lay because of a filthy coop. Predators get in through the unrepaired coop, and chicks escape from it. It was just too much trouble to fix in a timely fashion. The bad steward's wasteful practices always lead to delays, missed opportunities and, at best, poor production, although the bad steward will often never appear busier than when he is most unfaithful.

Shebna was a steward in charge of the king's house (Isa. 22:15), but he "rose up" in presumption. He refused to keep his appointed place and, from there, to learn the lessons of kingdom submission to divine order and the rule of love. It didn't matter that he'd been given the highest position of authority in the palace, barring only the king's. Second highest was not enough for Shebna. He could never be fully persuaded of the legitimacy of any real authority over him because he always thought too highly of himself and at least subconsciously believed he held an underivative, undelegated position, an original and superior position, one having its source only in himself. He was therefore "presumptuous enough to be building himself a tomb among those of the mighty" (Isa. 22:15, Ampl.). He sought continuously to exalt and save his own place, his own life, his own reputation, rather than to lay it down in submission to a power transcendent to himself. So Isaiah the prophet brought a stark message from Yahweh to Shebna: "I will thrust you from your office, and from your station shall you be pulled down" (Isa. 22:19, Ampl.). Instead of finding self-exaltation, he lost his place, his whole privileged life.

The name Shebna means "growth" or "tender youth." He is the child who, though an heir, differs nothing from a slave, or from a "steward" (Gal. 4:1). So he remained a carnal child, consumed with his own selfish ambitions and desires instead of looking to his king's concerns. And, as a child who never matured enough to differ at all from a slave, he remained a slave without any permanent place in the family (John 8:35). He stood as the antithesis to Eliakim, the man God set in Shebna's place, who became a pillar of fatherhood in Israel.

Shebna typifies, then, ministries who refuse to decrease from their own infantile, small-minded, yet overblown and pathologically individualistic, view of their gifts and their kingdoms—all built on inflated notions of their own self-importance. They have no need whatsoever of decreasing so that Christ's corporate kingdom might increase (John 3:27-30). They therefore remain subject to still going "out of the temple." Yet the Eliakims, those who overcome their fallen and infantile natures to fulfill their call to sonship, will serve as "pegs" set "in a *firm* place," liable, reliable, bound in the eternal covenant.

The bad steward, then, doesn't appreciate the privilege of participating in a purpose transcendent to his own personal interests and individual ambitions. Perhaps, like Gehazi, he even resents the fact that the resources he has access to are not ultimately his own to be used to serve himself with all his covetousness and ambitions. But whether he holds resentment in his heart or not, he certainly lacks the vision to place his resources in God's service. Without God's vision ablaze in his heart, even the well-intentioned child will lack that godly wisdom that will make the best use of his resources according to God's purpose; and he lacks such a vision because he won't *fully* submit to the parents (whether natural or spiritual) to whom God has given divine super*vision* over his life. Instead, he's got his own ideas and agenda about what's best and what needs to be done. Because such a child lacks God's wisdom, he will therefore always waste or even destroy, for he who is not busy gathering is busy scattering abroad (Luke 11:23). If he doesn't see the best way to use God's resources, including his own time, it's only because, rather than seeking the mind of God to know how to use them, he merely uses things as he sees fit, usually according to his own conceits and rationalizations. This has been true even of gifted ministers in the church. Ultimately, the bad steward cares little more than a hoot about God's purpose or vision but cares a great deal about himself. He sees the importance of neither the big nor the little matters in God's kingdom. Unseeing, uncaring, unthinking, disrespectful, he squanders and dissipates God's resources, including his own gifts and even his own life.

> Come, go to this [contemptible] *steward* and treasurer, to Shebna, who is over the house [but who *is presumptuous enough to be building himself a tomb among those of the mighty, a tomb worthy of a king*], and say to him, What business have you here? And whom have you entombed here, that you have the right to hew out *for yourself* a tomb here? He hews out a sepulcher *for himself on the height!* He carves out a dwelling *for himself* in the rock! Behold, the Lord will hurl you away violently, O you strong man; yes, He will take tight hold of you and He will surely cover you [with shame]. He will surely roll you up in a bundle [Shebna] and toss you like a ball into a large country; there you will die and there will be your splendid chariots, *you disgrace* to *your master's house!* And *I will thrust you from your office*, and *from your station will you be pulled down.* And in that day I will call My servant, Eliakim son of Hilkiah. And I will clothe him with your robe and will bind your girdle on him and will commit your authority to his hand; he shall be a father to the inhabitants of Jerusalem and to the house of Judah. And the key of the house of David I will lay upon his shoulder; he shall open and no one shall shut, he shall shut and no one shall open. And I will fasten him like a peg or nail in a firm place; and he will become a throne of honor and glory to his father's house. And they will hang on him the honor and the whole weight of [responsibility for] his father's house: the offspring and issue [of the family, high and low], every small vessel, from the cups even to all the flasks and big bulging bottles. (Isa. 22:15-24, Ampl.)

a. Wasteful

Such a wasteful child doesn't even begin to see the limits of his own creaturehood, nor does he appreciate the real importance and purpose of God's blessings or the desirability of living under God's sovereignty. He moves through life as though limitless resources were always available to him, as though he should be able to create whatever he wants or needs out of nothing, according to his will and on his own time schedule. Instead of gathering, he scatters. Instead of building up, he tears down. Instead of using, he abuses and squanders all resources. He does not strengthen what remains but weakens and dissipates everything that came to him through the labors of others. So now we know why the Greek word *apoleia*, as used in Mark 14:4 and Matthew 7:13, means both "waste" and "destruction."

The *lazy man* does not roast his game, but the diligent man prizes his possessions. (Prov. 12:27)

In the house of the wise are stores of choice food and oil, but *a foolish man devours all he has*. (Prov. 21:20)

Now this is what Yahweh Almighty says: "Give careful thought to your ways. You have planted much, but have harvested little. You eat, but never have enough. You drink, but never have your fill. You put on clothes, but are not warm. You earn wages, only to put them in a purse with holes in it." (Hag. 1:5-6)

I went past the field of *the sluggard*, past the vineyard of the man who lacks judgment; thorns had come up everywhere, the ground was covered with weeds, and the stone wall was in ruins. (Prov. 24:30-31)

And He also said to His disciples: "There was a certain rich man who had a steward, and an accusation was brought to him that this man was *wasting his goods*.

"So he called him and said to him, 'What is this I hear about you? Give an account of your stewardship, for you can no longer be steward.'" (Luke 16:1-2)

Jesus continued: "There was a man who had two sons. The younger one said to his father, 'Father, give me my share of the estate.' So he divided his property between them. Not long after that, the younger son got together all he had, set off for a distant country and there *squandered his wealth* in wild living." (Luke 15:11-13)

When they had all had enough to eat, He said to His disciples, "Gather the pieces that are left over. *Let nothing be wasted*." (John 6:12)

b. Destructive

The pride of self-centered love and ambition precurses destruction. The destructive child is the child who becomes offended at the least exposure of his sins, and so he deliberately tears down and pulls apart everything around him, including his own life. In his pride, he actively opposes the purpose of God. He becomes bitter against his parents and God because their love didn't pamper him or acquiesce to him in his selfishness but ministered to his needs and even exposed his sins. So he comes to see the purpose of God as an obstacle to his own will rather than as a channel for his and everyone else's fulfillment. Jesus described destructive people as standing in direct opposition to God's purposes (John 10:10).

Pride goes before destruction, and *a haughty spirit before a fall*. (Prov. 16:18)

Wisdom is better than weapons of war, but one sinner *destroys* much good. (Eccles. 9:18)

One who is slack in his work is brother to one who *destroys*. (Prov. 18:9)

He who robs his father or mother and says, "It's not wrong"—he is partner to him who *destroys*. (Prov. 28:24)

The nations were angry; and Your wrath has come. The time has come for judging the dead, and for rewarding Your servants the prophets and Your saints and those who reverence Your name, both small and great—and for *destroying those who destroy the earth*. (Rev. 11:18)

c. Unreliable

The unreliable child fails to meet needs when called upon to do so. He's too busy doing everything *he* thinks is important, which usually amounts to whatever builds up his own image and feelings of *self*-importance, rather than what those over him have told him is important. At any given time he can be found standing just about everywhere but in his place, and so he actually obstructs the fulfillment of God's purpose. In fact, he can seldom, if ever, be counted upon to stand in his assigned place, especially not when his services are needed. Koehler and Baumgartner state that the Hebrew word *haphak*, translated "unreliable" in Psalm 78:57, means "to fail to function." Like the "faulty" bow, the unreliable child snaps under the pull of the moment's need and fails to function in those tasks required of him. His arrow falls at his feet instead of striking the mark.

He also refuses to be trained to stand in his place, usually because he has notions of some higher place he thinks he should be standing in. So he finds no joy in the fulfillment of his responsibilities, which become onerous to him. He flees from the purpose of God rather than into that purpose. Instead, he seeks his own self-centered purpose, which he rationalizes as God's purpose.

> But they put God to the test and rebelled against the Most High; they did not keep His statutes. Like their fathers they were disloyal and faithless, as *unreliable* [*haphak*] as a faulty bow. (Ps. 78:56-57)
>
> The men of Ephraim, though armed with bows, *turned back* [*haphak*] on the day of battle. (Ps. 78:9)
>
> And he returned to the man of God, he [Naaman] and all his aides, and came and stood before him; and he said, "Indeed, now I know that there is no God in all the earth, except in Israel; now therefore, *please take a gift from your servant*." But he [Elisha] said, "As Yahweh lives, before whom I stand, I will receive nothing." And *he urged him to take it, but he refused* . . . .
> Then he said to him, "Go in peace." So he departed from him a short distance.

But Gehazi, the servant of Elisha the man of God, *said*, "Look, my master has spared Naaman this Syrian, while not receiving from his hands what he brought; but as Yahweh lives, *I will run after him and take something from him.*" So Gehazi pursued Naaman. When Naaman saw him running after him, he got down from the chariot to meet him, and said, "Is all well?"

And he said, "All is well. My master has sent me, saying, 'Indeed, just now two young men of the sons of the prophets have come to me from the mountains of Ephraim. Please give them a talent of silver and two changes of garments.'"

So Naaman said, "Please, take two talents." And he urged him, and bound two talents of silver in two bags, with two changes of garments, and handed them to two of his servants; and they carried them on ahead of him. When he came to the citadel, he took them from their hand, and stored them away in the house; then he let the men go, and they departed. Now he went in and stood before his master. *Elisha said to him, "Where did you go, Gehazi?"*

And he said, "Your servant did not go anywhere."

Then he said to him, "Did not my heart go with you when the man turned back from his chariot to meet you? *Is it time to receive money and to receive clothing, olive groves and vineyards, sheep and oxen, male and female servants?* Therefore *the leprosy of Naaman shall cling to you and your descendants forever." And he went out from his presence leprous, as white as snow.* (2 Kings 5:15-16, 19-27)

The word that Jeremiah the prophet spoke to Baruch [Jeremiah's secretary] the son of Neriah, when he had written these words in a book at the instruction of Jeremiah, in the fourth year of Jehoiakim the son of Josiah, king of Judah, saying, "Thus says Yahweh, the God of Israel, to you, O Baruch: 'You said, "Woe is me now! For Yahweh has added grief to my sorrow. I fainted in my sighing, and I find no rest."'

"Thus you shall say to him, 'Thus says Yahweh: "Behold, what I have built I will break down, and what I have planted I will pluck up, that is, this whole land. And *do you seek great things for yourself?* Do not seek them; for behold, I will bring adversity on all flesh," says Yahweh. "But I will give your life to you as a prize in all places, wherever you go."'" (Jer. 45:1-5)

Thus says Yahweh GOD of hosts: "*Go, proceed to this steward, to Shebna, who is over the house*, and say: 'What have you here, and whom have you here, that you *have hewn a sepulcher here, as he who hews himself a sepulcher on high, who carves a tomb for himself in a rock*? Indeed, Yahweh will throw you away violently, O mighty man, and will surely seize you. He will surely turn violently and toss you like a ball into a large country; there you shall die, and there your glorious chariots shall be the shame of your master's house. So *I will drive you out of your office, and from your position he will pull you down.*

'Then it shall be in that day, that I will call My servant Eliakim the son of Hilkiah; I will clothe him with your robe and strengthen him with your belt; I *will commit your responsibility into his hand.* He shall be a father to the inhabitants of Jerusalem and to the house of Judah. The key of the house of David I will lay on his shoulder; so he shall open, and no one shall shut; and he shall shut, and no one shall open. I will fasten him as a peg in a secure place, and he will become a glorious throne to his father's house.'" (Isa. 22:15-23)

Then the man who had received the one talent came. "Master," he said, "I knew that you are a hard man, harvesting where you have not sown and gathering where you have not scattered seed. So I was afraid and went out and hid your talent in the ground. See, here is what belongs to you."

His master replied, "You *wicked, lazy servant*! So you knew that I harvest where I have not sown and gather where I have not scattered seed? Well then, you should have put my money on deposit with the bankers, so that when I returned I would have received it back with interest.

Take the talent from him and give it to the one who has the ten talents. For everyone who has will be given more, and he will have an abundance. Whoever does not have, even what he has will be taken from him. And throw that *worthless servant* outside, into the darkness, where there will be weeping and gnashing of teeth." (Matt. 25:24-30)

At my first defense, no one *came to my support*, but everyone *deserted me*. May it not be held against them. (2 Tim. 4:16)

d. Unfaithful

The unfaithful child refuses to fulfill God's purpose for his life, often because he does not think it is important enough for someone as important as he sees himself. He looks inward for his own purposes rather than outward to God and the church, which he merely uses; and so he can seldom if ever be depended upon. In his heart, he refuses to walk in the faith that would enable him to accomplish God's desires because he's always seeking his own. The Hebrew word *maal*, translated "unfaithful," literally means an "act of treachery." One who is unfaithful will surely hurt those who depend on him in the time of need, just as surely as when a companion in arms betrays his fellow soldiers into enemy hands in time of battle because he has vacated his post and left his place in the collective task to do what pleases him as an individual, which usually means running from the battle. What pleases him is always more important than the task assigned him. Again, as with reliability and faithfulness, unreliability and unfaithfulness are closely related, the former emphasizing external action and the latter the condition of the heart. The unfaithful child will surely fail in reliability when put to the test.

Like a bad tooth or a lame foot is reliance on *the unfaithful* in times of trouble. (Prov. 25:19)

Yet they tempted and provoked the most high God, and kept not

His testimonies: But turned back, and *dealt unfaithfully* like their fathers: they were turned aside like a deceitful bow. (Ps. 78:56-57, KJV)

For there is *no faithfulness* in their mouth; their inward part is very wickedness; their throat is an open sepulchre; they flatter with their tongue. (Ps. 5:9, KJV)

"But this has all taken place that the writings of the prophets might be fulfilled." Then all the disciples *deserted* Him and fled. (Matt. 26:56)

"What do you think? There was a man who had two sons. He went to the first and said, 'Son, go and work today in the vineyard.' 'I will not,' he answered, but later he changed his mind and went.

   "Then the father went to the other son and said the same thing. He *answered, 'I will, sir,' but he did not go*." (Matt. 21:28-30)

F. Taking Initiative/ Waiting to Be Told

1. Taking Initiative

God holds out a spiritual inheritance, a mission, a purpose for each of us. He has designated the pattern for His Body and given each a place and function in that Body. In the fulfillment of those functions, He has sent forth His Spirit to empower us, His Word to direct us. God's people engage in a great corporate construction project, the raising up of an eternal temple to glorify God. Jesus Christ is the only Head of this Body; all others are members. So the completion of God's purpose on earth depends upon each member maintaining his direct relationship with the Head, standing in his place and pressing forward to fulfill his responsibilities.

To do this requires constant vigilance to take spiritual initiative. To take initiative means, of course, to initiate, to take "responsibility for beginning or originating." The root of this word is the Latin *initium*, meaning "beginning." This word in turn derives from the Latin *inire*, meaning "to go into, enter upon, begin."[38] God Himself is, of course, the true initiator of every good and perfect work. He has already ordained for us the works that He wills us to accomplish (Eph. 2:10). But we must *enter into* these works, and to do so requires initiative. God has given special initiatory ministries within His Body to impart the basic patterns of the church and Christian life as Scripture reveals these. God shows His goals, aims, projects, direction and so on for the Body as a whole, for many fellowships together or for individual fellowships through special ministries.* But even if God reveals through another member of the Body the task we must accomplish, each of us must still take spiritual initiative in doing God's purpose by God's Spirit.

The book of Nehemiah brings this into sharp focus. God prompted Nehemiah to rebuild the walls of Jerusalem. God had prepared others in Jerusalem to receive the Word He sent through Nehemiah. They, too, wept at the burnt and ravaged walls of the city. They, too, yearned to see the city once again restored and established in peace and strength. But God gave Nehemiah the faith, wisdom and spiritual boldness to *initiate* this

---

* See *Forming Christ's Body, Book One* by Blair Adams (Elm Mott, Tex.: Colloquium Press, 1977, 1992, 2011).

great project. God, in other words, gave Nehemiah His *plan*, *resources* and *authority* to accomplish the task. All those whose hearts burned to see this happen then turned to Nehemiah and joined him in the task at hand. Each then took his assigned place in building the walls. But on what did the completion of the task depend? It depended upon each member of this great task force exercising spiritual initiative in his place to see the work through to completion. To build each section of the wall required initiative: initiative in providing enough bricks and men and in ensuring that the job proceeded according to the God-given time set for completion. If each waited for Nehemiah to come around and say when he needed more bricks or more men, the job could never have been done.

Just so, each of us must take the full spiritual initiative in his place to complete what God has given into his hands. Spiritual initiative begins when a vibrant relationship with God's Spirit opens our eyes to His vision and the present need, then fixes the visionary's heart, mind and eyes on God's purpose. A deep feeling is the motivating force—faith working through love (Gal. 5:6). When our children can begin to initiate what God has given them to do and follow through on their own to fulfill their responsibilities, then parents can have confidence that their offspring are growing toward maturity of character in God.

But this initiative has nothing to do with taking initiative in the flesh in a self-originating effort to do something apart from the presence and guidance of God. Christian initiative is the initiative to follow the Holy Spirit, to do *God's* will, to respond to *God's* voice, to do our part in the completion of *God's* purpose. Because we live in vital relationship with God and see His purpose and our place in its fulfillment, we can do our work without being reminded and take action to meet all pertinent needs as they arise. The wax of worldliness has been melted from the ears of our hearts, so we hear God when He speaks directly to us, and we move with grace to do His bidding. Zeal drives us toward the vision we see up ahead (Isa. 62:6-7). So we move forward in our task without constant external prodding, for God's visionary love powerfully constrains us from within (2 Cor. 4:8-10, 13, 16-18; 5:14).

To take initiative marks the move from the realm of a slave to the realm of a son (Gal. 4:7; Titus 3:7): that is, when a child begins to take initiative, he begins to move into possession of his spiritual inheritance. So long as the child requires constant prodding and supervision from others, he "differs nothing from a slave," even though by inheritance he rightfully owns everything in his father's house (Gal. 4:1). Only as he comes out from under external prompting and permits the internal combustion of the Holy Spirit and its fire to propel his life does he take hold of his inheritance as a son. Birth into God's kingdom makes us His children, but a child under tutors, who "differs nothing from a slave" (Gal. 4:1-2), differs greatly from a child who has come into his "adoption" or, in the Hebrew idiom, son-placing, his *placing*-as-a-son. The slave does not "know" to do his master's will (John 15:15), but the mature heir knows and takes responsibility to do his Lord's will because as a son he recognizes that the master's estate belongs to him as well (Luke 15:31). Through this recognition and the fulfillment of the responsibility it entails, the true son takes tangible possession of his inheritance and enters into his spiritual birthright in the kingdom of his Father.

Of course, we must always remember that so long as he remains "a child," the heir can't enter into his inheritance (Gal. 4:1). As Scripture declares, he therefore *properly* remains on the "slave" level, which means that his initiative is severely circumscribed. Increasing maturity brings increasing initiative. So we must exercise extreme caution in expecting too much initiative from younger children. Childhood is far more the time of imitation and following others than it is a time of initiation and leading. So to expect too much, to stretch our children beyond their abilities, will distort both their perspective of their place and our relationship to them. Such a course might even encourage rebellion and self-centeredness in their hearts. In the world, parents all too readily expect too much initiative from their children simply because the parents want to renege on their responsibilities in child rearing. In the name of encouraging initiative, they leave their children to raise themselves. As parents we must remember that Paul says our children differ nothing from slaves. So they need continual attendance, supervision, covering, direction and guidance.

But we must also remember that as parents what we *aim* for is to train them up to walk in the way they should go, to walk that path of ever-increasing maturity, and so of ever-increasing initiative. They will only come to the real spiritual initiative that comes with true maturity if we carefully nurture them into ever-greater initiative in the limited but growing spheres God has ordained for them. Such growth requires careful supervision as well as responsible and abiding relationship, not only between parents and child but especially between the parents and God.

As children grow, full spiritual initiative in the fulfillment of responsibility precedes being "set" into their place—entering into their adoption—as fully reliable sons. This happened to Jesus at His baptism, when the voice of the Father spoke, declaring, "This is My beloved Son in whom I am well pleased. Listen to Him." These words resembled the traditional ancient Jewish announcement whereby a father declared that his son had entered into the full rights of his estate, that he was no longer merely as a servant in his father's house but now exercised the full authority and rights of the heir.

This is the level of spiritual maturity to which God desires to bring His people, the level at which we meet all the obligations of our spiritual inheritance. The slave cannot be entrusted with responsibility because he has no share and therefore little interest in the estate. He must be guided through every detail in every step he takes. But the son moves with initiative that comes from the sense of sharing in the inheritance. The son remains in submission to the father and to all those set in authority over the son by the father, but the son's submission does not nullify his participation in the father's estate. He remains an heir, a co-owner of the estate. He therefore sees the necessity of fulfilling his functions in the estate if he is to gain what is rightfully his.

The task God has given to each of us to accomplish in His kingdom is not just arbitrarily related to us. He has made us so that we can precisely fulfill that purpose: the very essence of our individual being directly ties to the purpose God has ordained for our lives. As we strive and strain to fulfill that purpose both individually and as members of a corporate Body, we become what God intended. So spiritual initiative proves necessary to fulfill God's purpose on every level, both to accomplish what God has given us to do and also to become the new creatures into which He would fashion us. As we participate with increasing intensity in God's purpose for our lives, our whole being becomes increasingly one with God. As we move into our spiritual inheritance in Christ, God shapes us into His exact image for our lives. So we see that our active participation in God's purpose, our actual possessing of our inheritance in Christ, is the process of entering into the fullness of our salvation. This active participation demands that we love Yahweh with all our heart, soul, mind and strength. Only by the full participation of every part of our being in God's purpose—only when His zeal consumes us completely (Isa. 62:1)—can we fulfill that purpose.

> To those who sold doves He said, "Get these out of here! How dare you turn My Father's house into a market!"
> His disciples remembered that it is written: *"Zeal for Your house will consume Me."* (John 2:16-17)

> *Never be lacking in zeal*, but keep your *spiritual fervor*, serving the Lord. (Rom. 12:11)

> Yahweh said to Moses, "Phinehas son of Eleazar, the son of Aaron, the priest, has turned My anger away from the Israelites; for *he was as zealous as I am for My honor among them*, so that in My zeal I did not put an end to them. Therefore tell him I am making My covenant of peace with him. He and his descendants will have a covenant of a lasting priesthood, because *he was zealous for the honor of his God* and made atonement for the Israelites." (Num. 25:10-13)

> Do not let your heart envy sinners, but *always be zealous for the fear of Yahweh.* (Prov. 23:17)

Of the increase of His government and peace there will be no end. He will reign on David's throne and over His kingdom, establishing and upholding it with justice and righteousness from that time on and forever. The zeal of Yahweh Almighty will accomplish this. (Isa. 9:7)

a. Fulfilling Responsibilities without Being Reminded

The responsible child won't despise the day of small things (Zech. 4:10). Rather, he trusts his parents who communicate a deep sense of both the practical and spiritual importance of his tasks, of the place of those tasks in God's purpose. He needs no reminding because he recognizes his work as part of the whole family's and community's worship and service to something greater than any single individual. So in all he does he seeks to honor God and his parents and exalt the Lord of all he knows, experiences and loves.

> Solomon sent back this message to Hiram: "You know that because of the wars waged against my father David from all sides, he could not build a temple for the Name of Yahweh his God until Yahweh put his enemies under his feet. But now Yahweh my God has given me rest on every side, and there is no adversary or disaster. I intend, therefore, to build a temple for the Name of Yahweh my God, as Yahweh told my father David, when He said, 'Your son whom I will put on the throne in your place will build the temple for My Name.' So give orders that cedars of Lebanon be cut for me. My men will work with yours, and I will pay you for your men whatever wages you set. You know that we have no one so skilled in felling timber as the Sidonians." (1 Kings 5:2-6)

> Some time later Joash decided to restore the temple of Yahweh. He called together the priests and Levites and said to them, "Go to the towns of Judah and collect the money due annually from all Israel, to repair the temple of your God. Do it now." But the Levites did not act at once.
>
> Therefore the king summoned Jehoiada the chief priest and said to him, "Why haven't you required the Levites to bring in from Judah and Jerusalem the tax imposed by Moses the servant of Yahweh and by the assembly of Israel for the Tent of the Testimony?"
>
> The men in charge of the work were diligent, and the repairs progressed under them. They rebuilt the temple of God according to its original design and reinforced it. (2 Chron. 24:4-6, 13)

> When Esther's words were reported to Mordecai, he sent back this answer: "Do not think that because you are in the king's house you alone of all the Jews will escape. For if you remain silent at this time, relief and deliverance for the Jews will arise from another place, but you and your father's family will perish. And who knows but that you have come to royal position for such a time as this?"
>
> Then Esther sent this reply to Mordecai: "Go, gather together all

the Jews who are in Susa, and fast for me. Do not eat or drink for three days, night or day. I and my maids will fast as you do. When this is done, I will go to the king, even though it is against the law. And if I perish, I perish." (Esther 4:12-16)

In the month of Nisan in the twentieth year of King Artaxerxes, when wine was brought for him, I took the wine and gave it to the king. I had not been sad in his presence before; so the king asked me, "Why does your face look so sad when you are not ill? This can be nothing but sadness of heart."

I was very much afraid, but I said to the king, "May the king live forever! Why should my face not look sad when the city where my fathers are buried lies in ruins, and its gates have been destroyed by fire?"

The king said to me, "What is it you want?"

Then I prayed to the God of heaven, and I answered the king, "If it pleases the king and if your servant has found favor in his sight, let him send me to the city in Judah where my fathers are buried so that I can rebuild it." (Neh. 2:1-5)

After the king was settled in his palace and Yahweh had given him rest from all his enemies around him, he said to Nathan the prophet, "Here I am, living in a palace of cedar, while the ark of God remains in a tent."

Nathan replied to the king, "Whatever you have in mind, go ahead and do it, for Yahweh is with you." (2 Sam. 7:1-3)

I have come to cast fire upon the earth, and how I wish that it were already kindled!

I have a baptism with which to be baptized, and how greatly and sorely I am urged—impelled, constrained—until it is accomplished! (Luke 12:49-50, Ampl.)

However, I consider my life worth nothing to me, if only I may finish the race and complete the task the Lord Jesus has given me— the task of testifying to the gospel of God's grace. (Acts 20:24)

Whatever your hand finds to do, do it with all your might, for in the grave, where you are going, there is neither working nor planning nor knowledge nor wisdom. (Eccles. 9:10)

b. Meeting Needs without Being Told

To honor parents means staying alert to opportunities to serve them and to see how to properly take initiative in doing so. Such a child is sensitive to the needs of others, and so, when he sees them, he'll move to meet such needs without being told. He also looks for opportunities to grow in his service, desiring always to further give himself to fulfill God's purpose in his life and in the family's and community's. His heart is full, so he shares with others out of the abundance of grace he himself experiences from the Holy Spirit moving in deep love through parents and family.

Now Naaman was the commander of the army of the king of Aram.

He was a great man in the sight of his master and highly regarded, because through him Yahweh had given victory to Aram. He was a valiant soldier, but he had leprosy.

Now bands from Aram had gone out and had taken captive a young girl from Israel, and she served Naaman's wife. She said to her mistress, "If only my master would see the prophet who is in Samaria! He would cure him of his leprosy." (2 Kings 5:1-3)

Men of Issachar, who understood the times and knew what Israel should do—200 chiefs, with all their relatives under their command; men of Zebulun, experienced soldiers prepared for battle with every type of weapon, to help David with undivided loyalty—50,000 . . . .

All these were fighting men who volunteered to serve in the ranks. They came to Hebron fully determined to make David king over all Israel. All the rest of the Israelites were also of one mind to make David king. (1 Chron. 12:32-33, 38)

Then he prayed, "O Yahweh, God of my master Abraham, give me success today, and show kindness to my master Abraham. See, I am standing beside this spring, and the daughters of the townspeople are coming out to draw water. May it be that when I say to a girl, 'Please let down your jar that I may have a drink,' and she says, 'Drink, and I'll water your camels too'—let her be the one You have chosen for Your servant Isaac. By this I will know that You have shown kindness to my master."

Before he had finished praying, Rebekah came out with her jar on her shoulder. She was the daughter of Bethuel son of Milcah, who was the wife of Abraham's brother Nahor. The girl was very beautiful, a virgin; no man had ever lain with her. She went down to the spring, filled her jar and came up again.

The servant hurried to meet her and said, "Please give me a little water from your jar."

"Drink, my lord," she said, and quickly lowered the jar to her hands and gave him a drink.

After she had given him a drink, she said, "I'll draw water for your camels too, until they have finished drinking." So she quickly emptied her jar into the trough, ran back to the well to draw more water, and drew enough for all his camels. (Gen. 24:12-20)

The prayer of Abraham's servant reveals his genuine burden to bring Isaac the kind of wife Abraham wanted for his son. Eliezer didn't go out with the attitude of a mere slave (and from Genesis 24:1-9, we gather that Abraham treated him more like a son because of this attitude). Eliezer didn't merely do what he was forced to do. Instead, he assumed even greater responsibility than he was told to take. Zeal marked his service to his master.

"And now let Pharaoh look for a discerning and wise man and put him in charge of the land of Egypt. Let Pharaoh appoint commissioners over the land to take a fifth of the harvest of Egypt during the seven years of abundance. They should collect all the food of these good years that are coming and store up the grain under the authority of Pharaoh, to be kept in the cities for food. This food should be held in reserve for the country, to be used during the seven years of famine that will come upon Egypt, so that the country may not be ruined by the famine."

The plan seemed good to Pharaoh and to all his officials. So Pharaoh asked them, "Can we find anyone like this man, one in whom is the spirit of God?"

Then Pharaoh said to Joseph, "Since God has made all this known to you, there is no one so discerning and wise as you." (Gen. 41:33-39)

Elisha sent a messenger to say to him, "Go, wash yourself seven times in the Jordan, and your flesh will be restored and you will be cleansed."

But Naaman went away angry and said, "I thought that he would surely come out to me and stand and call on the name of Yahweh his God, wave his hand over the spot and cure me of my leprosy. Are not Abana and Pharpar, the rivers of Damascus, better than any of the waters of Israel? Couldn't I wash in them and be cleansed?" So he turned and went off in a rage.

Naaman's servants went to him and said, "My father, if the prophet had told you to do some great thing, would you not have done it? How much more, then, when he tells you, 'Wash and be cleansed'!" So he went down and dipped himself in the Jordan seven times, as the man of God had told him, and his flesh was restored and became clean like that of a young boy. (2 Kings 5:10-14)

A righteous man cares for the needs of his animal, but the kindest acts of the wicked are cruel. (Prov. 12:10)

I also told them about the gracious hand of my God upon me and what the king had said to me.

They replied, "Let us start rebuilding." So they began this good work. (Neh. 2:18)

All the believers were together and had everything in common. Selling their possessions and goods, they gave to anyone as he had need. (Acts 2:44-45)

One day Peter and John were going up to the temple at the time of prayer—at three in the afternoon. Now a man crippled from birth was being carried to the temple gate called Beautiful, where he was put every day to beg from those going into the temple courts. When he saw Peter and John about to enter, he asked them for money. Peter looked straight at him, as did John. Then Peter said, "Look at us!" So the man gave them his attention, expecting to get something from them.

Then Peter said, "Silver or gold I do not have, but what I have I give you. In the name of Jesus Christ of Nazareth, walk." Taking him by the right hand, he helped him up, and instantly the man's feet and ankles became strong. He jumped to his feet and began to walk. Then he went with them into the temple courts, walking and jumping, and praising God. (Acts 3:1-8)

> In Lystra there sat a man crippled in his feet, who was lame from birth and had never walked. He listened to Paul as he was speaking. Paul looked directly at him, saw that he had faith to be healed and called out, "Stand up on your feet!" At that, the man jumped up and began to walk. (Acts 14:8-10)

> Some men came, bringing to Him a paralytic, carried by four of them. Since they could not get him to Jesus because of the crowd, they made an opening in the roof above Jesus and, after digging through it, lowered the mat the paralyzed man was lying on. When Jesus saw their faith, He said to the paralytic, "Son, your sins are forgiven." (Mark 2:3-5)

> When Jesus came into Peter's house, He saw Peter's mother-in-law lying in bed with a fever. He touched her hand and the fever left her, and she got up and began to wait on Him. (Matt. 8:14-15)

> After He had said this, He went on to tell them, "Our friend Lazarus has fallen asleep; but I am going there to wake him up." (John 11:11)

> During this time some prophets came down from Jerusalem to Antioch. One of them, named Agabus, stood up and through the Spirit predicted that a severe famine would spread over the entire Roman world. (This happened during the reign of Claudius.) The disciples, each according to his ability, decided to provide help for the brothers living in Judea. This they did, sending their gift to the elders by Barnabas and Saul. (Acts 11:27-30)

> And now, brothers, we want you to know about the grace that God has given the Macedonian churches. Out of the most severe trial, their overflowing joy and their extreme poverty welled up in rich generosity. For I testify that they gave as much as they were able, and even beyond their ability. Entirely on their own, they urgently pleaded with us for the privilege of sharing in this service to the saints. And they did not do as we expected, but they gave themselves first to the Lord and then to us in keeping with God's will. (2 Cor. 8:1-5)

> I thank God, who put into the heart of Titus the same concern I have for you. For Titus not only welcomed our appeal, but he is coming to you with much enthusiasm and on his own initiative. (2 Cor. 8:16-17)

As said, if we're God's children, then we're heirs, but we can only come into our inheritance through the initiative of the Holy Spirit. Only then can we truly advance His government.

> Of the increase of His government and peace there will be no end. He will reign on David's throne and over His kingdom, establishing and upholding it with justice and righteousness from that time on and forever. The zeal of Yahweh Almighty will accomplish this. (Isa. 9:7)

We can take the initiative to bring more and more under God's dominion and authority in the Spirit.

So on that day Moses swore to me, "The land on which your feet have walked will be your inheritance and that of your children forever, because you have followed Yahweh my God wholeheartedly."

Now then, just as Yahweh promised, He has kept me alive for forty-five years since the time He said this to Moses, while Israel moved about in the desert. So here I am today, eighty-five years old! I am still as strong today as the day Moses sent me out; I'm just as vigorous to go out to battle now as I was then. Now give me this hill country that Yahweh promised me that day. You yourself heard then that the Anakites were there and their cities were large and fortified, but, Yahweh helping me, I will drive them out just as He said. (Josh. 14:9-12)

So Joshua took this entire land: the hill country, all the Negev, the whole region of Goshen, the western foothills, the Arabah and the mountains of Israel with their foothills, from Mount Halak, which rises towards Seir, to Baal Gad in the valley of Lebanon below Mount Hermon. He captured all their kings and struck them down, putting them to death. (Josh. 11:16-17)

As the Philistine moved closer to attack him, David ran quickly toward the battle line to meet him. (1 Sam. 17:48)

Jonathan said to his young armor-bearer, "Come, let's go over to the outpost of those uncircumcised fellows. Perhaps Yahweh will act in our behalf. Nothing can hinder Yahweh from saving, whether by many or by few."

"Do all that you have in mind," his armor-bearer said. "Go ahead; I am with you heart and soul."

Jonathan said, "Come, then; we will cross over toward the men and let them see us. If they say to us, 'Wait there until we come to you,' we will stay where we are and not go up to them. But if they say, 'Come up to us,' we will climb up, because that will be our sign that Yahweh has given them into our hands."

So both of them showed themselves to the Philistine outpost. "Look!" said the Philistines. "The Hebrews are crawling out of the holes they were hiding in." The men of the outpost shouted to Jonathan and his armor-bearer, "Come up to us and we'll teach you a lesson."

So Jonathan said to his armor-bearer, "Climb up after me; Yahweh has given them into the hand of Israel."

Jonathan climbed up, using his hands and feet, with his armor-bearer right behind him. The Philistines fell before Jonathan, and his armor-bearer followed and killed behind him. In that first attack, Jonathan and his armor-bearer killed some twenty men in an area of about a half an acre.

Then panic struck the whole army—those in the camp and field, and those in outposts and raiding parties—and the ground shook. It was a panic sent by God.

Saul's lookouts at Gibeah of Benjamin saw the army melting away in all directions. (1 Sam. 14:6-16)

At that time David was in the stronghold, and the Philistine garrison was at Bethlehem. David longed for water and said, "Oh, that someone would get me a drink of water from the well near the gate of Bethlehem!" So the Three broke through the Philistine lines, drew water from the well near the gate of Bethlehem and carried it back to David. But he refused to drink it; instead, he poured it out before Yahweh. "God forbid that I should do this!" he said. "Should I drink the blood of these men who went at the risk of their lives?" Because they risked their lives to bring it back, David would not drink it.

  Such were the exploits of the three mighty men. (1 Chron. 11:16-19)

c. Pressing Through

A maturing child who learns to take proper initiative moves forward and presses through to do what he knows is right to do. This requires real faith. James indicated that faith without any acts of initiative is dead (James 2:26). And without this faith, it is impossible to please God (Heb. 11:6). With faith the child can strain and press through. One lexicon says that the Greek word *epekteinomai*, translated "straining" or "stretching forward," is used in Philippians 3:13 as a metaphor from foot racing. Rienecker defines this word as "to stretch one's self out for, to stretch one's self out toward. The metaphor is from the foot race and the word pictures the body of the racer bent forward, his hand outstretched toward the goal, and his eye fastened upon it." Of course, this is more than a metaphor. As Christians, we actually engage in a spiritual race and can only achieve our goal by straining and striving with everything in us (Heb. 12:1-2; 1 Cor. 9:24-27). Only when we give everything does the whole of our life fall into God's hands as He accepts our sacrifice and consumes it with the fire of His presence. Only if we see God in all our tasks do they become worth enough to us to consume our time, energy and effort. If they have no such value to us, then they can hardly be worth enough for God to consume by coming down in His presence.

> Not that I have already obtained all this, or have already been made perfect, but I press on to take hold of that for which Christ Jesus took hold of me. Brothers, I do not consider myself yet to have taken hold of it. But one thing I do: forgetting what is behind and straining toward what is ahead, I press on toward the goal to win the prize for which God has called me heavenward in Christ Jesus. All of us who are mature should take such a view of things. And if on some point you think differently, that too God will make clear to you. Only let us live up to what we have already attained. (Phil. 3:12-16)

> Some men came, bringing to Him a paralytic, carried by four of them. Since they could not get him to Jesus because of the crowd, they made an opening in the roof above Jesus and, after digging through it, lowered the mat the paralyzed man was lying on. When

Jesus saw their faith, He said to the paralytic, "Son, your sins are forgiven." (Mark 2:3-5)

Ask and it will be given to you; seek and you will find; knock and the door will be opened to you. For everyone who asks receives; he who seeks finds; and to him who knocks, the door will be opened. (Matt. 7:7-8)

And if you call out for insight and cry aloud for understanding, and if you look for it as for silver and search for it as for hidden treasure, then you will understand the fear of Yahweh and find the knowledge of God. (Prov. 2:3-5)

A man was there by the name of Zacchaeus; he was a chief tax collector and was wealthy. He wanted to see who Jesus was, but being a short man he could not, because of the crowd. So he ran ahead and climbed a sycamore-fig tree to see Him, since Jesus was coming that way. (Luke 19:2-4)

Blessed is the man who finds wisdom, the man who gains understanding . . . . She is a tree of life to those who embrace her; those who lay hold of her will be blessed. (Prov. 3:13, 18)

Then Moses and Aaron fell facedown in front of the whole Israelite assembly gathered there. Joshua son of Nun and Caleb son of Jephunneh, who were among those who had explored the land, tore their clothes and said to the entire Israelite assembly, "The land we passed through and explored is exceedingly good. If Yahweh is pleased with us, He will lead us into that land, a land flowing with milk and honey, and will give it to us. Only do not rebel against Yahweh. And do not be afraid of the people of the land, because we will swallow them up. Their protection is gone, but Yahweh is with us. Do not be afraid of them." (Num. 14:5-9)

But Joshua the son of Nun and Caleb the son of Jephunneh remained alive out of those men who went to spy out the land. (Num. 14:38, NASV)

When Yahweh was about to take Elijah up to heaven in a whirlwind, Elijah and Elisha were on their way from Gilgal. Elijah said to Elisha, "Stay here; Yahweh has sent me to Bethel."
  But Elisha said, "As surely as Yahweh lives and as you live, I will not leave you." So they went down to Bethel.
  The company of the prophets at Bethel came out to Elisha and asked, "Do you know that Yahweh is going to take your master from you today?"
  "Yes, I know," Elisha replied, "but do not speak of it."
  Then Elijah said to him, "Stay here, Elisha; Yahweh has sent me to Jericho."
  And he replied, "As surely as Yahweh lives and as you live, I will not leave you." So they went to Jericho.
  The company of the prophets at Jericho went up to Elisha and asked him, "Do you know that Yahweh is going to take your master from you today?"
  "Yes, I know," he replied, "but do not speak of it."

Then Elijah said to him, "Stay here; Yahweh has sent me to the Jordan."

And he replied, "As surely as Yahweh lives and as you live, I will not leave you." So the two of them walked on.

Fifty men of the company of the prophets went and stood at a distance, facing the place where Elijah and Elisha had stopped at the Jordan. Elijah took his cloak, rolled it up and struck the water with it. The water divided to the right and to the left, and the two of them crossed over on dry ground.

When they had crossed, Elijah said to Elisha, "Tell me, what can I do for you before I am taken from you?"

"Let me inherit a double portion of your spirit," Elisha replied.

"You have asked a difficult thing," Elijah said, "yet if you see me when I am taken from you, it will be yours—otherwise not."

As they were walking along and talking together, suddenly a chariot of fire and horses of fire appeared and separated the two of them, and Elijah went up to heaven in a whirlwind. Elisha saw this and cried out, "My father! My father! The chariots and horsemen of Israel!" And Elisha saw him no more. Then he took hold of his own clothes and tore them apart.

He picked up the cloak that had fallen from Elijah and went back and stood on the bank of the Jordan. Then he took the cloak that had fallen from him and struck the water with it. "Where now is Yahweh, the God of Elijah?" he asked. When he struck the water, it divided to the right and to the left, and he crossed over. (2 Kings 2:1-14)

Then a man named Jairus, a ruler of the synagogue, came and fell at Jesus' feet, pleading with Him to come to his house because his only daughter, a girl of about twelve, was dying.

As Jesus was on His way, the crowds almost crushed Him. And a woman was there who had been subject to bleeding for twelve years, but no one could heal her. She came up behind Him and touched the edge of His cloak, and immediately her bleeding stopped.

"Who touched Me?" Jesus asked.

When they all denied it, Peter said, "Master, the people are crowding and pressing against You."

But Jesus said, "Someone touched Me; I know that power has gone out from Me."

Then the woman, seeing that she could not go unnoticed, came trembling and fell at His feet. In the presence of all the people, she told why she had touched Him and how she had been instantly healed. Then He said to her, "Daughter, your faith has healed you. Go in peace." (Luke 8:41-48)

Just then a woman who had been subject to bleeding for twelve years came up behind Him and touched the edge of His cloak. She said to herself, "If I only touch His cloak, I will be healed."

Jesus turned and saw her. "Take heart, daughter," He said, "your faith has healed you." And the woman was healed from that moment. (Matt. 9:20-22)

As Jesus went on from there, two blind men followed Him, calling out, "Have mercy on us, Son of David!"

When He had gone indoors, the blind men came to Him, and He asked them, "Do you believe that I am able to do this?"

"Yes, Lord," they replied.

Then He touched their eyes and said, "According to your faith will it be done to you"; and their sight was restored. Jesus warned them sternly, "See that no one knows about this." (Matt. 9:27-30)

At that time I, Daniel, mourned for three weeks . . . .

A hand touched me and set me trembling on my hands and knees. He said, "Daniel, you who are highly esteemed, consider carefully the words I am about to speak to you, and stand up, for I have now been sent to you." And when he said this to me, I stood up trembling.

Then he continued, "Do not be afraid, Daniel. Since the first day that you set your mind to gain understanding and to humble yourself before your God, your words were heard, and I have come in response to them. But the prince of the Persian kingdom resisted me twenty-one days. Then Michael, one of the chief princes, came to help me, because I was detained there with the king of Persia. Now I have come to explain to you what will happen to your people in the future, for the vision concerns a time yet to come." (Dan. 10:2, 10-14)

Then Jesus told His disciples a parable to show them that they should always pray and not give up. He said: "In a certain town there was a judge who neither feared God nor cared about men. And there was a widow in that town who kept coming to him with the plea, 'Grant me justice against my adversary.'

"For some time he refused. But finally he said to himself, 'Even though I don't fear God or care about men, yet because this widow keeps bothering me, I will see that she gets justice, so that she won't eventually wear me out with her coming!'"

And the Lord said, "Listen to what the unjust judge says. And will not God bring about justice for His chosen ones, who cry out to Him day and night? Will He keep putting them off? I tell you, He will see that they get justice, and quickly. However, when the Son of Man comes, will He find faith on the earth?" (Luke 18:1-8)

Make every effort to enter through the narrow door, because many, I tell you, will try to enter and will not be able to. Once the owner of the house gets up and closes the door, you will stand outside knocking and pleading, "Sir, open the door for us."

But he will answer, "I don't know you or where you come from." (Luke 13:24-25)

Leaving that place, Jesus withdrew to the region of Tyre and Sidon. A Canaanite woman from that vicinity came to Him, crying out, "Lord, Son of David, have mercy on me! My daughter is suffering terribly from demon-possession."

Jesus did not answer a word. So His disciples came to Him and urged Him, "Send her away, for she keeps crying out after us."

He answered, "I was sent only to the lost sheep of Israel."
The woman came and knelt before Him. "Lord, help me!" she said.
He replied, "It is not right to take the children's bread and toss it to their dogs."
"Yes, Lord," she said, "but even the dogs eat the crumbs that fall from their masters' table."
Then Jesus answered, "Woman, you have great faith! Your request is granted." And her daughter was healed from that very hour. (Matt. 15:21-28)

From the days of John the Baptist until now, the kingdom of heaven has been forcefully advancing, and forceful men lay hold of it. (Matt. 11:12)

Let us acknowledge Yahweh; let us press on to acknowledge Him. As surely as the sun rises, He will appear; He will come to us like the winter rains, like the spring rains that water the earth. (Hosea 6:3)

2. Waiting to Be Told

The Bible instructs us to wait upon the Lord, to follow His Spirit. But this waiting is not a passive, static, mechanical inactivity. The word *qavah*, the root of the word translated as "wait" in Isaiah 40:31 (NASV) means to be intertwined as one strand in a multistrand rope. When thus "intertwined" with God's purpose, we see our part in His inheritance and all that's necessary to fulfill His will. So waiting on God demands vigilance, attentiveness, a dynamic sense of expectancy. It requires a conviction that God *will* answer; He *will* act; He *will* speak. To hear Him we must know with certainty that He rewards those who diligently seek Him (Heb. 11:6), that He wants to meet every real need, that He wants to act on our behalf. Passivity loses touch with the burden and reality of God. Then we must constantly be prodded, reminded, coaxed to take action. This is not waiting upon the Lord, trying to follow Him, but this waiting only works *against* God's purpose as we refuse to listen, to *pay* attention, to do what He tells us, unwilling to follow Him. To always balk when God speaks soon renders us dead to the Spirit, unresponsive to all needs and duties.

This is what Yahweh Almighty says: "These people say, 'The time has not yet come for Yahweh's house to be built.'"
Then the word of Yahweh came through the prophet Haggai: "Is it a time for you yourselves to be living in your paneled houses, while this house remains a ruin?" (Hag. 1:2-4)

God's Word is *active* and powerful (Heb. 4:12). To communicate means literally to "share"; and so to truly receive God's active Word to us requires coming into an active relationship. We must enter into God's Word to truly hear it, and we saw that "enter into" is one literal meaning of *initiate*. So to receive God's active Word is more than a passive event on our part. The ability to hear God's Word requires more than the mere use of intellect; it must include our emotions, our spirit, our whole being. God's Word is like a river bringing life. To hear that Word is to hear the call to a life that holds back nothing. When we throw ourselves completely into the hearing of the Word, it carries us along as it did holy men of God (2 Pet. 1:21); and where it carries us is into actions that make us *doers* of the Word. Any resistance within us to the Word that comes to us on this river of the Holy Spirit will re-route the Spirit around our lives, cut us off and leave us behind as the river carries others on to their destinies in God. In the end, the deadness of our resistance will stultify and destroy us. Ultimately, even external prodding and reminders can avail nothing against a stone firmly embedded in the river. To be directly and actively open to the direction and moving of the Spirit defines being a child of God, "for as many as are *led by the Spirit* of God, they are the sons of God" (Rom. 8:14, KJV).

a. Unresponsive to Needs and Meeting Responsibilities

The maturing child who can't find the initiative of the Spirit to propel him forward in God's purpose and Word is like a car with a dead battery that must be pushed to restart at every stoplight. Such a child may work well when he's told what to do and then reminded to do it, but as soon as no one any longer pushes him, he stalls and rolls to a stop. No vision of what he should be, how he should act or why this vision should ignite him—in other words, no inner combustible force—propels him forward to fulfill a purpose greater than himself. Neither can he have a very deep relationship with his parents and God, since his own vision is so insipid and powerless, and his parents' vision seems to have failed to fire his life as well.

> Do you not say, "Four months more and then the harvest"? I tell you, open your eyes and look at the fields! They are ripe for harvest. Even now the reaper draws his wages, even now he harvests the crop for eternal life, so that the sower and the reaper may be glad together. Thus the saying "One sows and another reaps" is true. I sent you to reap what you have not worked for. Others have done the hard work, and you have reaped the benefits of their labor. (John 4:35-38)

> Anyone, then, who knows the good he ought to do and doesn't do it, sins. (James 4:17)

> And He also said to His disciples: "There was a certain rich man who had a steward, and an accusation was brought to him that this man was wasting his goods." (Luke 16:1)

> This is what Yahweh Almighty says: "Give careful thought to your ways. Go up into the mountains and bring down timber and build

the house, so that I may take pleasure in it and be honored," says Yahweh.

"You expected much, but see, it turned out to be little. What you brought home, I blew away. Why?" declares Yahweh Almighty. "Because of My house, which remains a ruin, while each of you is busy with his own house." (Hag. 1:7-9)

Meremoth son of Uriah, the son of Hakkoz, repaired the next section. Next to him Meshullam son of Berekiah, the son of Meshezabel, made repairs, and next to him Zadok son of Baana also made repairs. The next section was repaired by the men of Tekoa, but their nobles would not put their shoulders to the work under their supervisors. (Neh. 3:4-5)

Then Jesus went with His disciples to a place called Gethsemane, and He said to them, "Sit here while I go over there and pray." He took Peter and the two sons of Zebedee along with Him, and He began to be sorrowful and troubled. Then He said to them, "My soul is overwhelmed with sorrow to the point of death. Stay here and keep watch with Me."

Going a little farther, He fell with His face to the ground and prayed, "My Father, if it is possible, may this cup be taken from Me. Yet not as I will, but as You will."

Then He returned to His disciples and found them sleeping. "Could you men not keep watch with Me for one hour?" He asked Peter. "Watch and pray so that you will not fall into temptation. The spirit is willing, but the body is weak." (Matt. 26:36-41)

I also learned that the portions assigned to the Levites had not been given to them, and that all the Levites and the singers responsible for the service had gone back to their own fields. So I rebuked the officials and asked them, "Why is the house of God neglected?" (Neh. 13:10-11)

Because for some reason he lacks the love that would compel a response, his heart may grow cold and lifeless, unable to be moved to help others in need.

What good is it, my brothers, if a man claims to have faith but has no deeds? Can such faith save him? Suppose a brother or sister is without clothes and daily food. If one of you says to him, "Go, I wish you well; keep warm and well fed," but does nothing about his physical needs, what good is it? (James 2:14-16)

If anyone has material possessions and sees his brother in need but has no pity on him, how can the love of God be in him? Dear children, let us not love with words or tongue but with actions and in truth. (1 John 3:17-18)

In reply Jesus said: "A man was going down from Jerusalem to Jericho, when he fell into the hands of robbers. They stripped him of his clothes, beat him and went away, leaving him half dead. A priest happened to be going down the same road, and when he saw the man, he passed by on the other side. So too, a Levite, when he came to the place and saw him, passed by on the other side." (Luke 10:30-32)

Then He will say to those on His left, "Depart from Me, you who are cursed, into the eternal fire prepared for the devil and his angels. For I was hungry and you gave Me nothing to eat, I was thirsty and you gave Me nothing to drink, I was a stranger and you did not invite Me in, I needed clothes and you did not clothe Me, I was sick and in prison and you did not look after Me."

They also will answer, "Lord, when did we see You hungry or thirsty or a stranger or needing clothes or sick or in prison, and did not help You?"

He will reply, "I tell you the truth, whatever you did not do for one of the least of these, you did not do for Me." (Matt. 25:41-45)

b. Not Moving Forward or Pressing Through

A child lacking initiative doesn't experience any inner momentum of grace. So he needs props, supports and external constraints and forces to impel him because he lacks internal conviction, vision, burden and strength.

For in just a very little while, "He who is coming will come and will not delay. But My righteous one will live by faith. And if he shrinks back, I will not be pleased with him." But we are not of those who shrink back and are destroyed, but of those who believe and are saved. (Heb. 10:37-39)

And that servant, which knew his lord's will, and prepared not himself, neither did according to his will, shall be beaten with many stripes. (Luke 12:47, KJV)

Anyone, then, who knows the good he ought to do and doesn't do it, sins. (James 4:17)

. . . But I gave them this command: Obey Me, and I will be your God and you will be My people. Walk in all the ways I command you, that it may go well with you. But they did not listen or pay attention; instead, they followed the stubborn inclinations of their evil hearts. *They went backward and not forward.* (Jer. 7:23-24)

Still another said, "I will follow You, Lord; but first let me go back and say good-by to my family."

Jesus replied, "No one who puts his hand to the plow and looks back is fit for service in the kingdom of God." (Luke 9:61-62)

The child without initiative often buries his coin in the ground because he does not trust his master.

Then the man who had received the one talent came. "Master," he said, "I knew that you are a hard man, harvesting where you have not sown and gathering where you have not scattered seed. So I was afraid and went out and hid your talent in the ground. See, here is what belongs to you."

His master replied, "You wicked, lazy servant! So you knew that I harvest where I have not sown and gather where I have not scattered seed? Well then, you should have put my money on deposit with the bankers, so that when I returned I would have received it back with interest.

"Take the talent from him and give it to the one who has the ten talents. For everyone who has will be given more, and he will have an abundance. Whoever does not have, even what he has will be taken from him." (Matt. 25:24-29)

Instead of gathering, he scatters, often draining the energy and lifeblood of others.

He who is not with Me is against Me, and he who does not gather with Me scatters. (Matt. 12:30)

But the men who had gone up with him said, "We can't attack those people; they are stronger than we are." And they spread among the Israelites a bad report about the land they had explored. They said, "The land we explored devours those living in it. All the people we saw there are of great size. We saw the Nephilim there (the descendants of Anak come from the Nephilim). We seemed like grasshoppers in our own eyes, and we looked the same to them." (Num. 13:31-33)

G. HUMILITY/PRIDE

1. Humility

It has been truly said that "genuine meekness is an inner gift arising from complete surrender to God. Everything depends on our finding this full surrender."[39] To truly see the magnitude of Jesus' sacrifice for us and our unworthiness of that sacrifice should incite the sacrificial giving of ourselves to God—it should begin this process of self-surrender. Thus Paul tied God's mercy to our sacrifice (Rom. 12:1-3). This recognition of the worthiness of God and others as measured against our own unworthiness, a recognition expressed through the action to which it impels us, is the true meaning of humility. To see this generates the determination to perfectly and precisely fulfill God's purpose for our lives. Heini Arnold characterizes "the humble man" as one who "yields himself wholly to God and wants to live, not in his own strength, but only through God and for His glory."[40] The humble man is driven to do God's perfect will so that others can *see* the reality of *His* salvation. When this burden truly consumes us till we feel compelled to give all we have and all we are, the attitude and experience of humility will begin to speak through our whole life. The Greek New Testament word *tapeinophrosune*, translated "humility," literally means "lowliness of mind." This means to have the mind of Christ as described in Philippians 2, where we see that Jesus gave everything of Himself for God's purposes. The humble person is not brazen or a renegade but a responsible person willing to "come into the light so that it may be seen plainly that what he has done has been done through God" (John 3:21). Without this meekness, authentic purity or victory over any sin is impossible because we have no awareness, no consciousness of what even belongs to God. The narcissistic self unconsciously feels entitled to all things and so gives no thought to what is due God or others and therefore what should be denied self. The self-centered person lives in his own strength. The humble person, however, assesses himself with the sober measure of God's judgment and leans on the Lord with all his heart. God's strength is then made perfect through the weakness of the humble (2 Cor. 12:9). Not thinking of himself more highly than he ought (Rom. 12:3), but with gratitude in his heart for any gifts and talents God has given him, the humble person serves these to his brothers in God's stead, recognizing the privilege that God has given him. Humility is not thinking evil of oneself; it is giving no thought for oneself at all, while still recognizing one's limitations and obligations. Neither is it an affectation, such as the softening of one's face and laying back of one's ears, like a whipped dog. It is a genuinely submissive attitude of the heart manifested in words and deeds. Nor is it thinking hatefully of oneself, which means you cannot then love others (Matt. 22:37-40). It is rather thinking so much of God and the needs and worth of others that little remains to think of oneself at all.

> David, wearing a linen ephod, danced before Yahweh with all his might, while he and the entire house of Israel brought up the ark of Yahweh with shouts and the sound of trumpets . . . .
> David said to Michal, "*It was before Yahweh, who chose me rather than your father or anyone from his house when he appointed me ruler over Yahweh's people Israel—I will celebrate before Yahweh. I will become even more undignified than this, and I will be humiliated in my own eyes.* But by these slave girls you spoke of, I will be held in honor." (2 Sam. 6:14-15, 21-22)

> For I am the least of the apostles and do not even deserve to be called an apostle, because I persecuted the church of God. But by the grace of God I am what I am, and His grace to me was not without effect. No, I worked harder than all of them—yet not I, but the grace of God that was with me. (1 Cor. 15:9-10)

> I baptize you with water for repentance. But after me will come one who is more powerful than I, whose sandals I am not fit to carry. He will baptize you with the Holy Spirit and with fire . . . . *He must increase, but I must decrease.* (Matt. 3:11; John 3:30)

> Then Peter said, "Silver or gold I do not have, but what I have I give you. In the name of Jesus Christ of Nazareth, walk." (Acts 3:6)

> When Jesus had entered Capernaum, a centurion came to Him, asking for help. "Lord," he said, "my servant lies at home paralyzed and in terrible suffering."
> Jesus said to him, "I will go and heal him."
> *The centurion replied, "Lord, I do not deserve to have You come under my roof.* But just say the word, and my servant will be healed. For I myself am a man under authority, with soldiers under me. I tell this one, 'Go,' and he goes; and that one, 'Come,' and he comes. I say to my servant, 'Do this,' and he does it."
> When Jesus heard this, He was astonished and said to those following Him, "I tell you the truth, I have not found anyone in Israel with such great faith. I say to you that many will come from the east and the west, and will take their places at the feast with Abraham, Isaac and Jacob in the kingdom of heaven. But the subjects of the kingdom will be thrown outside, into the darkness, where there will be weeping and gnashing of teeth."
> Then Jesus said to the centurion, "Go! It will be done just as you believed it would." And his servant was healed at that very hour. (Matt. 8:5-13)

> When Jesus had finished saying all this in the hearing of the peo-

ple, He entered Capernaum. There a centurion's servant, whom his master valued highly, was sick and about to die. The centurion heard of Jesus and sent some elders of the Jews to Him, asking Him to come and heal his servant. When they came to Jesus, they pleaded earnestly with Him, "This man deserves to have You do this, because he loves our nation and has built our synagogue." So Jesus went with them.

He was not far from the house when the centurion sent friends to say to Him: *"Lord, don't trouble Yourself, for I do not deserve to have You come under my roof. That is why I did not even consider myself worthy to come to You.* But say the word, and my servant will be healed. For I myself am a man under authority, with soldiers under me. I tell this one, 'Go,' and he goes; and that one, 'Come,' and he comes. I say to my servant, 'Do this,' and he does it."

When Jesus heard this, He was amazed at him, and turning to the crowd following Him, He said, "I tell you, I have not found such great faith even in Israel." Then the men who had been sent returned to the house and found the servant well. (Luke 7:1-10)

But who am I, and who are my people, that we should be able to give as generously as this? Everything comes from You, and we have given You only what comes from Your hand. We are aliens and strangers in Your sight, as were all our forefathers. Our days on earth are like a shadow, without hope. O Yahweh our God, as for all this abundance that we have provided for building You a temple for Your Holy Name, it comes from Your hand, and all of it belongs to You. (1 Chron. 29:14-16)

As you were lying there, O king, your mind turned to things to come, and the revealer of mysteries showed you what is going to happen. As for me, this mystery has been revealed to me, *not because I have greater wisdom than other living men,* but so that you, O king, may know the interpretation and that you may understand what went through your mind. (Dan. 2:29-30)

Pharaoh said to Joseph, "I had a dream, and no one can interpret it. But I have heard it said of you that when you hear a dream you can interpret it."

"I cannot do it," Joseph replied to Pharaoh, *"but God will give Pharaoh the answer he desires."* (Gen. 41:15-16)

Do not be wise in your own eyes; fear Yahweh and shun evil. (Prov. 3:7)

Jesus gave them this answer: "I tell you the truth, *the Son can do nothing by Himself;* He can do only what He sees His Father doing, because whatever the Father does the Son also does . . . .

"*By Myself I can do nothing;* I judge only as I hear, and My judgment is just, for *I seek not to please Myself but Him who sent Me."* (John 5:19, 30)

For *I did not speak of My own accord,* but the Father who sent Me commanded Me what to say and how to say it. I know that His command leads to eternal life. So whatever I say is just what the Father has told Me to say. (John 12:49-50)

> When Peter saw this, he said to them: "Men of Israel, why does this surprise you? *Why do you stare at us as if by our own power or godliness we had made this man walk?*" (Acts 3:12)

When we fulfill God's design for our lives, then truly no room remains for the flesh to glory in His presence.

> But God has chosen the foolish things of the world to put to shame the wise, and God has chosen the weak things of the world to put to shame the things which are mighty; and the base things of the world and the things which are despised God has chosen, and the things which are not, to bring to nothing the things that are, *that no flesh should glory in His presence.* (1 Cor. 1:27-29)

> Then Moses set up the courtyard around the tabernacle and altar and put up the curtain at the entrance to the courtyard. And *so Moses finished the work.*
> Then the cloud covered the Tent of Meeting, and *the glory of Yahweh filled the tabernacle. Moses could not enter the Tent of Meeting because the cloud had settled upon it, and the glory of Yahweh filled the tabernacle.* (Exod. 40:33-35)

God called Moses the meekest man on earth (Num. 12:3). Yet even he could not enter into the tabernacle when God's glory filled it. When Solomon dedicated the temple, the priests could not even minister.

> When the priests withdrew from the Holy Place, the cloud filled the temple of Yahweh. *And the priests could not perform their service because of the cloud, for the glory of Yahweh filled His temple.*
> Then Solomon said, "Yahweh has said that He would dwell in a dark cloud." (1 Kings 8:10-12)

When we have fulfilled everything according to God's perfect patterns (Heb. 8:5; Exod. 40:33-35; 1 Chron. 28:11-19, NASU), then God's glory can truly come forth: His presence can be fully revealed. But He can only fulfill all that He has ordained when we have truly emptied ourselves of all that seeks to glory in His presence. And we can only totally conform to and complete all He has ordained when we have poured ourselves out in this way. So in both of these senses, the fullness of God's glory will descend only when we have truly lowered and humbled ourselves before Him.

My own experience over the decades has led me to believe that almost every failure in the kingdom of God can ultimately be traced to a failure of humility and a triumph of pride, whether overt or subtle. The deceptions of pride are always obvious to those who observe it from the outside but almost never to those held captive within it. There are, however, certain guideposts by which to measure the degree of our captivity.

a. Esteeming Others Higher

When we truly walk in humility before God, we will esteem others higher than ourselves, knowing that only the grace of God makes us able to stand responsibly before Him. Because we have a true realization of what we are in the flesh, we can sincerely appreciate the mercy God extends to us when He allows us to participate in His kingdom. Yet at the same time, in our hearts we will recognize the gift that each and every one of our brothers and sisters is in Christ. We will see them as the precious souls for whom Jesus suffered and died. We will then earnestly seek every opportunity to serve them with all our hearts in their time of need.

> Then Saul ordered his attendants: "Speak to David privately and say, 'Look, the king is pleased with you, and his attendants all like you; now become his son-in-law.'"
> They repeated these words to David. But David said, "Do you think it is a small matter to become the king's son-in-law? *I'm only a poor man and little known.*" (1 Sam. 18:22-23)

> *Although I am less than the least of all God's people*, this grace was given me: to preach to the Gentiles the unsearchable riches of Christ, and to make plain to everyone the administration of this mystery, which for ages past was kept hidden in God, who created all things. (Eph. 3:8-9)

> Be kindly affectionate to one another with brotherly love, *in honor giving preference to one another.* (Rom. 12:10)

> Your attitude should be the same as that of Christ Jesus: who, being in very nature God, did not consider equality with God something to be grasped, *but made Himself nothing, taking the very nature of a servant*, being made in human likeness. And being found in appearance as a man, *He humbled Himself and became obedient to the point of death, even the death of the cross.* (Phil. 2:5-8)

> Do nothing out of selfish ambition or vain conceit, but *in humility consider others better than yourselves.* (Phil. 2:3)

> And Jonathan made a covenant with David because he loved him as himself. *Jonathan took off the robe he was wearing and gave it to David, along with his tunic, and even his sword, his bow and his belt.* (1 Sam. 18:3-4)

> Young men, in the same way *be submissive* to those who are older. All of you, *clothe yourselves with humility* toward one another, because, *"God opposes the proud but gives grace to the humble."* (1 Pet. 5:5)

> Jesus knew that the Father had put all things under His power, and that He had come from God and was returning to God; so He got up from the meal, took off His outer clothing, and wrapped a towel around His waist. After that, *He poured water into a basin and*

began to wash His disciples' feet, drying them with the towel that was wrapped around Him.

He came to Simon Peter, who said to Him, "Lord, are You going to wash my feet?"

Jesus replied, "You do not realize now what I am doing, but later you will understand."

"No," said Peter, "You shall never wash my feet."

Jesus answered, "Unless I wash you, you have no part with Me."

"Then, Lord," Simon Peter replied, "not just my feet but my hands and my head as well!"

Jesus answered, "A person who has had a bath needs only to wash his feet; his whole body is clean. And you are clean, though not every one of you." (John 13:3-10)

b. Peace

Humility blossoms into peace in our lives because we no longer strive for position or eminence or to validate ourselves or our gifts to others. In short, those seeking to prove *themselves* are headed toward the terrible snare of strife, competition, self-validation and self-exaltation. There is a vast difference between the pride of *proving oneself* and the humility that alone can make full *proof of our ministry*. In regard to the former, our fellowship and relationship with God more than fulfills every need. So we don't measure ourselves among ourselves but find true security and fulfillment in a Christ-centered life of love. Our dependence on God allows Him to sustain us in every circumstance and way. We trust in His abiding provision, whether it comes directly by His Spirit or through our brothers and sisters. So the increasingly dominant desire of our life is to fulfill God's will; and when we humbly and trustingly stand in the place of His perfect way, we know an equally perfect peace because our minds are stayed on Him.

> You will guard him and keep him in perfect and constant peace whose mind [both its inclination and its character] is stayed on You, because he commits himself to You, leans on You, and hopes confidently in You. (Isa. 26:3, Ampl.)

God's rulership, His government, in our lives is thus perfected through the growing perfection of our submission to our mission; and where His government rules, there His peace will rest (Isa. 9:7).

The Hebrew word translated "peace," *shalom*, literally means, according to Brown, Driver and Briggs, "completeness, soundness." True peace, the *shalom* of God, comes with completing God's work for us. "There remains, then, a Sabbath-rest for the people of God; for anyone who enters God's rest also rests from his own work . . . . Let us, therefore, make every effort to enter that rest" (Heb. 4:9-11). When we reach levels of completion, we will more and more know God's peace. Rienecker says that the Greek New Testament word *eirene*, translated "peace," is "equivalent to the Hebrew *shalom* indicating wholeness, prosperity, well being." Humility before God leads to a completeness in God and the "true riches" of peace with God.

> *Humble yourselves* before the Lord, and He will *lift you up.* (James 4:10)

> For this is what the high and lofty One says—He who lives forever, whose name is holy: "I live in a high and holy place, but also with *him who is contrite and lowly in spirit, to revive the spirit of the lowly and to revive the heart of the contrite.*" (Isa. 57:15)

> So Abram said to Lot, "*Let's not have any quarreling* between you and me, or between your herdsmen and mine, for *we are brothers.* Is not the whole land before you? Let's part company. If you go to the left, I'll go to the right; if you go to the right, I'll go to the left." (Gen. 13:8-9)

> Isaac reopened the wells that had been dug in the time of his father Abraham, which the Philistines had stopped up after Abraham died, and he gave them the same names his father had given them.
> Isaac's servants dug in the valley and discovered a well of fresh water there. But the herdsmen of Gerar quarreled with Isaac's herdsmen and said, "The water is ours!" So he named the well Esek, because they disputed with him. Then they dug another well, but they quarreled over that one also; so he named it Sitnah. He moved on from there and dug another well, and *no one quarreled over it.* He named it Rehoboth, saying, "Now Yahweh has given us room and we will flourish in the land." (Gen. 26:18-22)

> I want men everywhere to lift up holy hands in prayer, *without anger or disputing.* (1 Tim. 2:8)

> Salt is good, but if it loses its saltiness, how can you make it salty again? Have salt in yourselves, and *be at peace* with each other. (Mark 9:50)

> Let us therefore *make every effort to do what leads to peace* and to mutual edification. (Rom. 14:19)

> Finally, brothers, good-by. Aim for perfection, listen to my appeal, be of one mind, *live in peace.* And *the God of love and peace will be with you.* (2 Cor. 13:11)

> Hold them in the highest regard in love because of their work. *Live in peace with each other.* (1 Thess. 5:13)

> *Make every effort to live in peace with all men* and to be holy; without holiness no one will see the Lord. (Heb. 12:14)

> *Blessed are the peacemakers*, for they will be *called sons of God.* (Matt. 5:9)

> You will *keep in perfect peace him whose mind is steadfast*, because *he trusts* in You. (Isa. 26:3)

2. Pride

The proud man refuses to enter into the labors of the Lord, which require that humility precede true success. Instead, the proud person only seeks works that lift him up in his own eyes and the eyes of others. As a slick and fit racehorse he rejoices only in the applause of the crowd and finds no joy in the pull of the harness on the lumbering draft horse. If the applause vanishes, so, too, does his reason for going on. One Hebrew word translated as "pride" is *gaah*, which means "to mount up, to be majestic." Another word translated as "pride," *govah*, means "elation" and "grandeur," while *shachats*, also translated "pride," literally means "to strut," to stride with great boldness and self-confidence. When a person sees himself as "majestic" or as possessing "grandeur," he sees nothing of what he truly is, whether in God's eyes or the eyes of others. His pride becomes the scales covering his eyes, making him stumble blindly along without even the eyes of others to help guide him. Instead of walking humbly before God, he struts around the barnyard. He may wear a saccharine mask of false humility, but inwardly he strides self-confidently in his vanity and struts in his pride. *Alazoneia*, the Greek word translated as "pride" in the New Testament, literally means, according to Rienecker, "the braggadocio which exaggerates what it possesses in order to impress other people."

The braggart may learn to more subtly "exaggerate" his gifts without starkly boasting with overt words. Perhaps he does so by his self-important confidence and smug style in putting forth his gift in order to validate his preeminence and "impress others." But all the "braggadocio" is nonetheless embarrassingly present in spite of all his efforts to make it more palatable. The proud man presumptuously esteems himself above others and sees himself as always deserving far more than what God has given him or others will recognize. Inflated in his own eyes, he is unable to fulfill the function God ordained for him, even as he strives in his flesh to do so. In his heart, he scorns the boundaries and limits of God's place for him and exalts himself to a place of preeminence, all the while ignoring the less than grand responsibilities that God would place on him to keep him humble. He gives preference to his own schedule rather than the schedule of others over him. Thus he concerns himself mainly with those things that enhance his own image and appearance, then judges all others by his own superficial assessment.

> When He noticed how the guests picked the places of honor at the table, He told them this parable: "When someone invites you to a wedding feast, *do not take the place of honor,* for a person more

distinguished than you may have been invited. If so, the host who invited both of you will come and say to you, 'Give this man your seat.' Then, humiliated, you will have to take the least important place. But when you are invited, *take the lowest place*, so that when your host comes, he will say to you, 'Friend, move up to a better place.' Then you will be honored in the presence of all your fellow guests. For *everyone who exalts himself will be humbled, and he who humbles himself will be exalted*." (Luke 14:7-11)

When pride comes, then comes disgrace, but with humility comes wisdom. (Prov. 11:2)

But after Uzziah became powerful, his pride led to his downfall. He was unfaithful to Yahweh his God, and entered the temple of Yahweh to burn incense on the altar of incense. Azariah the priest with eighty other courageous priests of Yahweh followed him in. They confronted him and said, "It is not right for you, Uzziah, to burn incense to Yahweh. That is for the priests, the descendants of Aaron, who have been consecrated to burn incense. Leave the sanctuary, for you have been unfaithful; and you will not be honored by Yahweh God."

Uzziah, who had a censer in his hand ready to burn incense, became angry. While he was raging at the priests in their presence before the incense altar in Yahweh's temple, leprosy broke out on his forehead.

When Azariah the chief priest and all the other priests looked at him, they saw that he had leprosy on his forehead, so they hurried him out. Indeed, he himself was eager to leave, because Yahweh had afflicted him.

King Uzziah had leprosy until the day he died. He lived in a separate house—leprous, and excluded from the temple of Yahweh. Jotham his son had charge of the palace and governed the people of the land. (2 Chron. 26:16-21)

Pride only breeds quarrels, but wisdom is found in those who take advice. (Prov. 13:10)

Pride goes before destruction, a haughty spirit before a fall. (Prov. 16:18)

The *proud and arrogant man*—"Mocker" is his name; he *behaves with overweening pride.* (Prov. 21:24)

A man's pride brings him low, but a man of lowly spirit gains honor. (Prov. 29:23)

The eyes of the arrogant man will be humbled and *the pride of men brought low*; Yahweh alone will be exalted in that day. (Isa. 2:11)

The arrogance of man will be brought low and *the pride of men humbled*; Yahweh alone will be exalted in that day. (Isa. 2:17)

Let another praise you, and *not your own mouth*; someone else, and not your own lips. (Prov. 27:2)

Do not exalt yourself in the king's presence, and *do not claim a place among great men*; it is better for him to say to you, "Come up here," than for him to humiliate you before a nobleman. (Prov. 25:6-7)

Samuel said, "Although *you were once small in your own eyes*, did you not become the head of the tribes of Israel? Yahweh anointed you king over Israel. And He sent you on a mission, saying, 'Go and completely destroy those wicked people, the Amalekites; make war on them until you have wiped them out.' Why did you not obey Yahweh? Why did you pounce on the plunder and do evil in the eyes of Yahweh?" (1 Sam. 15:17-19)

Love Yahweh, all you His saints! Yahweh preserves the faithful but *abundantly repays the one who acts in pride.* (Ps. 31:23, ESV)

a. Worldliness

Glorying of the flesh—the worship of self and exalting it to the place of God—lies behind all worldliness. When a child is worldly, he tries to conform himself to the lapsed world's image and not to Christ's. His speech, his attitudes, his mannerisms, his actions, do not reflect the humility of the risen Christ but the pride of fallen man. One lexicon translates the New Testament word *kosmikos*—worldly—as "'of this world' (i.e., made of mundane materials, adapted to this visible world, local and transitory)." The worldly child does not set his eyes upon the unseen reality of faith but upon the visible, the carnal, that which is passing away. Every new fad, whether of speech, attitude, mannerism, activity or dress, he picks up immediately, like a chameleon changing its colors with its changing environment. Without an identity of his own, and therefore not knowing who he is, he desperately tries to define himself by every latest cue coming forth from the surrounding world. So peer fear becomes his mode of existence. Such a child conforms to many different images—he or she may imitate the neighborhood kids (who are in turn imitating TV or movie or music personalities), but the child may also be imitating more sedate or sophisticated images of the world. Sometimes this worldliness is the otherworldliness of "never-never land," of the American fairy princess waiting for her prince charming. Or it may be the arrogant world of the intellectual. The worldly child may be polite, have good manners, know the right things to do and say, but depth of love and concern for God and others is lacking, so consumed is he with nervously trying to second guess his peers and the latest trends. When you look at him or her, you find yourself wondering, "What is he or she really like?" A facade always seems to float before your eyes, and you want to see through it to find the real gift God made the child to be. Such a child is insecure in his relationship with God and his parents. He tries to please others by appearing to be someone he thinks they'll like or be impressed by, but he has no real relationship with either God or his parents, at least none in the depth necessary to permit him to truly be himself in God. This is why he turns to the world to find the identity that he has lost, or never found, in Christ. Again, he does not know who he really is; and therefore his identity, like the chameleon, will forever change with all the changing fashions and trends of the surrounding world.

> But the people refused to listen to Samuel. "No!" they said. "We want a king over us. *Then we will be like all the other nations*, with a king to lead us and to go out before us and fight our battles." (1 Sam. 8:19-20)

> Now he who received seed among the thorns is he who hears the word, and *the cares of this world* and the deceitfulness of riches choke the word, and he becomes unfruitful. (Matt. 13:22)

> Brothers, I could not address you as spiritual but as worldly—mere infants in Christ. . . . You are still worldly. *For since there is jealousy and quarreling among you, are you not worldly?* Are you not acting like mere men? (1 Cor. 3:1, 3)

> *They are from the world and therefore speak from the viewpoint of the world*, and the world listens to them. (1 John 4:5)

> You adulterous people, don't you know that friendship with the world is hatred toward God? *Anyone who chooses to be a friend of the world becomes an enemy of God.* (James 4:4)

> *Do not love the world or anything in the world.* If anyone loves the world, the love of the Father is not in him. For everything in the world—the cravings of sinful man, the lust of his eyes and the boasting of what he has and does—comes not from the Father but from the world. (1 John 2:15-16)

> *Do not conform any longer to the pattern of this world*, but be transformed by the renewing of your mind. Then you will be able to test and approve what God's will is—His good, pleasing and perfect will. (Rom. 12:2)

> . . . for Demas, *because he loved this world*, has deserted me . . . . (2 Tim. 4:10)

b. Smirking, Sneering and Proud Looks

Those who exalt themselves find no peace—only turmoil. Their pride causes anxiety and frustration everywhere they go. Their own inner conflicts will show in their countenance. Their pride may cause them to smirk at God's authority. To smirk means "to smile in a conceited" or "complacent way."[41] A person smirks because in his heart he thinks he "knows better" than anyone else—whether God or man. He has a private secret that he shares with no one but himself (or perhaps only with others who share his haughty attitude or whom he thinks he can bring under the reign of his arrogant spirit). He automatically presumes that only he could possibly have the true view and see the true implications of everything, at least everything of any "real" importance. If his parents ask him what he smirks about, he cannot possibly explain it because, to him, they simply aren't capable of understanding—after all, they're bound by those pride-shackling teachings of that "silly old church." So he shakes his head superiorly at them and half-heartedly tries to hide his smirk. His face subtly adjusts its very contours as the pride of his heart molds his features and flashes through his steely eyes. The smirker may even seem at times to be respectful and considerate. His silence often even passes for humility to the undiscerning. But some circumstance will arise that will precipitate his smirk—some occasion will provoke his heart of pride to manifest itself. Just as the rebellious woman spoken of in Proverbs has an "impudent face," so his face will show what lies hidden and lurking in his heart (Prov. 7:13, KJV).

A wicked man shows a bold face. (Prov. 21:29, NASV)

The wicked, in the *haughtiness of his countenance*, does not seek Him. All his thoughts are, "There is no God." His ways are always prosperous; he is haughty and Your laws are far from him; he *sneers* at all his enemies. (Ps. 10:4-5, NASV, NIV)

The Pharisees, who loved money, heard all this and were *sneering* at Jesus. (Luke 16:14)

The people stood watching, and the rulers even *sneered* at Him. They said, "He saved others; let Him save Himself if He is the Christ of God, the Chosen One." (Luke 23:35)

Whom are you mocking? At whom do you *sneer* and stick out your tongue? Are you not a brood of rebels, the offspring of liars? (Isa. 57:4)

When they heard about the resurrection of the dead, some of them *sneered*, but others said, "We want to hear you again on this subject." (Acts 17:32)

Haughty eyes and a proud heart, the lamp of the wicked, are sin! (Prov. 21:4)

A scoundrel and villain, who goes about with a corrupt mouth, who *winks with his eye, signals with his feet* and *motions with his fingers*, who plots evil with deceit in his heart—he always stirs up dissension. Therefore disaster will overtake him in an instant; he will suddenly be destroyed—without remedy. (Prov. 6:12-15)

He who *winks maliciously* causes grief, and a chattering fool comes to ruin. (Prov. 10:10)

He who *winks with his eye* is plotting perversity; he who *purses his lips* is bent on evil. (Prov. 16:30)

Their words and deeds are against Yahweh, defying His glorious presence. The *look on their faces* testifies against them; they parade their sin like Sodom; they do not hide it. (Isa. 3:8-9)

Whoever slanders his neighbor in secret, him will I put to silence; whoever has *haughty eyes and a proud heart*, him will I not endure. (Ps. 101:5)

There are six things Yahweh hates, seven that are detestable to

Him: *haughty eyes*, a lying tongue, hands that shed innocent blood, a heart that devises wicked schemes, feet that are quick to rush into evil, a false witness who pours out lies and a man who stirs up dissension among brothers. (Prov. 6:16-19)

For You will save the humble people, but will bring down *haughty looks*. (Ps. 18:27)

c. Exalted View of Self

The proud child has an inflated and exalted view of himself. He thinks of himself more highly than he ought to (Rom. 12:3). He does not perceive the proper limits and bounds of his own gifts and talents because he fastens his eyes upon himself rather than upon the Giver of those gifts and talents, a Giver Who stands so far above and beyond anything the proud child might aspire to. Such a child may use, or allow himself to be used by, God's gifts, but only to exalt himself, never to exalt God or truth. He will often take the gifts God deposited in his life and spread them out before the "monarch of the children of pride" to use as that wicked king pleases. He listens to every story his parents tell of their children, every testimony given in the church about families, to see if something in them might somehow exalt him and show how wonderful he is. Then he smiles 'humbly' if such a story does this, proud in his heart of his own works and person. But this sin may also be expressed in pouting or sulking or sullenness if the child feels that he has not received ample attention or praise or opportunity to display his self-aggrandizing gifts. It may also be seen in a swagger or some other indication that he takes pride in some accomplishment or status he believes to be his. He most often has firmly convinced himself (and perhaps a few others) that no one in the family or church appreciates his true worth; and indeed, no one can appreciate it, at least not as the child sees it, since he sees it as far above anything it actually is. So he must then *show* everyone how great his gift is, flaunt it, exalt himself and make everyone take due notice. If they don't, he may get mean, even violent, to show them that they *have* to take notice of him. He never sees that every one of his brothers and sisters in Christ is also a gift that Jesus in love has given to him. He therefore fails to esteem them more highly than himself (Phil. 2:3), nor does he see his own unworthiness to possess any place at all in the kingdom of God. If he does have any gifts, he will always have moved out way ahead of even God in the exercise of God's gift, and so he has even forgotten where the gift came from. Neither can he truly serve anyone in love because he considers everyone to be unworthy of the great sacrifice that he has made. Or else he appears to be busily serving everyone in love, ingratiating himself for his own selfish purposes, but refusing to truly submit himself to those above him in the Lord because this would be too abasing to his own great gifts. So even his appearance of being so busily loving and serving is merely self-exalting.

> Two men went up to the temple to pray, one a Pharisee and the other a tax collector. The Pharisee stood up and *prayed about himself*: "*God, I thank You that I am not like other men*—robbers, evildoers, adulterers—or even like this tax collector." (Luke 18:10-11)

> My brothers, as believers in our glorious Lord Jesus Christ, don't show favoritism. Suppose a man comes into your meeting wearing a gold ring and fine clothes, and a poor man in shabby clothes also comes in. If you show special attention to the man wearing fine clothes and say, "Here's a good seat for you," but say to the poor man, "You stand there" or "Sit on the floor by my feet," have you not discriminated among yourselves and become judges with evil thoughts?
> Listen, my dear brothers: *Has not God chosen those who are poor in the eyes of the world to be rich in faith and to inherit the kingdom He promised those who love Him*? But you have insulted the poor. Is it not the rich who are exploiting you? Are they not the ones who are dragging you into court? Are they not the ones who are slandering the noble name of Him to whom you belong?
> If you really keep the royal law found in Scripture, "Love your neighbor as yourself," you are doing right. But *if you show favoritism, you sin* and are convicted by the law as lawbreakers. (James 2:1-9)

> Do you see a man *wise in his own eyes*? There is more hope for a fool than for him. (Prov. 26:12)

> *You said in your heart, "I will ascend to heaven; I will raise my throne above the stars of God; I will sit enthroned on the mount of assembly, on the utmost heights of the sacred mountain. I will ascend above the tops of the clouds; I will make myself like the Most High."* But you are brought down to the grave, to the depths of the pit. (Isa. 14:13-15)

> He said, *"Is not this the great Babylon I have built as the royal residence, by my mighty power and for the glory of my majesty?"*
> The words were still on his lips when a voice came from heaven, "This is what is decreed for you, King Nebuchadnezzar: Your royal authority has been taken from you. You will be driven away from people and will live with the wild animals; you will eat grass like cattle. Seven times will pass by for you until you acknowledge that the Most High is sovereign over the kingdoms of men and gives them to anyone He wishes." (Dan. 4:30-32)

> A rich man may be *wise in his own eyes*, but a poor man who has discernment sees through him. (Prov. 28:11)

> Elisha sent a messenger to say to him, "Go, wash yourself seven times in the Jordan, and your flesh will be restored and you will be cleansed."
> But Naaman went away angry and said, "I thought that he would surely come out to me and stand and call on the name of Yahweh

his God, wave his hand over the spot and cure me of my leprosy. Are not Abana and Pharpar, the rivers of Damascus, better than any of the waters of Israel? Couldn't I wash in them and be cleansed?" So he turned and went off in a rage.

Naaman's servants went to him and said, *"My father, if the prophet had told you to do some great thing, would you not have done it? How much more, then, when he tells you, 'Wash and be cleansed!'"* (2 Kings 5:10-13)

On the appointed day Herod, wearing his royal robes, sat on his throne and delivered a public address to the people. *They shouted, "This is the voice of a god, not of a man." Immediately, because Herod did not give praise to God, an angel of the Lord struck him down,* and he was eaten by worms and died. (Acts 12:21-23)

For by the grace given me I say to every one of you: *Do not think of yourself more highly than you ought, but rather think of yourself with sober judgment,* in accordance with the measure of faith God has given you. (Rom. 12:3)

When they had pasture, they were filled; they were filled and their *heart was exalted*; therefore they forgot Me. (Hos. 13:6)

Don't let anyone deceive you in any way, for that day will not come until the rebellion occurs and the man of lawlessness is revealed, the man doomed to destruction. *He will oppose and will exalt himself over everything that is called God or is worshiped, so that he sets himself up in God's temple, proclaiming himself to be God.* (2 Thess. 2:3-4)

Self-exaltation pops up in presumptuousness, envy, jealousy, arguing, judging in the flesh, and it always ultimately evokes *krisis*, judgment.

For everyone who *exalts himself* will be humbled, and he who humbles himself will be exalted. (Luke 14:11)

d. Presumptuousness

According to Strong, the Hebrew word *aphal*, translated as "presumption," literally means "to swell, to be lifted up." In the New Testament, the word translated as "presumptuous" in the King James Version is *tolmetes*, which Rienecker translates as literally meaning "one who dares, one who is brazen . . . . The word smacks of the reckless daring that defies God and man." So in his pride, he who is presumptuous assumes, because of his exalted view of himself, that he can impetuously and cavalierly (even if secretly) do whatever he feels without waiting for direction from the Spirit or those the Spirit places in authority over him. He recognizes no limits, no restraints to his plans, purposes and actions. He does not think to ask permission because he cannot conceive of humbling himself enough to ask, much less say "please" to anyone. Who, after all, can possibly be worthy of such submission from so exalted a "gift"? The presumptuous person takes upon himself more than is warranted by his position or his abilities. He willfully steps beyond the limits that God would place upon him, convinced that he must meet every need and solve every problem through the power of his own person, his own fleshly nature, which he sees not as fleshly but as God's greatest gift to the world. So he inevitably steps out of his place and into that of another. Therefore not only does he fail to accomplish his own purpose in God, but he also prevents others from accomplishing theirs, crippling the whole purpose of God for the family or church. He obstructs the flow of the Spirit and prevents God from doing what He has ordained to accomplish through the intricate order of the Body and the other members of the Body, hence the severe judgment evoked by this sin. The presumptuous soul finally exalts himself above even the Holy Spirit. Since he seeks a higher place than he has been given, he rejects the order God gave and substitutes one of his own making, using the gift God gave him to ingratiate himself to others whom he will then subvert in order to only further exalt himself above every gift. He seeks to change God's work into his own, taking pride and glorying in the flesh while utterly convinced that he does the work of God. No wonder, then, that David prayed specifically to be kept from the "presumptuous sin."

> *Keep back Your servant also from presumptuous sins*; let them not have dominion over me. Then I shall be blameless, and I shall be innocent of great transgression. (Ps. 19:13)

> But Moses said, "Why are you disobeying Yahweh's command? This will not succeed! Do not go up, because Yahweh is not with you. You will be defeated by your enemies, for the Amalekites and Canaanites will face you there. Because you have turned away from Yahweh, He will not be with you and you will fall by the sword."
> *Nevertheless, in their presumption they went up toward the high hill country, though neither Moses nor the ark of Yahweh's covenant moved from the camp. Then the Amalekites and Canaanites who lived in that hill country came down and attacked them and beat them down all the way to Hormah.* (Num. 14:41-45)

> *But after Uzziah became powerful, his pride led to his downfall.* He was unfaithful to Yahweh his God, and entered the temple of Yahweh to burn incense on the altar of incense. Azariah the priest with eighty other courageous priests of Yahweh followed him in. They confronted him and said, "It is not right for you, Uzziah, to burn incense to Yahweh. That is for the priests, the descendants of Aaron, who have been consecrated to burn incense. Leave the sanctuary, for you have been unfaithful; and you will not be honored by Yahweh God."
> Uzziah, who had a censer in his hand ready to burn incense, became angry. While he was raging at the priests in their presence before the incense altar in Yahweh's temple, leprosy broke out on his forehead. When Azariah the chief priest and all the other priests looked at him, they saw that he had leprosy on his forehead,

so they hurried him out. Indeed, he himself was eager to leave, because Yahweh had afflicted him.

King Uzziah had leprosy until the day he died. He lived in a separate house—leprous, and excluded from the temple of Yahweh. Jotham his son had charge of the palace and governed the people of the land. (2 Chron. 26:16-21)

When they came to the threshing floor of Nacon, *Uzzah reached out and took hold of the ark of God*, because the oxen stumbled. Yahweh's anger burned against Uzzah because of his *irreverent act*; therefore God struck him down and he died there beside the ark of God. (2 Sam. 6:6-7)

I tell you the truth, *the man who does not enter the sheep pen by the gate*, but climbs in by some other way, is *a thief and a robber*. (John 10:1)

Don't let anyone deceive you in any way, for that day will not come until the rebellion occurs and the man of lawlessness is revealed, the man doomed to destruction. He will oppose and will *exalt himself* over everything that is called God or is worshiped, so that he sets himself up in God's temple, proclaiming himself to be God. (2 Thess. 2:3-4)

. . . *and especially those who walk according to the flesh in the lust* of uncleanness and despise authority. *They are presumptuous, self-willed*; they are not afraid to slander dignitaries; yet even angels, although they are stronger and more powerful, do not bring slanderous accusations against them in the presence of the Lord. But these men blaspheme in matters they do not understand. They are like brute beasts, creatures of instinct, born only to be caught and destroyed, and like beasts they too will perish. (2 Pet. 2:10-12, NKJV, NIV)

If a matter arises which is too hard for you to judge, between degrees of bloodguiltiness, between one judgment or another, or between one punishment or another, matters of controversy within your gates, then you shall arise and go up to the place which Yahweh your God chooses, and you shall come to the priests, the Levites, and to the judge there in those days, and inquire of them; they shall pronounce upon you the sentence of judgment.

You shall do according to the sentence which they pronounce upon you in that place which Yahweh chooses. And you shall be careful to do according to all that they order you.

According to the sentence of the law in which they instruct you, according to the judgment which they tell you, you shall do; you shall not turn aside to the right hand or to the left from the sentence which they pronounce upon you.

Now *the man who acts presumptuously and will not heed the priest who stands to minister there before Yahweh your God, or the judge, that man shall die. So you shall put away the evil person from Israel. And all the people shall hear and fear, and no longer act presumptuously*. (Deut. 17:8-13)

e. Envy and Jealousy

The child who envies another is neither satisfied with what God made him to be nor has he fulfilled what God gave him to do. Therefore he begins to hate those who are and do. Whereas jealousy can at times arise from an intense affection placed on others and can therefore, if it remains centered in God, mark at least one aspect of godly character (God describes Himself as a "jealous God"), envy arises from an inturned self-love that can only bear the fruit of hatred, even murder. Envy possesses enduring affection for no one except self. It often lies behind the mentality of the mob in revolt. Many, even of a more secular orientation, have noted that today's generation is marked by envy. Self-absorbed, demanding its "rights" and trumpeting its so-called victimizations, such a generation can only hate anyone or anything it perceives as having more of anything or as standing in the way of getting whatever the envious covets. Like Cain, an envious person thinks only of himself and cannot therefore conceive of becoming jealous—that is, zealous—for the things of God. So if anyone else does exhibit such a desire toward God, envy nurtures a murderous attitude toward the faithful that often expresses itself in rage, slander, lies, mocking, scoffing or else subtle subversion. As Jesus makes clear, murder is not merely the physical destruction of another but is hatred without cause against another (Matt. 5:21-22). Because envy has none of the restraints that the affection rooted in jealousy can potentially provide, its hatred, if not externally restrained, will, like Cain's, eventually end in murder, if in nothing else, in the destruction of the witness, reputation, accomplishments, position and function of others. In the end, envy must result in murder because it hates the people who stand in a place in which envy thinks it should stand, and so those people must be destroyed and removed. This is true whether done overtly as open slander and lies or as covert subversion and a willful ignoring of everyone else's authority and place.

An envious child cannot know godliness with contentment (1 Tim. 6:6), and so he constantly feels cheated, victimized and at a loss, even when he has everything he needs and perhaps much more than most, as was true of satan (Ezek. 28:12-17). Envy can be directed toward anyone or anything. It may have a particular focus at various times, zeroing in on particular wants and demands; but even when it gets what it wants, this never satisfies it. The envy of younger children looks resentfully at older children because, in envy's eyes, they somehow seem to have greater respect and responsibility; then it envies the younger children because they have fewer responsibilities, greater opportunity to play and seem to get more attention. The envious child is basically dissatisfied with *whatever* comes his way—whether it's what God and his parents give or what he has made himself to be. Envy can be manifested in a whining and complaining that never ceases, even when, over and over again, it gets what it wants. The Greek New Testament word that is translated as "envy," *phthonos,* means "pain felt and malignity conceived at the sight of excellence or happiness; malice." Love rejoices in the victories and joy of others; envy stews and agonizes over it. It opposes the very essence of the Spirit of Christ.

God describes Himself as jealous, and the Hebrew word translated "jealous," as seen, also means "zealous." Again, jealousy is a consuming, burning force. Since God is love, since He has made all things for Himself, for His purpose and His pleasure, He refuses to compromise or yield until all things come into perfect harmony and oneness with Him. His jealous love will not rest until He has cleansed His people from all that separates them from Him. But while this jealousy centered in God works toward our salvation, when jealousy becomes centered in the human heart and its lapsed purposes, it becomes a force for destruction, disintegration and death. As said, jealousy is also a powerful, all-consuming force. It desires to possess completely for itself whatever it fixes its attention upon and to remove whatever stands in its way or whatever would share in its accomplishment. The carnally jealous child stews in resentment and bitterness toward everyone who does not center their attention upon him. Carnal jealousy, like envy, seeks to destroy and tear down everything that competes with one's self. God's jealousy *raises* everything to His level. Mere human jealousy seeks to destroy what it cannot exclusively claim, possess or be, to *reduce* everything to the lowest common level, often masking itself in a crusade for "equality in all things," a crusade to "reveal the truth" and "expose the evil" of those who have done nothing more evil than become the object of envy and jealousy. While God's jealousy elevates the lowest level to "be like Him," human jealousy tries to degrade the reputation of the highest until it's brought down to the pit in which the envious and jealous slither. Yeats described the attitude in a poem:

> These are the clouds about the fallen sun,
> The majesty that shuts his burning eye:
> The weak lay hand on what the strong has done,
> Till that be tumbled that was lifted high . . . ,
> And all things at one common level lie.[42]

In the camp *they grew envious of Moses and of Aaron,* who was consecrated to Yahweh. The earth opened up and swallowed Dathan; it buried the company of Abiram. Fire blazed among their followers; a flame consumed the wicked. (Ps. 106:16-18)

Now Adam knew Eve his wife, and she conceived and bore Cain, and said, "I have acquired a man from Yahweh." Then she bore again, this time his brother Abel . . . . Now Abel kept flocks, and

Cain worked the soil. In the course of time Cain brought some of the fruits of the soil as an offering to Yahweh. But Abel brought fat portions from some of the firstborn of his flock. *Yahweh looked with favor on Abel and his offering*, but on Cain and his offering He did not look with favor. So *Cain was very angry, and his face was downcast.*

Then Yahweh said to Cain, "Why are you angry? Why is your face downcast? If you do what is right, will you not be accepted? But if you do not do what is right, sin is crouching at your door; it desires to have you, but you must master it."

Now Cain said to his brother Abel, "Let's go out to the field." And while they were in the field, Cain attacked his brother Abel and killed him.

Then Yahweh said to Cain, "Where is your brother Abel?"

"I don't know," he replied. "Am I my brother's keeper?" (Gen. 4:1-9, NKJV, NIV)

But as for me, my feet had almost slipped; I had nearly lost my foothold. *For I envied the arrogant when I saw the prosperity of the wicked.* (Ps. 73:2-3)

A heart at peace gives life to the body, *but envy rots the bones.* (Prov. 14:30)

Do not let your heart envy sinners, but always be zealous for the fear of Yahweh. (Prov. 23:17)

And I saw that *all labor and all achievement spring from man's envy of his neighbor*. This too is meaningless, a chasing after the wind. (Eccles. 4:4)

"Do you want me to release to you the king of the Jews?" asked Pilate, knowing *it was out of envy that the chief priests had handed Jesus over to him.* (Mark 15:9-10)

Furthermore, since they did not think it worthwhile to retain the knowledge of God, He gave them over to a depraved mind, to do what ought not to be done. They have become filled with every kind of wickedness, evil, greed and depravity. They are full of *envy,* murder, strife, deceit and malice. They are gossips . . . . (Rom. 1:28-29)

If anyone teaches false doctrines and does not agree to the sound instruction of our Lord Jesus Christ and to godly teaching, he is conceited and understands nothing. He has an unhealthy interest in controversies and arguments that result in *envy,* quarreling, malicious talk, evil suspicions. (1 Tim. 6:3-4)

It is true that *some preach Christ out of envy and rivalry*, but others out of good will. The latter do so in love, knowing that I am put here for the defense of the gospel. (Phil. 1:15-16)

Do not envy wicked men, do not desire their company; for their hearts plot violence, and their lips talk about making trouble. (Prov. 24:1-2)

Do not envy a violent man or choose any of his ways, for Yahweh detests a perverse man but takes the upright into His confidence. (Prov. 3:31-32)

Do not fret because of evil men or *be envious of the wicked*, for the evil man has no future hope, and the lamp of the wicked will be snuffed out. (Prov. 24:19-20)

Then he dreamed still another dream and told it to his brothers, and said, "Look, I have dreamed another dream. And this time, the sun, the moon, and the eleven stars bowed down to me."

So he told it to his father and his brothers; and his father rebuked him and said to him, "What is this dream that you have dreamed? Shall your mother and I and your brothers indeed come to bow down to the earth before you?"

And *his brothers envied him*, but his father kept the matter in mind . . . .

Now when they saw him afar off, even before he came near them, they conspired against him to kill him. (Gen. 37:9-11, 18)

Because the patriarchs were *jealous* of Joseph, they sold him as a slave into Egypt. But God was with him. (Acts 7:9)

You are still worldly. *For since there is jealousy and quarreling among you, are you not worldly?* Are you not acting like mere men? (1 Cor. 3:3)

Anger is cruel and fury overwhelming, but *who can stand before jealousy*? (Prov. 27:4)

When the men were returning home after David had killed the Philistine, the women came out from all the towns of Israel to meet King Saul with singing and dancing, with joyful songs and with tambourines and lutes. As they danced, they sang: "Saul has slain his thousands, and David his tens of thousands."

Saul was very angry; this refrain galled him. "They have credited David with tens of thousands," he thought, "but me with only thousands. What more can he get but the kingdom?" And *from that time on Saul kept a jealous eye on David.*

The next day an evil spirit from God came forcefully upon Saul. He was prophesying in his house, while David was playing the harp, as he usually did. Saul had a spear in his hand and he hurled it, saying to himself, "I'll pin David to the wall." But David eluded him twice. (1 Sam. 18:6-11)

When the Jews saw the crowds, *they were filled with jealousy* and talked abusively against what Paul was saying. (Acts 13:45)

The acts of the sinful nature are obvious: sexual immorality, impurity and debauchery; idolatry and witchcraft; hatred, discord, *jealousy*, fits of rage, selfish ambition, dissensions, factions and envy; drunkenness, orgies, and the like. I warn you, as I did before, that those who live like this will not inherit the kingdom of God. (Gal. 5:19-21)

f. Judging

When someone judges others according to the flesh, he forgets that he is a sinner saved by grace. He becomes ready to offer his opinions and views where they are neither warranted nor desired. His heart grows hard as he forgets the pit from which he himself has been dug. He constantly sees everyone else's flecks of failure but refuses to cast the beam of failure—pride—from his own eye. He fails to realize that God will judge him exactly as he judges others.

> Do not judge, or you too will be judged. *For in the same way you judge others, you will be judged*, and with the measure you use, it will be measured to you.
> Why do you look at the speck of sawdust in your brother's eye and pay no attention to the plank in your own eye? How can you say to your brother, "Let me take the speck out of your eye," when all the time there is a plank in your own eye? You hypocrite, first take the plank out of your own eye, and then you will see clearly to remove the speck from your brother's eye. (Matt. 7:1-5)

> You, therefore, have no excuse, *you who pass judgment on someone else, for at whatever point you judge the other, you are condemning yourself*, because you who pass judgment do the same things. Now we know that God's judgment against those who do such things is based on truth. So when you, a mere man, pass judgment on them and yet do the same things, do you think you will escape God's judgment? Or do you show contempt for the riches of His kindness, tolerance and patience, not realizing that God's kindness leads you toward repentance? (Rom. 2:1-4)

> *You, then, why do you judge your brother? Or why do you look down on your brother?* For we will all stand before God's judgment seat. It is written: "'As surely as I live,' says the Lord, 'Every knee will bow before Me; every tongue will confess to God.'"
> So then, each of us will give an account of himself to God.
> Therefore *let us stop passing judgment on one another*. Instead, make up your mind not to put any stumbling block or obstacle in your brother's way. (Rom. 14:10-13)

> My brethren, be not many masters, knowing that we shall receive the greater condemnation. (James 3:1, KJV)

> As the ark of Yahweh was entering the City of David, Michal daughter of Saul watched from a window. And when she saw King David leaping and dancing before Yahweh, *she despised him in her heart.*
> When David returned home to bless his household, Michal daughter of Saul came out to meet him and said, "How the king of Israel has distinguished himself today, disrobing in the sight of the slave girls of his servants as any vulgar fellow would!"
> David said to Michal, "It was before Yahweh, who chose me rather

than your father or anyone from his house when He appointed me ruler over Yahweh's people Israel—I will celebrate before Yahweh. I will become even more undignified than this, and I will be humiliated in my own eyes. But by these slave girls you spoke of, I will be held in honor."

And Michal daughter of Saul had no children to the day of her death. (2 Sam 6:16, 20-23)

To some who were *confident of their own righteousness and looked down on everybody else*, Jesus told this parable: "Two men went up to the temple to pray, one a Pharisee and the other a tax collector. The Pharisee stood up and *prayed about himself*: 'God, I thank you that I am not like other men—robbers, evildoers, adulterers—or even like this tax collector. I fast twice a week and give a tenth of all I get.'

"But the tax collector stood at a distance. He would not even look up to heaven, but beat his breast and said, 'God, have mercy on me, a sinner.'

"I tell you that this man, rather than the other, went home justified before God. *For everyone who exalts himself will be humbled, and he who humbles himself will be exalted*." (Luke 18:9-14)

So Joseph went after his brothers and found them near Dothan. But they saw him in the distance, and before he reached them, they plotted to kill him.

"Here comes that dreamer!" they said to each other. (Gen. 37:17-19)

David asked the men standing near him, "What will be done for the man who kills this Philistine and removes this disgrace from Israel? Who is this uncircumcised Philistine that he should defy the armies of the living God?". . .

When Eliab, David's oldest brother, heard him speaking with the men, he burned with anger at him and asked, "Why have you come down here? And with whom did you leave those few sheep in the desert? I know how conceited you are and how wicked your heart is; you came down only to watch the battle." (1 Sam. 17:26, 28)

So Obadiah went to meet Ahab and told him, and Ahab went to meet Elijah. When he saw Elijah, he said to him, "Is that you, you troubler of Israel?" (1 Kings 18:16-17)

Scripture says to judge only *in the Spirit* (1 Cor. 2:14-15). Such judgment is necessary because we must make many decisions in our lives, and we depend upon the Spirit of God to "judge" in such a way as to show us what to do and to say. Only the Spirit *always* judges rightly (1 Cor. 2:10-11). Scripture forbids us to judge in the flesh, with our carnal mind (Isa. 11:3-4; John 7:24). The motive of the flesh is always to "be as God." Therefore the flesh can never judge honestly but only out of pride, always desiring to be greater than someone else. The flesh can always see only partially; only God sees everything in its fullness, and so He alone can be the just Judge.

Paul also said that we are not to judge those outside the church (1 Cor.

5:12). And Peter similarly declared that judgment begins at the house of God (1 Pet. 4:17, NKJV). This is because to whom much is given, of them much is required (Luke 12:48). Moreover, Paul said if we would judge ourselves, we would not be judged at the end of the world. So if judgment begins at the house of God, it is only to save us from an eternal judgment.

g. Arguing

An argumentative child becomes oblivious to God-centered relationship. He sees his views, opinions or whatever he has set his mind to as more important than the people he argues with and the order of God. He is like Uzzah, who touches the ark because it's so obviously falling but has no regard for the order God has designated by which the ark may be approached (1 Chron. 13:6-14; 15:1-28). Such a child abandons trust in God and tries to push through his own wants, desires or views by the power of his flesh. The Hebrew word *reev*, translated "quarrel," literally means, according to one source, "a contest," and it is rooted in the meaning "to toss, to grapple, to wrangle." One exception *might* be in formal philosophy, but otherwise we can say that the difference between argument and discussion is that discussion is a mutual search for a common truth; argument is a "contest" to see who will win intellectually. It is therefore rooted in pride. Clearly, arguing destroys relationships, causing us to see the one with whom we argue as an opponent to be defeated so that our own flesh may prevail and be exalted.

> Do everything *without complaining or arguing*, so that you may become blameless and pure, children of God without fault in a crooked and depraved generation, in which you shine like stars in the universe. (Phil. 2:14-15)

> *Pride only breeds quarrels*, but wisdom is found in those who take advice. (Prov. 13:10)

> A greedy man stirs up dissension, but he who trusts in Yahweh will prosper. (Prov. 28:25)

> They came to Capernaum. When He was in the house, He asked them, "What were you arguing about on the road?" But they kept quiet *because on the way they had argued about who was the greatest.* (Mark 9:33-34)

> There are six things Yahweh hates, seven that are detestable to Him: haughty eyes, a lying tongue, hands that shed innocent blood, . . . a false witness who pours out lies and *a man who stirs up dissension among brothers.* (Prov. 6:16-17, 19)

> *Hatred stirs up dissension*, but love covers over all wrongs. (Prov. 10:12)

> A gentle answer turns away wrath, but *a harsh word stirs up anger.* (Prov. 15:1)

He who loves a quarrel loves sin; he who builds a high gate invites destruction. (Prov. 17:19)

An offended brother is more unyielding than a fortified city, *and disputes are like the barred gates of a citadel.* (Prov. 18:19)

It is to a man's honor to avoid strife, but *every fool is quick to quarrel.* (Prov. 20:3)

As charcoal to embers and as wood to fire, *so is a quarrelsome man for kindling strife.* (Prov. 26:21)

You are still worldly. *For since there is jealousy and quarreling among you,* are you not worldly? Are you not acting like mere men? (1 Cor. 3:3)

Don't have anything to do with foolish and stupid arguments, because you know they produce quarrels. *And the Lord's servant must not quarrel;* instead, he must *be kind to everyone,* able to teach, *not resentful.* (2 Tim. 2:23-24)

If you have played the fool and exalted yourself or if you have planned evil, clap your hand over your mouth!

For as churning the milk produces butter, and as twisting the nose produces blood, so *stirring up anger produces strife.* (Prov. 30:32-33)

Haughtiness brings God's judgment:

For whoever exalts himself will be humbled, and whoever humbles himself will be exalted. (Matt. 23:12)

Pride goes before destruction, a haughty spirit before a fall. (Prov. 16:18)

You save the humble, but *Your eyes are on the haughty to bring them low.* (2 Sam. 22:28)

Yahweh says, "The women of Zion are *haughty,* walking along with outstretched necks, flirting with their eyes, tripping along with mincing steps, with ornaments jingling on their ankles. Therefore Yahweh will bring sores on the heads of the women of Zion; Yahweh will make their scalps bald." (Isa. 3:16-17)

H. KINDNESS AND GENEROSITY/ MEANNESS AND GREED

1. Kindness and Generosity

The human heart, the scripture tells us, is desperately wicked, even deceitful above all things (Jer. 17:9). From it proceeds every evil (Matt. 15:17-20). No entirely good thing can be found to come from the fallen human nature (Rom. 7:18). So long as a person is centered in himself, his heart is hardened to one degree or another. But when we turn out from ourselves and toward God, and when His nature is engrafted within us, His heart and mind will come to be expressed through us. "God is love" (1 John 4:8), and Paul tells us that love is kind (1 Cor. 13:4). We see the kindness of love perfectly reflected in the life of Jesus Christ, in His tenderness, His care, His concern for everyone in need. He wept with tears of compassion for people (Luke 19:41-44). This supernatural kindness even to enemies, because it is so unnatural to fallen humanity, comes to be expressed spontaneously only from hearts infused by God's Spirit. *Chrestos*, the Greek word translated as "kindness," means literally "to furnish what is needed," what is "useful, profitable, good."

Sometimes, however, it is true that "what is needed" must take the form of anger, rebuke or chastisement. Therefore kindness should never be confused with that mere "niceness" that forever shows unlimited and undiscriminating tolerance to every form of iniquity, stubbornness, rebellion, pride and dishonesty. Scripture speaks repeatedly of God's anger against such sin. When Moses returned from the mountain of God to the Israelite camp to find the Israelites worshiping the golden calf, "his anger burned" (Exod. 32:19). When the Pharisees resented Jesus' acts of healing performed on the Sabbath, Mark reports that Jesus "looked around at them in anger and, deeply distressed at their stubborn hearts," performed a healing (Mark 3:5). When Jesus cleared the temple of the money changers and "those selling doves," He decried them for making God's house "a 'den of robbers'" (Matt. 21:12-13). Such godly anger actually reveals the kindness of God, for "wounds from a friend can be trusted, but an enemy multiplies kisses" (Prov. 27:6), and if a "righteous man" chastens us, it is to be considered "a kindness" (Ps. 141:5). In the Old Testament, the Hebrew word translated as "kindness" is *chesed*, the fulfillment in love of all our covenant obligations. In Matthew 11:30, when Jesus speaks of His yoke being gentle or easy, this is the word *chrestos*. The yoke symbolizes a certain bondage, in this case, of our bond service of love to Jesus. God expressed His kindness to us by making us His love-slaves, and our service to Him enables us to become channels of His kindness to others so that we might do those "good works, which God prepared in advance for us to do" (Eph. 2:10). He infuses His nature within us, which motivates us to give of ourselves completely and joyfully, pouring out everything we are and have in His service. As we pour ourselves out for our brothers and sisters in love, we will naturally express generosity. The Greek word *haplotes*, translated "generosity," has, according to Rienecker, the literal meaning of "simplicity" and "single-mindedness." It means a "true open-heartedness and generosity toward others in which there is no duplicity of motive." Arndt and Gingrich give the meaning of this word as "sincere concern." This "sincere concern" of the heart will naturally express itself in our demeanor and actions.

a. Considerate

The second commandment, like unto the first, is to love our neighbor as ourselves. When we obey this command through God's Spirit and grace, we no longer take only our own needs, burdens and desires into account when charting our course of action. Our frame of reference changes, and we feel the needs and burdens of our brothers and sisters as vitally and viscerally as our own. Rienecker translates the Greek word *gnosis*, which in 1 Peter 3:7 is translated "considerate" in the New International Version, as "Christian insight and tact, a conscious sensitivity to God's will." We are conscious and sensitive to the needs around us because God's love has entered our hearts. True consideration of others cannot come merely from the human will but rather becomes the spontaneous expression of only a transformed inner nature.

> How blessed is he who *considers* the helpless; Yahweh will deliver him in a day of trouble. Yahweh will protect him, and keep him alive, and he shall be called blessed upon the earth; and do not give him over to the desire of his enemies. Yahweh will sustain him upon his sickbed; in his illness, You restore him to health. (Ps. 41:1-3, NASU)

> And let us *consider* how we may spur one another on toward love and good deeds. (Heb. 10:24)

> He who oppresses the poor shows contempt for their Maker, but *whoever is kind to the needy* honors God. (Prov. 14:31)

> If you have any encouragement from being united with Christ,

if any comfort from His love, if any fellowship with the Spirit, if any tenderness and compassion, then make my joy complete by being like-minded, having the same love, being one in spirit and purpose. Do nothing out of selfish ambition or vain conceit, but in humility *consider others better than yourselves*. Each of you *should look not only to your own interests, but also to the interests of others*. (Phil. 2:1-4)

Before he had finished praying, Rebekah came out with her jar on her shoulder. She was the daughter of Bethuel son of Milcah, who was the wife of Abraham's brother Nahor. The girl was very beautiful, a virgin; no man had ever lain with her. She went down to the spring, filled her jar and came up again.

The servant hurried to meet her and said, "Please give me a little water from your jar."

"*Drink, my lord,*" she said, and quickly lowered the jar to her hands and *gave him a drink*.

After she had given him a drink, *she said, "I'll draw water for your camels too, until they have finished drinking."* So she quickly emptied her jar into the trough, ran back to the well to draw more water, and drew enough for all his camels. (Gen. 24:15-20)

But Jacob said to him, "My lord knows that the children are tender and that *I must care for* the ewes and cows that are nursing their young. If they are driven hard just one day, all the animals will die. So let my lord go on ahead of his servant, *while I move along slowly at the pace of the droves before me and that of the children,* until I come to my lord in Seir." (Gen. 33:13-14)

We *who are strong ought to bear with the failings of the weak and not to please ourselves. Each of us should please his neighbor* for his good, to build him up. (Rom. 15:1-2)

b. Merciful

This love and care that children of good character will give others does not come merely at the child's own convenience. Children faithful to express God's love will consistently share His mercy. In the New Testament, the Greek word translated as "mercy" corresponds to the Hebrew word *chesed*. To show mercy is to show *chesed*, to express the words and deeds of covenant love faithfully. It is a *mercy* towards all those we are in covenant relationship with when we keep covenant with them, when they can trust our love for them, when they can be sure that they can rely and depend upon our love and faithfulness. Strong says that *chesed* has a root meaning of "to bow." The proud heart can never truly show *chesed*, for true covenant faithfulness is rooted in humility.

Let not *mercy and truth* forsake you; *bind them around your neck, write them on the tablet of your heart.* (Prov. 3:3)

The merciful man does himself good, but the cruel man does himself harm. (Prov. 11:17, NASV)

So you, by the help of your God, return; *observe mercy and justice*, and wait on your God continually. (Hos. 12:6)

He has showed you, O man, what is good. And what does Yahweh require of you? To act justly and *to love mercy* and to walk humbly with your God. (Mic. 6:8)

Blessed are the merciful, for they will be shown mercy. (Matt. 5:7)

Be merciful, just as *your Father is merciful*. (Luke 6:36)

For I desire mercy, not sacrifice, and acknowledgment of God rather than burnt offerings. (Hos. 6:6)

He answered, "Haven't you read what David did when he and his companions were hungry? He entered the house of God, and he and his companions ate the consecrated bread—which was not lawful for them to do, but only for the priests. Or haven't you read in the Law that on the Sabbath the priests in the temple desecrate the day and yet are innocent? I tell you that one greater than the temple is here. If you had known what these words mean, '*I desire mercy*, not sacrifice,' you would not have condemned the innocent. For the Son of Man is Lord of the Sabbath." (Matt. 12:3-8)

Judgment without mercy will be shown to anyone who has not been merciful. Mercy triumphs over judgment! (James 2:13)

David asked, "Is there anyone still left of the house of Saul to whom I can *show kindness* for Jonathan's sake?"

Now there was a servant of Saul's household named Ziba. They called him to appear before David, and the king said to him, "Are you Ziba?"

"Your servant," he replied.

The king asked, "Is there no one still left of the house of Saul to whom I can show *God's kindness*?"

Ziba answered the king, "There is still a son of Jonathan; he is crippled in both feet."

"Where is he?" the king asked.

Ziba answered, "He is at the house of Makir son of Ammiel in Lo Debar."

So King David had him brought from Lo Debar, from the house of Makir son of Ammiel.

When Mephibosheth son of Jonathan, the son of Saul, came to David, he bowed down to pay him honor.

David said, "Mephibosheth!"

"Your servant," he replied.

"Don't be afraid," David said to him, "for I will surely *show you kindness* for the sake of your father Jonathan. I will restore to you all the land that belonged to your grandfather Saul, and you will always eat at my table." (2 Sam. 9:1-7)

He who is *kind* to the poor lends to Yahweh, and He will reward him for what he has done. (Prov. 19:17)

So Boaz said to Ruth, "My daughter, listen to me. Don't go and glean in another field and don't go away from here. Stay here with my servant girls. Watch the field where the men are harvesting, and follow along after the girls. I have told the men not to touch you. And whenever you are thirsty, go and get a drink from the water jars the men have filled."

At this, she bowed down with her face to the ground. She exclaimed, "Why have I found such *favor* in your eyes that you notice me—a foreigner?"

Boaz replied, "I've been told all about what you have done for your mother-in-law since the death of your husband—how you left your father and mother and your homeland and came to live with a people you did not know before. May Yahweh repay you for what you have done. May you be richly rewarded by Yahweh, the God of Israel, under whose wings you have come to take refuge." (Ruth 2:8-12)

Religion that God our Father accepts as pure and faultless is this: to *look after orphans and widows in their distress* and to keep oneself from being polluted by the world. (James 1:27)

c. Helpful

One of the key Greek New Testament words translated as "help" is *antilambanomai*, which is sometimes used in the Septuagint to mean "to enter into alliance with" or "taking up something," but it usually means to "help," "to share a task with someone" and "to help someone in his work." In the New Testament it is used to mean to "take someone's part by assisting, . . . come to the aid of, . . . help the weak," or to "take part in, devote oneself to, practise," "devote" oneself "to kindness," and also to "enjoy, benefit by."

Helping covers the rendering of acts of assistance to everyone in the Body of Christ. It consists of the whole range of helping activities performed in the Body, helping within the family, helping others in the church, helping in the work of various ministries within the church. These acts of assistance constitute the taking of someone's part in order to free him to carry out other tasks, for example, freeing a big sister so that she can help others in the family or church.

In reply Jesus said: "A man was going down from Jerusalem to Jericho, when he fell into the hands of robbers. They stripped him of his clothes, beat him and went away, leaving him half dead. A priest happened to be going down the same road, and when he saw the man, he passed by on the other side. So too, a Levite, when he came to the place and saw him, passed by on the other side. But a Samaritan, as he traveled, came where the man was; and *when he saw him, he took pity on him. He went to him and bandaged his wounds, pouring on oil and wine. Then he put the man on his own donkey, took him to an inn and took care of him.* The next day he took out two silver coins and gave them to the innkeeper. 'Look after him,' he said, 'and when I return, I will reimburse you for any extra expense you may have.'

"Which of these three do you think was a neighbor to the man who fell into the hands of robbers?"

The expert in the law replied, "The *one who had mercy on him.*"

Jesus told him, *"Go and do likewise."* (Luke 10:30-37)

Yahweh God said, "It is not good for the man to be alone. I will make *a helper* suitable for him." (Gen. 2:18)

If you come across your enemy's ox or donkey wandering off, be sure to take it back to him. *If you see the donkey of someone who hates you fallen down under its load, do not leave it there; be sure you help him with it.* (Exod. 23:4-5)

If one of your countrymen becomes poor and is unable to support himself among you, *help him as you would an alien or a temporary resident, so he can continue to live among you.* (Lev. 25:35)

Suppose a brother or sister is without clothes and daily food. *If one of you says to him, "Go, I wish you well; keep warm and well fed," but does nothing about his physical needs, what good is it?* In the same way, *faith by itself, if it is not accompanied by action, is dead.* (James 2:15-17)

Now the priest of Midian had seven daughters; and they came to draw water, and filled the troughs to water their father's flock.

Then the shepherds came and drove them away, but *Moses stood up and helped them, and watered their flock.* (Exod. 2:16-17, NASV)

The servant hurried to meet her and said, "Please give me a little water from your jar."

"Drink, my lord," she said, and quickly lowered the jar to her hands and gave him a drink.

After she had given him a drink, she said, "I'll draw water for your camels too, until they have finished drinking." So she quickly emptied her jar into the trough, ran back to the well to draw more water, and drew enough for all his camels. (Gen. 24:17-20)

I was eyes to the blind and feet to the lame. I was a father to the needy; I took up the case of the stranger. (Job 29:15-16)

Yes, and I ask you, loyal yokefellow, *help these women who have contended at my side in the cause of the gospel*, along with Clement and the rest of my fellow workers, whose names are in the book of life. (Phil. 4:3)

Now I urge you, brethren (you know the household of Stephanas, that they were the first fruits of Achaia, and that they have devoted themselves for ministry to the saints), that you also be in subjection to such men and *to everyone who helps in the work and labors.* (1 Cor. 16:15-16, NASV)

She opens her arms to the poor and extends her hands to the needy. (Prov. 31:20)

In everything I did, I *showed you that by this kind of hard work we must help the weak*, remembering the words the Lord Jesus Himself said: "It is more blessed to give than to receive." (Acts 20:35)

Praise be to the God and Father of our Lord Jesus Christ, the Father of compassion and the God of all comfort, who comforts us in all our troubles, *so that we can comfort those in any trouble with the comfort we ourselves have received from God.* For just as the sufferings of Christ flow over into our lives, so also through Christ our comfort overflows. If we are distressed, it is for your comfort and salvation; if we are comforted, it is for your comfort, which produces in you patient endurance of the same sufferings we suffer. And our hope for you is firm, because we know that just as you share in our sufferings, so also you share in our comfort. (2 Cor. 1:3-7)

d. Goodness

Kindness and generosity are necessarily tied to true goodness, the goodness not of man but of God. Goodness is *agathosune* (Gal. 5:22), which is defined as "active goodness" and which Strong identifies with "virtue." "It is character energized expressing itself in . . . active good." This type of active "zeal for goodness and truth" can be expressed in "rebuking, correcting, chastising." So if an older child, in love and from a true burden, helps to correct a younger, he is manifesting godly goodness. Arndt and Gingrich define *agathosune* as "goodness" and "uprightness" but also as "generosity." This type of generosity indicates more of giving in a spiritual sense than a desire to be generous in material things. Goodness, then, is the love of *God's* goodness, of *His* righteousness and love; it is an active desire to see it shared in the lives of others.

Therefore, *as we have opportunity, let us do good to all people*, especially to those who belong to the family of believers. (Gal. 6:10)

Our people *must learn to devote themselves to doing what is good*, in order that they may provide for daily necessities and not live unproductive lives. (Titus 3:14)

A good man obtains favor from Yahweh, but a man of wicked devices He will condemn. (Prov. 12:2)

But the fruit of the Spirit is love, joy, peace, patience, kindness, *goodness*, faithfulness, gentleness and self-control. Against such things there is no law. (Gal. 5:22-23)

For this very reason, make every effort to *add to your faith goodness; and to goodness*, knowledge; and to knowledge, self-control; and to self-control, perseverance; and to perseverance, godliness; and to godliness, brotherly kindness; and to brotherly kindness, love. (2 Pet. 1:5-7)

I myself am convinced, my brothers, that you yourselves are *full of goodness*, complete in knowledge and competent to instruct one another. (Rom. 15:14)

e. Brotherly Love (Sibling Love)

When Joseph finally revealed himself to his brothers, powerful waves of godly love swept over his soul, breaking forth in deep sobs that shook his whole body. These brothers had sold him into slavery; because of them he had spent years in prison. Only God's gracious mercy had brought him deliverance and brought victory out of their evil plottings. This overwhelming love that Joseph felt toward them was not something he set in motion by an act of his will. It swept over him as a power from outside himself, a power beyond his control, like rushing waters or winds. When the Bible speaks of God's love being "poured out" in our hearts (Rom. 5:5), this translates the Greek word *ekcheo*, which derives from *cheo*, meaning "to gush, spill." According to Rienecker, *ekcheo* "denotes both abundance and diffusion." Arndt and Gingrich give the literal translation of *cheo* as to "gush forth." This is the love of siblings we want to come forth in our children. When God's love burns in their hearts, children will truly love and care for each other not because of external constraint, but because God's love lives within them and they yearn to give expression to that love.

This love children feel in Christ should spontaneously pour forth on both their spiritual and their natural brothers and sisters.

> Now a man of the house of Levi married a Levite woman, and she became pregnant and gave birth to a son. When she saw that he was a fine child, she hid him for three months. But when she could hide him no longer, she got a papyrus basket for him and coated it with tar and pitch. Then she placed the child in it and put it among the reeds along the bank of the Nile. His sister stood at a distance to see what would happen to him.
>
> Then Pharaoh's daughter went down to the Nile to bathe, and her attendants were walking along the river bank. She saw the basket among the reeds and sent her slave girl to get it. She opened it and saw the baby. He was crying, and she felt sorry for him. "This is one of the Hebrew babies," she said.
>
> *Then his sister asked Pharaoh's daughter, "Shall I go and get one of the Hebrew women to nurse the baby for you?"*
>
> *"Yes, go," she answered. And the girl went and got the baby's mother.* (Exod. 2:1-8)

Then Joseph said to his brothers, "Come close to me." When they had done so, he said, *"I am your brother Joseph, the one you sold into Egypt!* And now, do not be distressed and do not be angry with yourselves for selling me here, because it was to save lives that God sent me ahead of you . . . . So then, it was not you who sent me here, but God. He made me father to Pharaoh, lord of his entire household and ruler of all Egypt. Now hurry back to my father and say to him, 'This is what your son Joseph says: God has made me lord of all Egypt. Come down to me; don't delay. You shall live in the region of Goshen and be near me—you, your children and grandchildren, your flocks and herds, and all you have . . . .'" Then he threw his arms around his brother Benjamin and wept, and Benjamin embraced him, weeping. *And he kissed all his brothers and wept over them.* (Gen. 45:4-5, 8-10, 14-15)

But Joseph said to them, *"Don't be afraid.* Am I in the place of God? You intended to harm me, but God intended it for good to accomplish what is now being done, the saving of many lives. So then, don't be afraid. I will provide for you and your children." *And he reassured them and spoke kindly to them.* (Gen. 50:19-21)

Do not seek revenge or bear a grudge against one of your people, but *love your neighbor as yourself.* I am Yahweh. (Lev. 19:18)

Love must be sincere. Hate what is evil; cling to what is good. *Be devoted to one another in brotherly love.* Honor one another above yourselves. (Rom. 12:9-10)

After David had finished talking with Saul, *Jonathan became one in spirit with David, and he loved him as himself.* From that day Saul kept David with him and did not let him return to his father's house. And Jonathan made a covenant with David because he loved him as himself. Jonathan took off the robe he was wearing and gave it to David, along with his tunic, and even his sword, his bow and his belt. (1 Sam. 18:1-4)

Jesus replied: "'Love the Lord your God with all your heart and with all your soul and with all your mind.' This is the first and greatest commandment. And the second is like it: 'Love your neighbor as yourself.' All the Law and the Prophets hang on these two commandments." (Matt. 22:37-40)

My command is this: Love each other as I have loved you. Greater love has no one than this, *that he lay down his life for his friends.* (John 15:12-13)

I give you a new commandment: love one another; just as I have loved you, you also must love one another. *By this love you have for one another, everyone will know that you are My disciples.* (John 13:34-35, JB)

You, my brothers, were called to be free. But do not use your freedom to indulge the sinful nature; rather, *serve one another in love.* (Gal. 5:13)

May the Lord *make your love increase and overflow for each other and for everyone else, just as ours does for you.* (1 Thess. 3:12)

Now about brotherly love we do not need to write to you, for *you yourselves have been taught by God to love each other.* And in fact, you do love all the brothers throughout Macedonia. *Yet we urge you, brothers, to do so more and more.* (1 Thess. 4:9-10)

Keep on loving each other as brothers. (Heb. 13:1)

Now that you have purified yourselves by obeying the truth so that you have sincere love for your brothers, *love one another deeply, from the heart.* (1 Pet. 1:22)

Finally, all of you, *live in harmony with one another;* be sympathetic, *love as brothers, be compassionate and humble.* (1 Pet. 3:8)

Above all, *love each other deeply,* because love covers over a multitude of sins. (1 Pet. 4:8)

Whoever loves his brother lives in the light, and there is nothing in him to make him stumble. (1 John 2:10)

We love because He first loved us. If anyone says, "I love God," yet hates his brother, he is a liar. For anyone who does not love his brother, whom he has seen, cannot love God, whom he has not seen. And He has given us this command: *Whoever loves God must also love his brother.* (1 John 4:19-21)

For this very reason, make every effort to add to your faith goodness; and to goodness, knowledge; and to knowledge, self-control; and to self-control, perseverance; and to perseverance, godliness; *and to godliness, brotherly kindness; and to brotherly kindness, love.* (2 Pet. 1:5-7)

Dear friends, let us love one another, for love comes from God. Everyone who loves has been born of God and knows God. Whoever does not love does not know God, because God is love. This is how God showed His love among us: He sent His one and only Son into the world that we might live through Him. This is love: not that we loved God, but that He loved us and sent His Son as an atoning sacrifice for our sins. Dear friends, since God so loved us, we also ought to love one another. No one has ever seen God; but *if we love one another, God lives in us and His love is made complete in us.* (1 John 4:7-12)

This love produces a oneness of heart and mind among brothers. Love is what "binds" our hearts together in unity. Paul calls this binding together in love "the bond of perfection" (Col. 3:14). This phrase consists of two Greek words. The first, *sundesmos,* means "that which binds together." The second, *teleiotes,* translated here as "perfection," conveys, according to Rienecker, "the full expression of the divine life in the community, devoid of bitter words and angry feelings, and freed from the ugly defects of immorality and dishonesty."

Therefore, as the elect of God, holy and beloved, put on tender mercies, kindness, humility, meekness, longsuffering; bearing with one another, and forgiving one another, if anyone has a complaint against another; even as Christ forgave you, so you also must do. *But above all these things put on love, which is the bond of perfection.* (Col. 3:12-14)

If you have any encouragement from being united with Christ, if any comfort from His love, if any fellowship with the Spirit, if any tenderness and compassion, *then make my joy complete by being like-minded, having the same love, being one in spirit and purpose.*

Do nothing out of selfish ambition or vain conceit, but in humility consider others better than yourselves. Each of you should look not only to your own interests, but also to the interests of others. (Phil. 2:1-4)

. . . that all of them may be one, Father, just as You are in Me and I am in You. May they also be in Us so that the world may believe that You have sent Me. I have given them the glory that You gave Me, that they may be one as We are One: I in them and You in Me. *May they be brought to complete unity* to let the world know that You sent Me and have loved them even as You have loved Me. (John 17:21-23)

Now when the Day of Pentecost had fully come, *they were all with one accord* in one place. (Acts 2:1)

So continuing daily with one accord in the temple, and breaking bread from house to house, they ate their food with gladness and simplicity of heart. (Acts 2:46)

So when they heard that, *they raised their voice to God with one accord* and said: "Lord, You are God, who made heaven and earth and the sea, and all that is in them." (Acts 4:24)

All the believers were one in heart and mind. No one claimed that any of his possessions was his own, but they shared everything they had. (Acts 4:32)

Live in harmony with one another. Do not be proud, but be willing to associate with people of low position. Do not be conceited. (Rom. 12:16)

May the God who gives endurance and encouragement *give you a spirit of unity among yourselves* as you follow Christ Jesus, so that with one heart and mouth you may glorify the God and Father of our Lord Jesus Christ. (Rom. 15:5-6)

Whatever happens, conduct yourselves in a manner worthy of the gospel of Christ. Then, whether I come and see you or only hear about you in my absence, *I will know that you stand firm in one spirit, contending as one man for the faith of the gospel.* (Phil. 1:27)

Finally, all of you, *live in harmony with one another*; be sympathetic, love as brothers, be compassionate and humble. (1 Pet. 3:8)

f. Sharing

"Sharing" is an English translation for a number of Greek New Testament words. One word translated "sharing" or "giving" is *metadidomi*. *Koinoneo*, also translated as "sharing," comes from *koinos*, which means literally "lying open to all." Our fellowship in Christ is to be a *koinonia*, a transparent life of giving everything of ourselves alongside the wholehearted giving of others in the Spirit. In some cases, this word means "close relationship," "fellowship." Like *koinoneo*, "sharing" connotes relationship, pointing to the context of covenant as the framework of true sharing.

Scripture admonishes us to give or share "with generosity." The word translated as "with generosity" in Romans 12:8 is *haplotes*, meaning with "sincerity," referring "to open-handed and open-hearted giving out of compassion and a singleness of purpose, not from ambition" or mechanical obligation. For us to share anything with others obviously entails the use of our own resources, and the admonition to share does not abrogate the commandment to be good stewards with these resources. It follows from this that it can be wrong to share with someone who will wantonly destroy what we give them or use it for destructive purposes. For example, it's wrong to give money to a drunkard so that he can buy alcohol with it; and it's wrong to share a toy with a child who will abuse or waste it, or hurt others with it. Again, sharing our possessions does not annul our need for responsible stewardship.

> When you reap the harvest of your land, do not reap to the very edges of your field or gather the gleanings of your harvest. Do not go over your vineyard a second time or pick up the grapes that have fallen. *Leave them for the poor and the alien.* I am Yahweh your God. (Lev. 19:9-10)

> Heal the sick, raise the dead, cleanse those who have leprosy, drive out demons. *Freely you have received, freely give.* (Matt. 10:8)

> All the believers were one in heart and mind. *No one claimed that any of his possessions was his own, but they shared everything they had.* With great power the apostles continued to testify to the resurrection of the Lord Jesus, and much grace was upon them all. There were no needy persons among them. For from time to time those who owned lands or houses sold them, brought the money from the sales and put it at the apostles' feet, and it was distributed to anyone as he had need. (Acts 4:32-35)

> Cornelius stared at him in fear. "What is it, Lord?" he asked. The angel answered, "Your prayers and *gifts to the poor* have come up as a memorial offering before God." (Acts 10:4)

> You yourselves know that these hands of mine have supplied my own needs and the needs of my companions. In everything I did, I showed you that by this kind of hard work we must help the weak, remembering the words the Lord Jesus Himself said: "*It is more blessed to give than to receive.*" (Acts 20:34-35)

> And now, brothers, we want you to know about the grace that God has given the Macedonian churches. Out of the most severe trial, their overflowing joy and their extreme poverty welled up in rich generosity. For I testify that they gave as much as they were able, and even beyond their ability. *Entirely on their own, they urgently pleaded with us for the privilege of sharing in this service to the saints.* And they did not do as we expected, but they gave themselves first to the Lord and then to us in keeping with God's will. (2 Cor. 8:1-5)

He who has been stealing must steal no longer, but must work, doing something useful with his own hands, *that he may have something to share with those in need.* (Eph. 4:28)

Command them to do good, to be rich in good deeds, and to be *generous and willing to share.* In this way they will lay up treasure for themselves as a firm foundation for the coming age, so that they may take hold of the life that is truly life. (1 Tim. 6:18-19)

If one of your countrymen becomes poor and is unable to support himself among you, *help him* as you would an alien or a temporary resident, so he can continue to live among you. (Lev. 25:35)

If there is a poor man among your brothers in any of the towns of the land that Yahweh your God is giving you, *do not be hardhearted or tightfisted toward your poor brother. Rather be openhanded and freely lend him whatever he needs.* Be careful not to harbor this wicked thought: "The seventh year, the year for canceling debts, is near," so that you do not show ill will toward your needy brother and give him nothing. He may then appeal to Yahweh against you, and you will be found guilty of sin. Give generously to him and do so without a grudging heart; then because of this Yahweh your God will bless you in all your work and in everything you put your hand to. There will always be poor people in the land. Therefore I command you to be openhanded toward your brothers and toward the poor and needy in your land.

If a fellow Hebrew, a man or a woman, sells himself to you and he serves you six years, in the seventh year you must let him go free. *And when you release him, do not send him away empty-handed. Supply him liberally from your flock, your threshing floor and your winepress. Give to him as Yahweh your God has blessed you.* Remember that you were slaves in Egypt and Yahweh your God redeemed you. That is why I give you this command today. (Deut. 15:7-15)

Nehemiah said, "Go and enjoy choice food and sweet drinks, and *send some to those who have nothing prepared.* This day is sacred to our Lord. Do not grieve, for the joy of Yahweh is your strength." (Neh. 8:10)

So Boaz said to Ruth, "My daughter, listen to me. Don't go and glean in another field and don't go away from here. Stay here with my servant girls. Watch the field where the men are harvesting, and follow along after the girls. I have told the men not to touch you. And whenever you are thirsty, go and get a drink from the water jars the men have filled."

At this, she bowed down with her face to the ground. She exclaimed, "Why have I found such favor in your eyes that you notice me—a foreigner?"

Boaz replied, "I've been told all about *what you have done for your mother-in-law since the death of your husband*—how you left your father and mother and your homeland and came to live with a people you did not know before. *May Yahweh repay you for what you have done. May you be richly rewarded by Yahweh,* the God of

Israel, under whose wings you have come to take refuge." (Ruth 2:8-12)

A generous man will prosper; he who refreshes others will himself be refreshed. (Prov. 11:25)

A generous man will himself be blessed, for he shares his food with the poor. (Prov. 22:9)

If your enemy is hungry, *give him food to eat;* if he is thirsty, *give him water to drink.* In doing this, you will heap burning coals on his head, and *Yahweh will reward you.* (Prov. 25:21-22) [How much more, then, *should we share with our brothers and sisters?*]

Share with God's people who are in need. Practice hospitality. (Rom. 12:13)

Therefore, *as we have opportunity, let us do good to all people,* especially to *those who belong to the family of believers.* (Gal. 6:10)

What good is it, my brothers, if a man claims to have faith but has no deeds? Can such faith save him? *Suppose a brother or sister is without clothes and daily food. If one of you says to him, "Go, I wish you well; keep warm and well fed," but does nothing about his physical needs, what good is it?* In the same way, *faith by itself, if it is not accompanied by action, is dead.* (James 2:14-17)

Cast your bread upon the waters, for after many days you will find it again. *Give portions* to seven, yes to eight, for you do not know what disaster may come upon the land. (Eccles. 11:1-2)

Is it not to *share your food with the hungry and to provide the poor wanderer with shelter—when you see the naked, to clothe him, and not to turn away from your own flesh and blood?*
   . . . *And if you spend yourselves in behalf of the hungry and satisfy the needs of the oppressed, then your light will rise in the darkness, and your night will become like the noonday.* (Isa. 58:7, 10)

Give to the one who asks you, and do not turn away from the one who wants to borrow from you. (Matt. 5:42)

Jesus answered, "If you want to be perfect, go, sell your possessions and give to the poor, and you will have treasure in heaven. Then come, follow Me." (Matt. 19:21)

Give, and it will be given to you. A good measure, pressed down, shaken together and running over, will be poured into your lap. For with the measure you use, it will be measured to you. (Luke 6:38)

Remember this: Whoever sows sparingly will also reap sparingly, and whoever sows generously will also reap generously. *Each man should give what he has decided in his heart to give, not reluctantly or under compulsion, for God loves a cheerful giver.* And God is able to make all grace abound to you, so that in all things at all times, having all that you need, you will abound in every good work. As it is written: "He has scattered abroad His gifts to the poor; His righteousness endures forever." (2 Cor. 9:6-9)

He who gives to the poor will lack nothing, but he who closes his eyes to them receives many curses. (Prov. 28:27)

God's Word admonishes us to reject the selfishness and covetousness that often manifests itself in meanness and greed and to reward those who overcome these works of the flesh.

But select capable men from all the people—men who fear God, trustworthy *men who hate dishonest gain*—and appoint them as officials over thousands, hundreds, fifties and tens. (Exod. 18:21)

You know *we never used flattery, nor did we put on a mask to cover up greed*—God is our witness. (1 Thess. 2:5)

Do nothing out of selfish ambition or vain conceit, but in humility consider others better than yourselves. (Phil. 2:3)

And *do not forget to do good and to share with others*, for with such sacrifices God is pleased. (Heb. 13:16)

g. Simplicity

Haplotes, the Greek word we discussed above, can also mean "with simplicity." "The term sometimes means *liberality* (cf. 2 Cor. 8:2; 9:11, 13). But elsewhere it means simplicity, in the sense of singlemindedness of heart, of motive and of purpose."[43]

Simplicity regulates our inner motives and desires towards the things of the world. It limits and channels them in such a way as to allow us to hear the Word of God. In other words, simplicity subordinates our hearts and minds to God's will and so eliminates the competing ambitions or competing desires that would divert us from the course God would put us on. It thus removes some of the main barriers to hearing the Word, such as the cares of this world and the deceitfulness of riches:

Now he who received seed among the thorns is he who *hears the word*, and *the cares of this world and the deceitfulness of riches choke the word*, and he becomes unfruitful. (Matt. 13:22)

Jesus said, "Let your eye be *single*." He warned that "you can't serve two masters." That word "single" in Matthew 6:22, KJV is the word *haplous*, the root of *haplotes*, "simplicity." The Bible commands us in Corinthians to walk in simplicity and not duplicity.

For our boasting is this: the testimony of our conscience that we conducted ourselves in the world in *simplicity [haplotes] and godly sincerity*, not with fleshly wisdom but by the grace of God, and more abundantly toward you. (2 Cor. 1:12)

Paul says again in Corinthians that he's afraid that believers will be deceived as Eve was by the serpent, that they'll be led away from the "simplicity," *haplotes*, that is supposed to mark our devotion to Christ.

> But I fear, lest somehow, as the serpent deceived Eve by his craftiness, so your minds may be corrupted from *the simplicity [haplotes] that is in Christ.* (2 Cor. 11:3)

When this simplicity governs our relationship to the world and the things of the world, it puts to death the lust of the flesh, the lust of the eyes and the pride of life.

> *Do not love the world or the things in the world. If anyone loves the world, the love of the Father is not in him.* For all that is in the world—the lust of the flesh, the lust of the eyes, and the pride of life—is not of the Father but is of the world. And the world is passing away, and the lust of it; but *he who does the will of God abides forever.* (1 John 2:15-17)

To have true simplicity is thus to possess singlemindedness of heart toward God. It means that we are truly centered in God, are able to "buy as though [we do] not possess, and" that we can "use this world as not misusing it." For we recognize that "the form [fashion] of this world is passing away" (1 Cor. 7:30-31). For anyone who walks before God in good conscience, in heartfelt conformity to His will, "simplicity" and "sincerity of heart" will follow and will govern one's "conduct . . . in the world" (2 Cor. 1:12). This will counterbalance and overcome the pulls exerted by the world's "fashions." People who live like this are "in the world" but "not of the world" (John 17:14-18) and so express God to the world because they do not "trust in uncertain riches but in the living God" (1 Tim. 6:17). This rootedness in God explains why simplicity and trust in God sever us from an inordinate desire for the things of the world and instead declare: "This is how I stand with the world": the "world is crucified to me, and I am crucified to the world" (Gal. 6:14). Simplicity severs the believer from the world and even from the world's very dynamic. It's the step of reduction that takes the believer out of Egypt so he can come into Canaan, out of the kingdoms of the world so he can enter the kingdom of God.

To live the simple life does not mean, however, living a destitute life deprived of essential needs. Simplicity is good in a specific sense, just as purity, honesty, kindness, loyalty, generosity, courage and love are good. Again, simplicity's good resides in the fact that it is the "virtue which regulates our attitude to material things." It is rooted in and sustained by love, which is to say it is rooted in and sustained by God (1 John 4:8, 16). So simplicity is holy. It is the same *attitude* toward the material world of which Jesus spoke when He said, "Blessed are the poor in spirit for theirs is the kingdom of heaven" (Matt. 5:3). When our attitude toward material things is governed by simplicity, we may seem to lose a few things of that world, which usually only clutter our lives and choke out love, but what we gain is a kingdom of love, peace and joy—a realm of relationships with God, nature and our fellow man, a kingdom never known to us before (Rom. 14:17; 1 Tim. 6:6-11; Heb. 13:5; Phil. 4:11-13). Like all the other virtues named above, only love can bring us to simplicity, but the teaching of simplicity—to give rather than to receive, to lose one life that we might find a better, to possess less while having more to enjoy (Acts 20:35; Luke 9:23-24; Acts 4:32-33; Phil. 2:1-8)—this is a positive teaching, not a negative one.

Then He said to His disciples, "Therefore I say to you, do not worry about your life, what you will eat; nor about the body, what you will put on. Life is more than food, and the body is more than clothing. Consider the ravens, for they neither sow nor reap, which have neither storehouse nor barn; and God feeds them. Of how much more value are you than the birds? And which of you by worrying can add one cubit to his stature? If you then are not able to do the least, why are you anxious for the rest? Consider the lilies, how they grow: they neither toil nor spin; and yet I say to you, even Solomon in all his glory was not arrayed like one of these. If then God so clothes the grass, which today is in the field and tomorrow is thrown into the oven, how much more will He clothe you, O you of little faith? And do not seek what you should eat or what you should drink, nor have an anxious mind. For all these things the nations of the world seek after, and your Father knows that you need these things. But *seek the kingdom of God, and all these things shall be added to you.* Do not fear, little flock, for it is your Father's good pleasure to give you the kingdom. Sell what you have and give alms; provide yourselves money bags which do not grow old, a treasure in the heavens that does not fail, where no thief approaches nor moth destroys. For *where your treasure is, there your heart will be also.*" (Luke 12:22-34)

Now *godliness with contentment is great gain.* For we brought nothing into this world, and it is certain we can carry nothing out. And *having food and clothing, with these we shall be content.* But those who desire to be rich fall into temptation and a snare, and into many foolish and harmful lusts which drown men in destruction and perdition. For the love of money is the root of all kinds of evil, for which some have strayed from the faith in their greediness, and pierced themselves through with many sorrows. But you, O man of God, flee these things and pursue righteousness, godliness, faith, love, patience, gentleness. Fight the good fight of faith, lay hold on eternal life, to which you were also called and have confessed the good confession in the presence of many witnesses. (1 Tim. 6:6-12)

Listen, my beloved brethren: Has God not chosen the poor of this world to be *rich in faith* and *heirs of the kingdom which He promised to those who love Him?* (James 2:5)

Bondservants, be obedient to those who are your masters according to the flesh, with fear and trembling, *in sincerity [simplicity] of heart, as to Christ*; not with eyeservice, as men-pleasers, but as bondservants of Christ, *doing the will of God from the heart,* with goodwill doing service, as to the Lord, and not to men, knowing that whatever good anyone does, he will receive the same from the Lord, whether he is a slave or free. And you, *masters, do the same* things to them, giving up threatening, knowing that your own Master also is in heaven, and there is no partiality with Him. (Eph. 6:5-9)

Bondservants, obey in all things your masters according to the flesh, not with eyeservice, as men-pleasers, *but in sincerity [simplicity] of heart*, fearing God. And whatever you do, do it heartily, as to the Lord and not to men, knowing that from the Lord you will receive the reward of the inheritance; *for you serve the Lord Christ.* (Col. 3:22-24)

So continuing daily with one accord in the temple, and breaking bread from house to house, they ate their food with gladness and *simplicity of heart*, praising God and having favor with all the people. And the Lord added to the church daily those who were being saved. (Acts 2:46-47)

2. Meanness and Greed

The mean child considers only himself. Everyone and everything around him merely become a means to further his self-centered ends. The Greek New Testament word *astorgos*, translated in 2 Timothy 3:3 as "without love," literally means "without family affection, without love of kindred, destitute of love," especially for those in one's own family. Rienecker also translates this word as "without tenderness. It refers to the lack of the feelings of natural tenderness, as seen in a mother who exposes or kills her child, a father who abandons his family, or children who neglect their aged parents" or abandon them. *Astorgos*, in other words, is the opposite of *chesed*. Selfishness and envy, arrogance and covetousness rush in to fill the vacuum in the heart devoid of God's love. To love requires engaging in the battle of prayer, seeking God to give us *His* love and fighting off the enemies of love. If we don't enter *this* battle for love, we will lose the war for our souls. But the self-centered child feels no compassion for anyone else, and so he gives no consideration to their needs or thoughts or feelings or to his own arrogant words. Even when his intent is not deliberately malicious, his self-centeredness continually hurts those around him. In both the Old Testament Hebrew and the New Testament Greek, words we translate as "greed" mean literally "plunder." The plunderer takes everything as though it were rightfully his, including other people's positions, reputation and happiness, for he is incapable of considering any right or need but his own.

a. Hurting Others and Mercilessness

The ugly consequences of self-centeredness include envy and jealousy, and these always in turn result in hurting others who get in the way of our selfish ambition to obtain whatever we covet or to justify our failures to get that which we covet. Rienecker states that the Greek word *pleonexia*, translated as "greed," literally means "the insatiable desire to have more even at the expense of harming others." We come to regard people not as subjects, feeling, thinking, living human beings who are like ourselves and with whom we should ideally enter relationship, but merely as objects for manipulation, things to be used for our self-centered purposes. We feel no compassion or mercy, then, but we become insensitive and unfeeling—it is as though we become the mere objects that we have tried to convince ourselves that others are for us.

> The *wicked man craves evil*; his neighbor *gets no mercy from him.*
> (Prov. 21:10)

> He *lies in wait* near the villages; *from ambush he murders the innocent, watching in secret for his victims.* He *lies in wait* like a lion in cover; he *lies in wait to catch the helpless*; he catches the helpless and drags them off in his net. *His victims are crushed*, they collapse; they fall under his strength. He says to himself, "God has forgotten; He covers His face and never sees." (Ps. 10:8-11)

> Therefore, the kingdom of heaven is like a king who wanted to settle accounts with his servants. As he began the settlement, a man who owed him ten thousand talents was brought to him. Since he was not able to pay, the master ordered that he and his wife and his children and all that he had be sold to repay the debt.
> The servant fell on his knees before him. "Be patient with me," he begged, "and I will pay back everything." The servant's master took pity on him, canceled the debt and let him go.
> But *when that servant went out, he found one of his fellow servants who owed him a hundred denarii. He grabbed him and began to choke him.* "Pay back what you owe me!" he demanded.
> His fellow servant fell to his knees and begged him, "Be patient with me, and I will pay you back."
> *But he refused. Instead, he went off and had the man thrown into prison until he could pay the debt.* When the other servants saw what had happened, they were greatly distressed and went and told their master everything that had happened.
> Then the master called the servant in. "You wicked servant," he said, "I canceled all that debt of yours because you begged me to. Shouldn't you have had mercy on your fellow servant just as I had on you?" In anger his master turned him over to the jailers . . . until he should pay back all he owed.
> *This is how My heavenly Father will treat each of you unless you forgive your brother from your heart.* (Matt. 18:23-35)

Our hearts become the bad fruit that Jesus spoke of in Matthew 7:17 because we are totally rooted in ourselves. No true goodness that would serve our brothers and sisters can come from such hearts.

Judah said to his brothers, "What *will we gain if we kill our brother and cover up his blood*? Come, let's sell him to the Ishmaelites and not lay our hands on him; after all, he is our brother, our own flesh and blood." His brothers agreed.

So when the Midianite merchants came by, his brothers pulled Joseph up out of the cistern and sold him for twenty shekels of silver to the Ishmaelites, who took him to Egypt. (Gen. 37:26-28)

But *your eyes and your heart are set only on dishonest gain, on shedding innocent blood and on oppression and extortion.* (Jer. 22:17)

Woe to him who builds his realm by unjust gain to set his nest on high, to escape the clutches of ruin! (Hab. 2:9)

A *greedy man brings trouble to his family*, but he who hates bribes will live. (Prov. 15:27)

What causes fights and quarrels among you? Don't they come from your desires that battle within you? You want something but don't get it. You kill and covet, but you cannot have what you want. You quarrel and fight. You do not have, because you do not ask God. When you ask, you do not receive, because you ask with wrong motives, that you may spend what you get on your pleasures. (James 4:1-3)

Adam lay with his wife Eve, and she became pregnant and gave birth to Cain. She said, "With the help of Yahweh I have brought forth a man." Later she gave birth to his brother Abel.

Now Abel kept flocks, and Cain worked the soil. In the course of time Cain brought some of the fruits of the soil as an offering to Yahweh. But Abel brought fat portions from some of the firstborn of his flock. Yahweh looked with favor on Abel and his offering, but on Cain and his offering He did not look with favor. *So Cain was very angry, and his face was downcast.*

Then Yahweh said to Cain, "Why are you angry? Why is your face downcast? If you do what is right, will you not be accepted? But if you do not do what is right, sin is crouching at your door; it desires to have you, but you must master it."

Now Cain said to his brother Abel, "Let's go out to the field." And while they were in the field, Cain attacked his brother Abel and killed him.

Then Yahweh said to Cain, "Where is your brother Abel?"

"I don't know," he replied. "Am I my brother's keeper?"

Yahweh said, "What have you done? Listen! Your brother's blood cries out to Me from the ground." (Gen. 4:1-10)

Do not be like Cain, who belonged to the evil one and murdered his brother. And why did he murder him? Because his own actions were evil and his brother's were righteous. (1 John 3:12)

With his mouth *the godless destroys his neighbor*, but through knowledge the righteous escape. (Prov. 11:9)

For *they cannot sleep till they do evil; they are robbed of slumber till they make someone fall.* They *eat the bread of wickedness and drink the wine of violence.* (Prov. 4:16-17)

Blessings crown the head of the righteous, *but violence overwhelms the mouth of the wicked.* (Prov. 10:6)

A kind man benefits himself, but *a cruel man brings trouble on himself.* (Prov. 11:17)

From the fruit of his lips a man enjoys good things, but *the unfaithful have a craving for violence.* (Prov. 13:2)

A *violent man* entices his neighbor and leads him down a path that is not good. (Prov. 16:29)

The *violence of the wicked will drag them away*, for they refuse to do what is right. (Prov. 21:7)

Do not say, "I'll do to him as he has done to me; I'll pay that man back for what he did." (Prov. 24:29)

Do not repay anyone evil for evil. Be careful to do what is right in the eyes of everybody. If it is possible, as far as it depends on you, live at peace with everyone. *Do not take revenge*, my friends, but leave room for God's wrath, for it is written: "It is Mine to avenge; I will repay," says the Lord. On the contrary: "If your enemy is hungry, feed him; if he is thirsty, give him something to drink. In doing this, you will heap burning coals on his head." (Rom. 12:17-20)

The merciless person is finally so completely absorbed into the black hole of self-centeredness that he can only radiate hate and derision toward all those around him who would in any way impede his total inturning into himself.

Anyone who claims to be in the light *but hates his brother is still in the darkness.* . . . But *whoever hates his brother is in the darkness and walks around in the darkness*; he does not know where he is going, because *the darkness has blinded him.* (1 John 2:9, 11)

This is how we know who the children of God are and who the children of the devil are: Anyone who does not do what is right is not a child of God; nor is anyone who does not love his brother.

This is the message you heard from the beginning: We should love one another. *Do not be like Cain, who belonged to the evil one and murdered his brother. And why did he murder him? Because his own actions were evil and his brother's were righteous.* Do not be surprised, my brothers, if the world hates you. We know that we have passed from death to life, because we love our brothers. *Anyone who does not love remains in death. Anyone who hates his brother is a murderer*, and you know that no murderer has eternal life in him. (1 John 3:10-15)

At one time we too were foolish, disobedient, deceived and

enslaved by all kinds of passions and pleasures. *We lived in malice and envy, being hated and hating one another.* (Titus 3:3)

b. Covetousness/Greed

As noted, selfishness and covetousness lead to greed and meanness. Covetousness often drives those who are consumed with self. The covetous not only refuse to share, but they also seek to possess, hold onto and grasp everything unto themselves. Their *only* concern often narrows to self-interest and gratifying their own immediate desires. They want everything for themselves and desire anything new that comes along—all simply because someone else has it or wants it, even if the other person may truly need it while the covetous person has no need for it whatsoever. The covetous person affirms his own value simply by trying to possess everything possible: he thinks he deserves it all, and so he grasps it because to him it shows his "worth." The covetous child will seldom ask permission but will instead demand what he wants in order to fulfill his lusts and pride. One lexicon defines the Greek word *pleonektes*, translated "covetous," as literally "eager to have more . . . , i.e., to have what belongs to others."[44] This lexicon further says that the word describes someone who is "often cruel as well as grasping."[45] So the covetous will frequently (even if only in his own mind) belittle, hate and slander anyone who has what the covetous wants. This is true even if the covetous needs nothing of what might be saving the life of those he envies and hates. He couldn't care less about what might help someone else live—if he doesn't have it, then no one should.

In fact, covetousness stoked the fires of original sin. The Fall came with the temptation to desire, to covet, the fruit of the forbidden tree. Man and woman grasped to possess the power and wisdom of God. Thus, covetous greed lay at the root of death. Envy and violence follow, just as in the first murder of Abel by his envious brother, Cain. It isn't surprising, then, that covetousness has even been seen by historians and sociologists as a central motive force in the development of all that is destructive in the history of human culture. A group of scholars at a number of major American and European universities has pursued insights introduced by the seminal work of Stanford University's René Girard. Girard presented "mimetic rivalry" as a primary dynamic of human civilization. Covetousness feeds this rivalry and leads to envy, hostility, scapegoating, violence, war, conquest and subjugation.[46] It rests not even on coveting actually needed goods but merely on coveting the luxuries and possessions of those that others enviously fixate on as "role models." The mass of people accepts these role models as worthy of emulation, of "mimesis" or mimicry. The role models thus assume the position of a kind of cultural priesthood. In short, the individual member of a given communal order wants the *status* possessed by the role model. So the mimic's desire for what the role model possesses doesn't arise because the mimic *needs* these goods but rather because of the *status* associated with the possession of them and because of his view of his own godlike worth. Material goods thus become valuable as mere symbols of *status*. This readily suggests an unseen, nonphysical and spiritual dimension behind this powerful human drive, a dynamic that grasps at something beyond merely physical possessions.

In other words, while greed is often directed *toward* physical things, greed *itself* is not a physical thing. You can't, in other words, put greed in a cup and gulp it down. Greed is metaphysical. *Meta* means "beyond." So greed's roots go beyond the physical. Greed, of course, seldom *sees* anything beyond the material, but the greed itself does not come from what it directs its avarice toward, which would mean it had limits. Rather, it comes from the human heart, and therefore it knows no limits. It never says, "That's enough" or, "That's too much." It always wants "more, more, more."

We may think that our attitudes toward material things do not involve any spiritual considerations, but Scripture refutes this claim. James said that the source of "bitter envy and self-seeking" was not "from above" but rather from below, being "earthly, sensual, *demonic*." Thus greed has a spiritual source: when we yield to such attitudes, we yield to demonic spirits. This spiritual element to desire explains why material things can never permanently satisfy greed. It is unending in its desire. In this sense it is, again, metaphysical. It's *inside* of us. Jesus said that out of the heart proceeds murder and *avarice* (Matt. 15:19).

The "Preacher" of Ecclesiastes said, "Whoever loves money never has money enough; whoever loves wealth is *never satisfied*." *Satis* is the Latin word "enough," and there is never enough for the greedy person. The rich man of Jesus' parable demonstrates this: he had all he needed, but he wanted more. This is what motivated him to ask, "What shall I do now?" In his greedy mind, it was simply time for him to pull down his already full barns and build larger ones. All he could imagine was making room to grasp for more. So greed can never be merely controlled—it can only be mortified, killed. That's why covetousness is idolatry: it makes the individual into a worshiper within a lapsed world's system of never-ending greed, of a never-satisfied consumerism, a system based on mimetic rivalry, status and position, a system that worships a great, singular, magnified black hole of Self, as well as all of its lesser, subsidiary expressions.

By yielding to covetousness, greed, self-seeking and envy, a believer throws off the restraints of simple living that come through yielding to and trusting in God rather than in riches. To walk in God's love and "let brotherly love continue" means to find the place of "conduct . . . without covetousness," a place of "contentment with such things that we have" (Heb. 13:1, 5; see also 1 Tim. 6:6-8; Phil. 4:11-12; Luke 3:14). So covetousness and greed stand opposite contentment and simplicity. The latter is the disposition of heart that regulates one's own attitude toward material things by keeping our lives singlemindedly and sincerely centered in God.

Jesus told the Laodicean church that they saw themselves as "rich, increased with goods" and in "need of nothing"—that is, in need of nothing from God because all their material desires were being met through a materialistic world. But the Lord then said that in reality they were "wretched, miserable, poor, blind and naked." Their greed for the material things of the world blinded them to the spiritual (or the *meta*physical) dynamic behind their self-seeking greed. In their love of, and faith in, riches they became idolaters, placing material things and money ahead of God. But their worship of material things blinded them to the spiritual forces moving through their own hearts and planting in them the desire for those things.

Because they couldn't *see* the dynamic that motivated them, they didn't recognize that they were participating in what the Bible calls a "mystery," a myth (Rev. 17:5). The word "myth," as we have so often said over the years, is rooted in the Greek word *muo*, which means "that which the eyes and ears are closed to." Because of their greed, the Laodiceans couldn't see their own participation in a system that was much larger than themselves and their petty desires, a system that, as a "secret mystery," was controlling their blind actions through their attitudes, thoughts and feelings about material possessions and wealth. So they boasted in their freedom, while they were actually slaves. This is why the Lord described them as "wretched, miserable, poor, blind and naked." They were perishing because the "god of this world had blinded their minds" (2 Cor. 4:4).

We, too, must recognize the possibility that, imagining ourselves free, we may actually be enslaved. Scripture tells us that "friendship with the world," the dynamic of which is "earthly, sensual and demonic," is *enmity* with God" (James 3:14–4:4). *Enmity* means "implacably opposed," an opposition that *nothing* can ever reconcile. Yet what precisely is unalterably opposed to God? It is, of course, satan and his kingdom—the antagonists of "all that is called God or is worshiped" (2 Thess. 2:4). So when people come to the place where they "love the world and the things of the world" and let the world and material possessions fill their lives rather than seeking God to fill their lives, Paul explicitly states that they're sacrificing to demons and not to God (1 Cor. 10:20-21). This is so because, according to the first epistle of John, "the *whole* world lies under the control of the evil one."* Only this can explain why, when we're spiritually betrothed to God and His Christ, Scripture describes covetousness not only as "idolatry" but as "fornication," "adultery," "harlotry":† as James said, "You *adulterers and adulteresses*, don't you know that friendship with this world is enmity with God?" (James 4:4).

To love money, to love this world and its goods, is to sell your soul, to desacralize and profane your life for a mess of pottage (Heb. 12:16). A desacralized life of materialism denies the God who is Spirit (John 4:24). The word *desacralized* means "not marked by sacrifice." Instead of sacrificing our lives to God, as we're commanded by Paul and Peter (Rom. 12:1-3; 1 Pet. 2:5), we choose another god, an idol, and to that desacralized, and therefore secular and seemingly spiritually neutral, idol we offer everything. We desire to get rich, be powerful, be happy in a worldly way, to be something in the eyes of the world and to do all of this outside God, in the realm of materialism, of secularism, of things sacrificed not to the living God but to what we perceive as being *merely* material objects, yet that are in truth idols (Acts 15:29; 1 Cor. 10:19-22). These idols then serve for us a mimetic function, raising our status, our value and worth in our climb to a place of pseudo-godhood. These idols of materialism thus become our substitutes for the true and living God, who alone can give life meaning and worth.

We can understand, then, why Paul links this idolatry, this sacrifice to idols, with making sacrifices to something much deeper and darker, to an underlying spiritual power, to diabolical forces that seek to supplant the primacy of God in the hearts and minds of human beings. Paul has already repeatedly identified "covetousness [as] idolatry" (Eph. 5:3, 5; Col. 3:5). Then in 1 Corinthians 8, Paul speaks directly about idols:

> Now concerning *things offered to idols* . . . , we know that *an idol is nothing in the world*, and that there is *no other God but one*. For even if there are so-called gods, whether in heaven or on earth (*there are many gods and many lords*), yet for *us* there is *one God*, the Father, of whom are all things, and we for Him; and one Lord Jesus Christ, through whom are all things, and through whom we live. (1 Cor. 8:1, 4-6)

Indeed, "there are many gods," Paul says. "But for *us* there is only one." This certainly counters any claim that other powers simply don't exist. So it can't be interpreted as meaning that there aren't other gods, that is, spiritual powers that seek to fill the place of God in people's lives. But rather for *us*, for those who truly believe in the Biblical God, there is only

---

* 1 John 5:19; see also Matt. 4:8-9; 2 Cor. 4:4; John 12:31; 14:30; 16:11.

† Exod. 20:17; James 4:4; Eph. 5:5; Col. 3:5; Rev. 17:2; 18:3.

one. Again, however, Paul is not denying that "many lords" do exist. That's why he went on to tell the Corinthians in chapter 10:

> What am I saying then? That an *idol* is anything, or what is *offered to idols* is anything? Rather, that the things which the Gentiles sacrifice they *sacrifice to demons* and not to God, and I do not want you to have fellowship with demons. You cannot drink the cup of the Lord and the cup of demons; you cannot partake of the Lord's table and of *the table of demons*. Or do we provoke the Lord to jealousy? Are we stronger than He? (1 Cor. 10:19-22)

Paul is explaining that an idol has no power in itself. Rather, he's saying that people who sacrifice to such idols—who expend themselves and their resources on them—aren't merely offering something up to a piece of stone, to some material object. But the things that the Gentiles sacrifice to these idols, "they sacrifice to demons and not to God." So he explains that he doesn't want us to be a partaker of demons. He's saying this to Christians who have the Holy Spirit. He's telling them that they cannot eat from both "the table of the Lord" and "the table of demons." If they die, then God must then give them over to these other lordships—to these "many lords," which Paul has already identified two chapters earlier (1 Cor. 8:1, 4-6). So if they allow covetousness to remain in their hearts and thereby seek prestige and status for their lives through the possession of material goods that have, in fact, become idols for them, then they will be brought under the influence and power of the spiritual forces—the "many gods and many lords"—that rule through these inordinate desires of the human heart.

So someone may think he is his own lord, but God will give him over to other lordships that he then must serve. And these will eventually swallow up every last vestige of the person's independence and quasi-lordship. If God is not fully Lord, other lordships, other principalities, other powers, will begin to exercise real dominion in a person's life through obsessions, compulsions and addictions, especially in relation to material things. It may not be the thing in and of itself that is evil, the "stone," but what stands behind it and influences us through it certainly is evil. This is the sin of materialism, of covetousness which becomes idolatry.

In Colossians, Paul writes again of these principalities and powers:

> As you therefore have received Christ Jesus the Lord, so walk in Him, rooted and built up in Him and established in the faith, as you have been taught, abounding in it with thanksgiving. Beware lest anyone cheat you through philosophy and vain [or empty] deceit, according to the tradition of men, according to the elementary *principles* of the world, and not according to Christ. For in Him dwells all the fullness of the Godhead bodily; and you are complete in Him, who is *the head of all principality and power. Therefore, if you died with Christ from the basic principles of the world, why, as though living in the world, do you subject yourselves to regulations— "Do not touch, do not taste, do not handle," which all concern things*

which perish with the using—according to the commandments and doctrines of men? These things indeed have an appearance of wisdom in self-imposed religion, false humility, and neglect of the body, but are of no value against the indulgence of the flesh. (Col. 2:6-10, 20-23)

The word *stoicheia* ("principles") here was used throughout the ancient world to indicate "powers," powers that were "understood as exercising rule and authority over and within the world of humanity."[47] According to Bauer, Danker, Arndt and Gingrich, in both Colossians 2:8 and Galatians, this word carries the meaning of "transcendent" (or, rather, "metaphysical" or "supernatural") "powers that are in control over events in this world, elements, elemental spirits." Swanson also attributes to both scriptures the meaning of "basic principles" and "elementary truths," a definition that Arndt further clarifies as pertaining to "things that constitute the foundation of learning, *fundamental principles*."[48] In this sense, the word is also said to mean "any first things from which others in a series, or a composite whole, take their rise."[49] It seems, then, that what Scripture asserts here, even against the most bloated and inflated views of human pride and arrogance on behalf of human intelligence, is that all of the philosophies of the world, the human traditions of this world, the intellectual principles, worldviews and mind-sets of the human world, as well as the economic, political and religious paradigms and structures of the world—all of these "first principles," the entire framework of the world system—is not only inspired by supernatural principles or forces but also "lies," as John explicitly stated concerning "the whole world," "under the control of the evil one" (1 John 5:19). These particular powers or forces therefore enable satan to fashion the very framework of lapsed human thinking. Thus "elementary principles" has also been translated as "elemental forces" or "elemental spirits of the universe" (RSV/NRSV, NEB, REB, Moff.). And Paul has, in the previous chapter of Colossians, already set the stage for his discussion of these cosmic powers, speaking of "all things . . . that are in heaven and that are on earth, *visible and invisible*, whether *thrones or dominions or principalities or powers*" (Col. 1:16). So it seems that "visible" powers, systems, structures and dominions are ordered and controlled by "invisible" powers.

To repeat, John declared that "the whole world is under the control of the evil one" (1 John 5:19)—under the power of satan. And Paul makes clear in repeated passages throughout the New Testament that the world is divided up into realms that lie under the authority of the various principalities and powers.

> For *we* do not *wrestle* against flesh and blood, but *against principalities, against powers, against the rulers of the darkness of this age, against spiritual hosts of wickedness* in the heavenly places. (Eph. 6:12; see also Col. 1:16; 1 Cor. 15:24-26; Eph. 1:19-23)

Scripture, ancient literature and history* have all shown, then, that the world is divided up in a division and specialization of labor under these elemental principles, principalities and powers. For instance, according to ancient Sumerian texts, some principalities or powers were seen as exercising dominion over carnal lust; others had dominion over other similar areas of human desires; still others over human relationships; others specifically over relationships between men and women; others had dominion over still other areas of life, such as medicine.[50] Others "taught the people (the art of) . . . bracelets, decorations (shadowing of the eye) with antimony, ornamentation, the beautifying of the eyelids, all kinds of precious stones and all coloring tinctures and alchemy."[51] Others had dominion over writing and metallurgy.[52] One power "showed the children of the people (how to make) the instruments of death (such as) the shield, the breastplate and the sword for warfare and all (the other) instruments of death . . . [and] through their agency (death) proceeds against the people who dwell upon the earth."[53] Under the influence of these powers, it was said millennia ago that humans "began fighting in order to take captive and to kill each other, . . . to build fortified cities and walls and towers, so that (one) man will be raised up over the people, to set up the first kingdoms to go to war, people against people, and nation against nation, and city against city . . . . And they began to take captive cities and to sell male and female slaves."†[54] In all these activities, so the ancient writings record, these "cruel spirits assisted them [human beings] and led them astray so that they might commit sin and pollution."[55] These powers even had specified areas of work under their dominion, such as farming or various crafts and businesses.[56] This all expresses a different lordship from, and opposing counterparts to, God's lordship in every area of life.

So how are we to discern which power—God or His adversaries— exercises dominion over each area of our own lives? The key lies in Paul's statement: "The things which the Gentiles sacrifice, they sacrifice unto demons and not unto God." So how then do you know which deity you are sacrificing to? The determinant is not intellect or competence or skill or success or even dedication to your work. It's your motivation. If your work, your life, your relationships, are rooted in pride and the self-images of the world or in competitive lust for the things of the world, then James says you stand in "enmity against God" (James 4:1-4). If you are consumed with competitiveness and mimetic rivalry and envy, with "keeping up with the Joneses," then Paul says that your "covetousness is idolatry" (Eph. 5:5; Col. 3:5). So you are sacrificing to the wrong god, to demons (1 Cor.

---

* See *Two Powers, Two Kingdoms, Two Worlds* (2004, 2011, 2013) and *Descent to Civilization* (1995, 2003, 2008) both by Blair Adams (Elm Mott, Tex.: Colloquium Press). Also see 1 Enoch 7:1–8:4; 69:1-16; Jubilees 11:2-6; 15:30-32.

† See *Descent to Civilization.*

10:19-22). You may be a hard worker, a good businessman, an excellent craftsman, but you will nonetheless be eventually bound by obsessions rooted in envy, competition and covetousness—all of which oppose the very purpose and nature of God (James 4:4).

All these scriptures tell us that if we move and live according to the *principles* that work behind the scenes to rule the world (Eph. 6:10-12; Col. 2:8; Gal. 4:3, 8-9), then we're going to eventually sever from the Headship and the lordship that's *in Christ* (Col. 2:18-20, NIV). To enter into the dominion of Christ's lordship requires an active, *continuing* decision on our part: "As you received Christ as Lord, so walk *in Him* as Lord" (Col. 2:6). This lordship of Christ, then, cannot be compulsory. We must *walk* it out voluntarily. We must voluntarily enter the kingdom of God's redeeming love where humility and God's self-giving love come to rule our lives. To refuse to do this is to remain under the dominion of the principalities and powers—the "many gods and many lords"—that oppose God's rule. This makes us subject to God's judgment through those opposing powers (Rom. 2:1-11; 1 Cor. 5:5).

But even this judgment is, at least in part, something we do to ourselves through our own decisions about who or what we'll serve. So we see how Paul in the first chapter of Romans repeatedly tells us that God gives people "*over* to those things that are not convenient" and that this is how the "wrath of God comes on the children of disobedience" (Rom. 1:24, 26, 28). So when we reject God's noncoercive but nonetheless absolute lordship, something begins to happen inside of us—in our attitudes, our thinking, our perspective, our worldview. As John says, we then "speak according to the viewpoint of the world" (1 John 4:5, NIV). In contrast to those who speak from this perspective, John says of those who are under the lordship of Christ: "But we are of God and we know the whole world is under the control of the evil one." So there is a viewpoint radically opposed to that of God, a viewpoint that God gives us over to (2 Thess. 2:10-12) when we place ourselves under these counterposed lordships and influences, these powers that rule through covetousness, pride and greed.

In Colossians, after admonishing us to walk in Christ's lordship, Paul goes on to say that "*in Him* dwells all the fullness of the Godhead bodily; and you are complete *in Him*, who is the head of all *principality and power*" (Col. 2:8-10). Is Christ, then, the head of all *demonic* activity? In one sense, some might answer, "Yes," but only in the sense that He's conquered death, and so He has power over all these "principalities" and "powers" that once ruled through death (1 Cor. 15:24-28; Heb. 2:14-15). But this power doesn't redeem or change them or their kingdoms; rather, it's the supernatural power of His Holy Spirit—His love—to draw us *out* of those kingdoms in a great Passover exodus and into the alternative "kingdom of the Son of His love." So even these evil powers, like Pharaoh, by disciplining the heirs of salvation and driving them out of Egypt (Exod. 11:1; 12:31-32), ultimately will serve the purpose of redeeming love for those who will endure in that love (Matt. 24:13). This is true even though these demonic forces won't serve this purpose willingly. This is even evidenced by Paul's instruction to "turn" the man from the Corinthian church "over to satan for the destruction of the flesh" so that he might be saved on the day of judgment (1 Cor. 5:5). For the obedient and righteous, God's kingdom is, of course, a safe haven from these forces of destruction. But we must overcome their threats of death and destruction the same way Jesus did—through nonviolent and nonresistant love.*

So in the first two chapters of Colossians, Paul speaks of being "in Him" (Christ) 11 times (Col. 1:2, 14, 17, 19, 28; 2:3, 6, 7, 9, 10, 11). In direct contrast, the larger context of both of these chapters refers to being under these other powers. So we can either find our refuge *in* Christ and His Body, or we inescapably stand under these other powers. There is a refuge *in Him*, and there are holy angels of God that give us wisdom and that minister to those of us who are the heirs of salvation (Heb. 1:13-14). But God's kingdom has invaded and been planted in a dimension of darkness, and covetousness has always been a principal vehicle through which this dark dominion continues to rule over human lives. Thus Paul tells Timothy that "the love of money is the *root* of all evil" (1 Tim. 6:10).

"Come out from among them," Paul writes in 2 Corinthians 6, "and be separate and I will receive you. Touch not the unclean thing" (2 Cor. 6:17). Don't "touch" it by letting such metaphysical drives as covetousness influence your attitudes toward the things of the world. "For," Paul asked, "what fellowship has light with darkness? Or believers with unbelievers? *Or the temple of God with idols?*" Whose temple you are (2 Cor. 6:14-16; 1 Cor. 3:16-17). "Flee idolatry," Paul warns over and over again, and yet he says an idol is nothing. So why flee idolatry? As we've seen, Paul also says, "Covetousness is idolatry" (Eph. 5:3, 5; Col. 3:5). So covetousness *is* idolatry, and yet an idol in itself is nothing. But when you sacrifice in idolatry, you're sacrificing to demons and not to God (1 Cor. 10:20-22) because greed binds a soul to the material realm over which the principalities, powers and "the rulers of this dark world" have dominion.†

A deeper insight into the nature of this bondage emerges with a new level of insight into the polytheistic Greek demon-god Eros. This demon-god was identified as the spirit behind every form of unrestrained desire, including incest, fornication, sodomy, adultery, gluttony, bestiality,

---

* Isa. 53:3-9; Matt. 5:9-12, 38-48; Luke 9:51-56; Matt. 26:51-53; John 18:36; Rom. 12:9-21; 1 Pet. 3:8-9; 1 Thess. 5:15.

† Eph. 6:12; 2:2; John 12:31; 14:30; 16:11; Acts 26:18; Col. 1:13.

romantic fantasy and other physical idolatries and perversions, but he was also the spiritual power ruling over greed and covetousness. The Greeks viewed Eros as the first god created from chaos, which then acted as a "demiurgic catalyst in the creation of the world."[57] So Eros was seen as the central self-creative principle of the immanent world, a principle that supplanted the Hebrews' "divine principle *ruah elohim*."[58] Eros, in other words, at the tree of desire, replaced the Spirit of the transcendent God who, in Genesis, brought forth the heavens and the earth and then "rested." Desire, in contrast, never rests, is never satisfied. So in place of a personal, monotheistic transcendence as the Creator, as the nonphysical Spirit who brings cohesion and peace to existence, in polytheism it is Eros who is portrayed as bringing forth and, through little more than an animal-like coupling, binding together all things by his power. So his power is the power of irrepressible lust rising like deadly fumes from the breakdown of all other transcendently given orders of relationship. His power arises, in other words, from chaos and represents the disruption of the God-ordered world at "rest," at peace (Gen. 1:31–2:3). So Eros is the epitome of restlessness. This is true whether this lust is directed toward wealth, goods, power, vainglory or the flesh of other people. Eros is the ultimate ruler of those controlled by covetousness and greed, including nominal believers who profess to follow the Spirit of God but who are actually gripped by the insatiable desire for material things.

So, through our own lust and unbridled desires, covetousness makes us servants of a demonic dominion—it places us under the lordship of satan. Didn't the devil offer Jesus "all the kingdoms of the world and their glory" if only Jesus would "*fall down and worship*" the devil? That's why Paul says, "'Come out and be separate and I will receive you,' says the Lord" and, "Touch not the unclean thing. For what part *has the temple of God with idols?*"

To sum up, anyone who *covets is sacrificing to idols, and to sacrifice to idols is to sacrifice to demons*. At least, Paul says so. It means we're participating in a *system* that is run, planned, set up and executed by satan; but we're to be the temple of God, not a house of idolatry. Why, then, does Paul repeat over and over again that covetousness is idolatry?—Because covetousness is so pervasive, so evasive, so powerful, so easily slipped into that few forces can more easily gain control of us. But, again, when we're covetous, then Paul says we're sacrificing to idols—we're sacrificing to demons. So to be seduced by it is to place ourselves in great spiritual danger. We're simply trying to eat from the Lord's table and from satan's table, too. This means we turn our backs on what God wants to be to us as His people—we shun and "neglect so great a salvation" (Heb. 2:2-3), while at the same time placing ourselves under the dominion of darkness. Yet all the while God is pleading with us, "I will be a Father to you, and you will be My sons and daughters," if only you will "come out from among them and be separate" (2 Cor. 6:17-18). But to love the world or the things of the world means, John wrote, to lose this love of the Father (1 John 2:15-17). God wants to come into a fathering relationship with us, but to enter this relationship means fleeing idolatry, fleeing the rule of covetousness over our lives, with all its many desires for all the things of this world, and extricating ourselves by God's grace from the system that entangles us in the world, the system that takes us down to death and hell in a candy-cane carriage.

We've seen that Paul tells us we're "complete" in Christ (Col. 2:9-10). Now to be complete means to be whole, wholly sanctified "in spirit, soul and body" (1 Thess. 5:23). Completeness by definition covers everything—the *whole*. And so to be whole, also by definition—now think about this—means that the whole of whatever we're speaking of is covered by what we're referring to. So to say, for example, "This whole thing is complete in itself" means on some level that it is self-sufficient. If all of life is covered by what we're talking about, then the whole of that life is complete and self-sufficient in regard to our topic. So if we're "*complete*" in something, then whatever brings that completeness is sufficient in and of itself. We can conclude, then, that in the completeness and wholeness of Christ is self-sufficiency, not leaning upon what would make us partakers of a system run by something totally opposed to and at enmity with God. So the Scripture is *full* of admonition, warning, rebuke, about everything that would tie us to such a world and to such a system.* These admonitions are not peripheral to the Word of God. They are part and parcel of what Paul meant when he said, "You are complete" in Christ (Col. 2:10). So if our *whole* life is to be lived in Christ and we are "complete in Him," then our whole life should be self-sufficient in Christ—not dependent on the world or its systems and provisions.

And what happens when we are *not* complete, whole and sufficient in Christ? Our loyalties become divided. So Matthew records, "Jesus . . . said to them: 'Every *kingdom divided against itself* is brought to *desolation*'" (Matt. 12:25). A house and a kingdom "*divided against itself cannot stand*." Remember our earlier quotes:

> For even if there are so-called gods, whether in heaven or on earth (as *there are many gods and many lords*), yet *for us there is one God, the Father, of whom are all things, and we for Him; and one Lord Jesus Christ, through whom are all things, and through whom we live.* (1 Cor. 8:5-6)

> You cannot drink the cup of the Lord and the cup of demons; you cannot partake of the Lord's table and of the table of demons. Or

---

* 2 Tim. 2:4; 1 Tim. 6:6-12; 1 John 2:15-17; James 4:1-5; 2 Cor. 6:14-18; Rev. 18:1-5.

do we provoke the Lord to jealousy? Are we stronger than He?
(1 Cor. 10:21-22)

So only for those who truly dwell in the temple—who are not under those other principalities and powers—can it be said that there's *only one God*. And this doesn't happen merely because we've mentally assented to some facts about Jesus' life. *Our whole life must assent to His lordship.* Otherwise, we are divided against ourselves, and we will be given over to other lords and other gods—gods in charge of attitudes, gods in charge of feelings, gods in charge of thoughts, gods and lords in charge of human activities and relationships. So we cannot toy with covetousness—it will either uproot us from the kingdom of God, or we will completely uproot it from our hearts, minds and lives, preparing the way for God's pure and holy love to control our thoughts, feelings and desires. Only when His love takes complete control of our inner man can we be completely His and thereby "complete in Him."

In Galatians 4, Paul writes:

> I say that the heir, as long as he is a child, differs nothing from a slave, though he is master of all, but is under guardians and stewards until the time appointed by the father. Even so we, when we were children, were in bondage under the *elements* of the world.
> (Gal. 4:1-3)

Here's that word again—the word "elements" is *stoicheia*. It means, to repeat, "elementary principles" or "basic principles." But, as seen, the word carries connotations far greater than that, indicating "*world powers*" or "*elemental powers* or *principalities*." The word implicitly contains within itself the *principles* by which these powers rule people who live in "bondage under *the elements of the world*."

After Paul speaks of the power of these "elements of the world," he goes on to tell us of the alternative kingdom Christ has come to bring:

> And when the fullness of the time had come, God sent forth His Son, born of a woman, born under the law, to redeem those who were under the law, that we might receive the adoption as sons. And because you are sons, God has sent forth the Spirit of His Son into your hearts, crying out, "Abba, Father!" (Gal. 4:4-6)

As shown, Jesus, in a sense, is the head of all principalities and powers because He's conquered death by submitting His righteous life unto death and thereby overcoming its power. This does not mean in any sense that Jesus personally relates to these powers—it only means He has defeated them through the agony of His sinless life on the cross (Col. 2:13-15). *So our task is to put the entirety of our lives into both His sacrificial death and His resurrection life in order that He might release us from the accusations of these destroying forces—their accusations against our guilt—and their actual dominion over our thinking and lives. God can, of course, overturn* *these powers in His own realm of dominion,* but God originally gave man and woman a bona fide gift of dominion over this earth (Gen. 1:26-28; Ps. 8:4-6; 115:16; 1 Cor. 15:21-28; Eph. 1:17-23). And God's gifts and callings are irrevocable (Rom. 11:29; Heb. 2:5-9). So when man and woman surrendered their dominion to satan's dominion of death in the garden (Gen. 1:26-30; 3:1-7), justice demanded that God honor that freely made decision. Therefore, as the ancient *Christus Victor* view of the atonement points out,* there is also a dominion of satan, and without Christ we are inevitably held by that malevolent dominion. This is why God had to incarnate *Himself*: "God was *in* Christ reconciling the world unto Himself" (2 Cor. 5:19). Through Christ's death and resurrection, He liberated us from the wrath of God, which is expressed in the wrath of the *elohim†*— not by God personally in the full expression of His essential nature (love) that was expressed in Jesus Christ, but only by God *impersonally* acting through the laws of His creation or the *elohimic* "host" of heaven. God no more *personally* moves through the judgment of this host than He *personally* moves through a she-bear defending her cubs against an intruder into her territory. So this "territory" of judgment is the impersonal realm administered by the lesser *elohim*, the angels, whether fallen or righteous, into whose hands this dominion fell. Jesus came to pull us out of that impersonal dominion of death and judgment by creating another dominion and kingdom here on earth into which people could escape. The writer of Hebrews said that "through death He [Jesus] destroyed him who had the *power* of death, that is, the devil, and *released* those who *through fear of death* were all their lifetime subject to bondage" (Heb. 2:14-15). In Acts Jesus tells Paul, on the road to Damascus, that "I now send you [Paul] to *open their eyes*, in order to *turn them from darkness to light*, and *from the power of satan to God*" (Acts 26:17-18). And in Colossians Paul writes that "He has *delivered* us *from the dominion of darkness* and *conveyed us into the kingdom of the Son* of His love" (Col. 1:13). We're not supposed to be members and citizens of the world anymore, or of that kingdom or "dominion of darkness," but members and citizens of this alternative kingdom, the "kingdom of the Son of His love." Jesus, not the "many gods and many lords" that Paul referred to, is supposed to be the Lord of love for our *entire* life. But covetousness would try to bring us under the latter, malevolent lordship.

We can now review some of the previously quoted passages and bring out their implications more fully. We read again when Paul says:

---

* See The Minister's Dialectical Handbook of Theology and Doctrine *On Atonement, Justification and the Law, Book One: Atonement and the Law* by Blair Adams (Elm Mott, Tex.: Colloquium Press, 1996, 2005).

† See *Beyond Violence, Beyond Pacifism* by Blair Adams (Elm Mott, Tex.: Colloquium Press, 1988, 2003, 2008).

> God sent forth His Son . . . to *redeem* those who were under the law, that we might receive the adoption as sons. And because you are sons, God has sent forth the Spirit of His Son into your hearts, crying out, "Abba, Father!" Therefore you are no longer a slave but a son, and if a son, then an heir of God through Christ. But then, indeed, when you did not know God, you served *those gods that by nature are not really gods.* (Gal. 4:4-8)

Here Paul is undoubtedly talking about the same thing that he was talking about in 1 Corinthians 8 and that he was talking about in Colossians. He's telling us again and again that there are principalities; there are dominions and powers of spiritual darkness—rulers of this dark world. So as long as our lives are lived in darkness, we are under "the dominion of darkness" (Col. 1:13, NIV), in bondage to "the rulers of the *darkness* of this age" (Eph. 6:12). This is the case whether we realize it or not. And most often we don't because it is in the very nature of darkness to blind us. If we walk in partial darkness, then we see only partially. So even believers often fail to clearly see the nature of the conflict. They think the material realm is safe because it does not involve *direct* interaction with evil spirits. But such a direct interaction wouldn't be much of a temptation to *believers*—it would not, in other words, be a deception powerful enough to "deceive the very elect" (Matt. 24:24). But the seemingly nonspiritual, material realm is the very realm of idolatry, and that's why it is so deceptive—because, as Paul said, an idol in itself seems to be nothing, so it can easily pull us into sacrificing to powers that are far more than nothing if we let them rule our lives through materialism and greed. So idolatry is how the material realm is being used by principalities and powers to incite feelings of envy, status, pride, independence, obsessions that fill our lives and take the place of God.

Yet many believers too often see reality materialistically, ignoring its spiritual dimension. They fail in this way for many reasons, but we can mention four of the main ones: one, because such a view is natural to the natural man, and these believers are either infants or carnal (1 Cor. 2:14; 3:1); two, because they've been trained and conditioned and programmed by the very culture of the world in which they live to view reality materialistically; three, because they live their entire lives in the unremitting materialism of an economic system given to such a view; four, because they've never made an exodus from the kingdoms given to this view and entered a comprehensive Christian community life that constitutes the alternative kingdom of God; and so on. But in any case, they're unconscious of the spiritual dimension behind the material. They're in a stupor, drunk on materialism (Rev. 17:1-5; 18:1-4), and this has occurred in such a way that they sink deeper and deeper into it while remaining unconscious of the spiritual powers behind it. They therefore don't even see the *spiritual* battle (Eph. 6:10-18), much

less what its nature is or the role that covetousness and greed play in
it.

They don't even see that the material realm, *the realm of matter, is
precisely the realm of the malevolent spirit that they're adulterously serving.*
Indeed, the word *"matter,"* the root of *materialism*, is itself rooted in
the Latin word *mater*, which means "mother." In the ancient world, the
materialist realm of the *mater* was seen as the world of the great pagan
mother goddess (who "sits as a queen," the "queen of heaven," the *"mother
of harlots,"* Jer. 7:18; Rev. 17:1-5; 18:7). The pagans saw the mother
goddess as the whole material earth and everything that has its origins
from below, including the great commercial empires built on exploiting
the earth's (the magna mater's) resources. All this was counterposed to the
realm above of the *pater*, the Father, the Giver of the *pattern* of the temple
and all human relationships ordered from above. Jesus clearly expressed
the opposition between these two realms when He declared that He had
come to do His *Father's* will, and then He laid down His life to fulfill
that spiritual purpose. So we cannot claim to have surrendered completely
to Jesus and experience His freedom so long as we greedily cling to this
material world (1 John 2:15-17; James 4:4).

Therefore those who serve the realm of *mater* are serving a different
spirit. They're serving a different kingdom. If they claim to follow God,
then they're dividing the kingdom of God against itself and desolating it
through the wine of their fornication, their adulteries with the world (Rev.
17:1-5; 18:2-5). The material world all seems so pragmatic and nonspiritual, so innocently secular and materialistic: "I'm just making a living,"
people say. But *how*, and has your vocation (literally "calling") in the world
taken the place of God and His calling in your life? "I'm just amusing
myself," you say, but on *what*, and what is it doing to your thinking, your
attitudes, your relationships, your ethics, your worldview? People whose
lives are consumed with material things are serving a spiritual power—
"gods who are by nature no gods."

That's why God is saying: "Come out of her, My people." That's why
it describes those in the church of Laodicea as "blind, wretched, naked,
poor, miserable." That's why it says that what the Bible calls "Babylon,"
which is the apostate kingdom adulterated by the systems of the world,
"has put all the nations under her magic spell." People don't see the reality of what they're doing—they're under a spell, entranced. She's called
"mystery, Babylon." It's all supposedly based on simply a pragmatic "materialism." Yet it's much more—a "mystery" lies hidden beneath the surface
of materialism. Scripture describes this system as being comprised of all
"the *merchants*" and "*rulers*" of the earth (Rev. 18:1-20). So it's both an
economic ("merchants") system and a political ("rulers") system. In fact,

it's this entire secular world that's supposedly completely removed from the spiritual. It's the same world that says the church should confine itself to a little private, compartmentalized area where people can sip a spiritual drink once or twice a week (or year) and then live out the rest of their lives firmly rooted, motivated, driven and absorbed in a materialistic, secular order that allegedly has nothing to do with spiritual matters. But that's not the way the Bible speaks of Babylon. For it reveals this world's political and economic—its *secular*—system to be a religious and spiritual system, even the habitation of demonic powers (Rev. 18:1-5). In fact, Scripture says that if you can't see this spiritual dimension inherent in the world system, it only means you're "drunk on the wine of her fornication," that you're under her "spell" because of your adulteration by and adultery with the world (Rev. 17:1-5; James 4:4, Ampl.). And this is what blinds you to the whole dynamic of this system, which is spiritual to the core. All today's vaunted individualism largely rests on the implicit acceptance of the lie that we can be our own god (Gen. 3:1-5; 2 Thess. 2:9-12), isolating ourselves from the kingdom of God, separating ourselves from God and His people, from *His* spiritual world. We so completely "privatize" our religion that we won't even impose it upon ourselves, even as we continue to rapidly descend to what is "earthly, sensual and devilish"—into raw and unremitting materialism and the covetousness that drives it (James 3:15; 4:4). Paul concludes the Galatians passage we just read:

> But now after you have known God, or rather are known by God, how is it that you turn again to these weak and beggarly *elements* [world powers], to which you desire again to be *in bondage*? (Gal. 4:9)

Here we see that same word, *stoicheia*. Paul is telling us that if we "turn" to these "world powers," to the god of this world (2 Cor. 4:4), we will inevitably find ourselves in bondage. And our desires, our covetousness and greed, are what will bring us into this bondage, as James said:

> Where do wars and fights come from among you? Do they not come from your desires for pleasure that war in your members? You *lust and do not have*. You murder and *covet* and *cannot obtain*. You fight and war. Yet you do not have because you do not ask. You ask and do not receive, because you ask amiss, that you may spend it *on your pleasures. Adulterers and adulteresses!* Do you not know that friendship with the world is enmity with God? Whoever therefore wants to be a friend of the world makes himself an enemy of God. Or do you think that the Scripture says in vain, "The Spirit who dwells in us *yearns jealously*"? But He gives more grace. Therefore He says: "God resists the proud, but gives grace to the humble." Therefore submit to God. Resist the devil and he will flee from you. Draw near to God and He will draw near to you. Cleanse your hands, you sinners; and purify your hearts, you double-minded. Lament and mourn and weep! Let your laughter

be turned to mourning and your joy to gloom. Humble yourselves in the sight of the Lord, and He will lift you up. (James 4:1-10)

The climactic book of Scripture, the book of Revelation, extensively and horrifically describes just how the whole world will be brought into bondage to an economic and political system of idolatry, of spiritual bondage:

> I stood on the sand of the sea. And I saw a beast rising up out of the sea, having seven heads and ten horns, and on his horns ten crowns, and on his heads a blasphemous name. Now the beast which I saw was like a leopard and his feet were like those feet of a bear, . . . his mouth like the mouth of a lion. The dragon gave him his power, his throne, and his great authority. And I saw one of his heads as if it had been mortally wounded, and his deadly wound was healed. And all the world marveled and followed the beast. So they worshiped the dragon [this is a political, Statist power and a certain form of government] who gave authority to the beast; and they worshiped the beast, saying, "Who is like him? And who can make war with him?" He was given a mouth speaking great things and blasphemies. (Rev. 13:1-5)

Then the passage goes on to say:

> It was granted to him to make war with the saints and to overcome them. And authority was given him over every tribe, tongue, and nation . . . . If anyone has an ear, let him hear. He who leads into captivity shall go into captivity; he who kills with the sword must be killed with the sword. Here is the perseverance and the faith of the saints. (Rev. 13:7, 9-10)

> All those whose names have not been written in the Book of Life of the Lamb slain from the foundation of the world are going to worship him. (Rev. 13:8)

And here is the critical part for our discussion of covetousness:

> I saw another beast coming up out of the earth, and he had two horns like a lamb and spoke like a dragon. And he exercises all the authority of the first beast in his presence, and causes the earth and those who dwell in it to worship the first beast, whose deadly wound was healed. He performs great signs, so that he makes fire come down from heaven on the earth in the sight of men. And he *deceives those who dwell on the earth* by those signs which he was granted to do in the sight of the beast, telling those who dwell on the earth to make an image of the beast . . . . He was granted power to give breath to the image . . . , that the image of the beast should speak and cause as many as would not worship the image of the beast to be killed. He causes all, small, great, rich and poor, free and slave, to receive a mark on their right hand or on their foreheads, *that no one may buy or sell except he who has the mark or the name of the beast.* (Rev. 13:11-17)

So what is the sanction portrayed here, or that enforces the ultimate act of idolatry? *It's an economic sanction—you won't be able to buy or sell.* You won't be able to participate in the materialistic system that will finally be revealed as all along having belonged to a spiritual monstrosity in a secularly political guise that only unveils its spiritual dimension at the very end. If we are so deeply rooted in it that we have turned our backs on every provision of God, how will we escape if we "neglect so great a salvation" (Heb. 2:2-3)? And what is it that will keep us rooted in that system, ignoring God's call to come out of her? Is it not consistently shown to be covetousness in one form or another? No wonder, then, Paul repeatedly called it "idolatry," and God listed its avoidance as one of the ten governing principles for the world (Exod. 20:17; Rom. 13:9; Col. 3:5).

John writes then in the next chapter of Revelation, after describing those who receive this mark of economic sanction, that "the smoke of their torment will ascend forever and ever" (Rev. 14:11). There is, in other words, no hope for these people. They're consigned to eternal punishment. They have *accepted their permanent place in the system of ultimate idolatry in the context of the dominion of darkness and death.* Yet this is only the culmination of that idolatry. But what could possibly lead people to follow along in each step that will finally culminate in this eternal bondage? *"Covetousness which is idolatry."* This is what causes people to keep following until they are eternally captive: *"the love of money which is the root of all evil."*

> *Woe to you who are rich,* for you have received your consolation. (Luke 6:24)

> Now as He was going out on the road, one came running, knelt before Him, and asked Him, "Good Teacher, what shall I do that I may inherit eternal life?" So Jesus said to him, "Why do you call Me good? No one is good but One, that is, God. You know the commandments: 'Do not commit adultery,' 'Do not murder,' 'Do not steal,' 'Do not bear false witness,' 'Do not defraud,' 'Honor your father and your mother.'" And he answered and said to Him, "Teacher, all these things I have kept from my youth." Then Jesus, looking at him, loved him, and said to him, *"One thing you lack: Go your way, sell whatever you have and give to the poor, and you will have treasure in heaven; and come, take up the cross, and follow Me."* But he was sad at this word, and went away sorrowful, for he had great possessions. Then Jesus looked around and said to His disciples, *"How hard it is for those who have riches to enter the kingdom of God!"* And the disciples were astonished at His words. But Jesus answered again and said to them, "Children, how hard it is for those who *trust in riches* to enter the kingdom of God! It is easier for a camel to go through the eye of a needle than for a rich man to enter the kingdom of God." And they were greatly astonished, saying among themselves, "Who then can be saved?" But Jesus looked at them and said, "With men it is impossible, but not with God; for with God all things are possible." (Mark 10:17-27)

Then one from the crowd said to Him, "Teacher, tell my brother to divide the inheritance with me." But He said to him, "Man, who made Me a judge or an arbitrator over you?" And He said to them, *"Take heed and beware of covetousness, for one's life does not consist in the abundance of the things he possesses."* Then He spoke this parable to them, saying: "The ground of a certain rich man yielded plentifully. And he thought within himself, saying, 'What shall I do, since I have no room to store my crops?' So he said, 'I will do this: I will pull down my barns and build greater.' And he said, 'I will say to my soul, "Soul, you have many goods laid up for many years; take your ease; eat, drink, and be merry."' But God said to him, 'Fool! This night your soul will be required of you; then whose will those things be that you have provided?' So is *he who lays up treasure for himself, and is not rich toward God."* Then He said to His disciples, "Therefore I say to you, *don't worry about your life, what you will eat; nor about the body, what you will put on. Life is more than food, and the body is more than clothing.* Consider the ravens, for they neither sow nor reap, which have neither storehouse nor barn; and God feeds them. Of how much more value are you than the birds? And which of you by worrying can add one cubit to his stature? If you then are not able to do the least, why are you anxious for the rest? . . . Do not seek what you should eat or what you should drink, nor have an anxious mind. For all these things the Gentiles of the world [or the nations] seek after, and your Father knows that you have need of these things. But seek ye first the kingdom of God. Sell what you have and give alms; provide yourselves money bags which do not grow old, a treasure in the heavens that does not fail, where no thief approaches nor moth destroys. *For where your treasure is, there will your heart be also."* (Luke 12:13-34)

Godliness with contentment is great gain. For we brought nothing into this world, and it is certain we can carry nothing out. But having food and clothing, with these we shall be content. But those who desire to be rich fall into temptation and a snare, and into many foolish and harmful lusts which drown men in destruction and perdition. For the love of money is the root of all kinds of evil, for which some have strayed from the faith in their *greediness,* and pierced themselves through with many sorrows. But you, O man of God, flee these things and pursue righteousness, godliness, faith, love, patience, gentleness. Fight the good fight of faith, lay hold on eternal life . . . . Command those who are rich in this present age not to be haughty, *nor to trust in uncertain riches but in the living God* . . . . Let them do good, that they be rich in good works, ready to give, willing to share, storing up for themselves a good foundation for the time to come, that they may lay hold on eternal life. (1 Tim. 6:6-12, 17-19)

Let *the lowly brother glory in his exaltation, but the rich in his humiliation,* because as a flower of the field he will pass away. For no sooner has the sun risen with a burning heat than it withers the grass; its flower falls, and its beautiful appearance perishes. *So the rich man also will fade away in all his pursuits.* (James 1:9-11)

Has God not chosen the poor of this world to be rich in faith and heirs of the kingdom? (James 2:5)

Now come, you rich, weep and howl for your miseries that are coming upon you! Your riches are corrupted, and your garments are moth-eaten. Your gold and silver are corroded, and their corrosion will be a witness against you and will eat your flesh like fire. You have heaped up treasure in the last days . . . . You have lived on the earth in pleasure and luxury; you have fattened your hearts as in a day of slaughter. (James 5:1-3, 5)

If I have made gold my hope, or said to fine gold, "You are my confidence [—I'm going to succeed in this. I'm putting my trust in this—]; If I have rejoiced *because my wealth was great,* and because *my hand had gained much;* . . . so that my heart has been secretly enticed, and my mouth has kissed my hand; this would also be an iniquity deserving of judgment, for *I would have denied God who is above."* (Job 31:24-25, 27-28)

When you have eaten and are full, then you shall bless Yahweh your God for the good land which He has given you. Beware that you do not forget Yahweh your God by not keeping His commandments . . . lest—when you have eaten and are full, and have built beautiful houses and dwell in them; and when your herds and your flocks multiply, and your silver and your gold are multiplied, and all that you have is multiplied; when your heart is lifted up, and you forget Yahweh your God who brought you out of the land of Egypt, from the house of bondage; who led you through that great and terrible wilderness, in which were fiery serpents and scorpions and thirsty land where there was no water; who brought water for you out of the flinty rock; who fed you in the wilderness with manna, which your fathers did not know, that He might humble you and that He might test you, to do you good in the end—then you say in your heart, "My power and the might of my hand have gained me this wealth." And you shall remember Yahweh your God, for *it is He who gives you power to get wealth, that He may establish His covenant.* (Deut. 8:10-18)

The only reason God gives us this power to obtain wealth is so that we may accomplish the *purpose of His covenant.* It's not for our own purposes, to feed our covetous desires and allow us to "get ahead" of our neighbors. If we have no incentive to work except to acquire things for ourselves, then we have no incentive but selfishness and pride:

He who *hastens to be rich* will not go unpunished. (Prov. 28:20)

Will you set your eyes on that which is not? *For riches certainly make themselves wings; they fly away like an eagle toward heaven.* (Prov. 23:5)

A man with an evil eye *hastens after riches.* (Prov. 28:22)

Behold, the days are coming when all that is in your house, and *what your fathers have accumulated until this day, shall be carried to Babylon; nothing shall be left of it.* They shall take away your sons who will descend from you, whom you will beget; and they will be eunuchs in the palace of the king of Babylon. (Isa. 39:6-7)

There is one who makes himself rich, yet has nothing; and one who makes himself poor, yet has great riches. (Prov. 13:7)

By faith Moses, when he became of age, refused to be called the son of Pharaoh's daughter, choosing rather to suffer affliction with the people of God than to enjoy the passing pleasures of sin, *esteeming the reproach of Christ greater riches than all the treasures in Egypt; for he looked to the reward.* (Heb. 11:24-26)

The kingdom of heaven is *like treasure hidden in a field*, which a man found and hid; and for joy over it he goes and sells *all* that he has and buys that field. (Matt. 13:44)

No one can serve two masters; for either he will hate the one and love the other, or else he will be loyal to the one and despise the other. *You cannot serve God and mammon.* (Matt. 6:24)

You cannot bow down to—genuflect before—mammon and then go to the table of the Lord.

Now the Pharisees, who were *lovers of money*, heard these things, and they derided Him. And He said to them, "You are those who justify yourselves before men, but God knows your hearts. For what is highly esteemed among men is an abomination in the sight of God." (Luke 16:14-15)

There was a certain *rich man*, who was clothed in purple and fine linen and fared sumptuously every day. But there was a certain beggar named Lazarus, full of sores, who was laid at his gate, desiring to be fed with the crumbs which fell from the rich man's table. Moreover the dogs came and licked his sores. So it was that the beggar died, and was carried by the angels to Abraham's bosom. The rich man also died and was buried. And being in torments in Hell, he lifted up his eyes and saw Abraham afar off, and Lazarus in his bosom. Then he cried and said, "Father Abraham, have mercy on me, and send Lazarus that he may dip the tip of his finger in water and cool my tongue; for I am tormented in this flame." But Abraham said, "Son, *remember that in your lifetime you received your good things*, and likewise Lazarus evil things; but now he is comforted and *you are tormented*. And besides all this, between us and you there is a great gulf fixed, so that those who want to pass from here to you cannot, nor can those from there pass to us." (Luke 16:19-26)

Where do wars and fights come from among you? Do they not come from your desires for pleasure that war in your members? You lust and do not have. You murder and covet and cannot obtain. You fight and war. Yet you do not have because you do not ask. You ask and do not receive, because you ask amiss, that you may spend it on your pleasures. Adulterers and adulteresses! Do you not know that friendship with the world is enmity with God? Whoever therefore wants to be a friend of the world makes himself an enemy of God. Or do you think that the Scripture says in vain, "The Spirit who dwells in us yearns jealously"? But He gives more grace. Therefore He says: "God resists the proud, but gives grace to the humble." (James 4:1-6)

Do not love the world or the things in the world . . . . All that is in the world [all of it]—the lust of the flesh, the lust of the eyes, and the pride of life—is not of the Father. (1 John 2:15-16)

One of the seven angels who had the seven bowls came and talked with me, saying to me, "Come, I will show you the judgment of the great harlot who sits upon many waters, with whom the kings of the earth committed fornication, and the inhabitants of the earth were made drunk with the wine of her fornication." . . . I saw a woman sitting on a scarlet beast which was full of names of blasphemy, having seven heads and ten horns. The woman was *arrayed in purple and scarlet, and adorned with gold and precious stones and pearls,* having in her hand a golden cup full of abominations and the filthiness. (Rev. 17:1-4)

I saw another angel coming down from heaven, having great authority, . . . and he cried mightily with a loud voice, saying, "Babylon the great is fallen, is fallen, and has become *a dwelling place of demons, a prison for every foul spirit, and a cage for every unclean and hated bird!* All the nations have drunk of the wine of the *wrath* of her fornication, the kings of the earth have committed fornication with her, and the merchants of the earth have become rich through the abundance of her luxury." And I heard another voice from heaven saying, "Come out of her, my people, lest you share in her sins, and lest you receive of her plagues." (Rev. 18:1-4)

We are supposed to "come out" "of Babylon." But what does that mean? As in Revelation 13, John here describes a political system ("the *kings* of the earth"), and he's describing an economic system ("the *merchants* of the earth"), and then he immediately says to "come out of her." As he continues, he keeps describing the same system with its great riches and luxuries of international trade, this great city and all the ships of the merchants who have become rich through her trade. And the time of her desolation comes—in one hour she is made desolate. Then the scripture says,

Rejoice apostles, prophets. Thus with violence the great city of Babylon shall be overthrown. (Rev. 18:20-21).

The similarity of these passages to one in Ezekiel is striking and even alarming.

Son of man, say to the *prince of Tyre,* "Because your heart is lifted up, and *you say, 'I am a god, I sit in the seat of gods, in the midst of the seas,'* yet you are a man, and not a god, though *you set your heart as the heart of a god* . . . . *You have gained riches for yourself,* and *gathered gold and silver* into your treasuries; by your great *wisdom in trade* you have *increased your riches,* and *your heart is lifted up because of your riches* . . . . But you shall be thrown down into the Pit." (Ezek. 28:2, 4-5, 8)

This king, described as gaining great "riches" through his "wisdom in trade," is then revealed to be satan, who says, "I am a god." And what Ezekiel says will be done for the prince (principality) of Tyre, satan, is the same as what will be done to Babylon—it will be burned up.

> Take up a lamentation for the *king of Tyre*, and say to him, . . . "*You were the seal of perfection*, full of wisdom and perfect in beauty. *You were in Eden, the garden of God* . . . . You were *the anointed cherub who covers*; . . . *you were on the holy mountain of God*; . . . *You were perfect* in your ways from the day you were created, *till iniquity was found in you. By the abundance of your trading you became filled with violence* within, and you sinned; therefore *I cast you as a profane thing out of the mountain of God*; and *I destroyed you, O covering cherub* . . . . Your heart was lifted up because of your beauty; you corrupted your wisdom for the sake of your splendor . . . . You defiled your sanctuaries by the multitude of your iniquities, by the *iniquity of your trading*; therefore I brought fire from your midst." (Ezek. 28:12-18)

Satan's very fall has to do, then, with his covetousness for wealth through commerce and "trading." Thus Jesus declared,

> Whoever desires to come after Me, let him deny himself, and take up his cross, and follow Me. For whoever desires to save his life will lose it, but whoever loses his life for My sake and the gospel's will save it. For *what will it profit a man if he gains the whole world, and loses his own soul*? (Mark 8:34-36)

In this last scripture, the Lord succinctly reveals the nature of the activity of greed—the metaphysical power of greed, the working of the covetousness that is idolatry: the "whole world" is not big enough to satisfy greed. So you can "gain the whole world and lose [your] own soul." Or, "What will a man give *in exchange for* his soul?" This is the ultimate "trading" that satan is carrying on—the "exchange" of the world for every soul who will sell him- or herself for the "world and the things of the world" and thereby sacrifice "the love of the Father" (1 John 2:15-17) and their own souls. This is the ultimate system of "exchange." Jesus states it clearly: in giving ourselves to covetousness, we're exchanging our souls for the world and the things of the world. So, to "come out of her" means to come out of participation in this entire commercial system based on greed and covetousness and to turn to a life of completeness, wholeness and self-sufficiency in Christ (Col. 2:9-10). That's why Jesus, Paul, James and others said to lay hold of eternal life by fleeing from this world and all its enticements.

> *Whoever is ashamed of Me and My words* in this adulterous and sinful generation, *of him the Son of Man also will be ashamed* when He comes in the glory of His Father. (Mark 8:38)

> These are the ones sown among thorns; they are the ones who hear the word, and *the cares of this world, the deceitfulness of riches, and*

the desires for other things entering in choke the word, and it becomes unfruitful. (Mark 4:18-19)

Concerning *things offered to idols*: . . . if anyone thinks that he knows anything, he knows nothing yet as he ought to know . . . . Concerning the eating of *things offered to idols, we know that an idol is nothing in the world, and that there is no other God but one.* (1 Cor. 8:1-2, 4)

Now these things became our examples, to the intent that we should not lust after evil things. [But] *do not become idolaters* as were some of them . . . . Are not those who eat of the sacrifices partakers of the altar? What am I saying then? That an idol is anything, or what is offered to idols is anything? Rather, that the *things which the Gentiles sacrifice they sacrifice to demons and not to God*, and *I do not want you to have fellowship with demons. You cannot drink the cup of the Lord and the cup of demons; you cannot partake of the Lord's table and of the table of demons. Or do we provoke the Lord to jealousy?* (1 Cor. 10:6-7, 19-22)

This you know, that no fornicator, unclean person, nor *covetous man, who is an idolater,* has any inheritance in the kingdom of Christ and God. Let no one deceive you . . . , for because of these things the wrath of God comes upon the sons of disobedience. (Eph. 5:5-6)

Therefore put to death your members which are on the earth: fornication, uncleanness, passion, evil desire, and *covetousness, which is idolatry.* Because of these things the wrath of God is coming upon the sons of disobedience. (Col. 3:5-6)

Do *not be unequally yoked together with unbelievers.* For what fellowship has righteousness with lawlessness? And what communion has light with darkness? And what accord has Christ with Belial? Or what part has a believer with an unbeliever? And what agreement has the temple of God with idols? For you are the temple of the living God. As God has said: "I will dwell in them and walk among them. I will be their God, and they shall be My people." Therefore "*Come out from among them and be separate* . . . . *Do not touch what is unclean*, and I will receive you." (2 Cor. 6:14-17)

Jesus continued: "There was a man who had two sons. The younger one said to his father, 'Father, give me my share of the estate.' So he divided his property between them. Not long after that, the younger son got together all he had, set off for a distant country and there *squandered his wealth in wild living.*" (Luke 15:11-13)

Some time later there was an incident involving a vineyard belonging to Naboth the Jezreelite. The vineyard was in Jezreel, close to the palace of Ahab king of Samaria. Ahab said to Naboth, "Let me have your vineyard to use for a vegetable garden, since it is close to my palace. In exchange I will give you a better vineyard or, if you prefer, I will pay you whatever it is worth."

But Naboth replied, "Yahweh forbid that I should give you the inheritance of my fathers."

So Ahab went home, sullen and angry because Naboth the Jezreelite had said, "I will not give you the inheritance of my fathers." He lay on his bed sulking and refused to eat.

His wife Jezebel came in and asked him, "Why are you so sullen? Why won't you eat?"

He answered her, "Because I said to Naboth the Jezreelite, 'Sell me your vineyard; or if you prefer, I will give you another vineyard in its place.' But he said, 'I will not give you my vineyard.'"

Jezebel his wife said, "Is this how you act as king over Israel? Get up and eat! Cheer up. I'll get you the vineyard of Naboth the Jezreelite." So she wrote letters in Ahab's name, placed his seal on them, and sent them to the elders and nobles who lived in Naboth's city with him. In those letters she wrote: "Proclaim a day of fasting and seat Naboth in a prominent place among the people. But seat two scoundrels opposite him and have them testify that he has cursed both God and the king. Then take him out and stone him to death."

So the elders and nobles who lived in Naboth's city did as Jezebel directed in the letters she had written to them. They proclaimed a fast and seated Naboth in a prominent place among the people. Then two scoundrels came and sat opposite him and brought charges against Naboth before the people, saying, "Naboth has cursed both God and the king." So they took him outside the city and stoned him to death. Then they sent word to Jezebel: "Naboth has been stoned and is dead."

As soon as Jezebel heard that Naboth had been stoned to death, she said to Ahab, "Get up and take possession of the vineyard of Naboth the Jezreelite that he refused to sell you. He is no longer alive, but dead." When Ahab heard that Naboth was dead, he got up and went down to take possession of Naboth's vineyard. (1 Kings 21:1-16)

The heart of the covetous closes to the needs of others. This condition in the heart of anyone destroys them unless it is uprooted.

> *The sluggard's craving will be the death of him*, because his hands refuse to work. *All day long he craves for more*, but *the righteous give without sparing*. (Prov. 21:25-26)

> *Whoever loves money never has money enough; whoever loves wealth is never satisfied with his income*. This too is meaningless. (Eccles. 5:10)

> *You shall not covet your neighbor's house. You shall not covet your neighbor's wife, or his manservant or maidservant, his ox or donkey, or anything that belongs to your neighbor.* (Exod. 20:17)

> I have seen a grievous evil under the sun: *wealth hoarded to the harm of its owner*, or wealth lost through some misfortune, so that when he has a son there is nothing left for him. Naked a man comes from his mother's womb, and as he comes, so he departs. He takes nothing from his labor that he can carry in his hand. (Eccles. 5:13-15)

A greedy man stirs up dissension, but he who trusts in Yahweh will prosper. (Prov. 28:25)

When *the woman saw that the fruit of the tree was good for food and pleasing to the eye, and also desirable for gaining wisdom, she took some and ate it. She also gave some to her husband, who was with her, and he ate it.* Then the eyes of both of them were opened, and they realized they were naked; so they sewed fig leaves together and made coverings for themselves. (Gen. 3:6-7)

In the spring, at the time when kings go off to war, David sent Joab out with the king's men and the whole Israelite army. They destroyed the Ammonites and besieged Rabbah. But David remained in Jerusalem.

One evening David got up from his bed and walked around on the roof of the palace. *From the roof he saw a woman bathing. The woman was very beautiful*, and David sent someone to find out about her. The man said, "Isn't this Bathsheba, the daughter of Eliam and the wife of Uriah the Hittite?" *Then David sent messengers to get her.* She came to him, and he slept with her. (She had purified herself from her uncleanness.) Then she went back home. The woman conceived and sent word to David, saying, "I am pregnant."

So David sent this word to Joab: "Send me Uriah the Hittite." And Joab sent him to David. When Uriah came to him, David asked him how Joab was, how the soldiers were and how the war was going. Then David said to Uriah, "Go down to your house and wash your feet." So Uriah left the palace, and a gift from the king was sent after him. But Uriah slept at the entrance to the palace with all his master's servants and did not go down to his house.

When David was told, "Uriah did not go home," he asked him, "Haven't you just come from a distance? Why didn't you go home?"

Uriah said to David, "The ark and Israel and Judah are staying in tents, and my master Joab and my lord's men are camped in the open fields. How could I go to my house to eat and drink and lie with my wife? As surely as you live, I will not do such a thing!"

Then David said to him, "Stay here one more day, and tomorrow I will send you back." So Uriah remained in Jerusalem that day and the next. At David's invitation, he ate and drank with him, and David made him drunk. But in the evening Uriah went out to sleep on his mat among his master's servants; he did not go home.

In the morning *David wrote a letter to Joab and sent it with Uriah. In it he wrote, "Put Uriah in the front line where the fighting is fiercest. Then withdraw from him so he will be struck down and die."*

So while Joab had the city under siege, he put Uriah at a place where he knew the strongest defenders were. Then the men of the city came out and fought with Joab. And some of the people of the servants of David fell; and Uriah the Hittite died also . . . .

When the wife of Uriah heard that Uriah her husband was dead, she mourned for her husband. And when her mourning was over, *David sent and brought her to his house, and she became his wife and bore him a son. But the thing that David had done displeased Yahweh.*

Then Yahweh sent Nathan to David. And he came to him, and said to him: *"There were two men in one city, one rich and the other poor. The rich man had exceedingly many flocks and herds. But the poor man had nothing, except one little ewe lamb which he had bought and nourished; and it grew up together with him and with his children. It ate of his own food and drank from his own cup and lay in his bosom; and it was like a daughter to him. And a traveler came to the rich man, who refused to take from his own flock and from his own herd to prepare one for the wayfaring man who had come to him; but he took the poor man's lamb and prepared it for the man who had come to him."*

So David's anger was greatly aroused against the man, and he said to Nathan, "As Yahweh lives, the man who has done this shall surely die! And he shall restore fourfold for the lamb, because he did this thing and because he had no pity."

Then Nathan said to David, "You are the man! Thus says Yahweh God of Israel: 'I anointed you king over Israel, and I delivered you from the hand of Saul. I gave you your master's house and your master's wives into your keeping, and gave you the house of Israel and Judah. And if that had been too little, I also would have given you much more! Why have you despised the commandment of Yahweh, to do evil in His sight? *You have killed Uriah the Hittite with the sword; you have taken his wife to be your wife, and have killed him with the sword of the people of Ammon . . . .*

So David said to Nathan, "I have sinned against Yahweh." . . .

And Nathan said to David, "Yahweh also has put away your sin; you shall not die." (2 Sam. 11:1-17, 26-27; 12:1-9, 13)

c. Selfishness

Selfishness traps those who center their hearts and minds in themselves and all their desires and wants. Since their chief desire is to serve self, God's life in them dies. And not only do they covet material things: *everything* must be centered in themselves. A selfish child wants everything to revolve around himself. He craves the attention of others, their praise, their recognition, their concern and so on. Nonetheless, he offers nothing of himself to others. He wants to take everything in and give nothing back—like an animate black hole, ingesting everything and letting nothing out. Jude spoke of such people when he said:

These men are blemishes at your love feasts, eating with you without the slightest qualm—shepherds *who feed only themselves*. They are clouds without rain, blown along by the wind; autumn trees, without fruit and uprooted—twice dead. They are wild waves of the sea, foaming up their shame; wandering stars, for whom blackest darkness has been reserved forever. (Jude 12-13)

I urge you, brothers, to watch out for those who cause divisions and put obstacles in your way that are contrary to the teaching you have learned. Keep away from them. *For such people are not serving our Lord Christ, but their own appetites. By smooth talk and flattery they deceive the minds of naive people.* (Rom. 16:17-18)

Do not withhold good from those who deserve it, when it is in your power to act. Do not say to your neighbor, "Come back later; I'll give it tomorrow"—when you now have it with you. (Prov. 3:27-28)

If a man *shuts his ears to the cry of the poor*, he too will cry out and not be answered. (Prov. 21:13)

If *anyone has material possessions and sees his brother in need but has no pity on him, how can the love of God be in him?* (1 John 3:17)

Turn my heart toward Your statutes and *not toward selfish gain.* (Ps. 119:36)

But among you there must not be even a hint of sexual immorality, or of any kind of impurity, *or of greed*, because these are improper for God's holy people. (Eph. 5:3)

Put to death, therefore, whatever belongs to your earthly nature: sexual immorality, impurity, lust, evil desires and *greed*, which is idolatry. (Col. 3:5)

An unfriendly man pursues *selfish ends*; he defies all sound judgment. (Prov. 18:1)

I was enraged by his *sinful greed*; I punished him, and hid My face in anger, yet he kept on in his willful ways. (Isa. 57:17)

Do not eat the food of a *stingy* man, do not crave his delicacies; for he is the kind of man who is always thinking about the cost. "Eat and drink," he says to you, but his heart is not with you. You will vomit up the little you have eaten and will have wasted your compliments. (Prov. 23:6-8)

And He told them this parable: "The ground of a certain *rich man* produced a good crop. He thought to himself, 'What shall I do? I have no place to store my crops.'

"Then he said, 'This is what I'll do. I will tear down my barns and build bigger ones, and there I will store all my grain and my goods. *And I'll say to myself, "You have plenty of good things laid up for many years. Take life easy; eat, drink and be merry."'*

"But God said to him, 'You fool! This very night your life will be demanded from you. Then who will get what you have prepared for yourself?'

"This is how it will be with anyone who stores up things for himself but is not rich toward God." (Luke 12:16-21)

d. Selfish Ambition

The spiritual black hole not only refuses to give anything out while holding on to what it takes in, but it also greedily and omnivorously reaches out to consume everything it can suck in. And so, too, does selfishness give rise to an ambition that destroys all it touches. The self-centered child becomes the self-aggrandizing child who tries to bring more and more under his own control and influence simply for the sake of building himself up in his own eyes, simply for the sake of having more, more, more. According to Rienecker, *eritheia*, translated "selfish ambition," means "the ambition which has no conception of service and whose only aims are profit and power."

> But if you harbor bitter envy and *selfish ambition* in your hearts, do not boast about it or deny the truth. Such "wisdom" does not come down from heaven but is earthly, unspiritual, of the devil. *For where you have envy and selfish ambition, there you find disorder and every evil practice.* (James 3:14-16)

> The former preach Christ out of selfish ambition, not sincerely, supposing that they can stir up trouble for me while I am in chains. (Phil. 1:17)

> In the course of time, Absalom provided himself with a chariot and horses and with fifty men to run ahead of him. He would get up early and stand by the side of the road leading to the city gate. Whenever anyone came with a complaint to be placed before the king for a decision, Absalom would call out to him, "What town are you from?" He would answer, "Your servant is from one of the tribes of Israel." Then Absalom would say to him, "Look, your claims are valid and proper, but there is no representative of the king to hear you." And Absalom would add, *"If only I were appointed judge in the land! Then everyone who has a complaint or case could come to me and I would see that he gets justice."*
> Also, whenever anyone approached him to bow down before him, Absalom would reach out his hand, take hold of him and kiss him. *Absalom behaved in this way toward all the Israelites who came to the king asking for justice, and so he stole the hearts of the men of Israel.*
> At the end of four years, Absalom said to the king, "Let me go to Hebron and fulfill a vow I made to Yahweh. While your servant was living at Geshur in Aram, I made this vow: 'If Yahweh takes me back to Jerusalem, I will worship Yahweh in Hebron.'"
> The king said to him, "Go in peace." So he went to Hebron.
> Then Absalom sent secret messengers throughout the tribes of Israel to say, "As soon as you hear the sound of the trumpets, then say, 'Absalom is king in Hebron.'". . .
> A messenger came and told David, "The hearts of the men of Israel are with Absalom." Then David said to all his officials who were with him in Jerusalem, "Come! We must flee, or none of us will escape from Absalom. We must leave immediately, or he will move quickly to overtake us and bring ruin upon us and put the city to the sword." (2 Sam. 15:1-10, 13-14)

> Listen to another parable: There was a landowner who planted a vineyard. He put a wall around it, dug a winepress in it and built a watchtower. Then he rented the vineyard to some farmers and went away on a journey. When the harvest time approached, he sent his servants to the tenants to collect his fruit.
> The tenants seized his servants; they beat one, killed another, and

stoned a third. Then he sent other servants to them, more than the first time, and the tenants treated them the same way. Last of all, he sent his son to them. "They will respect my son," he said. But when the tenants saw the son, they said to each other, "This is the heir. Come, let's kill him and take his inheritance." (Matt. 21:33-38)

After Jesus was born in Bethlehem in Judea, during the time of King Herod, Magi from the east came to Jerusalem and asked, "Where is the one who has been born king of the Jews? We saw His star in the east and have come to worship Him."
When King Herod heard this he was disturbed, and all Jerusalem with him. When he had called together all the people's chief priests and teachers of the law, he asked them where the Christ was to be born . . . .
Then Herod called the Magi secretly and found out from them the exact time the star had appeared. He sent them to Bethlehem and said, "Go and make a careful search for the child. *As soon as you find Him, report to me, so that I too may go and worship Him."*. . .
And having been warned in a dream not to go back to Herod, [the Magi] returned to their country by another route . . . .
When Herod realized that he had been outwitted by the Magi, he was furious, and he gave orders to kill all the boys in Bethlehem and its vicinity who were two years old and under, in accordance with the time he had learned from the Magi. (Matt. 2:1-4, 7-8, 12, 16)

To share unselfishly is out of the question when self sits on the throne.

People curse the *man who hoards grain*, but blessing crowns him who is willing to sell. (Prov. 11:26)

They *covet fields and seize them, and houses, and take them. They defraud a man of his home, a fellowman of his inheritance.* (Mic. 2:2)

I have seen a grievous evil under the sun: *wealth hoarded to the harm of its owner.* (Eccles. 5:13)

He who gives to the poor will lack nothing, but *he who closes his eyes to them receives many curses.* (Prov. 28:27)

e. Tattling

Instead of finding joy from loving his brothers and sisters, the self-centered child secretly rejoices in their failures and wrongdoings, often even slyly encouraging it, so he can then elevate himself by tattling on them. Children should certainly report the hidden sins in which other children take pride. But are they doing so from a sense of what is right, what is owed to God, to the other child, to their parents and to the community of the faithful, or to exalt themselves in their own or their parents' eyes at their brother's expense? The tattler delights in tearing down others because when they are brought low, he sees himself as exalted. He thinks he'll win parental esteem by tattling.

> It is the glory of God to conceal a matter; to search out a matter is the glory of kings. (Prov. 25:2)

> Love does not delight in evil but rejoices with the truth. (1 Cor. 13:6)

> Finally, brothers, whatever is true, whatever is noble, whatever is right, whatever is pure, whatever is lovely, whatever is admirable— if anything is excellent or praiseworthy—think about such things. (Phil. 4:8)

f. Slander/Gossip

The evil impulse that leads to tattling, if not uprooted from the heart of the child, will cause him eventually to even invent problems to tell on, that is, to engage in slander. "Slanderer" or "talebearer" is the English translation of the Hebrew word *rakil*. According to Strong, *rakil* literally means "a scandal-monger" "traveling about." *Rakil* comes from the root word *rakal*, which means "to travel for trading," as a "merchant." The scandal-monger is like a merchant going about trading in tales about others. Every merchant seeks a profit for himself, and the slanderer perversely believes his lies against others will somehow lead to his profit; he thinks tearing down the image of others will exalt his own false facade. One of the Greek New Testament words for "slander" is *blasphemia*, from which the word *blasphemy* is derived. *Blasphemia* comes from the Greek word *blapto*, "to injure," and *pheme*, "speech." *Thayer's Greek-English Lexicon* defines *blasphemia* as "railing, reviling," "slander, detraction, speech injurious to another's good name." *Thayer's* further defines the verb form of this word, *blasphemeo*, as "to speak reproachfully, rail at, revile, calumniate." (Webster tells us that *calumniate* means "to spread false and harmful statements about; slander."[59]) The slanderer seeks to deliberately tear down what he hates and opposes, but the angels of judgment hate his malicious practice.

> This is especially true of those who follow the corrupt desire of the sinful nature and despise authority.
> *Bold and arrogant, these men are not afraid to slander celestial beings*; yet even angels, although they are stronger and more powerful, do not bring slanderous accusations against such beings in the presence of the Lord. But these men blaspheme in matters they do not understand. They are like brute beasts, creatures of instinct, born only to be caught and destroyed, and like beasts they too will perish. (2 Pet. 2:10-12)

> . . . nor thieves nor the greedy nor drunkards *nor slanderers* nor swindlers will inherit the kingdom of God. (1 Cor. 6:10)

> For I am afraid that when I come I may not find you as I want you to be, and you may not find me as you want me to be. I fear

that there may be quarreling, jealousy, outbursts of anger, factions, *slander, gossip,* arrogance and disorder. (2 Cor. 12:20)

Get rid of all bitterness, rage and anger, brawling and *slander,* along with every form of malice. (Eph. 4:31)

Brothers, do not slander one another. Anyone who speaks against his brother or judges him speaks against the law and judges it. When you judge the law, you are not keeping it, but sitting in judgment on it. (James 4:11)

If an enemy were *insulting* me, I could endure it; if a foe were raising himself against me, I could hide from him. But it is you, a man like myself, my companion, my close friend, with whom I once enjoyed sweet fellowship as we walked with the throng at the house of God . . . .
  My companion attacks his friends; he violates his covenant. *His speech is smooth as butter, yet war is in his heart; his words are more soothing than oil, yet they are drawn swords.* (Ps. 55:12-14, 20-21)

"Beware of your friends; do not trust your brothers. For every brother is a deceiver, and every friend *a slanderer.* Friend deceives friend, and no one speaks the truth. They have taught their tongues to lie; they weary themselves with sinning. You live in the midst of deception; in their deceit they refuse to acknowledge Me," declares Yahweh. (Jer. 9:4-6)

You use your *mouth for evil and harness your tongue to deceit. You speak continually against your brother and slander your own mother's son.* (Ps. 50:19-20)

But this I confess unto thee, that after the way which *they call heresy,* so worship I the God of my fathers, believing all things which are written in the law and in the prophets. (Acts 24:14, KJV)

My enemies say of me in malice, "When will he die and his name perish?" Whenever one comes to see me, he speaks falsely, *while his heart gathers slander; then he goes out and spreads it abroad.* (Ps. 41:5-6)

I will set before my eyes no vile thing. The deeds of faithless men I hate; they will not cling to me. Men of perverse heart shall be far from me; I will have nothing to do with evil. *Whoever slanders his neighbor in secret, him will I put to silence;* whoever has haughty eyes and a proud heart, him will I not endure. My eyes will be on the faithful in the land, that they may dwell with me; he whose walk is blameless will minister to me. No one who practices deceit will dwell in my house; *no one who speaks falsely will stand in my presence.* Every morning I will put to silence all the wicked in the land; I will cut off every evildoer from the city of Yahweh. (Ps. 101:3-8)

They said, "Come, let's make plans against Jeremiah; for the teaching of the law by the priest will not be lost, nor will counsel from the wise, nor the word from the prophets. So come, let's *attack him with our tongues and pay no attention to anything he says."* (Jer. 18:18)

Do not go about spreading slander among your people. Do not do anything that endangers your neighbor's life. I am Yahweh.

Do not hate your brother in your heart. Rebuke your neighbor frankly so you will not share in his guilt. (Lev. 19:16-17)

He who conceals his hatred has lying lips, and *whoever spreads slander is a fool.* (Prov. 10:18)

He went on: "What comes out of a man is what makes him 'unclean.' For from within, out of men's hearts, come evil thoughts, sexual immorality, theft, murder, adultery, greed, malice, deceit, lewdness, envy, *slander,* arrogance and folly. All these evils come from inside and make a man 'unclean.'" (Mark 7:20-23)

I have made you a tester of metals and My people the ore, that you may observe and test their ways. They are all hardened rebels, *going about to slander.* They are bronze and iron; they all act corruptly. The bellows blow fiercely to burn away the lead with fire, but the refining goes on in vain; the wicked are not purged out. They are called rejected silver, because Yahweh has rejected them. (Jer. 6:27-30)

A gossip betrays a confidence, but a trustworthy man keeps a secret. (Prov. 11:13)

A perverse man stirs up dissension, *and a gossip separates close friends.* (Prov. 16:28)

The words of a gossip are like choice morsels; they go down to a man's inmost parts. (Prov. 18:8)

A *gossip* betrays a confidence; so avoid a man *who talks too much.* (Prov. 20:19)

Without wood a fire goes out; *without gossip a quarrel dies down.* (Prov. 26:20)

Furthermore, since they did not think it worthwhile to retain the knowledge of God, He gave them over to a depraved mind, to do what ought not to be done. They have become filled with every kind of wickedness, evil, greed and depravity. They are full of envy, murder, strife, deceit and malice. *They are gossips, slanderers,* God-haters, insolent, arrogant and boastful; they invent ways of doing evil; they disobey their parents; they are senseless, faithless, heartless, ruthless. Although they know God's righteous decree that those who do such things deserve death, they not only continue to do these very things but also approve of those who practice them. (Rom. 1:28-32)

As for younger widows, do not put them on such a list. For when their sensual desires overcome their dedication to Christ, they want to marry. Thus they bring judgment on themselves, because they have broken their first pledge. Besides, they get into the habit of being idle and going about from house to house. And not only do they become idlers, *but also gossips* and busybodies, saying things they ought not to. (1 Tim. 5:11-13)

g. Jesting

The Greek word *eutrapelia* means "coarse jesting" or "buffoonery." Paul warns against this form of speaking and acting in Ephesians 5:4. Rienecker claims that this word implies "deceptive speech, so formed that the speaker easily contrives to wriggle out of its meaning or engagements" (*eutrapelia* means literally "easily turning, from *eu*, well, *trepo*, to turn"). Ephesus was known as a center for such "facetious orators." The word generally denoted a characteristic approved by the ancient pagan Greeks (identified as "flexibility" by Pericles and "versatility" by Aristotle) but viewed entirely negatively in the New Testament.

To jest in the sense Scripture condemns is to use a joking manner to disguise a desire to hurt someone. This form of joking results from an unwillingness to take responsibility for one's real intent and meaning. It is a deception, a coverup, behind which someone hides what he really wants to say, pretending that the person to whom he speaks hasn't properly understood. The speaker says that he's merely "teasing" or "kidding," which is actually "low-level jeering done with a small smile as you speak."[60] With a short laugh and a slap on the back, the coarse jester covers up feelings of envy and such with quips, "Oh, I see that you're sewing a dress that can double as a sack to store potatoes in—just joking" or, "Boy, your singing really hit the high notes. I thought at first a screech owl had flown into the room—just kidding." It is a form of cruelty, a desire to hurt someone else, masquerading as harmless fun. When someone "kids" in this way, he refuses to take seriously the thoughts and feelings expressed by someone else, dismissing those thoughts and feelings with a confidence and authority deriving not from the Spirit but from the flesh. Instead of respecting someone's attempt to give expression to the feelings of his heart, the jester reacts with a self-exalting mockery that lifts him up by putting down his brother or sister. "Oh, were you playing a *song* on the fiddle or just tuning up?" "Next time you tell a joke, maybe you could let me know when I'm supposed to laugh." "Did you mean to carve this design, or did your chisel just slip?"

When someone "kids" in this way, he tries to do what Jesus says one can never do, that is, to "serve two masters at once." In this case, the one kidding is "putting down this person at the same time" that the jester smiles "to show that" the person he kids "would be a poor sport to take" the "kidding amiss."[61] Of course, the only master served by this kind of behavior is the one who works through deception.

If the "smile doesn't work," such subtle cruelty generally escalates by asking, "'Can't take kidding?' If even that doesn't work to generate just the satisfying mix of shame and passivity which bullies enjoy in a child's face, you can add, 'I'll tell you one thing: you're not going to get very far in this world without a sense of humor.'"[62]

People often fall into habitual types of kidding "routines" that "give a little pleasure and don't seem to do any harm at the moment" but actually do much harm, for the joke comes at the expense of someone else.[63] None of this is to imply, of course, that one can never joke with someone else. The key lies in the motive, and the motive will manifest itself in the way that someone jokes and the effects of his words: a good joke never hurts someone else. Remember that *eutrapelia* refers to "deceptive speech" behind which someone hides the hurt he really intends. When a child jests in this way, he intends, however subtly, to hurt the "object" of his remarks, and he does actually turn that person into an object rather than respecting and loving him as a brother. It takes considerable meanness to engage in such jesting.

> Like a madman *shooting firebrands* or *deadly arrows* is a man who deceives his neighbor and says, *"I was only joking!"* (Prov. 26:18-19)

> Nor should there be filthiness, nor foolish talking, *nor coarse jesting*, which are not fitting, but rather giving of thanks. (Eph. 5:4, NIV, NKJV)

> Like one who takes away a garment on a cold day, or like vinegar poured on soda, is *one who sings songs to a heavy heart.* (Prov. 25:20)

> When Sanballat heard that we were rebuilding the wall, he became angry and was greatly incensed. He *ridiculed* the Jews, and in the presence of his associates and the army of Samaria, he said, "What are those feeble Jews doing? Will they restore their wall? Will they offer sacrifices? Will they finish in a day? Can they bring the stones back to life from those heaps of rubble—burned as they are?" Tobiah the Ammonite, who was at his side, said, "What they are building—if even a fox climbed up on it, he would break down their wall of stones!" (Neh. 4:1-3)

> From there Elisha went up to Bethel. As he was walking along the road, some youths came out of the town and *jeered* at him. "Go on up, you baldhead!" they said. "Go on up, you baldhead!" (2 Kings 2:23)

> Then the governor's soldiers took Jesus into the Praetorium and gathered the whole company of soldiers around Him. They stripped Him and put a scarlet robe on Him, and then twisted together a crown of thorns and set it on His head. They put a staff in His right hand and knelt in front of Him and *mocked* Him. "Hail, king of the Jews!" they said. (Matt. 27:27-29)

I. NONVIOLENCE, NONRESISTANCE/VIOLENCE

1. Nonviolence, Nonresistance

In any discussion of Christian identity or of Christian ethics, and even of individual Christian character, the issue of violence and non-violence would seem, on the face of it, to stand at the forefront. Yet to even open such an issue to discussion at times further seems almost inevitably to lead straight into controversy. In short, no other ethical issue can rouse such conflicting responses and yet at the same time so determinatively influence such a great range of human character traits and profound social changes. While Christians unanimously oppose unjust wars of aggression, many regard defensive combat, both on a personal level and on the civil and national level, as not only acceptable but also as exemplary of a number of positive character traits. A brother who will not physically defend his little sister against bullies, or a husband who will not use force to defend his family against aggressors, many will look upon as a coward. Many, in fact, view courage, honor, self-sacrifice, generosity, initiative and other character traits as associated with moral virtue in defending the weak and vulnerable through the use of physical force.

At the very least, such an association complicates teaching believers, whether children or adults, Jesus' admonition to "turn the other cheek," to "love your enemies," to "not resist evil" and to not "return evil for evil but good for evil." It does so, first of all, because most Christians find it difficult to ignore the clear example and teachings of Jesus and the early Christians. Historians and scholars from every persuasion tell us, for instance, that not only Jesus but also the first Christians for over 175 years made no effort to physically defend themselves, their wives or children from unjust attacks and persecution.[64] And to turn for examples directly from Scripture, the Saul who, after his conversion (as Paul), wrote most of the New Testament books that follow the book of Acts met no physical resistance when, in Acts 8:3, "he made havoc of the church, entering every house, and dragging off men *and women*, committing them to prison." Nor, after his own conversion, did Paul himself offer any physical resistance at any time to those who persecuted him, even beating him until he was left for dead (Acts 14:19; 16:22-23; 21:30-32; 2 Cor. 11:23-27). Rather, he saw being "persecuted" and even "struck down" (2 Cor. 4:9) as "carrying about in the body the dying of the Lord Jesus, that the life of Jesus also may be manifested in our body" (2 Cor. 4:10). Instead of seeking to physically defend himself or other persecuted Christians, he willingly accepted physical suffering as an opportunity to "know" the Lord "and the power of His resurrection, and the fellowship of His sufferings, being conformed to His death, if, by any means, I may attain to the resurrection from the dead" (Phil. 3:10-11).

This portrait of what constitutes courage (as well as honor, self-sacrifice, generosity and initiative) stands in stark contrast to the one given above based on violence. This second portrait ultimately derives from the scriptural examples of nonviolence that come from the life of the One who was Himself given "all power in heaven and on earth" (Matt. 28:18), yet who came to earth as the Lamb of God and whose suffering life on earth Christians are explicitly told to model their own lives after.

> He who says he abides in Him *ought himself also to walk just as He walked.* (1 John 2:6)

> Servants, be submissive to your masters with all fear, not only to the good and gentle, but also to the harsh. For this is commendable, if because of conscience toward God one endures grief, suffering wrongfully. For what credit is it if, when you are beaten for your faults, you take it patiently? But when you do good and suffer, if you take it patiently, this is commendable before God. *For to this you were called, because Christ also suffered for us, leaving us an example, that you should follow His steps*: "Who committed no sin, nor was deceit found in His mouth"; who, when He was reviled, did not revile in return; when He suffered, He did not threaten, but committed Himself to Him who judges righteously. (1 Pet. 2:18-23)

It is in this Man alone, the Word made flesh in whom all things consist (Col. 1:17), that we can see the scripturally consistent view of all positive Biblical character traits. Jesus' life shows how all these work together under *every* circumstance, including those cases that would, for many people, involve physical violence in self-defense.

To recognize as Christians our call to become part of, and to prepare our children to become part of, what Jesus called a "kingdom . . . not of this world" is to understand why, as our Lord's servants, we are *not* called upon to "fight."

> Thus Jesus answered Pilate, saying: "*My kingdom is not of this world. If My kingdom were of this world, My servants would fight,* so that I should not be delivered to the Jews; but now *My kingdom is not from here.*" (John 18:36)

In this light, it becomes evident why no discussion of Christian character and ethics can be complete without coming to grips with the question of a Christian's attitude toward violence. As we'll see, one's attitude toward violence goes to the core of his or her Christianity. It reveals, for one thing, whether God's own nature, as a love that conquers death (1 John 4:8, 16; Song of Sol. 8:6-7), has truly transformed the believer, whether he has authentically surrendered his life to God's control and whether he, empowered by the same Spirit of love that drove Jesus to lay down His life for people, will choose to lay down, rather than seek to preserve (Matt. 16:24-26; Luke 14:26-33), the believer's own life. And if believers claim that they should choose this path of self-sacrifice, this would naturally then mean that they would also, by the same faith, avail themselves of the most effectual power for defending the weak and vulnerable (Eph. 6:10-18; 2 Cor. 10:3-6), a power so great that, Paul tells us, had those spiritual powers who crucified the Lord of glory known what they were releasing against themselves through the crucifixion, they would not have put Jesus to death (1 Cor. 2:6-8). This, of course, is, again, the power of God's *self-sacrificing* love "shed abroad in our hearts by the Holy Spirit" (Rom. 5:5, KJV), the love that defines God's very nature.

And we should always also remember that, in dealing with this issue of violence and nonviolence, more than mere principles serve to guide Christians: a perfect, living *example* has also been given to the church in the life of its Head, Jesus. So, beyond following in His steps, only "Christ *in* us" constitutes our "hope of glory" (Col. 1:27). Therefore Jesus didn't just give us precepts; He exemplified them with a life, commanded us to follow Him and then empowered us with the Spirit to do so. He not only *said*, "Love your enemies," "Turn the other cheek," "Do not resist evil" and, "If My kingdom were of this world, then My servants would fight, but now My kingdom is not from here" (Matt. 5:38-48; John 18:36); but He also then *lived out* these precepts and did not resist evil when He was mocked, beaten and even tortured to death on the cross. Furthermore, as seen, both Peter and John declared that Jesus' suffering for doing good was given to *us* as "an *example*," that we should "walk in His steps" (1 Pet. 2:19-23; 1 John 2:6). Moreover, Paul said "Do not return evil for evil, but good for evil" (Rom. 12:17, 21) and, "the weapons of *our* warfare *are not carnal*, but mighty through God" (2 Cor. 10:4, KJV). This would seem to straightforwardly rule out the Christian use of "carnal weapons." As noted, the first-century church, when faced with persecution, also put these nonviolent precepts into practice.*

This call to believers to "walk in His steps," picking up "our cross" and "following Him," runs contrary to the impulse of the lapsed human nature, controlled as it is by "the fear of death" (Heb. 2:15). Fallen human flesh,

---

* Of course, many questions arise, but we've answered these in Apologetic Handbook *On Violence and Nonviolence* by Blair Adams (Elm Mott, Tex.: Colloquium Press, 1988, 2005, 2012).

like most of the animal world, will move by natural instinct to seek to defend itself and its own at all costs, even if it ultimately seeks only to defend its social image in the eyes of others. Of course, as mentioned, many find no difficulty in condemning aggression when it merely pursues self-ambition. Such people will, however, still justify violence in self-defense. Yet Jesus did not call His followers to merely repudiate aggression, nor was His life an example of merely nonaggression. He, while perfectly innocent, nonetheless did not defend Himself against violent men. So Jesus did not advocate killing in *self*-defense—He taught, instead (and with His very life), that we must die to self-interest and self-preservation (Matt. 16:24-26).

This reveals why a nonresistant conviction actually becomes a test of authentic conversion—because only those who are truly converted and who have authentically made Jesus the Lord of their lives can ever even hope to surrender *all* their own godhood and authority, even their very lives, to Him (Luke 14:26-33; Rev. 12:11, KJV). In other words, only authentic Christians even *could* ever lay down their own lives, or surrender the lives of their loved ones, in redeeming love for those who are lost, just as the Father did through *His Son* Jesus. And we must remember that Jesus Himself commanded us to be perfect in our love, *just as* our Father in heaven is perfect in His (Matt. 5:48). What Christian can ignore, then, that our Father "so loved the world that He gave His only begotten Son" (John 3:16)? Without this love, no one can hope to be nonviolent. So the question becomes a question of love, of whether we actually do have the Father's love. If we haven't cultivated out of our hearts the weeds of pride, selfishness, contempt, disdain, mockery and hatred for others, as well as encountered, been filled with and sustained by the love of God burning and alive in our hearts through the Holy Spirit (Rom. 5:5, KJV), then we can in no way hope in a crisis to maintain nonviolence and nonresistance toward those who would attack either us or those we *do* love. The natural instinct that is the cause of a fallen world and all its violence will, then, sadly prevail over *super*natural love. And such a natural man can never even understand, much less live out, the things of the Spirit of God—they are "foolishness" to him (1 Cor. 2:14).

Given all this, then, we can train up our children, even before they are converted, in the way that they should go. We can teach them as we do so that the goal is always to internalize the attitudes and responses but, above all, the love of God that will be shed abroad in their hearts by the Holy Spirit (Rom. 5:5, KJV). This is the ultimate source *and* goal. All of these they'll be learning to pursue in their minds, hearts, conduct and lives. The immediate goal, therefore, is to help them see and overcome feelings of pride, selfishness, fear, contempt, anger and so on that feed violence in their lives, as well as in their reactions to people and circumstances, so that the love of God can triumph in their lives just as it did in the Lord Jesus' life.

Countervailing Powers: The Order of Conservation

Even believers who hold nonviolent convictions are *not*, however, called to be *political* activists lobbying for or even advocating a national policy of pacifism or of anything else. In short, as believers, we neither deny the reality of evil in this world nor seek to disarm nations through political advocacy, political agendas or political activism. Furthermore, claims that would deny any even temporary purpose whatsoever to a nation or "kingdom of this world" defending itself against tyranny, such as in the British and American response to Hitler's aggression, should be seriously scrutinized from a thoroughly New Testament perspective, a perspective that sees purposes falling to the kingdom of God that differ greatly from those various and diverse purposes falling to the kingdoms of this world (Matt. 22:21; John 18:36; Rom. 13:1-8). But we should also equally doubt any claim that would make the kingdom of God, which Jesus said is "*not* of this world," in any way synonymous with any of the kingdoms of this world, which John described as universally "under the control of the evil one" (1 John 5:19). This confusion of two realms that were so explicitly separated by Jesus (John 18:36; Matt. 22:21) has ramified into great confusion in the church's position vis-à-vis the world, even in regard to the nature, extent and limits of the church's own power and identity.

Yes, God is *ultimately* "in charge" of history and will triumph, but only by the essential power of His own nature, which John declared to be agape love (1 John 4:8, 16). So we must not only keep in mind that Jesus Himself still called satan the "prince" or "ruler" of this world (John 12:31; 14:30; 16:11), but we must also understand why He did so. Then we must include in this understanding why, even years after Jesus' triumphant resurrection and the church's birth, Paul was still referring to satan as "the god of this world" (2 Cor. 4:4).

God's perfect order of creation has been violated by sin and the Fall. So that order has indeed now shifted in its adjustment to meet the needs created by so great a catastrophe (Rom. 8:19-23). Part of that adjustment in God's originally perfect design is its temporary ordering of forces in such a way that the countervailing powers of nations in a lapsed world now rise up against other aggressor nations to temporarily limit *any* international power that would make itself final and absolute. This may in certain times and instances *conserve* some limited measure of a peace such as the world gives (John 14:27). Just as the principle of division of powers was designed to serve as a checks-and-balances system within the U.S. government, so, too, the countervailing forces of "nation against nation" can temporarily keep in check the ever-present tendency of tyranny to reach inescapable, global and totalitarian proportions. But this can never be a permanent solution to the human condition. In fact, in the end, it only promises to contribute to the ever-mounting problems.

Yet these countervailing powers find their place in God's order of conservation and restraint in a *fallen* and *impermanent* world—not within His order of perfection, which is the church, the repository of God's very nature on the earth (Eph. 1:22-23; 4:11-16; Col. 1:16-19; 1 Pet. 2:5; 1 Tim. 3:15). Just because two dogs fight over who will eat the cat and may, through their dogfight, open an opportunity to thereby "free" the cat doesn't mean that God is *personally* on the side of either dog. Rather, the very order of things in a *fallen* world—as now *ordained*—requires this way of the world until a new heaven and new earth come into existence. Within the New Testament church, however, resides God's own Spirit, and this impartation of God's *essential* nature calls forth a radically different standard for that church, a standard heretofore unknown in the world or even in Old Testament Israel.

This radically different standard is necessary because God's essential nature, which now resides in the church, is *never* described as hate or wrath, but rather the Bible declares that "God *is* love" (1 John 4:8, 16). Neither is His power "the power of death," which Scripture precisely designates as *satan's* power (Heb. 2:14-15). Rather, God's power is the power of life (John 3:16; 10:10; 14:6; 2 Tim. 1:10; 1 John 5:11-13). The kingdom of heaven is itself described in such terms: eternal *life* (Matt. 25:32-34, 41, 45-46; John 17:1-3). Neither God nor His kingdom is touched by death. Rather, Christ came to *destroy* the power of death (2 Tim. 1:10; Rom. 5:14, 21; Rev. 21:4).

The patterns God gave people to live by in the Old Testament were for a people who, although *situationally* visited and used by the power of God's self-sacrificial love, had not been reconstituted (rebirthed) in their very nature by the essential nature of God, a promise that was reserved for the consummation of the New Covenant.* So these Old Testament patterns provided for a still-fallen world, not a redeemed one; and a fallen people could never live up to God's essential nature. He therefore "conserved" them in the law of "an eye for an eye." But this law did not express God in His essence. If it could have done so, Paul said, Christ need not have come and died (Gal. 2:21; 3:21-24). Hence Jesus' requirement that Christian righteousness would have to "*exceed* the righteousness of the scribes and Pharisees," who purported to live by Old Testament Law. And this new righteousness would be expressed in very specific ways that contrasted radically with the Old Testament way: not "an eye for an eye" but in

---

* John 7:37-39; Heb. 11:39-40; Jer. 31:31-34; Ezek. 11:19-20; 36:26-27; Joel 2:28-32; Luke 24:49; Acts 1:5, 8; 2:1-4, 14-21, 33, 38-39; Gal. 3:14-16, 29; 4:28-29.

"turning the other cheek," not in "hating" our enemies but in "loving" them.

> Jesus went on to say "that *unless your righteousness exceeds the righteousness of the scribes and Pharisees, you will by no means enter the kingdom of heaven.*" (Matt. 5:20)

> *You have heard that it was said, "An eye for an eye and a tooth for a tooth." But I tell you not to resist an evil person.* But *whoever slaps you on your right cheek, turn the other to him also.* If anyone wants to sue you and take away your tunic, let him have your cloak also. And whoever compels you to go one mile, go with him two. Give to him who asks you, and from him who wants to borrow from you do not turn away. *You have heard that it was said, "You shall love your neighbor and hate your enemy." But I say to you, love your enemies, bless those who curse you, do good to those who hate you, and pray for those who spitefully use you and persecute you, that you may be sons of your Father in heaven;* for He makes His sun rise on the evil and on the good, and sends rain on the just and on the unjust. For if you love those who love you, what reward have you? Do not even the tax collectors do the same? And if you greet your brethren only, what do you do more than others? Do not even the tax collectors do so? Therefore you shall be perfect, just as your Father in heaven is perfect. (Matt. 5:38-48)

So the Old Testament *natural* battles fought by faith, along with all the ensuing victories wrought by the angelic and the telluric *elohim* (Ps. 8:5; 2 Kings 1:2; Ps. 82:6-7; Exod. 21:6; 22:8-9, 28), remain essential and valuable only when understood in light of their *spiritual* application in the New (1 Cor. 10:1-11). They are types of the reality to come in the New Covenant, the mere shadow of that reality (Heb. 8:5), the mere seed of the fully germinated and matured plant (Mark 4:26-29). And the New Testament says that what is old—the Law—is "fading," "passing away" and becoming "obsolete" (2 Cor. 3:7-11; Heb. 8:13; 10:1-7). Just as the true temple is not now stone but people, and just as the seed of natural Israel has sprouted above the natural ground in the resurrected life of Jesus to become His corporate Body of human souls (Zech. 6:9-13), so now the weapons of our warfare, as Paul insisted, are no longer fleshly but spiritual (2 Cor. 10:4). When Jesus came and then ascended, He gave His people His Spirit so that we can be like Him (Eph. 4:7-16). Therefore John says: "This is how we know we are in Him: Whoever claims to live in Him must walk as Jesus did" (1 John 2:6). And Peter declared: "For to this you were called, *because Christ* also *suffered* for us, *leaving us an example* that you should follow in His steps" (1 Pet. 2:21). And, of course, Jesus went like a lamb to the slaughter, and He told us to turn the other cheek, to resist not evil, to pick up our cross and follow Him.*

So, again, another far greater order now exists beyond the old order

---

* Isa. 53:7; Acts 8:32-35; Matt. 5:39; Rom. 12:17-21; Luke 9:23.

of mere conservation (Heb. 9:8-10, NIV); and it, too, has a purpose on the earth—indeed, the greatest of all purposes. While the order of conservation serves at best as an increasingly less effective "holding pattern" (Gal. 3:21-26), temporarily restraining human self-destructive tendencies from reaching genocidal or totalitarian proportions, the other order that came with the New Covenant embodied in Christ's self-sacrifice, the order of redemption, reaches toward an eternal goal to open the only avenues for *God's very nature* to come to us as a transcendent, unfolding and self-giving love. This unique and powerful love now invades human hearts, changing us from fallen, violence-prone creatures to sons of God able to not only conserve or hold back but also to be increasingly transformed and redeemed. The old order had only the negating power to destroy enemies. The new order possesses the positive power of God's love and life, which can transform enemies into brothers and sisters.

The weapons of these two orders could hardly differ more: while earthly nations, as the agents of wrath, wage war with weapons of destruction in exerting the countervailing powers that conserve, perhaps at times even temporarily holding back worldwide violence on some level, believers modeled after Christ and His first-century followers fight only *spiritual* battles on behalf of a kingdom "*not of this* world" (John 18:36).* They use "weapons" Paul describes as "not carnal but mighty through God" (2 Cor. 10:4, KJV)—the "weapons" of love, hope, faith, prayer, truth, which pull down the strongholds of lies, hatred and violence.

So secular polities and economies provide neither our paradigms for power nor the mediums in which we can truthfully live out our lives. Rather, we move in the free associations of a transcendent society reaching out to *all* peoples. We avoid the love-destroying competition of an immanently and economically centered culture. We reject the compulsion of a totally politicized culture where the nation becomes a whole people's religion, a veritable substitute for the kingdom of God. In such thoroughly politicized cultures, religious worship of and devotion to the Biblical Lord Jesus in His own corporate Body is marginalized and finally replaced by a religious worship of and devotion to the State. Such devotion is then often called "patriotism," a word frequently used in the same way Hitler used it to incite worship of the Nazi State. Such exaltation of the cult of nationalism distorts the believer's ability to see those of other opposing nations as his potential brothers worthy of Christ's suffering redemption. It tends to void Christ's Great Commission to go into "*all* the nations," preaching the "gospel of the kingdom," the "kingdom . . . not of this world"

---

* As shown extensively in *Beyond Violence, Beyond Pacifism*, this means that no doctrines of "dual citizenship" can justify Christians using violence in the sphere of the world while remaining nonviolent only in the context of the church.

(Matt. 24:14; 28:18-20; Mark 16:15; John 18:36). Samuel Johnson long ago called such patriotism, "the last refuge of a scoundrel."[65]

We do not, however, disrespect, condemn or seek to negate any temporary purpose or even temporary necessity of the old order of conservation as it applies to the unenlightened, the unconverted or the only nominally converted, all of whom have yet to know the tender mercy of a God who would prepare them for life in His singular kingdom. Only a utopian idealism utterly out of touch with reality can believe that police and military force serve no necessary purpose in a fallen and unredeemed world. Yet, as said, God has a greater purpose than in merely backing the efforts of people to endlessly (and, increasingly, futilely or even counterproductively) attempt to restrain evil; and that purpose won't be achieved through political or military means, through orders of compulsion, coercion or physical violence. Rather, to fulfill this distinct and supernatural function is precisely what God has called the church to accomplish by stepping out of places of authority in the world systems of natural power and into the world of supernatural power made manifest in love.*

To not merely restrain evil but to conquer it completely requires the redemptive love and mercy that Jesus Himself demonstrated by submitting His life even to violent men, not defending it by doing violence in return (John 18:36). Jesus said that he who has been forgiven much loves much, and it is for this reason—the fact that believers have been forgiven much, not that we are in any way superior—that Christians have also been appointed to manifest the order of redemption by exhibiting to others the same love, mercy and forgiveness shown to them by Jesus and His Body.

Again, then, while we do not condemn those in the military or police, and even deeply respect those who have shown themselves worthy of respect by their integrity of character and sacrifice, nonetheless, Christians, as forgiven and redeemed men and women, must devote themselves *completely* only to another order, one that holds out the hope of redemption and the only possible everlasting peace to this world.

The Center of God's Purpose

The writer of Hebrews states: "Inasmuch then as the children have partaken of flesh and blood, He Himself likewise shared in the same, that *through death* He might *destroy him* who had the *power of death*, that is, *the devil*" (Heb. 2:14).

In this scriptural reference to the "power of death," that word translated "power" is, in the Greek, *kratos*. It is the same word that appears in *demos-*

---

* John 18:36; Rom. 12:1-2; 2 Cor. 6:14-18; Rev. 18:4; 1 John 2:15-17; James 4:4.

kratos, democracy (literally, "people-power"), or in *aristocracy*, or in all similarly rooted words denoting rulership and authority. It is often found in the most worldly contexts, expressing a power such as is exercised through the threat of coercion and violence against the disobedient or even against the dissident. And *kratos* here in this passage is explicitly shown by the immediate context to carry the meaning of that very kind of violent power.

So the writer of Hebrews is saying that satan possesses a rulership and authority, and this rulership exerts itself through the "*power* of death" and the "fear of death." Everyone who's read even a children's story-Bible knows what the serpent's promise was: "You will not surely *die*" (Gen. 3:1-5). But he, being, as Jesus said, "a liar and murderer from the beginning" (John 8:44), knew all along that the man and woman would, indeed, die and that their disobedience to God would therefore place them under satan's own realm of dominion, the dominion or power of death. This dominion totally relied on dealing out death in order to control people, and then ruling the world through the fear of it. Even merely the fear of that dominion's violence, even merely its *threats* of death, have played a crucial role in its rule.

So what, then, is satan's source of power? The book of Hebrews goes on to immediately make the source of the devil's power explicit, speaking of the sum total of humanity "who all their lives were *held in bondage by their fear of death*" (Heb. 2:15). Death, as said, stands as the power behind satan's kingdom of fear.

The fifth chapter of John's first epistle declares: "We know that we are of God, and *the whole world* [or every kingdom of this world] *lies under the rule of the wicked one*" (1 John 5:19). His rule by the "fear of death" is therefore seen as pervasive and ubiquitous. As already shown, Jesus Himself furthermore called satan both "the *prince* of this world" and "the *ruler* of this world" (John 12:31; 14:30; 16:11, NIV, NKJV). And we said that even *after* the resurrection, even *after* satan's declared defeat and the coming of the kingdom of God, Paul *still* called satan the "*god of this world*" (2 Cor. 4:4, KJV). Yes, *all* the kingdoms of this world belong to him; and all these kingdoms rule through the compulsory, even coercive, power behind which stands an explicit or implicit threat of death—again, this is the threat of what the New Testament pinpoints precisely as satan's power (Heb. 2:14-15).*

---

* Modern sociology concurs with the Biblical perspective of the nature of the authority of the State. As sociologist and professor of law Jacques Ellul thoroughly showed, "Every State is founded on violence and cannot maintain itself save by and through violence."[66] The German sociologist Max Weber also defined the State precisely in terms of its coercive power: "A compulsory political association with continuous organization . . . will be called a 'State' . . . in so far as its administrative staff successfully upholds a claim to the *monopoly*

So we cannot, situated in our own time and place in history, when so many are increasingly religiously devoted to nations that preserve themselves through the threat of violence and the fear it evokes, remind ourselves too often of Jesus' own words: "My kingdom is not of this world. If My kingdom were of this world, My servants would *fight* . . . . But now My kingdom is from another place" (John 18:36, NIV). Did not Jesus here make the ultimate distinction between, on the one hand, those kingdoms secured by the threat of death through carnal weapons and, on the other hand, His own kingdom, which both Paul and John said came to conquer death and destroy the works of the devil (2 Tim. 1:10; 1 John 3:8)? And that kingdom is now supposed to begin "within you" (Luke 17:20-21) and to then begin "advancing" (Matt. 11:12, NIV) "on earth as it is in heaven" (Matt. 6:10).

When Jesus spoke His words to Pilate about His kingdom, that particular Roman official immediately challenged, "You are a *king then!*" "*Yes,*" Jesus replied, "I have come *to bear witness* to the *truth*" (John 18:36-37). So notice that this exchange reveals a position contrary to the claim that Jesus' kingship or kingdom comes by striving against Caesar's with Caesar's carnal weapons (2 Cor. 10:3-5). Especially must we believe this to be the case since Christ had already declared, "Render unto Caesar the things that are Caesar's, and render unto God the things that are God's" (Matt. 22:21). With these words, and those Christ had spoken to Pilate, Jesus sharply distinguished between what belongs to those two realms of authority, those two *different* and *counterposed* kingdoms of Caesar and God. Moreover, He insisted that we "cannot serve two masters" (Matt. 6:24)—we must choose one kingdom or another, one lord or another. Either Jesus is Lord, or Caesar is Lord. One king "fights" with swords, the other King with "weapons" of "truth." And Paul said that even this truth must be spoken in love, not with a blood-stained sword in our hand to back it up (John 18:36; Eph. 4:15). So only such truth, as both Jesus and Paul insisted, can demolish strongholds in human hearts and minds (John 8:31-32; 14:6; 18:36-37; 2 Cor. 6:7; 10:3-6). Only this truth can cut to the root of human needs and problems.

And so this truth does not try to negate evil by merely using violence to simply prune the evil tree, thereby producing a greater crop by cutting

---

of the *legitimate* use of physical force in the enforcement of its order . . . . The threat of force, and in case of need its actual use, is the method which is specific to political associations . . . . Thus it is possible to define the 'political' character of a corporate group only in terms of the *means* peculiar to it, the use of force."[67] Dr. Kenneth Kaunda, founding president of Zambia, gave the *Realpolitik* view: "Some people draw a comforting distinction between 'force' and 'violence'. . . . I refuse to cloud the issue by such word-play . . . . The power which establishes a State is violence; the power which maintains it is violence; the power which eventually overthrows it is violence . . . . Call an elephant a rabbit only if it gives you comfort to feel that you are about to be trampled to death by a rabbit."[68]

off only a few people who presently bear its poisonous fruit, or who are controlled and thus also victimized by it. Instead, Jesus' kingdom lays the ax at the root of evil, at the very root of its power to intimidate by the threat of violence, thus overcoming evil with good (Rom. 12:19-21). It thereby delivers satan's human captives "from the dominion of darkness" (Col. 1:13), from the "power of death," transforming them by the power of light and love. So Paul says that Jesus "abolished death and brought life and immortality to light through the gospel" (2 Tim. 1:10).

Paul further showed what lies at the core of this clash of kingdoms when he wrote that he desired "to make all see what is the fellowship of the mystery, which from the beginning of the ages [from the very first when satan established his rule, or authority, or *kratos*, of death] has been hidden in God who created all things through Jesus Christ* to the intent that now *through the church the manifold wisdom of God* might be *made known to the principalities and powers* in the heavenly places, *according to the eternal purpose*" (Eph. 3:8-11).

Paul unveils here God's unique and extraordinary activity through *the church*, the church through which God desires to display His supreme wisdom *to* all the rulers and principalities of this dark world, a world ruled by the sword and the threat of death. And this manifestation of a wisdom far beyond such a dark rule is called God's "eternal purpose."

Paul goes on in this chapter to say, "*Therefore* I ask that you do not lose heart because of *my tribulations* . . . . *I bow* my knees to the Father of our *Lord* Jesus Christ, from whom the *whole family in heaven* and earth is named" (Eph. 3:13-15). So, God is doing something through the church that will fulfill His "eternal purpose," and this church is ruled "not by might nor by power" but relationally by the familial love and truth that comes through God's own Spirit moving through His own corporate Body. And because of this, Paul admonishes his readers to "not lose heart because of [his] *tribulations*" (Eph. 3:13), that is, don't lose heart because of Paul's *sufferings* and *trials*—because of, in other words, all the persecution and slander he suffers at the hands of the *kratos* of violence and death in bearing the cross of Christ and "filling up the afflictions" that belong to the One who conquers death through nonresistant, self-sacrificing love (Col. 1:24). Jesus, Paul, John and Peter all say over and over, in many ways and circumstances, that this *familial rule* of God's "*whole* family in heaven and on *earth*" will not be established by the sword but by a love so supernaturally powerful that it lays down its life for others, suffering

---

* How did God create all things through Christ? Well, it is recorded, "God *said*, 'Let there be light.'" So it was the *Word* that went forth to create, but "the Word was made flesh" in Jesus (John 1:14, KJV). So through that creative Word, God created all things through Christ, who *is* the *Word* made flesh, "the light of the world" (John 8:12; 9:5).

the consequences by following the nonresistant path of the cross, a path that Jesus Himself followed in "tribulations," "sufferings," "persecutions" and "trials." So, this suffering in doing good *constitutes* our very obedience to the gospel (2 Thess. 1:3-8)—it represents our unflagging faith, in the face of suffering, persecution and "tribulations," our faith that life and love shall ultimately overcome death and hatred.

The Lamb on the Throne

What, then, is it that God desires to reveal "*through* the church" and "to" these principalities and powers? That is, what activity or attainment will prove so crucial and all-encompassing that it can be termed His "eternal purpose"? The answer will explain why these verses in Ephesians 3 speak of two vital matters: God's "eternal purpose" and our "sufferings." These both somehow come together in Paul's thinking. As Paul made explicit elsewhere, "We must through *much tribulation enter into the kingdom of God*" (Acts 14:22, KJV). But this doesn't yet make clear the "eternal purpose."

To find that clarity, we must also see that this suffering and God's eternal purpose for His kingdom are connected to the strikingly *paradoxical* nature of how the One who is described as now sitting on the throne of the kingdom of God lived His life (Rev. 5:6; 7:17). He indeed sits as the Lord of lords and the King of kings (1 Tim. 6:14-15; Rev. 17:14; 19:16). But this is where the incongruities and problems arise, especially for a world whose paradigms all rest on raw power. Crucifixion for both Romans and Jews represented the ultimate expression of absolute rejection. So how, people have asked down through the centuries, could the *King* of the universe be the same person as the "Lord" who has the pierced hands and feet of a condemned *slave*, a man who bears the horrific stigmata of someone designated as a criminal, an "*enemy of the State*" whose status has fallen beneath classification of what is accepted as human? How could the face of the Lord of universal dominion ever be battered by His so-called subjects until it is unrecognizable as the face of a human being (Isa. 52:14)? How, instead of the most dazzling crown or most luxurious robe ever worn by royalty, could His brow be jabbed and torn by a mocking crown of thorns, His back beaten and bloodied to the bone by the blunt scepter of brute force, His side stabbed straight to the heart? How, in short, is it that the *Crucified* One sits on the *throne*? How can a *slaughtered Lamb* be "Lord of lords" and "King of kings?"

Even many, if not most, believers still fail to understand the paradox all this carries for their own lives, a paradox residing in the fact that *nonresistant* suffering was necessary to establish Christ's kingship over the kind of kingdom God sent Him to build. As Hegel said, "What is familiar, precisely because it is *familiar*, is not known."[69] Yet at least for believers, a remedy for the current blindness and ignorance, which took hundreds of years to evolve to this impasse, and both of which rest on little more than unexamined assumptions, resides in asking and answering one key question: what, for Christians, given the indisputable fact of Christ's nonresistant suffering, can be the meaning of the world's endless natural striving and competition, a striving for power, wealth, supremacy and exaltation through intellectual, psychological, social, economic or political manipulation and even through armed might? What is the meaning of the worship of force, a worship implicit in how people always and forever ultimately seek *political* solutions to every problem?

First, if an implicit death threat lies behind all power based on coercive force, as indeed (again, according to sociologist Max Weber and historian William McNeill[70]) all political power ultimately does, then Christ's life and triumphant death in the end declare that all the world's power—the *kratos* of violence, compulsion and death, the very power of satan himself—is *nothing* in the face of God's nonresistant love. I say this simply because God's abused, spurned love, as incarnated in the resurrected Christ, is (from a Biblical viewpoint) so plainly what triumphed and took its place on the *throne* of the *whole* universe—the betrayed, battered, bruised, tortured, slandered, humiliated, forsaken, nonresisting, Lord of love conquered (through His resurrection) the death that all worldly power is ultimately predicated upon (Phil. 2:5-8). If this is so, what, then, can that power now threaten the Lord of life with—fear, torture and death? No, He's already met and conquered all of them. And so, the perhaps greatest irony of all is that it was precisely *through* all these *nonresistant sufferings* that He conquered the ultimate power held by the enemy, the power held by the enslaver of every soul who ever lived or will live. Jesus, to repeat, conquered *death* through *nonresistant love.*

What, therefore, can self-professed Christians conclude from all this? They can plainly see that the King of kings, the Lord of lords, the One who sits on the throne, the One whom Peter declared to be their "example" and of whom Peter also said that they should "walk in His steps" (1 Pet. 2:18-24), is the *Crucified* One. So their *Supreme* Ruler never relied on the power of death, on what Scripture calls the power of satan (Heb. 2:14-15). He never turned to the kind of destructive power that ultimately determines who rules in a world built largely by war, which is the world of these kingdoms under the dominion of the one who holds the "power of death" (1 John 5:19; Heb. 2:14-15).

God, then, had no desire to demonstrate what Scripture describes as the power of God's archenemy. Rather, God's eye was set on death's antithesis: His eternal purpose has been to show forth the superior power of a self-sacrificing, supernatural love that leads to eternal *life*, not the power of death that leads to eternal death.

To begin with, the simple but startling fact is that, contrary to prevalent human assumptions, Jesus didn't come to establish justice *in the kingdoms of this world.** Jesus knew that, in a fallen world, it was possible to make justice a constituent and constitutional part *only* of the other kingdom that *He* had come to establish. And this latter kingdom, again, He declared to be "not of this world." If He had come to bring justice to the world systems—that is, to what the apostle John dared to call the "evil one's" systems (1 John 5:19)—then He would never have announced the coming of a new and different, totally counterposed kingdom, one that did not depend on the power of armed conflict or coercive brute force (Matt. 5:1-10, 20-48; 18:1-4; 19:23-30; John 3:3-8; 18:36). Rather, He would have simply worked within the existing kingdoms and their systems of power— within their *stoicheia*, to use Paul's Greek term (Col. 1:13; 2:8, 15, 20; Eph. 3:10; 6:12; Gal. 4:3, 8-9).

More concretely, if Jesus had been bringing justice *to the world*, He would never have submitted to His own crucifixion by that world, since His execution was certainly the greatest of all the *injustices* ever committed on earth, as Peter clearly saw (Matt. 16:21-23; Acts 2:22-36; 1 Pet. 2:20-24). Instead, however, Jesus did *submit to* the world's injustice. Not only this, but the injustices also continued against His immediate followers and then against a multitude of others on down through the centuries to the present day, exactly as the New Testament foretold.† Democide, the slaughter of people by their own governments, was, according to R. J. Rummel's exhaustive research, the number one cause of death in the twentieth century,[72] a century that saw more Christians persecuted and killed for their faith than in any other era of history.[73] So Jesus didn't come to end injustice in the kingdoms of the world, in the kingdoms that the New Testament portrayed as ultimately belonging to *satan*. If He did, then He failed and still continues to *increasingly* fail after 2,000 years.

Why, then, isn't God bringing justice to this world's kingdoms? Again, simply because His "kingdom is not of this world"—it is not of a world that freely gave itself to satan's brutal control and that God refuses to *force*

---

* As two of America's leading Christian scholars on church-State relations, Derek H. Davis and Matthew McMearty, have pointed out, not one word of Scripture shows that Jesus "advocated the overthrow of the Roman government, or even its adjustment, in favor of a more theocratic order." Jesus "never identified Himself with any particular form of [civil] government, nor did He even remotely suggest that it was the duty of human government to aid His mission." This was because "the temporal was for Him far less important than the eternal; thus He focused on the spiritual rather than the physical aspects of Kingdom building. The idea of a 'Christian' nation [based on *any* polity of this world], it seems, was foreign to Him."[71]

† Luke 21:12; John 15:18-20; 16:2-3; 2 Tim 3:10-13; 1 Pet. 2:18-25; 3:9-17.

under His own noncoercive control. Instead, people are now being "called out" of systems of coercive violence, and called to an exodus *from* the coercive power systems of this world and *into* a "kingdom not of this world." The very message of the church is contained in the meaning of its Greek name, *ekklesia*—"called-out ones." So God never intended to make righteousness and justice prevail in an intrinsically unjust world or in all its lapsed kingdoms, which had willingly given themselves to the rule of "the Attacker," "the Destroyer," "the King of Terrors" (Rev. 9:11; Job 18:14). Rather, Jesus intended to enter such a world with the power of a radically different and redemptive love, a love that He would pour out in the supernaturally transforming experience of the Holy Spirit (Rom. 5:5). Through that new power, He would *call out* a people, a church (an *ekklesia*), for His name, a people who would live their lives in *another* kingdom under the new lordship of His supernatural love. Only such a love *in such a kingdom* could ever hope to bring justice. The very sign that the kingdom has "come upon you" is that satan and his rule of brute force are utterly "cast out," but only cast out of the kingdom that would be *God's* (Matt. 12:28; John 12:31).

Paul talked about this new life lived in a new community (or a new communion) of relationships, one built on a love that sacrifices everything. This is what he said testified to God's "eternal purpose" to all "the principalities and powers" that ruled by brute force and the "fear of death" (Eph. 3:10-11). This testimony, or "witness," would also draw all who longed to make a spiritual and relational exodus *out* of a world marked by cruelty, hatred, lies, slander and violence. Through this exodus, through this spiritually powerful baptism of fire into "Christ [their] Passover," they would leave one world and enter another, the kingdom of God (1 Cor. 10:1-4; 5:7; Rom. 6:3-5).

And so Isaiah prophesied: "Behold! My Servant whom I uphold, My Elect One in whom My soul delights! I have put *My Spirit* upon Him; He will *bring forth justice* to the Gentiles" (Isa. 42:1). The coming of justice appears, then, only as it is inextricably tied to the coming work of God's great anointing Spirit within His own kingdom—thus, according to Jesus' explicit words, only those who receive the gift of His own supernatural Spirit would inwardly change to a degree sufficient to constitute "entering the kingdom of God" (John 3:3, 5, 8). And so only they will ever find a kingdom of true justice, a discovery that ultimately comes only because "*mercy* has triumphed *over justice*." Mercy triumphs in the sense of freeing such a people from the just claim over their lives by the one "who has the power of death" (James 2:13; Heb. 2:14-15).

So mercy could only be found, then, in the kingdom of those who have likewise been transformed by this supernatural power of God's love. Thus the Isaiah passage announcing the coming of the Anointed Servant who will bring justice goes on to say, "He will not cry out, nor raise His voice, nor cause His voice to be heard in the street. A bruised reed He will not break, and smoking flax He will not quench; He will bring forth justice in truth" (Isa. 42:2-3, NKJV). There is, in short, no coercion, no brute force used to bring this justice that Jesus brings. Jesus, not Caesar, is the Lord of this new kingdom ruled by love, a unique love coming in the power and life of the Holy Spirit and casting out the rule of the fear of death (Heb. 2:14-15). So, as Paul stated, no one can make this claim that Christ is Lord over them and that they are part of this new kingdom "*except by the Holy Spirit*" (1 Cor. 12:3). If the Spirit does not come powerfully into a person's life and continue to lead them (Rom. 8:9-14), then Jesus is not their Lord; and their lives will soon be ruled by the same old type of lapsed, human-centered reasoning that ends up always rationalizing self-preservation and self-interest at the expense of God's love and purpose.

So Jesus didn't come to convert either satan or those who willfully, even after seeing the clear nature of the conflict, choose to serve satan or his dominion of death. Rather, He came, in John's words, to "destroy the works of satan," but only *within* a called-out people who would submit to Christ's course of discipleship in the kingdom of God (1 John 3:8; Matt 28:18-20). God would accomplish this in us through the power of self-sacrificing love, which is the power of the Holy Spirit (Rom. 5:5), the very power and love that defines the nature of God Himself (1 John 4:8, 16). And, again, that's exactly why this world, one over which Jesus said satan rules, will itself be destroyed in its own violence, its elements finally melting in a fervent heat; and this will be inspired and energized by the same destructive force from satan that first brought death into the world (2 Pet. 3:10-12). So satan himself, and all those given over to him, will become the very instruments of destructive wrath that God's gift of freedom must allow as the world eats the fruit of its own ways in its own self-engendered judgment and collapse.* Does God care? Yes. Does God want to save us from this fate? Yes. That's why He robed Himself in human flesh, came in the likeness of a man and suffered unto death to bring the end of death.

Since, then, Jesus came and established a new standard and kingdom of justice, one rising from redemptive love, we can therefore no longer seek for merely the law, and its righteous, external retribution, to justify us. The measure for our conscience is now the *Lamb* of God. Our standard of measure is not, in short, the shadow but the fulfilled reality—"the *measure* of the stature of the *fullness of Christ*" Himself (Eph. 4:13). Christians now therefore seek refuge in the secret place of the Most High—in the inner court of God's temple (Rev. 11:1-2), in the Body of Christ (Col. 3:3). We

---

* Prov. 1:31; 22:8, NIV; Hos. 8:7; Job 4:8, NIV; 5:13; Gal. 6:7-9; 1 Cor. 3:19.

are no longer wedded to the Old Covenant that confined worship to the outer courts, *outside* the place of God's direct habitation. Rather, we have died with Christ to what we were once married to (Rom. 7:1-4; 6:3-8; Col. 2:20). We can therefore no longer serve as agents of the Law's wrath (Rom. 4:14-16).

Again, Jesus said that we would "by no means enter" His kingdom "unless our righteousness exceeds the righteousness of the scribes and Pharisees" (Matt. 5:20). And it was in that very passage that He also declared: "You have heard that it was said, 'An eye for an eye and a tooth for a tooth.' But I tell you not to resist an evil person . . . . I say to you, *love your enemies*" (Matt. 5:38-39, 44).

So, for those of us who truly desire to participate in the redeemed corporate Body of Christ, who long to come into God's presence in the inner court and stand at His mercy seat, if we then exact retributive justice, we can only stand condemned for completely disregarding the new standard of a righteousness rising from God's love and mercy; and this therefore makes us unjust as well. In Jesus' parable of the unmerciful servant in Matthew 18, a steward had been forgiven a tremendous debt and unhesitatingly set free from his obligation. Yet when he in turn attempted to exact payment for another legitimate—that is, another "just"—debt, he became "unjust" himself "*in view of [the] mercy*" that had been shown him. Even though the particular debt for which he demanded payment was legitimate, he had incurred a higher obligation in the forgiveness granted to his own debt, a higher obligation to show mercy (Matt. 18:21-35). In this parable, the servant forfeited the grace extended to him by his master because the servant refused, in turn, to show mercy to others. Instead, he had demanded from his debtor a "just" repayment. Jesus warned that we, too, shall forfeit grace unless the mercy extended to us, rather than our bitter demands that justice be exerted against a fallen world, controls our thoughts and deeds (Matt. 18:35).

So, Jesus came to bring an alternative kingdom *to* the world. In this kingdom, He would "conquer" the fallen nature by the power of love and truth. At least this conquest of love would occur in all those who are "of the truth," in all those who have received His same Spirit, in all who can therefore hear His voice and who joyfully surrender their entire lives to the rule of His love. That's why He declares to them, "Come *out* of her, My people" (Rev. 18:4); or, in Paul's words, "Come *out from* among them and *be separate*" (2 Cor. 6:17); and, again, "*Be not conformed* to the patterns of this world, *but be transformed* . . ." (Rom. 12:2).

This also suggests why Jesus never intended to use the church to force justice onto the unwilling and *fallen* kingdoms of satan's world, why He never tried to forcibly convert satan and his world, which included all the kingdoms that, according to Scripture, *still* to this day lie under death's dominion.* After all, how could justice ever reign in a world bound by death except within a separate kingdom temporarily planted in such a world in order to call people out of that world's system? So Jesus, instead, told His own followers to turn away from "the patterns of this world," not to try to forcibly change either these patterns or that world (John 17:14-17; 18:36; Rom. 12:1-2). Rather, believers should themselves be "transformed" by an ever-renewing spiritual experience, an experience that began in such a powerful encounter with God that it would bring their rebirth into another world—into the kingdom of God. And in this kingdom alone would justice come to reign (Rom. 12:2; 2 Cor. 3:18; John 3:3, 5).

No doubt many may view justice as indeed eventually coming to the world in the end. But this will only happen when the world, consolidated and homogenized economically, socially and politically under its prince of darkness, "melts" in "fervent heat," when it reaps what it has sown in the self-induced holocaust that its own lapsed wisdom brings to pass. Then, at last, it will have exerted to the ultimate its dominion of death. But *now* redeeming love still calls people out. It still calls on them to separate themselves unto God and to enter a "kingdom . . . not of this world." So the church has a higher calling than trying to force justice on a world that holds justice in contempt. Rather, the church is to call people to completely die to one world and to come to a miraculous new life in another. The church is to facilitate the impartation of God's very nature and righteousness, bringing an utterly uprooted and regenerated people into conformity to the image of God's self-sacrificing Son† And for those who have received this abundant mercy from God, He calls them to His own higher standard of love, of suffering and of mercy (Matt. 5:20-48). As God joins them together in every aspect of their lives, their God-composed relationships and the ordered life they live together will ever mature toward the full manifestation of the celestial kingdom on earth.

Indeed, Jesus came to establish—*through the church*—the triumph of that power that constitutes the very essence of God. "God is love," John wrote. Therefore Jesus said, "Father, forgive them," not, "Father, bring justice to this situation and destroy these evil people." Further, it is not merely Jesus who had to suffer. He Himself said that *we* must pick up our crosses "daily" and follow Him, even suffering for doing good (Luke 9:23-24; 1 Pet. 2:15-25). So Paul made clear the need for Christians to "complete what was lacking in the afflictions of Christ" (Col. 1:24). And

---

* 1 John 5:19; Matt. 4:8-10; Col. 1:13, NASU; Acts 26:15-18, NASU.

† John 3:3, 5; Rom. 8:29; 2 Cor. 3:18; Titus 3:4-6; Phil. 2:5-8.

thus did Peter later declare that Christ *crucified* is the "*example*" for all Christians and that they "should follow His steps" (1 Pet. 2:19-24).

Deliverance from the Dominion of Death

If, however, believers are not called to establish God's justice, His righteous rule, in the kingdoms of this world—specifically by taking over this world's means of rulership, then exactly how *could* this child born to Mary sit on the "*throne*" of any kingdom, as Luke suggests He will (Luke 1:31-33)? Almost any people, especially those whose entire thinking and way of life have been weighed down and shaped by some pyramidal political and cultural power structure such as Rome's, would assume that this new king would work from the top of the totemic political hierarchy down. They would have assumed that his ascendancy might come through any number of means: manipulating money, propaganda, sloganeering, electioneering, social prowess, psychological finesse, ballot box stuffing; or in a *coup d'état* through the direct use of armed might, political parlaying, conventional or unconventional warfare and conquest. Or at least he might use the show and threat of all these latter forces, forces ultimately rooted in violence and death, to leverage himself into a position of power. Either way, he could merely change the economic and political order into one appropriate to his own agenda by establishing a new government more to his liking. That government would then surely try to *appear* to bring justice to bear against its selectively chosen evil, at least, in short, according to the definitions of justice and evil that fit such a leader's own agenda. And these definitions of justice and evil would have to be such that he could manipulate or educate the people to accede to (usually, this means some affected form of *social* justice). But, according to this scenario, he might also surely be working behind the scenes, as Machiavelli instructed, clandestinely implementing his goals. He would, in this view, become a Machiavellian master of manipulation through education and propaganda, but also he would be more than willing to use brute force to crush the recalcitrant. He would no doubt further be expected to administer a form of governmental aid in which the "rich" and "mighty" (likely with the exception of those who firmly held the reins of power) would now be compelled to share that wealth and power with the "lowly," at least on some token level, such as in Augustus's "bread and circuses," again, all in a great (if empty) show of concern for "social justice" and the welfare of the masses. This would keep the proletariat happy with food and entertainment while it kept the rich depleted enough not to become too powerful or bothersome. And it even seems, given the magnitude of Israel's centuries-old messianic expectations, that all of this would ultimately have to be presented as a *global* government with some sort of at least quasi-religious or civil-religious trappings. But how would this differ from what countless demagogues, politicos, tyrants, oppressors and charlatans have always proposed?

This is indeed pretty much how the Herodians, the Pharisees, the Sadducees, the Essenes and the Zealots all, to one degree or another, in one way or another, were assessing Jesus. But He was not coming out well in their assessment, since He did not fit any of these molds. Natural Israel had, in short, taken for granted that God would deal with the miseries of humanity's many subjugations at the hands of tyrannical or demagogic powers on the same old superficial level, the same level on which people have always unsuccessfully dealt with such miseries—by simply trying to find deliverance from the *current* expression of subjugation, from the *immediately present form* that the power of coercive force, of conquering armies and of the threat of death and destruction and economic woe had then beset Yahweh's once again subjugated people.

Yet a crucial, most often overlooked problem returns to thorn Christians who would accept such a foregone conclusion: it would essentially mean that the transcendent God of the Hebrew Scriptures would be resorting to exactly the same dynamic by which His implacable enemy (in order to establish his own self-serving definitions of what was 'just' and 'unjust') had always ruled—compulsory force against compulsory force, and may the most forceful, brutal, death-dealing and destructive force win. In short, nothing about such a view would differ in the essential nature of its exertion of power from what is explicitly depicted in Scripture as satan's power, which the Bible plainly describes as death and its threat (Heb. 2:14-15). To put the problem differently, the God of life would be using, for His highest purposes, the power that Scripture explicitly declares belongs to satan—"the power of death" and the fear it engenders (Heb. 2:14-15), a power that lies at the core of every political dominion, as Weber showed.

What Jesus called the "prince" or "ruler of this world" held people in "bondage" through this "fear of death" (John 12:31; 14:30; 16:11, KJV; Heb. 2:14-15). This "king of terrors" was said to have long ago tricked people into separating from the God who is life, thus bringing them under the dominion of death (Gen. 3:1-7; Job 18:11-14). Now, because they had sold themselves to satan in treachery against God, satan could come at them under the banner of law and justice (Rom. 4:15; 7:5, 7-11, 13-14, 22-25). He could, in short, legitimately claim that nothing but the blood that signaled this death could satisfy this bloodthirsty, wrathful "god of this world" and his "just" claim that his dominion of death must rule over all people (John 12:31; 14:30; 16:11; 2 Cor. 4:4; Col. 1:13; Rev. 12:12). And so nothing else could free people from his grip. But the Hebrew Scriptures show that the transcendent God, Yahweh, had never been pleased with such sacrifices (Ps. 40:6-8; 51:16-17; 1 Sam. 15:22; Mic. 6:6-8). The New

Testament also declares His displeasure in them (Heb. 10:1-9; Matt. 9:13; 12:7).

Yes, God had freely given people a stewardship dominion over the earth (Gen. 1:26-28; Ps. 8:4-6; 115:16). But they, in turn, had freely handed it over to the king of death.* And so now responsible freedom and justice required that the world's new brutal ruler somehow *freely* release his *justly* gained captives. If God could simply trump everyone's freedom by brute force, then how could real love triumph over brute force in the world? Such a course would have denied love as the most powerful force in the universe—only death and its raw coercion could claim that title, since God Himself would have had to finally resort to it in order to win the conflict when love proved impotent in the face of satan's power of death.

Therefore, since this "God *is* love" (1 John 4:8, 16), and He "cannot deny Himself" (2 Tim. 2:13), He had to win this battle by the love that defined His own life, character and power—not by the brute force, violence and death that defined His archenemy's power. That's one reason why, with the coming of the New Covenant (Jer. 31:31-34; Heb. 8:8-12; 10:16-17), God had declared His unwillingness to accept temporary and substitutionary animal sacrifices, sacrifices unable to change human nature from rebellion against God to a oneness with Him that was created and maintained by covenantal love (Heb. 10:1-4; John 17:20-26; 1 John 4:7-16). So these old sacrifices had at best only year by year temporarily covered that lapsed human nature's baser workings, forestalling the ultimate claims of satan's dominion of death (Heb. 9:12-15). But God had always wanted to put an *end* to these sacrifices and especially to the death that lay behind them.†

For the same reasons, God would now offer His people not merely another temporary relief from the current expression of a rule rooted in the power of all evil—a rule manifesting itself through the kingdoms of this world. It would not, in short, be one more temporary respite from the dominion of destruction and death.‡

So, the change Jesus now proposed in His gospel was so radical, so unprecedented, that, in John the Baptist's words, it laid "the ax" at the very "*root.*" It would, in short, completely crush the head, or source, of this malevolent force that ruled the world through the fear of death (Heb. 2:14-15; 1 John 5:18-19). It would thereby destroy the strength and power of what the New Testament called the "*last* enemy"—death itself (Isa. 25:7-8; 1 Cor. 15:24-28, 50-57; Rev. 20:11-14). God, then, would sunder the root

---

* Gen. 3:1-6; Isa. 14:12-17; Ezek. 28:2-19; Ps. 2:1-3; 1 Tim. 2:14; Rom. 7:23-24; 8:19-23; Eph. 6:10-12; Col. 2:13; Heb. 2:14-15.

† Heb. 10:1-9; Hos. 6:6; Matt. 9:13; Rom. 6:14; 1 Cor. 15:50-57.

‡ Ps. 2:1-12; 1 John 5:19; Heb. 2:14-15; Acts 26:18; Col. 1:13.

authority of the one who has the power of death by destroying that power (Heb. 2:14-15; 2 Tim. 1:10). He would crush its head (Gen. 3:15, NIV), its *kephalē*, its *source* of authority, its ability to threaten violence and death. This was the authority that always exerted itself in all the world's contests of coercive might, where one coercive kingdom after another perpetually threatened other coercive kingdoms with "the power of death."

God's highest work, therefore, cannot at all resemble this death-force, since the Bible describes this as *satan's* very source of dominion (Heb. 2:14-15). Again, God's power instead resides in a redemptive love that leads to "eternal life," not in a brute force that threatens the world with ever-increasing displays of death and destruction. Therefore, God was about to do something never before seen on earth; and at the end of it, death would have no more dominion (Rom. 6:8-14; 1 Cor. 15:53-56).

Yes, God would indeed introduce into the world a great departure point from political and economic power, but the change would not come in any context having to do with the kingdoms of this world, or in rivalry with them over material wealth or any form of raw force. Jesus' radical commandments concerning the uses of power and wealth would only freely *come to fruition within His* own *new* kingdom, a kingdom that was "not of this world," a kingdom ruled only by God's love and entered only by a freely made choice to accept this rule of love in our lives.

Furthermore, these radical changes would come in a unique way. This is made clear in the Beatitudes and the rest of the Sermon on the Mount, which is Jesus' "summary text" of what has been called the Christian "catechism of conduct and life." John Stott pinpointed the singular way in which, "right at the beginning of" this epochal discourse, "Jesus contradicted all human judgments and all nationalistic expectations of the kingdom of God. The kingdom is given to the poor, not the rich; the feeble, not the mighty; to little children humble enough to accept it, not to soldiers who boast that they can obtain it by their own prowess."[74] Through this inversion of all natural expectations, Jesus laid down a new constitution for a new humanity, a constitution manifest in lives utterly transformed by God and serving as the standard and pattern of the new and revolutionary kingdom that He proclaimed, one into which individuals were to be supernaturally reconstituted, reborn, so as to no longer be "mere men" (John 3:3-5; 1 Cor. 3:3; Col. 1:13).

The "good news," then, was apparently to be much greater than anything Israel or the Gentile world could have imagined. The Christian "good news" is that the King of life has come to reign in a new kingdom of love, peace and joy through the extraordinary power of the Spirit, and that death shall no longer have dominion in this alternative kingdom. Messiah will deliver us from the "hand of our enemies," even from the greatest enemy, from the one that stands behind all other enemies, the enemy that rules all the kingdoms of this world through the threat of violence and its inherent ability to engender "the fear of death" (1 Cor. 15:24-28; Heb. 2:14-15). God desires to accomplish this deliverance so "that we might serve Him *without fear*," without even the "fear of death" or any of its subsidiary fears, so that we might live "in holiness and righteousness before Him all the days of our life . . . to give *light* to those who sit in *darkness* and the *shadow of death*, to *guide* our feet *into the way of peace*" (rather than the path of war). This is the way of reconciliation with the God who is life (Luke 1:5-6, 11-55, 67-75, 79). So God, coming to earth as the "Prince of *Peace*" (Isa. 9:6-7), has, as Paul would later write, "*delivered* us from the *dominion of darkness* ["and the shadow of death"] and conveyed us into the *kingdom* of the Son of *His love*, in whom we have *redemption* through His blood, the *forgiveness* of sins" (Col. 1:13-14).

Victory over this "enemy" will not come, then, through the way of carnal warfare but only through "the way of peace," of "peace on earth and goodwill toward men" (Luke 1:79; 2:14). But this is not a peace as this world gives (John 14:27), which usually only amounts to a tension of countervailing forces of violence held in fragile balance (John 14:27).* It is not the Pax Romana or Pax Britannica or Pax Americana. It is the "Pax" encircled by a crown of thorns, a peace that can confront a world of unending suffering, trials, tragedies and tribulations precisely *because* it knows it has overcome death and can therefore walk on through its valleys of shadows.

And so Luke writes, not unlike Paul's quote we just read, that Jesus "has come to open their eyes, in order to turn them *from darkness* to light, and from *the power of satan to God*, that they may receive *forgiveness* of sins and an inheritance among those who are *sanctified by faith in Me*" (Acts 26:18). Since Hebrews plainly states that the "power of satan" is "death" (Heb. 2:14-15), and since this "darkness" Luke writes of is made synonymous with this power, the "darkness" spoken of here must refer to the "shadow" of satan's power of death, the encircling shadows or darkness of every scudding fear in human life that points to, or ultimately rests upon and arises out of, the fear of death, the fear of an eternal darkness.

So this "dark" power of satan is the "*shadow* of death" (Luke 1:79), "the *fear* of death" (Heb. 2:14-15). God, therefore, calls believers to participate in Christ's victory *over* death, as opposed to participating *in* the "power of

---

* But as the context of Jesus' words about giving peace to His disciples makes clear, this peace is tied to the coming of the presence of God in their lives, the *paraclete*, the Holy Spirit that will stay with them and teach them everything of God (John 14:26); and this coming Holy Spirit was inextricably tied to the coming kingdom of God (John 3:3-8).

death," that is, as opposed to participating in violence. To so participate in Christ, we must not seek to "save our lives," for then we shall surely lose them to the fear of death (Luke 9:23-25). Rather, we must willingly lay down our lives in love for our brothers to find the life that is in Christ alone (Matt. 16:24-26; Rom. 12:1-3; Phil. 1:21). Again, since we have been forgiven much, God calls us to love much (Luke 7:47), with a supernatural love that overcomes our natural instincts and fleshly urges to defend ourselves and even all those with whom we feel the closest identification (Luke 14:26-33). As our children experience more and more of the forgiveness of God, as they experience in the depth of their being the reality of His mercy, they, too, will receive the grace to love with such an overcoming love.

The Dynamic of Self-Preservation

After Peter confessed Jesus as Messiah, Jesus told him that upon that revelation He would build His church and that He would give to Peter the keys to this kingdom. But then Peter, immediately after his initial sensitivity to the Spirit, instantly fell back into a mere natural mind-set, telling Jesus he would never let Him die at the hands of His enemies. He insisted, instead, that he would preserve Jesus' life at all cost. And Jesus, in response to something buried in this very statement, pierced Peter with the startling words, "Get behind Me, *satan*. You are an *offense* to Me" (Matt. 16:13-25). The first sentence is, of course, an exact repetition of the words He spoke to satan when the devil offered Him all the kingdoms of this world (Matt. 4:10).

So what, many will surely want to know, precisely *did* provoke this stinging rebuke from Jesus? Hadn't Peter merely pledged himself to, in the lofty language of our world today, 'defend the innocent,' to ensure the 'triumph of justice' and to protect Jesus' own freedom to pursue life, liberty and happiness in the face of 'cruel, oppressive forces'? Yet Jesus rebuked Peter precisely *because* this zealous disciple had told Jesus *not* to sacrifice Himself, that He should *not* give up His innocent life, that He should instead preserve it at all cost. In this exchange, then, Jesus seemed to be condemning Peter's notion of *self-preservation and survival at any cost as actually having its origins in the viewpoint of Jesus' archadversary* (Matt. 16:23), *that this is in fact the very dynamic through which Christ's antitype rules his kingdoms.*

Yet how could this be?—Mainly because self-preservation is the root instinct by which "the fear of death," *the key to satan's power, rules all human life* (as the twentieth century's foremost sociologist also insisted[75]). And Jesus immediately intensifies His rebuke by emphasizing this very point, "If anyone desires to come after Me, let him *deny himself, take up his cross,* and *follow Me. For whoever desires to save his life will lose it*, but whoever *loses his life for My sake* will find it. For what profit is it to a man if he gains *the whole world*, and loses his soul? Or what will he give in exchange for his soul?" (Matt. 16:24-26).

In Matthew 4, Jesus first proclaimed that everyone must "repent, for the *kingdom* of heaven is at hand" (Matt. 4:17). Then in the next chapter, Jesus begins to describe the kind of attitudes and conduct the rule of this kingdom will produce in human lives (Matt. 5). In that chapter Jesus insisted, "Your righteousness [must now] *exceed* the righteousness of the scribes and the Pharisees" (Matt. 5:20). Believers, in short, would have to *enter* and live out their lives *in* the only righteous man who ever lived, the only altogether "perfect man" in whom *we* are corporately supposed to become "the measure of the stature of the fullness of Christ" (Eph. 4:13). To enter the rule of Christ's love, confessing His Lordship over our lives, *was* to enter the kingdom, born of the same Spirit that gave Him birth (Matt. 1:18-21), called by the same name as we are immersed into the identity of His sacrificial death (Rom. 6:3).

So it was after Jesus said our righteousness must "exceed" that of "the scribes and the Pharisees" that He also went on to say, to repeat, "You have heard that it was said, an eye for an eye," but "I say to you *love* your *enemies*." Only then could His disciples "be sons of the Most High. For *He is kind to the unthankful* and *the evil*" (Matt. 5:20, 38, 44; Luke 6:35). Even the command to "*be therefore perfect*" could be stated at the end of this passage only because the kingdom of God had come in the life of Jesus (Matt. 5:48; 6:10). So they could not enter the kingdom unless they confessed, sought and lived out the *direct* rule of God's love in their own hearts and lives just as Jesus did;* and believers would have to live such a life by placing its demands above the demands of *every* other loyalty in this world, including that to their nation, to their family and even to their own lives. *The conclusion to be drawn is that self-preservation and the kingdom of God simply do not mix—rather, the kingdom demanded self-sacrifice and self-denial for the sake of a redeeming love, not self-preservation.*

Nonresistant Love: The Supreme Force

What, then, characterizes this coming kingdom that Jesus began to describe in the Sermon on the Mount? For one thing, this kingdom would usher in an utterly new way of individual and corporate life. Jesus' kingdom would be revolutionary in this most fundamental way— it would require the *spiritual and therefore internal* transformation of the *human* spirit by *God's* Spirit so that it could be made to be like God's.

---

*John 3:3, 5; Col. 2:6; Phil. 2:5-8; 1 John 2:6; 3:16; 4:17; 1 Pet. 2:19-24.

And this revolutionary spiritual vision would be expressed through the kingdom's new social order rooted in self-sacrificing love. It was *not*, then, revolutionary in any primarily political or economic or secularly social sense. But it would be revolutionary in its new way of informing human minds and lives, in its teachings that were rooted in and flowing from the numinous presence and agape experience of the transcendent God Himself. It would be revolutionary in the whole new cultural, economic and social configuration that would come into existence merely as a result of this powerful transformation and the numinous relational shift to the primacy of redemptive love that followed it.

Never would there be another association of people in which *every* idea it put forth could have such untold consequences in the way these *spiritually* driven ideas empowered the transformation of human lives. This was mainly because in no other social order was it possible that any and every idea could come saturated in the numinous presence of God, carrying in its inherent and all-powerful love its own potency not only to inspire but also to work deep change in its recipients.

If it was revolutionary, it was because it was ruled by the God who *is* perfect love. This rule would not be forced but would take root through a personal, direct encounter and powerfully experienced relationship flowing from God and into *every* human life in His kingdom. And its love would cover every *area* of each of those lives—all of which together would be brought into a newly re-created social order of loving relationships among this people, a people now empowered and familially arranged in His living order by the love of God Himself. And this empowerment would begin on the day when God came to live within each soul through the supernatural power of the Holy Spirit (Acts 1:8; 2:1-4).

Agape love would necessarily now rule lifestyle, education, dress, daily existence from birth to death, even the way people sustained themselves and rested from their labors by conforming to His already given patterns. No area of life would any longer be lived unto self. Rather, every area would become an occasion for invoking God's love: within families, within the larger Christian community, among community leaders, between believers and the surrounding world—even in believers' relationship with creation. The kingdom of the crucified and resurrected Christ would establish a new ethic, a new individual and social rule and a new living order of self-sacrificing love—an order, ethic and rule that the forces and cultures of death could threaten but never ultimately defeat, an ethic and rule that could be bruised but never crushed.

How could death defeat this kingdom? Such a kingdom's life came from the very Spirit that had raised Christ from the dead (Rom. 8:11). Christ had conquered death by first submitting to death in nonresisting obedience to the God of love. The powerful cohering strength of God's love overcame death's decomposing power. And so Christ rose from the dead. Now this power was breaking forth in His own *corporate* Body, a Body of people whose life *was Christ's* life, a Body over which He reigned as Head (Zech. 6:12; Phil. 1:21). The lordship of Jesus, which believers first pledged themselves to in baptism (Rom. 6:3-5; 10:8-10; 1 Pet. 3:21, NIV), would now work itself out in their lives and relationships. It would disciple and conform them to the image of Christ's love (Matt. 28:18-20; Rom. 8:29; 2 Cor. 3:18), until the rule of that death-conquering redemptive love was wholly established "on earth as it is in heaven" (Matt. 6:10; 1 Cor. 12:4-6, 11-14, 18, 24). This was to become the intense focus of even the believer's prayers (Matt. 6:9-13).

The now enthroned ruler of this new kingdom, in utter contrast to all the kingdoms of the world, was called by John the Baptist, "the Lamb." Nothing could have been more upside down to the world's often predatory empowerment mentality than for a leader to be called "the Lamb." Even more to the point, He was the *sacrificial* Lamb, the *crucified* Christ. This could scarcely proclaim more clearly the astounding message that, in the end, nonresistant and self-sacrificing love will prevail over all the world's powers of physical force and violence, that the very nature of the Hebrew God—which is said to be life and love, rather than the power to kill—is the supreme force in the universe.

This situates the new kingdom's authority not in the wealthiest, nor in those with the most worldly power and status, nor in those with the greatest worldly presence and prestige, but in the One slandered and crucified as a humiliated criminal, the One who was so empathetic with others that He utterly humbled and abandoned Himself in a way unthinkable to most. The Lord of all the universe saw His reputation utterly ruined as He became a servant and laid down His life in a total and even scandalous self-loss (Phil. 2:5-8). And yet this is precisely what constitutes redeeming love's great empowerment, an empowerment nothing like that of any polity or economy of the world. It does not even remotely resemble the empowerment of a secular collective rooted in political and economic images. It could hardly differ more. Nor is it the empowerment of individual fame, fortune and influence.

Those who seek personal empowerment in cultural forms that rest on the paradigms of a lapsed world, a world wracked by ruthless competition and violence, will never find congenial a place in Jesus' alternative kingdom. And this kingdom's love and service paradigm is precisely what brought the ultimate loss of face to God Himself, His rejection as someone worthy to even live in a world whose every institution was solely of human manufacture. So Jesus unequivocally declared that such self-centered people "cannot be [His] disciples." They are not *able* to do so because they are simply looking and longing for the wrong things in the wrong place (Luke 14:26-33; Matt. 6:24-34). They are, in truth, following a spirit counterposed to everything for which God's own life on earth stood.

In contrast, the kingdom of God offered different answers than had ever been proposed by the great civilizations of the world. These answers were unlike anything with which such a world confronts the great questions of history and the problems of human existence. Yes, these questions include problems about social justice and freedom, but on a far different level than self-aggrandizing, heroic posturings. For instance, from the kingdom's perspective, the ultimate denial of all human freedoms is death—death even denies human beings (at least in any positive sense) the power to determine the span of their own days. But before Jesus came, no one in history had (or could have) dealt head-on, and with their entire life, with this absolute crushing of human freedom by death. A true resurrection of the dead—not just being raised to die again, as in the myths of many pagan deities, or even with Lazarus, but being resurrected to an "indestructible life"—*that* was unheard of in *any* religion. Therefore it was far more than astounding—it was more like the dawn of a new creation. That's why early Christians responded to the problem of death by first entering through spiritual rebirth, into the living Christ. Then they totally and increasingly surrendered to the One who alone conquered death.

Because Jesus kept His life free from all the attitudes, thoughts and conduct that brought death's sting to humanity in the first place, He could face death with an overcoming courage that He now offers to all who follow Him in His sacrificial obedience to the Holy Spirit, to the Spirit of life. By being "crucified with Christ" (Gal. 2:20; Rom. 6:3-8), as Paul said, by entering a pledge in baptism to His self-sacrificing death, they could now avail themselves of His sinless sacrifice and thus be covered from any just claim that death might make on their souls. If they lived in the power and life of the Holy Spirit, they could therefore hope to experience the culmination of that death-defying power in the great resurrection of the dead.

So they saw offered to them the power to face the question of violence and oppression as Jesus did—with suffering. Violent resistance to threats of violence only worships at the same old altar of brute force that has always brought continued injustice, renewed anger and the further mush-rooming of such violence. On the other hand, suffering in Christ promised the confrontation and overcoming of death by the resurrection power of the Holy Spirit as it prevailed over even the worst that injustice might deal out.

In regard to the other everyday problems common to human life, the new community of Christ offered similarly unique answers. For instance, what about problems of money and poverty? Early Christians responded with voluntary giving and sharing, a giving governed by the need of the recipient and not by what the giver's selfish nature might dictate. Many Christians would even sacrifice to the point of hurting along with those in need (Heb. 11:23-26; 2 Cor. 8:1-4). Likewise, to entangled questions people had about authority, Christian leaders would respond by laying down their own lives in sacrificial service, leading through example and precept, perfecting every member's gift in the fullest possible corporate realization of the rule of redeeming love. This became the same rule of love that constituted God's kingdom.

Whatever sphere of life was to be dealt with, the Lord of love came to establish His reign of love. And all these spheres together made up the kingdom over which the King of redemptive love would rule. "From faith to faith," victory to victory, "glory to glory" (Rom. 1:17; 2 Cor. 3:18), God would reveal more and more of His eternal purpose in human lives, establishing His kingdom on earth as it is in heaven. And this purpose was to show the triumph of love's rule over the rule of fear, brute force, selfishness, violence and death.

Jesus therefore declared, "Pick up your cross and follow Me" precisely because the cross so exactly expressed God's love marching against and overcoming death through Christ. And it is still supposed to do this today through Christ's own *corporate* Body. That is, in truth, the very nature of God's love. And this love is not only self-sacrificing but also a *holy* love, a pure love, one that reaches far beyond even the greatest expressions of natural affection. It is the love that urges us to lay down our lives for others because God did so when He clothed Himself in the human life of Jesus. He thus founded a kingdom in this world that would become a city of refuge for all those captive to the dynamic of death, a death that history repeatedly shows as ultimately ruling all the world's kingdoms by violence and fear, by all the mechanisms and measures of a self-preservation that lays its cost totally at the feet of those it chooses to call its enemies. Only in Christ, then, could all of these captives hope to escape this "dominion of death" by fleeing into the refuge of love and life, into God's kingdom, into Christ's own self-sacrificing Body, into the only true freedom.

It is crucial to see, then, that Jesus did not conquer this power of death by appropriating more of that power than His adversary possessed. Rather, "*through* death" He conquered death. That is, by freely sacrificing His *own* life, not taking another's, He "destroyed him who had the power of death" (Heb. 2:14). He did so the moment He rose from the dead (2 Tim. 1:10). Through His own death, then, Jesus thereby "abolished death" and "brought life and immortality to light through the gospel" (1 Cor.

15:20-28). The victory came *not* through a greater show of raw might and brute force, but, again, through the ultimate display of a nonresistant and self-sacrificing love, a love that rose triumphant over the power of death and the grave. When Paul saw this true power of God, he immediately determined to know and preach nothing but "Christ crucified" (1 Cor. 2:2).

Paul knew who sits as King on the throne of this kingdom—the *Suffering* Servant who died the *scandalous* death of a criminal, of a total reject of society. And this suffering One is *still* on the throne today. For He took "the form of a *bondservant* and . . . *humbled Himself* and became *obedient unto death*—the *death of the cross. Therefore* God highly exalted Him . . . so that every knee should *bow* . . . and . . . every tongue *confess* that *He*," this Man humbled to the marrow, "*is Lord*" (Phil. 2:7-11).

Pride is the mechanism of a self-view that must rely on self-preservation at all cost, while humility is the mechanism of a view that can surrender self entirely to God's rule of agape. "Survival at all cost" or "Sacrifice the full cost"—these ultimately seem to be the only two real options (Luke 9:23-27; 14:26-33; Rom. 12:1-3; 1 Pet. 2:5). We can pretend, when we stand *outside* our confrontations with the inevitable crises of life, that we have more subtle choices that fall into shades of gray. But when those crises become ultimate, we will have only two—until we finally have none at all.

True Faithfulness

We can conclude, then, that nonresistant Christian love keeps on trusting God in active faith, no matter what life may confront the believer with, or what God may require of him. And that love even keeps on believing God in complacent trust when nothing else can be *done* to curtail the evil that comes against us, when all that we *can* do *has* been done. When the spikes of those who hate us pierce our hands and nail our ability to minister to God's people to the cross, serious Christians don't even then exert active faith to call "twelve legions of angels" or rise up to call down fire from heaven or otherwise "blow the enemy away" (Matt. 26:53; Luke 9:54-56). Rather, they simply keep speaking the truth; they keep exposing the lies; they keep bringing to light the hidden things of darkness (Eph. 5:8-16; 1 Cor. 4:5). But if all else seems to fail and our image is hanging stripped and naked and vulnerable on a cross of scandal, we surrender in our nonresistant trust of love, in our trust in God, even as we keenly feel those piercing spikes of rejection, slander and hatred. And when the situation has brought us to "the last enemy," death, we still trust love to have its way, regardless of what the circumstances may look like. We trust even when the knife point rests at the throat of the very promise and purpose of God in our lives, just as it was once poised over Isaac.

We should take care, however, not to deceive ourselves—Jesus said we cannot serve two masters (Matt. 6:24). Remember what Jesus said toward the middle of the Sermon on the Mount—that we're going to serve one master and kingdom or the other? All believers must decide if Jesus is to truly be Lord. We must decide if we want to break the enemy's hold on our lives and make our exodus from his dominion of death and enter God's life instead. To do so, we must leave behind the "power" of satan in this world and be reborn of water and Spirit (John 3:3-5). And such a rebirth must come in such experiential magnitude that its rising *tsunami* of power carries us right into the kingdom of God (John 3:3, 5). Then we must "take up our cross," following the example Jesus gave us in His own life (1 Pet. 2:21). We must obey Jesus when He said, "Deny yourself," sacrifice even your own life (Luke 9:23-25; 14:26-33), which then also means we'll finally come to *live for* love. Why? Because that's the only way the dominion of death will ever be broken—by the power of God's love triumphing over our every fear of death. This is true whether our fears are for our own lives—*our* image, *our* career, *our* possessions, *our* reputation— or for *our* loved ones. Again, this shows why a conviction of nonresistant love marks true conversion: only someone truly determined to surrender his life completely to God can follow the crucified Lord all the way to Calvary.

To remind God's children of all this encourages them to truly come to Biblical repentance and faith. A goal will rise before them, if they will be honest concerning the deepest impulses of their hearts, that they can then press toward as they seek to know Jesus and to be like Him.

> For though we walk in the flesh, *we do not war according to the flesh.* For the weapons of our warfare are not carnal but mighty in God for pulling down strongholds, casting down arguments and every high thing that exalts itself against the knowledge of God, bringing every thought into captivity to the obedience of Christ, and being ready to punish all disobedience *when your obedience is fulfilled.* (2 Cor. 10:3-6)

> *For we do not wrestle against flesh and blood, but against principalities, against powers, against the rulers of the darkness of this age, against spiritual hosts of wickedness in the heavenly places.* (Eph. 6:12)

> Jesus answered, "My kingdom is not of this world. If My kingdom were of this world, My servants would fight, so that I should not be delivered to the Jews; but now My kingdom is not from here." (John 18:36)

> You have heard that it was said, "An eye for an eye and a tooth for a tooth." *But I tell you not to resist an evil person.* But whoever slaps you on your right cheek, *turn the other to him also.* If anyone wants to sue you and take away your tunic, let him have your cloak also. And whoever compels you to go one mile, go with him two. Give

to him who asks you, and from him who wants to borrow from you do not turn away. You have heard that it was said, "You shall love your neighbor and hate your enemy." But I say to you, *love your enemies, bless those who curse you, do good to those who hate you, and pray for those who spitefully use you and persecute you, that you may be sons of your Father in heaven*; for He makes His sun rise on the evil and on the good, and sends rain on the just and on the unjust. For if you love those who love you, what reward have you? Do not even the tax collectors do the same? And if you greet your brethren only, what do you do more than others? Do not even the tax collectors do so? Therefore you shall be perfect, just as your Father in heaven is perfect. (Matt. 5:38-48)

Let love be without hypocrisy. Abhor what is evil. Cling to what is good. Be kindly affectionate to one another with brotherly love, in honor giving preference to one another; not lagging in diligence, fervent in spirit, serving the Lord; rejoicing in hope, *patient in tribulation*, continuing steadfastly in prayer; distributing to the needs of the saints, given to hospitality. *Bless those who persecute you; bless and do not curse.* Rejoice with those who rejoice, and weep with those who weep. Be of the same mind toward one another. Do not set your mind on high things, but associate with the humble. Do not be wise in your own opinion. *Repay no one evil for evil.* Have regard for good things in the sight of all men. If it is possible, as much as depends on you, live peaceably with all men. Beloved, *do not avenge yourselves*, but rather give place to wrath; for it is written, "Vengeance is Mine, I will repay," says the Lord. Therefore "*If your enemy is hungry, feed him; if he is thirsty, give him a drink*; for in so doing you will heap coals of fire on his head." *Do not be overcome by evil, but overcome evil with good.* (Rom. 12:9-21)

Now it came to pass, when the time had come for Him to be received up, that He steadfastly set His face to go to Jerusalem, and sent messengers before His face. And as they went, they entered a village of the Samaritans, to prepare for Him. But they did not receive Him, because His face was set for the journey to Jerusalem. And when His disciples James and John saw this, they said, "*Lord, do You want us to command fire to come down from heaven and consume them*, just as Elijah did?" *But He turned and rebuked them, and said, "You do not know what manner of spirit you are of. For the Son of Man did not come to destroy men's lives but to save them."* And they went to another village. (Luke 9:51-56)

And suddenly, one of those who were with Jesus stretched out his hand and drew his sword, struck the servant of the high priest, and cut off his ear. *But Jesus said to him, "Put your sword in its place, for all who take the sword will perish by the sword.* Or do you think that I cannot now pray to My Father, and He will provide Me with more than twelve legions of angels?" (Matt. 26:51-53)

But I say to you who hear: *Love your enemies, do good to those who hate you, bless those who curse you, and pray for those who spitefully use you. To him who strikes you on the one cheek, offer the other also.*

And from him who takes away your cloak, do not withhold your tunic either. Give to everyone who asks of you. And from him who takes away your goods do not ask them back. (Luke 6:27-30)

Finally, all of you be of one mind, having compassion for one another; love as brothers, be tenderhearted, be courteous; *not returning evil for evil or reviling for reviling, but on the contrary blessing, knowing that you were called to this*, that you may inherit a blessing. (1 Pet. 3:8-9)

For we know Him who said, *"Vengeance is Mine; I will repay,"* says the Lord. And again, "The Lord will judge His people." (Heb. 10:30)

See that no one renders evil for evil to anyone, but always pursue what is good both for yourselves and for all. (1 Thess. 5:15)

2. Violence

It is hopefully evident by now that violence can never express love simply because it's love's very antithesis. Violence is impelled not by love but by fear. Fear arises from faithlessness and breeds hatred against what we fear. So the Bible speaks of the faithless man as a violent man (Prov. 13:2): fear and violence feed each other because the essence of fear is self-preservation at all costs. Once you choose violence as a defense, you must then be willing to escalate more and more, to always go your enemy one better in destructiveness or inflicting pain. That's why the world's instruments of violence continue to grow in their destructive power, until today the nations of the world have developed weapons capable of destroying all humanity many times over. Once you choose the course of destruction to defend that which you claim to love, you must be willing to pursue such a course even if you see destroyed everything worth loving. So tens of thousands of innocent children have been incinerated at Hamburg, Dresden, Tokyo, Hiroshima, Nagasaki and elsewhere, all in the name of defending the innocent.[76]

Whatever such a world does, the few Christians who cling to Christ's nonviolent teachings cannot rely upon human wisdom and strength for their defense (1 Cor. 1:17–2:16). The path of a violent defense may be rational and logical if based on certain narrowly human-centered assumptions situated in the captive kingdoms of death, but, ironically, it can now lead to the destruction of all that humanity seeks to defend, of everything worth defending; and surely in the larger view, that is neither rational nor logical. Even if we were to win such a battle, we would lose the larger and ultimate "war," the war within ourselves, the war for the triumph of love and mercy over hatred and cruelty. To win the war against war, we must die to the fear of death in all its forms. Only then can we beat both war and death by not playing the game according to their rules: if nonviolence loses this war in the hearts of Christians, they will then simply become like the destroyer they claim to oppose and seek to overcome—we will deny our true faith.

So we can only defend the precious things God has given us in a way consistent with His own nature if we follow the path of perfect submission to His will, the path Jesus walked. Because He walked the path, when the multitude tried to throw Him from the hilltop of Nazareth, He could pass through the mob unharmed. Since "it was not His time," God protected Him until the time arrived when His death would glorify the Father and serve the love of God to others. The Lord has laid out such a path of faith for each of us as well. All this admittedly calls for a supernatural faith in God, the faith of Abraham, a faith we as serious Christians should presumably already be seeking daily (Rom. 1:17; 4:12; 9:30-32; Heb. 11:6).

> A man shall eat well by the fruit of his mouth, but *the soul of the unfaithful feeds on violence.* (Prov. 13:2)

> Do not be deceived, God is not mocked; for whatever a man sows, that he will also reap. (Gal. 6:7)

> And suddenly, one of those who were with Jesus stretched out his hand and drew his sword, struck the servant of the high priest, and cut off his ear. But Jesus said to him, "Put your sword in its place, for *all who take the sword will perish by the sword.* Or do you think that I cannot now pray to My Father, and He will provide Me with more than twelve legions of angels?" (Matt. 26:51-53)

> He who leads into captivity shall go into captivity; *he who kills with the sword must be killed with the sword.* Here is the patience and the faith of the saints. (Rev. 13:10)

> For with what judgment you judge, you will be judged; and with the measure you use, it will be measured back to you. (Matt. 7:2)

Child Training, Play and Violence

The Scripture makes clear, and the experience of every parent confirms, the corruption in the heart of every soul, even from our mother's womb.* Children, especially boys, easily fall into violence with each other in all sorts of circumstances, through greed, impatience or sometimes just "playing around." In the competitive culture of a materialistic world, such attitudes are natural and reinforced. Parents in such a world teach their children to "defend themselves" aggressively, not to be "cowards"; or else they use other terms denigrating an unwillingness to fight physically. Many consider it good to be "tough," competitive and even forcefully assertive.

---

*Jer. 17:9; Ps. 14:2-3; 51:5; 53:3; Eccles. 7:20; Rom. 3:10-12, 23; 1 John 1:8-10.

We're all aware, too, of the ubiquitous violence of our surrounding culture, from the attitudes expressed in so many of the books, in media games, even in educational materials designed for children and simply in the statistics of crime and violence. Everywhere we turn, satan's violence is glorified—in media, in history books, in daily conversation and recreation.

To not only protect our children from such attitudes but also to even seek to create a contrasting Biblical attitude towards violence requires a full commitment to uproot and overcome everything that glorifies violence. This is a difficult task, particularly because there have been men who were in some measure honorable, including historical figures as well as Old Testament heroes, who did employ violence. But we must learn to see that God now wants us to battle against the greater enemies of the spiritual realm and of our own spiritual nature. We must learn to see how true courage lies in the willingness to face and overcome all evil impulses that would lead us to harm others. Each must first face these attitudes in his or her own heart, but if we do, we can find the grace to help others overcome them as well.

As we all know, games of violence and war are a normal part of childhood play in the predominant culture. In such games, the "good guys" are stronger and beat the "bad guys." It takes an entirely different perspective to instill a Biblical attitude toward *all* violence. We must remember that "culture heroes" are *not* God's heroes, and we must consistently avoid nurturing such images and attitudes in children.

Of course, children need times to play and relax and to read stories. But these times must serve to re-*create* our children's energies for constructive activity in ways that build them up in the purpose of God. This will prove impossible in the absence of a sacralized form, which comes to each child as the patterns for relationship with parents and other adults and children. Without such form and direction, our children's playtime will serve only to destroy their character as their life dissipates in foolishness and worse. As a rule, a game, toy, book, audio disc or program should encourage peaceful, constructive activity and should encourage a spirit of unity (in contrast to a competitive spirit) among all the children playing together. *All* our children's activities will either build them up or tear them down, not only spiritually but also in many other ways. So books and activities should not lead children into unreal fantasy worlds, many of them characterized by violence and strange or familiar spirits.

As noted, such material usually portrays the violence exerted by the hero as the triumph of the "good," but as Christians, we should reexamine such claims and the use of such books, games and other play activities. To repeat, whatever positive characteristics, such as courage, we see in such stories should be presented in the context of the true courage needed to overcome spiritual enemies within ourselves, such as the inclination towards violence in the child's own heart.

Instead of permitting "play" in the form of "shooting" others with toy guns, we should rather direct our children in pastimes that ultimately encourage them toward the joyous, liberating reality of Jesus. In everything, we should nurture in our children the ability to take dominion over the world in the name of Jesus Christ and the love He poured out at Calvary. Fantasy, much of which contains some form of violence, does the opposite of that. Children should emulate Jesus—the Lamb of God. This means training them to "walk as He walked."

Do to others as you would have them do to you. (Luke 6:31)

Blessed are the peacemakers, for they will be called sons of God. (Matt. 5:9)

Repay no one evil for evil. Have regard for good things in the sight of all men. If it is possible, as much as depends on you, *live peaceably with all men.* Beloved, *do not avenge yourselves*, but rather give place to wrath; for it is written, "Vengeance is Mine, I will repay," says the Lord. Therefore *"If your enemy is hungry, feed him; if he is thirsty, give him a drink; for in so doing you will heap coals of fire on his head."* Do not be overcome by evil, but overcome evil with good. (Rom. 12:17-21)

See that no one renders evil for evil to anyone, but always pursue what is good both for yourselves and for all. (1 Thess. 5:15)

Finally, all of you be of one mind, having compassion for one another; love as brothers, be tenderhearted, be courteous; not returning evil for evil or reviling for reviling, but on the contrary blessing, knowing that you were called to this, that you may inherit a blessing. For "He who would love life and see good days, let him refrain his tongue from evil, and his lips from speaking deceit. Let him turn away from evil and do good; *let him seek peace and pursue it.* For the eyes of the Lord are on the righteous, and His ears are open to their prayers; but the face of the Lord is against those who do evil." And who is he who will harm you if you become followers of what is good? (1 Pet. 3:8-13)

Remind them to be subject to rulers and authorities, to obey, to be ready for every good work, to speak evil of no one, *to be peaceable, gentle, showing all humility to all men.* (Titus 3:1-2)

But the wisdom that comes from heaven is first of all pure; then *peace-loving, considerate, submissive, full of mercy* and good fruit, impartial and sincere. *Peacemakers who sow in peace raise a harvest of righteousness.* (James 3:17-18)

As a prisoner for the Lord, then, I urge you to live a life worthy of the calling you have received. *Be completely humble and gentle*; be patient, bearing with one another in love. Make every effort to keep the unity of the Spirit through the *bond of peace.* (Eph. 4:1-3)

J. PATIENCE/IMPATIENCE

1. Patience

The same love that brings forth kindness, generosity and peace also brings forth patience. When a child learns patience, we know that God has begun to rule his life. God so controls him that his flesh doesn't break out of the gentle bounds of God's Word. The literal meaning of the Greek New Testament word *hupomone*, which is translated "patience," is "an abiding under." The patient child "abides under" the authority of his parents and the authority of God. He doesn't obey his flesh but the Spirit. Because he continually senses God's faithful covering, he doesn't give way to anxiety but patiently waits. Patience enables us to persevere in the will of God in hopeful expectation. "Through faith and patience" God's people "inherit what has been promised" (Heb. 6:12). Patience enables us to enter into the fullness of God's inheritance for us, not stopping short, but moving forward in abiding faith until the birthright becomes ours in its entirety.

a. Self-Control

The patient child is self-controlled. Whims, habits and external compulsions having their origin in the flesh or in satan don't control him. Such extraneous forces don't influence him, and so he can respond to the leading of God's Spirit as the Spirit wills. His will surrenders not to the will of man or satan, but to the will of God.

> Better a patient man than a warrior, a *man who controls his temper* than one who takes a city. (Prov. 16:32)

> A fool gives full vent to his anger, but a *wise man keeps himself under control*. (Prov. 29:11)

> *"In your anger do not sin"*: Do not let the sun go down while you are still angry. (Eph. 4:26)

> For this very reason, make every effort to add to your faith goodness; and to goodness, knowledge; *and to knowledge, self-control; and to self-control, perseverance*; and to perseverance, godliness . . . . (2 Pet. 1:5-6)

> But the fruit of the Spirit is love, joy, peace, patience, kindness, goodness, faithfulness, gentleness and *self-control*. Against such things there is no law. (Gal. 5:22-23)

A patient man has great understanding, but a quick-tempered man displays folly. (Prov. 14:29)

When you sit to dine with a ruler, note well what is before you, and *put a knife to your throat if you are given to gluttony.* Do not crave his delicacies, for that food is deceptive. (Prov. 23:1-3)

Do not be quickly provoked in your spirit, for anger resides in the lap of fools. (Eccles. 7:9)

The end of all things is near. Therefore be clear minded and *self-controlled* so that you can pray. (1 Pet. 4:7)

In your patience possess your souls. (Luke 21:19)

b. Mannerly

The very notion of a temple suggests a form. God gives such forms to help us stay within the bounds of His nature, which is love. A mannerly child willingly and joyfully restrains himself within the boundaries and forms God has set for him in his love for others. Thus to be "courteous," the English translation of the Greek word *philophron*, means to be "friendly" and derives from the root word *phrao*, which means to "rein in or curb." Because Christians recognize the sinful human nature, they also recognize the necessity to bring that nature within God-given forms and restraints that would stop that nature short of conflict and mutual destruction. Forms of politeness and mannerliness express our recognition of the inescapably destructive consequences of any absolute freedom from all forms. These forms help prompt our flesh to honor our fellow man while restraining our own carnal man. To truly know the evil in human hearts is to recognize the highly volatile potential in all human relationships. Forms of courtesy place limits upon us that permit us to truly live at peace with others. To ignore those forms invites conflict, discord and violence. To abide within these forms is, as James Thompson has said, to

> inject into daily intercourse qualities that plane off the rough edges and blunt the jagged points of human contact. They provide a means whereby people convey mutual respect for fellow travelers as they pass through this world. Manners impose . . . order upon human contacts that otherwise resemble something akin to particles violently repelling one another inside an atom.[77]

They define relationships so one becomes a participant "in the drama of life," a drama whose plot and purpose is brought into focus by our very conformity to the final rules of manners.[78] To ignore these assents to the arbitrariness and purposelessness of life. To throw down the rules of courtesy constitutes a declaration of hatred and war, a willingness to do violence to another. It says you are throwing away all restraint, that you will no longer look upon this person as even a potential friend, with whom you might share a common life, but that you are "outlawing" them forever, permanently consigning them to the category of an implacable and unredeemable enemy. There is hardly a worse judgment you could make against another human being.

So the Bible says that being unmannerly is one of the characteristics opposed to love. Love

> is not conceited—arrogant and inflated with pride; it is not rude (*unmannerly*), and does not act unbecomingly. Love [God's love in us] does not insist on its own rights or its own way, for it is not self-seeking. (1 Cor. 13:5, Ampl.)

To be sure, everyone has seen an all too formal politeness that spoke only of inward pride in one's superiority as a part of a "better class" of "the polite." But the fact that such people exist doesn't condone a rejection of manners. If anything, it points to an even greater need for a genuine mannerliness that does not merely externally restrain evil in our hearts, but which truly reflects a transformation where mannerliness manifests genuine love and patience. Yes, we can be polite in outward manners without feeling one positive thing in our hearts toward another human being, but surely the habit of good manners is still better than its lack. A savage or barbaric heart is no better for being unmannerly. Manners at least help keep us alive and in relationship long enough until the Holy Spirit can fill the empty form of a hollow politeness.

> Finally, all of you be of one mind, having compassion for one another; love as brothers, be tenderhearted, *be courteous.* (1 Pet. 3:8)

> If you find honey, eat just enough—too much of it, and you will vomit. (Prov. 25:16)

> Seldom set foot in your neighbor's house—too much of you, and he will hate you. (Prov. 25:17)

> The lips of the righteous know *what is fitting*, but the mouth of the wicked only what is perverse. (Prov. 10:32)

c. Endurance and Perseverance

Patience indicates a faith greater than a mere seed planted in shallow soil that withers in the heat of trial. Rather, we "run with *patience* the race that is set before us" (Heb. 12:1, KJV). We endure and persevere until we overcome. Patience allows the child to endure because love lies behind patience (1 Cor. 13:4-8), and love always endures (1 Cor. 13:7). Love rooted in God cannot be shaken; it remains steadfast, a tree planted by the waters. This is one reason why redemptive love can only be known in covenant. Only in covenant bonds does love have the opportunity to make known its durable nature—that it endures all things, that it never fails. A child who has endurance has thus begun to enter into some measure of the reality of God's covenant love.

To endure is to persevere. The New Testament Greek words generally translated by these English words indicate "steadfastness" in "enduring evils" or "to bear up under" a heavy "load"—for example, *kakopatheo*, "to suffer evil" (2 Tim. 2:3) and *hupomeno*, "to remain under" (Heb. 12:2). Only love can empower us to do this in victory.

> Love is *patient*, love is kind. It does not envy, it does not boast, it is not proud. It is not rude, it is not self-seeking, it is not easily angered, it keeps no record of wrongs. Love does not delight in evil but rejoices with the truth. It always protects, always trusts, always hopes, *always perseveres*. Love never fails. (1 Cor. 13:4-8)

> And you will be hated by all for My name's sake. But *he who endures to the end will be saved*. (Matt. 10:22)

> *Endure hardship as discipline*: God is treating you as sons. For what son is not disciplined by his father? (Heb. 12:7)

> For this is commendable, if because of conscience toward God one *endures grief, suffering wrongfully*. (1 Pet. 2:19)

> *And endurance (fortitude) develops maturity of character*—that is, approved faith and tried integrity. And character [of this sort] produces [the habit of] joyful and confident hope of eternal salvation. (Rom. 5:4, Ampl.)

> *Endure hardship with us like a good soldier of Christ Jesus*. No one serving as a soldier gets involved in civilian affairs—he wants to please his commanding officer. Similarly, if anyone competes as an athlete, he does not receive the victor's crown unless he competes according to the rules. The hardworking farmer should be the first to receive a share of the crops. Reflect on what I am saying, for the Lord will give you insight into all this. (2 Tim. 2:3-7)

> So Joshua fought the Amalekites as Moses had ordered, and Moses, Aaron and Hur went to the top of the hill. As long as Moses held up his hands, the Israelites were winning, but whenever he lowered his hands, the Amalekites were winning. When Moses' hands grew tired, they took a stone and put it under him and he sat on it. Aaron and Hur held his hands up—one on one side, one on the other—so that *his hands remained steady till sunset*. So Joshua overcame the Amalekite army with the sword . . . .He said, "For hands were lifted up to the throne of Yahweh. Yahweh will be at war against the Amalekites from generation to generation." (Exod. 17:10-13, 16)

> *Blessed is the man who perseveres under trial*, because when he has stood the test, he will receive the crown of life that God has promised to those who love Him. (James 1:12)

> Then Jesus told His disciples a parable to show them that they should always pray and not give up. He said: "In a certain town there was a judge who neither feared God nor cared about men.

And there was a widow in that town *who kept coming to him with the plea*, 'Grant me justice against my adversary.'

"For some time he refused. But finally he said to himself, 'Even though I don't fear God or care about men, yet because this widow keeps bothering me, I will see that she gets justice, so that she won't eventually wear me out with her coming!'"

And the Lord said, "Listen to what the unjust judge says. And will not God bring about justice for His chosen ones, who cry out to Him day and night? Will He keep putting them off? I tell you, He will see that they get justice, and quickly. However, when the Son of Man comes, *will He find faith on the earth*?" (Luke 18:1-8)

As you know, we *consider blessed those who have persevered.* You have heard of Job's perseverance and have seen what the Lord finally brought about. The Lord is full of compassion and mercy. (James 5:11)

Therefore, since we are surrounded by such a great cloud of witnesses, let us throw off everything that hinders and the sin that so easily entangles, and *let us run with perseverance the race marked out for us.* (Heb. 12:1)

Consider it pure joy, my brothers, whenever you face trials of many kinds, because you know that the testing of your faith develops perseverance. *Perseverance must finish its work so that you may be mature and complete, not lacking anything.* (James 1:2-4)

When the storm has swept by, the wicked are gone, *but the righteous stand firm forever.* (Prov. 10:25)

God "will give to each person according to what he has done." To those who by *persistence in doing good* seek glory, honor and immortality, He will give eternal life. (Rom. 2:6-7)

d. Overcoming

Endurance requires more than passivity. It actively withstands all wrongful opposition, but it also surmounts that opposition with love. The only defense in our spiritual battles becomes an "offense" of love. The Greek New Testament verb *nikao* is translated "overcome." The noun form, *nike*, according to Arndt and Gingrich means "victory" or "the means for winning a victory." To truly endure the enemies' assaults means to overcome our enemies by loving them as ourselves (Matt. 5:44). Beyond this, the Christian must also overcome the world. So his whole way of life comprises a series of successive victories over the patterns and powers of the kingdoms of this world. He must struggle his way up the inclined plane of events and history even as all the world around him slides down this slippery slope and toward the abyss. In addition, he must be stretching out his hands to the right and left, offering to catch hold of any who might desire help in stopping their downward slide. The child, too, must learn early on to start overcoming the seemingly small obstacles in his path—including those erected by friends and playmates, but, above all, by his own flesh. Everything the child overcomes, every time he overcomes, will strengthen him to overcome further and greater opposition in the future. Only by sticking to the overcoming way will he learn to live a prevailing life in God's grace.

> Do not be overcome by evil, but *overcome evil with good.* (Rom. 12:21)

> For everyone born of God overcomes the world. *This is the victory that has overcome the world, even our faith.* (1 John 5:4)

> He who has an ear, let him hear what the Spirit says to the churches. *To him who overcomes, I will give the right to eat from the tree of life,* which is in the paradise of God. (Rev. 2:7)

> *To him who overcomes, I will give the right to sit with Me on My throne,* just as I overcame and sat down with My Father on His throne. (Rev. 3:21)

> *He who overcomes will inherit all this,* and I will be his God and he will be My son. (Rev. 21:7)

2. Impatience

Refusal to submit to the guidance of those with vision, wisdom and maturity always results in impatience. The Hebrew word *qatsar,* translated "impatience" in Numbers 21:4, literally means, according to Brown, Driver and Briggs, "to come short of." The impatient child or disciple "comes short" of the vision of God because he falls short of submitting fully to those who have it. He cannot see that God has truly provided, truly seen ahead (*provideo*). This Hebrew word *qatsar* also has the meaning "to harvest." Thus, such a child always wants to "harvest" *right now* whether it is in God's time or not (Mark 4:26-29; Acts 1:7). He can't patiently await the full harvest and doesn't really believe it will even come. He doesn't submit himself to the seasons of God but tries to force something to completion before God's time. He becomes anxious to have what he wants when he wants it. He sees no purpose in restraining his flesh and will. He hurries his parents and everyone close to him, all of whom he sees as obstacles to his wish fulfillments. Such impatience has nothing to do with wanting to see the will of God done. Rather, it merely marks a frustration with everything that hinders the child's own will from ruling. Such a child refuses to wait on the Lord in the Spirit because he doesn't care about God's purpose or God's people but only his own agenda.

a. Temper Fits

Temper fits, quitting, whining and the anger of frustration simply express the child's unrestrained flesh. When the impatient child's will is in the least obstructed, he often reacts with such temper fits in a last-ditch effort to get his way, particularly if he thinks that such methods have worked at all in the past. Like all impatient children, he wants immediate satisfaction for his appetites, unwilling to wait for the appointed time of the harvest that could bring fulfillment. But even a hint of concession to his outbursts will only further hurt the child and will require even more prolonged and persistent efforts to redress.

> The acts of the sinful nature are obvious: sexual immorality, impurity and debauchery; idolatry and witchcraft; hatred, discord, jealousy, *fits of rage*, selfish ambition, dissensions, factions and envy; drunkenness, orgies, and the like. I warn you, as I did before, that those who live like this will not inherit the kingdom of God. (Gal. 5:19-21)

> A *fool shows his annoyance* at once, but a prudent man overlooks an insult. (Prov. 12:16)

> A patient man has great understanding, but a *quick-tempered man displays folly*. (Prov. 14:29)

> Do not make friends with a *hot-tempered man*, do not associate with *one easily angered*, or you may learn his ways and get yourself ensnared. (Prov. 22:24-25)

> Stone is heavy and sand a burden, but *provocation by a fool* is heavier than both. (Prov. 27:3)

> A *fool gives full vent to his anger*, but a wise man keeps himself under control. (Prov. 29:11)

> An *angry man stirs up dissension*, and a hot-tempered one commits many sins. (Prov. 29:22)

> Get rid of all bitterness, *rage and anger*, brawling and slander, along with every form of malice. (Eph. 4:31)

> Like a city whose walls are broken down is a man who *lacks self-control*. (Prov. 25:28)

> A wise man fears Yahweh and shuns evil, but a fool is hotheaded and reckless. *A quick-tempered man does foolish things*, and a crafty man is hated. (Prov. 14:16-17)

> A *hot-tempered man stirs up dissension*, but a patient man calms a quarrel. (Prov. 15:18)

> Better a patient man than a warrior, a man who *controls his temper* than one who takes a city. (Prov. 16:32)

> A *hot-tempered man must pay the penalty*; if you rescue him, you will have to do it again. (Prov. 19:19)

For I am afraid that when I come I may not find you as I want you to be, and you may not find me as you want me to be. I fear that there may be quarreling, jealousy, *outbursts of anger*, factions, slander, gossip, arrogance and disorder. (2 Cor. 12:20)

"In your anger do not sin": Do not let the sun go down *while you are still angry*. (Eph. 4:26)

b. Quitting

Whereas the impatient child flies into fits of rage to have his own will satisfied, he also permits even the slightest of obstacles to deter him from his goal in God. Again, he lacks vision, faith in God's provision, and would rather be doing something else anyway. So any excuse will do to stop him from doing God's will. The New Testament Greek word *hupostello*, translated "shrink back," can, according to one lexicon, illustrate "lowering a sail and so slackening the course, and hence of being remiss in holding the truth." The quitter literally lets the wind—which is, of course, the Spirit—out of his sails, and so he sits stagnantly in the dark doldrums of his own faithlessness.

But *Jonah ran away from Yahweh* and headed for Tarshish. He went down to Joppa, where he found a ship bound for that port. After paying the fare, he went aboard and sailed for Tarshish to flee from Yahweh. (Jon. 1:3)

But my righteous one will live by faith. And if he *shrinks back*, I will not be pleased with him. (Heb. 10:38)

Jesus replied, *"No one who puts his hand to the plow and looks back is fit for service in the kingdom of God."* (Luke 9:62)

"You have said harsh things against Me," says Yahweh.
  "Yet you ask, 'What have we said against You?'"
  "You have said, 'It is futile to serve God. What did we gain by carrying out His requirements and going about like mourners before Yahweh Almighty?'" (Mal. 3:13-14)

c. Frustration

The child feels frustrated when, sensing that his sacrifice is unacceptable to the Lord, he refuses to repent and then offer an acceptable sacrifice. Instead, he insists upon presenting the same unacceptable and faithless offering so often that it begins to mark his character and even personality. In his heart he contends that what he has given is good enough and that further efforts required to do the job right are just too great a price to pay.

But Abel brought fat portions from some of the firstborn of his flock. Yahweh looked with favor on Abel and his offering, but on Cain and his offering He did not look with favor. So *Cain was very angry, and his face was downcast.*

Then Yahweh said to Cain, "Why are you angry? Why is your face downcast? If you do what is right, will you not be accepted? But if you do not do what is right, sin is crouching at your door; it desires to have you, but you must master it." (Gen. 4:4-7)

Refrain from anger and turn from wrath; do not fret—it leads only to evil. (Ps. 37:8)

Yahweh watches over the alien and sustains the fatherless and the widow, but *He frustrates the ways of the wicked.* (Ps. 146:9)

As man comes, so he departs, and what does he gain, since he toils for the wind? All his days he eats in darkness, *with great frustration, affliction and anger.* (Eccles. 5:16-17)

But *Jonah was greatly displeased and became angry.* He prayed to Yahweh, "O Yahweh, is this not what I said when I was still at home? That is why I was so quick to flee to Tarshish. I knew that You are a gracious and compassionate God, slow to anger and abounding in love, a God who relents from sending calamity. Now, O Yahweh, take away my life, for it is better for me to die than to live." (Jon. 4:1-3)

K. Sobriety/Foolishness

1. Sobriety

Sobriety is our English word for the Greek New Testament word *sophrosune*, meaning literally "soundness of mind." This word also denotes self-control, self-mastery—specifically self-control over the passions, wants and desires. One lexicon speaks of it as a "habitual inner self-government, with its constant rein on all . . . passions." Arndt and Gingrich speak of it as both "reasonableness" and "good judgment, moderation" and "self-control." To be sober in this sense means to walk in recognition of God's reality. It is to live under the control of the Spirit. When we walk humbly before God, we see, feel and walk in this place of sobriety, of reality. We are not drunk on the delusions of the world. James explains that a perfect man, one under the Spirit's control, will have a controlled tongue. Sobriety, recognition of God's reality, will bring dominion over our most unruly member, the tongue. Our words will be fitting and appropriate. Because we aren't drunk on the world's delusions, we don't speak as drunkards but soberly, holding our tongues unless we truly have something worthwhile to say.

a. Holding the Tongue

Guard your steps when you go to the house of God. Go near to listen rather than to offer the sacrifice of fools, who do not know that they do wrong.

 Do not be quick with your mouth, do not be hasty in your heart to utter anything before God. God is in heaven and you are on earth, so let your words be few. As a dream comes when there are many cares, so the speech of a fool when there are many words. (Eccles. 5:1-3)

It is good for a man to bear the yoke while he is young. Let him sit alone *in silence,* for Yahweh has laid it on him. (Lam. 3:27-28)

We all stumble in many ways. *If anyone is never at fault in what he says, he is a perfect man, able to keep his whole body in check.* (James 3:2)

My lips will not speak wickedness, and *my tongue will utter no deceit.* (Job 27:4)

Keep your tongue from evil and *your lips from speaking lies.* (Ps. 34:13)

The mouth of the righteous man utters wisdom, and his tongue speaks what is just. (Ps. 37:30)

Set a guard over my mouth, O Yahweh; keep watch over the door of my lips. (Ps. 141:3)

Wisdom is found on the lips of the discerning, but a rod is for the back of him who lacks judgment . . . . *When words are many, sin is not absent, but he who holds his tongue is wise* . . . . *The lips of the righteous nourish many,* but fools die for lack of judgment . . . . *The mouth of the righteous brings forth wisdom,* but a perverse tongue will be cut out. *The lips of the righteous know what is fitting,* but the mouth of the wicked only what is perverse. (Prov. 10:13, 19, 21, 31-32)

From the fruit of his lips a man is filled with good things as surely as the work of his hands rewards him . . . . *Reckless words pierce like a sword, but the tongue of the wise brings healing.* (Prov. 12:14, 18)

He who guards his lips guards his soul, but *he who speaks rashly will come to ruin.* (Prov. 13:3)

The tongue of the wise commends knowledge, but the mouth of the fool gushes folly . . . . *The tongue that brings healing is a tree of life, but a deceitful tongue crushes the spirit* . . . . *The lips of the wise spread knowledge;* not so the hearts of fools . . . . *A man finds joy in giving an apt reply—and how good is a timely word!* (Prov. 15:2, 4, 7, 23)

A wise man's heart guides his mouth, and his lips promote instruction. (Prov. 16:23)

A man of knowledge uses words with restraint, and a man of understanding is even-tempered. Even a fool is thought wise if he keeps silent, and discerning if he holds his tongue. (Prov. 17:27-28)

The words of a man's mouth are deep waters, but the fountain of wisdom is a bubbling brook. (Prov. 18:4)

He who guards his mouth and his tongue keeps himself from calamity. (Prov. 21:23)

Therefore this is what Yahweh says:
  "If you repent, I will restore you that you may serve Me; *if you utter worthy, not worthless, words, you will be My spokesman.* Let this people turn to you, but you must not turn to them." (Jer. 15:19)

A word aptly spoken is like apples of gold in settings of silver . . . . Through patience a ruler can be persuaded, and a gentle tongue can break a bone. (Prov. 25:11, 15)

She speaks with wisdom, and faithful instruction is on her tongue. (Prov. 31:26)

My heart is stirred by a noble theme as I *recite my verses for the king; my tongue is the pen of a skillful writer.* (Ps. 45:1)

. . . a time to tear and a time to mend, *a time to be silent and a time to speak* . . . . (Eccles. 3:7)

Words from a wise man's mouth are gracious, but a fool is consumed by his own lips. (Eccles. 10:12)

The remnant of Israel will do no wrong; *they will speak no lies, nor will deceit be found in their mouths.* They will eat and lie down and no one will make them afraid. (Zeph. 3:13)

Make a tree good and its fruit will be good, or make a tree bad and its fruit will be bad, for a tree is recognized by its fruit. You brood of vipers, how can you who are evil say anything good? *For out of the overflow of the heart the mouth speaks.* The good man brings good things out of the good stored up in him, and the evil man brings evil things out of the evil stored up in him. But I tell you that *men will have to give account on the day of judgment for every careless word they have spoken.* For by your words you will be acquitted, and by your words you will be condemned. (Matt. 12:33-37)

Do not let any unwholesome talk come out of your mouths, but only what is helpful for building others up according to their needs, that it may benefit those who listen. (Eph. 4:29)

Let your conversation be always full of grace, seasoned with salt, so that you may know how to answer everyone. (Col. 4:6)

My dear brothers, take note of this: Everyone should be quick to listen, *slow to speak* and slow to become angry . . . . If anyone considers himself religious and yet does not keep a tight rein on his tongue, he deceives himself and his religion is worthless. (James 1:19, 26)

The mouth of the righteous is a fountain of life, but *violence overwhelms the mouth of the wicked.* (Prov. 10:11)

The tongue of the righteous is choice silver, but the heart of the wicked is of little value. (Prov. 10:20)

A man who lacks judgment derides his neighbor, *but a man of understanding holds his tongue.* (Prov. 11:12)

A gentle answer turns away wrath, but a *harsh word stirs up anger.* (Prov. 15:1)

Pleasant words are a honeycomb, sweet to the soul and healing to the bones. (Prov. 16:24)

From the fruit of his mouth a man's stomach is filled; with the harvest from his lips he is satisfied. *The tongue has the power of life and death,* and those who love it will eat its fruit. (Prov. 18:20-21)

Likewise *the tongue is a small part of the body, but it makes great boasts.* Consider what a great forest is set on fire by a small spark. *The tongue also is a fire, a world of evil among the parts of the body. It corrupts the whole person, sets the whole course of his life on fire, and is itself set on fire by hell.* (James 3:5-6)

Do you see *a man who speaks in haste?* There is more hope for a fool than for him. (Prov. 29:20)

The same Spirit that enables us to control our tongues also enables us to control our attitudes and actions.

> Even a child is known by his actions, by whether his conduct is pure and right. (Prov. 20:11)

By God's grace we can be calm, deliberate and careful.

b. Calm

Calmness comes from self-control—over our tongue and therefore over our whole being (James 3:2). The root of the Greek word used in the New Testament for "calmness" is *galene*, which literally means "tranquility." Calmness goes beyond the absence of anxiety or fretfulness or not getting upset by adverse circumstances. Calmness expresses a positive state of being, the fruit of self-control, which is itself a fruit of the Spirit. The lexicon says the Greek word for "smiling" derives from this word and that this word brought to mind "the calm of the sea, the smiling ocean being a favourite metaphor of the poets." Arndt and Gingrich similarly define *galene* as "a calm on the lake." So calmness outwardly manifests a deep inner peace and tranquility that come from bringing our inner thoughts, feelings and attitudes, as well as our outward expression of these, under the control of God's Spirit. The calmness of a great body of water is a powerful, overawing force; storms, winds, earthquakes and so on rock and shatter the ocean's peace, but ultimately the calm prevails, absorbing the turmoil into itself. This is the calmness God would bring to His people; it ultimately prevails against all obstacles and opposition, no matter how great the storms it must confront may be.

> Better a *patient man* than a warrior, a man who *controls his temper* than one who takes a city. (Prov. 16:32)

> A man of knowledge *uses words with restraint*, and a man of understanding is *even-tempered*. (Prov. 17:27)

> If a ruler's anger rises against you, do not leave your post; *calmness can lay great errors to rest*. (Eccles. 10:4)

> You will keep in perfect peace him whose mind is steadfast, because he trusts in You. (Isa. 26:3)

> But you will have a son who will be *a man of peace and rest*, and I *will give him rest* from all his enemies on every side. His name will be Solomon, and *I will grant Israel peace and quiet during his reign*. He is the one who will build a house for My Name. He will be My son, and I will be his Father. And I will establish the throne of his kingdom over Israel forever. (1 Chron. 22:9-10)

> All your sons will be taught by Yahweh, and great will be your children's *peace*. (Isa. 54:13)

c. Deliberateness

Our English word *deliberate* comes from the Latin *deliberare*. It means "to weigh well." The second element of this word derives from the word *libra*, meaning "a balance" or "a pair of scales." Thus *deliberate* means to accurately weigh a course or a deed or a judgment in the balanced reasoning of God before we proceed with it. The Hebrew word in the Old Testament that is translated "plan" is *charash*. One source tells us that it literally means "to engrave, to plow." It stands opposed to a rash and careless leaping into words or deeds. Sometimes we must reach decisions quickly, but even then, as always, the Spirit must control us. We can only fully weigh the proper course of action in the balance of God's truth through the guidance of His Spirit. Noah, Moses and Solomon all received God's direction on exactly how to do what God had commanded (Gen. 6:14-16; Exod. 25:9; 1 Kings 6:11-13). They had to first respond and then deliberate in order to carry out and finish the work. Such deliberateness proceeds only in full possession of all faculties, aware of the extent and limits of our resources, of the challenges of the circumstances and of all else germane to the situation at hand. In God, deliberateness may cause us to proceed against impossible conditions that demand God's miraculous intervention, but then we can recognize more clearly the greatness of God in our midst. David's challenge of Goliath was made in full awareness of the magnitude of the task before him. So he could nonetheless charge forward to the battle line with deliberateness, glorifying the God who would grant him victory because he was sure of God's presence in his deed. Jesus admonished us to count the cost before proceeding in any serious action (Luke 14:28), but He also reminded us that while with man the task may be impossible, with God, all that falls within the approval of His will is possible (Matt. 19:26; Luke 18:26-27).

> Do not those who plot evil go astray? *But those who plan what is good* find love and faithfulness. (Prov. 14:22)

> The heart of the righteous *weighs its answers*, but the mouth of the wicked gushes evil. (Prov. 15:28)

> *Make plans by seeking advice; if you wage war, obtain guidance.*
>   A gossip betrays a confidence; so avoid a man who talks too much. (Prov. 20:18-19)

> Suppose one of you wants to build a tower. Will he not *first sit down and estimate the cost to see if he has enough money to complete it*? For if he lays the foundation and is not able to finish it, everyone who sees it will ridicule him, saying, "This fellow began to build and was not able to finish." (Luke 14:28-30)

d. Carefulness

The Old Testament word translated "careful" is *shamar*, which literally means "to hedge around something" and "to watch (as a watchman of cattle or sheep)." So it also carries the connotation of "protecting." This word is first used in Genesis 2:15, where it denotes the care that man was to take in tending the Garden of Eden. Carefulness obviously will mark those who tend or care for something. So carefulness calls for alertness, sobermindedness, as well as an ability to make a full and accurate assessment of what needs to be done and how to do it. Only the Spirit can give us the grace to recognize the full extent of the needs we must responsibly meet and then show us exactly how and when to effectively meet them. The root of the New Testament Greek word for "careful" is a word we've already met in our study of courtesy, *phrao*, which means "to rein in or curb." Carefulness, then, denotes self-control in our own lives as well as dominion in the Spirit over that for which we are responsible.

> Do you not know that in a race all the runners run, but only one gets the prize? *Run in such a way as to get the prize. Everyone who competes in the games goes into strict training. They do it to get a crown that will not last; but we do it to get a crown that will last forever.* Therefore I do not run like a man running aimlessly; I do not fight like a man beating the air. (1 Cor. 9:24-26)
>
> *The wisdom of the prudent is to give thought to their ways,* but the folly of fools is deception. (Prov. 14:8)
>
> A simple man believes anything, but *a prudent man gives thought to his steps.* (Prov. 14:15)
>
> Now Yahweh, God of Israel, keep for Your servant David my father the promises You made to him when You said, "You shall never fail to have a man to sit before Me on the throne of Israel, if only your sons are *careful in all they do to walk before Me* as you have done." (1 Kings 8:25)
>
> *Be very careful, then, how you live*—not as unwise but as wise. (Eph. 5:15)
>
> Do not repay anyone evil for evil. *Be careful to do what is right* in the eyes of everybody. (Rom. 12:17)
>
> Be sure you know the condition of your flocks, *give careful attention to your herds.* (Prov. 27:23)

2. Foolishness

Foolishness suggests a lack of dominion over one's tongue, the consequences of which affect the whole man. The Bible describes the tongue as the most difficult member to control (James 3:7-8). One source states that the Greek word for "foolishness," *anoetos*, denotes "one who does not govern his lusts" and stands "in contrast with *sophron*, sober-minded, self-controlled." Hort states that the Greek word *aphron*, also translated "foolish," means "a reckless and inconsiderate habit of mind." Thus foolishness marks a lack of self-control, an inability to govern one's self, which must be most obviously manifested in an inability to control that member most difficult to gain dominion over. If not brought under dominion, the tongue inevitably gives vent to foolishness. Speaking too much, interrupting, silliness, wildness, fleshly boldness, loquaciousness and unmannerliness—all mean an inability to respond to or honor God or parents, all of which in turn mark the "fool."

> Now when the people saw that Moses delayed coming down from the mountain, the people gathered together to Aaron, and said to him, "Come, make us gods that shall go before us; for as for this Moses, the man who brought us up out of the land of Egypt, we do not know what has become of him." . . .
> And he received the gold from their hand, and he fashioned it with an engraving tool, and made a molded calf. Then they said, "This is your god, O Israel, that brought you out of the land of Egypt!"
> So when Aaron saw it, he built an altar before it. And Aaron made a proclamation and said, "Tomorrow is a feast to Yahweh."
> Then they rose early on the next day, offered burnt offerings, and brought peace offerings; and the people sat down to eat and drink, and *rose up to play*. (Exod. 32:1, 4-6)

a. Speaking Too Much

The child who speaks too much does so because he esteems himself too highly. He values his own words above the words of wisdom God would speak to him through his parents and others. He has too little or no respect for others—literally, he does not "look at" them "again": he does not discern and value their true importance for him because he is too filled with his own self-importance. So his foolishness, as seen, manifests itself in a lack of self-control. His words "gush" out. Proverbs 15:2 says that "the mouth of the fool gushes folly." And according to Brown, Driver and Briggs, in Proverbs 15:28, the words of the wicked figuratively "burst out with reckless utterance." In his foolish pride the child believes himself wiser than his parents, so he sees no point in having a hearing ear and being silent and receiving their instruction.

> If *only you would be altogether silent! For you, that would be wisdom.* (Job 13:5)

> The tongue of the wise commends knowledge, *but the mouth of the fool gushes folly.* (Prov. 15:2)

> As a dream comes when there are many cares, so *the speech of a fool when there are many words.* (Eccles. 5:3)

> Words from a wise man's mouth are gracious, but *a fool is consumed by his own lips.* At the beginning his words are folly; at the end they are wicked madness—and the fool multiplies words. No one knows what is coming—who can tell him what will happen after him? (Eccles. 10:12-14)

> *When words are many, sin is not absent*, but he who holds his tongue is wise. (Prov. 10:19)

> If you have been trapped by what you said, *ensnared by the words of your mouth*, then do this, my son, to free yourself, since you have fallen into your neighbor's hands: Go and humble yourself; press your plea with your neighbor! (Prov. 6:2-3)

> *A fool's talk brings a rod to his back*, but the lips of the wise protect them. (Prov. 14:3)

> Stay away from a foolish man, for *you will not find knowledge on his lips.* (Prov. 14:7)

> *A fool's lips bring him strife*, and his mouth invites a beating. *A fool's mouth is his undoing*, and his lips are a snare to his soul. (Prov. 18:6-7)

> *He who answers before listening—that is his folly and his shame.* (Prov. 18:13)

> A gossip betrays a confidence; so *avoid a man who talks too much.* (Prov. 20:19)

> Better a poor man whose walk is blameless than a *fool whose lips are perverse.* (Prov. 19:1)

> Every word of God is flawless; He is a shield to those who take refuge in Him. *Do not add to His words, or He will rebuke you and prove you a liar.* (Prov. 30:5-6)

> You brood of vipers, how can you who are evil say anything good? For out of the overflow of the heart the mouth speaks. The good man brings good things out of the good stored up in him, and the evil man brings evil things out of the evil stored up in him. *But I tell you that men will have to give account on the day of judgment for every careless word they have spoken.* For by your words you will be acquitted, and by your words you will be condemned. (Matt. 12:34-37)

b. Interrupting

A child who interrupts disdains the words of others. He cuts them off before they can be completed because he holds them in contempt, at least when compared to his view of the importance of his own words. His speech cannot be seasonable or appropriate because he does not have a hearing ear to receive wisdom—he does not perceive his parents' place "in the Lord," so their words are to him merely a nuisance—a hindrance and an obstacle to his being heard.

> *He who answers before listening—that is his folly and his shame.*
> (Prov. 18:13)

> "But I have had God's help to this very day, and so I stand here and testify to small and great alike. I am saying nothing beyond what the prophets and Moses said would happen—that the Christ would suffer and, as the first to rise from the dead, would proclaim light to His own people and to the Gentiles."
> At this point Festus *interrupted* Paul's defense. "You are out of your mind, Paul!" he shouted. "Your great learning is driving you insane." (Acts 26:22-24)

c. Silliness

The literal meaning of the Hebrew word *ivvelet*, which is translated "folly," is "silliness." As shown in the scriptures below, to be "silly" is a very serious matter. But we should distinguish between legitimate joy or mirth on the one hand and the silliness that the Bible condemns on the other. Silliness manifests itself in an undisciplined, unthoughtful manner and is rooted in foolishness. The Greek word *morologia*, which is translated "foolish talk" in Ephesians 5:4, literally means "the talk of a moron," one who is completely insensitive to God. Legitimate fun stays within the bounds of the Spirit. The Bible says a "cheerful heart" is like "medicine" (Prov. 17:22), bringing enjoyment and re-creation to our lives. It strengthens us so that we can fulfill God's purpose. Foolishness throws us out of the bounds of the Spirit and destroys God's purpose.

> Wise men store up knowledge, but *the mouth of a fool invites ruin.*
> (Prov. 10:14)

> *The woman Folly is loud; she is undisciplined and without knowledge.*
> She sits at the door of her house, on a seat at the highest point of the city, calling out to those who pass by, who go straight on their way. "Let all who are simple come in here!" she says to those who lack judgment. "Stolen water is sweet; food eaten in secret is delicious!" But little do they know that the dead are there, that her guests are in the depths of the grave. (Prov. 9:13-18)

> Every prudent man acts out of knowledge, but *a fool exposes his folly.* (Prov. 13:16)

> The wisdom of the prudent is to give thought to their ways, *but the folly of fools is deception.* (Prov. 14:8)

> The wealth of the wise is their crown, but *the folly of fools yields folly.* (Prov. 14:24)

> The discerning heart seeks knowledge, but *the mouth of a fool feeds on folly.* (Prov. 15:14)

> *Folly delights a man who lacks judgment,* but a man of understanding keeps a straight course. (Prov. 15:21)

> Understanding is a fountain of life to those who have it, *but folly brings punishment to fools.* (Prov. 16:22)

> *A man's own folly ruins his life,* yet his heart rages against Yahweh. (Prov. 19:3)

> *Folly is bound up in the heart of a child,* but the rod of discipline will drive it far from him. (Prov. 22:15)

> *The schemes of folly are sin,* and men detest a mocker. (Prov. 24:9)

> Though you grind a fool in a mortar, grinding him like grain with a pestle, *you will not remove his folly from him.* (Prov. 27:22)

d. Wildness

The Hebrew word *pereh,* translated "wild," can carry the sense of "*running* wild." It refers to a "wild donkey," not one that is domesticated to serve. This is how the Bible applies the term to Ishmael. Brown, Driver and Briggs say that Ishmael was called "a wild donkey of a man" because he was a "free nomad." But though his father Abraham was also a "free nomad," Abraham walked in obedience to the Spirit. Ishmael used the life of the nomad as an opportunity to serve the flesh. He followed his own desires wherever they would lead him and remained unsubmitted to the Spirit. Since he walked without submitting to anything outside of himself, since he refused to be yoked or harnessed to serve, Ishmael was likened to a wild donkey. He "ran" helter-skelter and uncontrolled through the purposes of God, like the proverbial bull in a china shop.

> Like a city whose walls are broken down is a *man who lacks self-control.* (Prov. 25:28)

> The angel of Yahweh also said to her:
> "You are now with child and you will have a son. You shall name him Ishmael, for Yahweh has heard of your misery.
> "He will be *a wild donkey of a man*; his hand will be against everyone and everyone's hand against him, and he will live in hostility toward all his brothers." (Gen. 16:11-12)

> Moses saw that the people were *running wild* and that Aaron had let them get out of control and so become a laughingstock to

their enemies. So he stood at the entrance to the camp and said, "Whoever is for Yahweh, come to me." And all the Levites rallied to him.

Then he said to them, "This is what Yahweh, the God of Israel, says: 'Each man strap a sword to his side. Go back and forth through the camp from one end to the other, each killing his brother and friend and neighbor.'" The Levites did as Moses commanded, and that day about three thousand of the people died. (Exod. 32:25-28)

He must be one who manages his own household well, keeping his *children under control* with all dignity. (1 Tim. 3:4, NASV)

A deacon must be the husband of but one wife and must *manage his children and his household well.* (1 Tim. 3:12)

e. Boldness in the Flesh

Boldness in the flesh comes from a false confidence in the child's own abilities and powers. He isn't broken to God's will, walking in humble faith. Rather, he boldly asserts himself without fear of God, without love or wisdom.

A wicked man puts up *a bold front*, but an upright man gives thought to his ways. (Prov. 21:29)

This is especially true of those who follow the corrupt desire of the sinful nature and despise authority. *Bold and arrogant*, these men are not afraid to slander celestial beings. (2 Pet. 2:10)

They have *lied about Yahweh;* they said, "He will do nothing! No harm will come to us; we will never see sword or famine. The prophets are but wind and the word is not in them; so let what they say be done to them." (Jer. 5:12-13)

Cush was the father of Nimrod, who grew to be a mighty warrior on the earth. He was a mighty hunter before Yahweh; that is why it is said, "Like Nimrod, a *mighty hunter before Yahweh*." The first centers of his kingdom were Babylon, Erech, Akkad and Calneh, in Shinar. From that land he went to Assyria, where he built Nineveh, Rehoboth Ir, Calah and Resen, which is between Nineveh and Calah; that is the great city. (Gen. 10:8-12)

Korah son of Izhar, the son of Kohath, the son of Levi, and certain Reubenites—Dathan and Abiram, sons of Eliab, and On son of Peleth—*became insolent and rose up against Moses.* With them were 250 Israelite men, well-known community leaders who had been appointed members of the council. They came as a group to *oppose Moses and Aaron and* said to them, "You have gone too far! The whole community is holy, every one of them, and Yahweh is with them. Why then do you set yourselves above Yahweh's assembly?" (Num. 16:1-3)

Then the *prophet Hananiah took the yoke off the neck of the prophet Jeremiah and broke it* . . . .

> Then the prophet Jeremiah said to Hananiah the prophet, "Listen, Hananiah! *Yahweh has not sent you, yet you have persuaded this nation to trust in lies.* Therefore, this is what Yahweh says: 'I am about to remove you from the face of the earth. This very year you are going to die, because *you have preached rebellion against Yahweh.*'"
>
> In the seventh month of that same year, Hananiah the prophet died. (Jer. 28:10, 15-17)

Of course, boldness in the Spirit is good and commended in the Word of God: this boldness rests on brokenness of the will of the flesh as well as trust and faith in God.

> Now when they saw the *boldness* of Peter and John, and perceived that they were uneducated and untrained men, they marveled. And they realized that they had been with Jesus. (Acts 4:13)

> "Now, Lord, look on their threats, and grant to Your servants that with *all boldness* they may speak Your word, by stretching out Your hand to heal, and that signs and wonders may be done through the name of Your holy Servant Jesus."
>
> And when they had prayed, the place where they were assembled together was shaken; and they were all filled with the Holy Spirit, and they spoke the word of God with boldness. (Acts 4:29-31)

> . . . in whom we have *boldness* and access with confidence through faith in Him. (Eph. 3:12)

> . . . according to my earnest expectation and hope that in nothing I shall be ashamed, but that with *all boldness*, as always, so now also Christ will be magnified in my body, whether by life or by death. (Phil. 1:20)

> For those who have served well as deacons obtain for themselves a good standing and great *boldness* in the faith which is in Christ Jesus. (1 Tim. 3:13)

> Therefore, brethren, having *boldness* to enter the Holiest by the blood of Jesus . . . . (Heb. 10:19)

> Let us therefore come *boldly* unto the throne of grace, that we may obtain mercy, and find grace to help in time of need. (Heb. 4:16, KJV)

> Love has been perfected among us in this: that we may have *boldness* in the day of judgment; because as He is, so are we in this world. (1 John 4:17)

L. Victory and Joy/
Sulking and Pouting

1. Victory and Joy

People walk in victory when they walk in faith: "This is the victory that has overcome the world, even our faith" (1 John 5:4). Faith carries us into the joy of the Lord, which in turn enables us to triumph over every circumstance. Moreover, "the joy of Yahweh is our strength" (Neh. 8:10). Through faith we manifest all the positive characteristics discussed in this book, and when we walk in this all-encompassing faith, victory and joy permeate our lives. The Greek word *nike*, translated "victory" in the New Testament, can also be translated "conquest." It suggests overcoming in a battle: through faith in Christ we are made overcomers. God's grace to complete His purpose works upon us through the effort to walk in that grace to perfect our character so we can "fight the fight of faith." Then we can hope to say with Paul, "I have fought the good fight, I have finished the race, I have kept the faith" (2 Tim. 4:7). Joy comes by pressing on to victory. Full victory, meaning "conquest," comes only with completion. Only when the enemy is completely subdued and dominion over the land is total do we enjoy full victory, and that complete victory will give us complete joy. The fruit of the Spirit grows in our hearts as we, through the Spirit, gain victory over the flesh, the devil and the world. When we sense the approach of total completion, then the sense of triumph and joy also grows in our hearts. In fact, one of the Hebrew words translated "joy" is the word *teruah*, literally meaning "a battle cry." Another Hebrew word for "joy" in the Old Testament, *rua*, means "triumph." Our joy will grow in this world as we move resolutely forward in God's purpose for our lives; the ultimate cry of victory and joy will resound in our hearts when we see our last enemy, death, lying at our feet.

> But thanks be to God! He gives us the *victory* through our Lord Jesus Christ. (1 Cor. 15:57)

> For everyone born of God overcomes the world. *This is the victory that has overcome the world, even our faith.* (1 John 5:4)

> He holds *victory* in store for the upright, He is a shield to those whose walk is blameless, for He guards the course of the just and protects the way of His faithful ones. (Prov. 2:7-8)

> The *prospect of the righteous is joy*, but the hopes of the wicked come to nothing. (Prov. 10:28)

But thanks be to God, *who always leads us in triumphal procession in Christ* and through us spreads everywhere the fragrance of the knowledge of Him. (2 Cor. 2:14)

. . . being *strengthened with all power according to His glorious might* so that you may have great endurance and patience, and *joyfully giving thanks to the Father*, who has qualified you to share in the inheritance of the saints in the kingdom of light. (Col. 1:11-12)

Nehemiah said, "Go and enjoy choice food and sweet drinks, and send some to those who have nothing prepared. This day is sacred to our Lord. Do not grieve, *for the joy of Yahweh is your strength*." (Neh. 8:10)

In this you *greatly rejoice*, though now for a little while you may have had to suffer grief in all kinds of trials. These have come so that your faith—of greater worth than gold, which perishes even though refined by fire—may be proved genuine and may result in praise, glory and honor when Jesus Christ is revealed. Though you have not seen Him, you love Him; and even though you do not see Him now, you believe in Him and are filled with an *inexpressible and glorious joy*, for you are receiving the goal of your faith, the salvation of your souls. (1 Pet. 1:6-9)

a. Brightness

Our countenance is bright because we experience the joy of Yahweh. Another Hebrew word in the Old Testament that is translated "joy" is *samach*, which literally means "brighten up." The Old Testament word for "cheerful," *yatab*, means literally "to be good, to be well, to be beautiful, to be pleasant, to be lovely, to be glad." The joy that comes from victory will be visible on our faces as we open more to the Lord in transparency in all of our relationships.

A happy heart makes the *face cheerful*. (Prov. 15:13)

All who were sitting in the Sanhedrin looked intently at Stephen, and they saw that *his face was like the face of an angel*. (Acts 6:15)

A *cheerful look* brings joy to the heart, and good news gives health to the bones. (Prov. 15:30)

Who is like the wise man? Who knows the explanation of things? *Wisdom brightens a man's face and changes its hard appearance.* (Eccles. 8:1)

b. Eagerness

When we are filled with faith and victory, we become eager to do God's work. We see God's vision, and we feel impelled to work to realize it. "Eagerness" is one translation of the Greek word *zelos*, which derives from *zeo.* This literally means "to be hot" or "boil." Like the disciples on the road to Emmaus, our hearts "burn within us" as God opens His Word to us. We are exhorted by God's Word to "fan into flame" the gifts that lie within us. The words "fan into flame" come from the Greek word *anazopurein*, which Rienecker literally translates as "to stir up smoldering embers into a living flame, to keep at white heat." The word means both to "kindle afresh" and "to keep a full flame." When our hearts blaze with the love and vision of God, we can't suppress our "eagerness" to do God's will.

> I know your deeds, that *you are neither cold nor hot. I wish you were either one or the other!* So, because *you are lukewarm—neither hot nor cold*—I am about to spit you out of My mouth. (Rev. 3:15-16)

> That is why I am so *eager* to preach the gospel also to you who are at Rome. (Rom. 1:15)

> And here is my advice about what is best for you in this matter: Last year you were the first not only to give but also to have the desire to do so. Now finish the work, so that your *eager willingness* to do it may be matched by your completion of it, according to your means. (2 Cor. 8:10-11)

> . . . who gave Himself for us to redeem us from all wickedness and to purify for Himself a people that are His very own, *eager to do what is good.* (Titus 2:14)

> Who is going to harm you if you are *eager to do good*? (1 Pet. 3:13)

c. Courage

The English word *courage* derives from the Latin word *cor*, meaning "heart." So to have courage literally means to have "heart." Godly courage is not merely something in our minds but something that comes from our hearts, from our relationship with God, something from God that fires our emotions. Peter said he would lay down his life for Jesus, but when the time came, he lacked the courage, or the heart, to do so because he lacked the necessary depth of relationship with God. So in his fear he resorted to violence. Later, in the book of Acts, Peter stood courageously in the face of persecution because he had gone on to enter into a much deeper relationship with God through the Spirit (Acts 4:13).

The New Testament Greek word translated "courage" is *parrhesia*, which, according to Rienecker, means "the courage appropriate to the free man, which acts openly even in a hostile atmosphere." Through his deep relationship with God, Peter now found the "freedom" to stand "openly" for Jesus. The book of Daniel describes those who "know their God" as "strong" (Dan. 11:32). The word "strong" is *chazaq*, the same Hebrew word often translated "courage." To "know" God means to enter into an intimate relationship of purest love with and for Him. In this relationship, love "casts out fear" (1 John 4:18). The Hebrew word translated "courage" literally means "to fasten upon," "to seize," "to conquer" and "to be strong." Joshua and Caleb had the courage to conquer Canaan because, through their relationship with God, they could overcome fear of the giants in Canaan. God referred to Caleb as "My servant" who "follows Me wholeheartedly." Because he followed "wholeheartedly," Caleb trusted the Lord with all his heart. When we have that kind of relationship with God through His Spirit, we can literally "fasten upon" and "seize" the victory over fear and all else.

> When they saw the *courage* of Peter and John and realized that they were unschooled, ordinary men, they were astonished and they took note that these men had been with Jesus. (Acts 4:13)

> But Christ is faithful as a son over God's house. And we are His house, if we *hold on to our courage* and the hope of which we boast. (Heb. 3:6)

> Be on your guard; stand firm in the faith; *be men of courage*; be strong. (1 Cor. 16:13)

> I have told you these things, so that in Me you may have peace. In this world you will have trouble. *But take heart!* I have overcome the world. (John 16:33)

> Joshua son of Nun and Caleb son of Jephunneh, who were among those who had explored the land, tore their clothes and said to the entire Israelite assembly, "The land we passed through and explored is exceedingly good. If Yahweh is pleased with us, He will lead us into that land, a land flowing with milk and honey, and will give it to us. Only do not rebel against Yahweh. And *do not be afraid* of the people of the land, because we will swallow them up. Their protection is gone, but Yahweh is with us. *Do not be afraid of them.*" (Num. 14:6-9)

> "*Be strong and courageous.* Do not be afraid or terrified because of them, for Yahweh your God goes with you; He will never leave you nor forsake you."
>   Then Moses summoned Joshua and said to him in the presence of all Israel, "*Be strong and courageous,* for you must go with this people into the land that Yahweh swore to their forefathers to give them, and you must divide it among them as their inheritance." (Deut. 31:6-7)

> Yahweh gave this command to Joshua son of Nun: "*Be strong and courageous,* for you will bring the Israelites into the land I promised them on oath, and I Myself will be with you." (Deut. 31:23)

> "*Be strong and courageous,* because you will lead these people to inherit the land I swore to their forefathers to give them. Be strong and very courageous. Be careful to obey all the law My servant Moses gave you; do not turn from it to the right or to the left, that you may be successful wherever you go . . . . Have I not commanded you? *Be strong and courageous.* Do not be terrified;

do not be discouraged, for Yahweh your God will be with you wherever you go . . . . Only *be strong and courageous!*" (Josh. l:6-7, 9, 18)

With flattery he will corrupt those who have violated the covenant, but the people who know their God will *display strength and take action.* (Dan. 11:32, NIV, NASV)

Then you will have success if you are careful to observe the decrees and laws that Yahweh gave Moses for Israel. *Be strong and courageous. Do not be afraid or discouraged.* (1 Chron. 22:13)

David also said to Solomon his son, "*Be strong and courageous*, and do the work. *Do not be afraid or discouraged*, for Yahweh God, my God, is with you. He will not fail you or forsake you until all the work for the service of the temple of Yahweh is finished." (1 Chron. 28:20)

Be strong and courageous. Do not be afraid or discouraged because of the king of Assyria and the vast army with him, for there is a greater power with us than with him. (2 Chron. 32:7)

But Jesus immediately said to them: "*Take courage! It is I. Don't be afraid.*" (Matt. 14:27)

He saw the disciples straining at the oars, because the wind was against them. About the fourth watch of the night He went out to them, walking on the lake. He was about to pass by them, but when they saw Him walking on the lake, they thought He was a ghost. They cried out, because they all saw Him and were terrified.
  Immediately He spoke to them and said, "*Take courage! It is I. Don't be afraid.*" (Mark 6:48-50)

The following night the Lord stood near Paul and said, "*Take courage!* As you have testified about Me in Jerusalem, so you must also testify in Rome." (Acts 23:11)

But now I urge you to *keep up your courage*, because not one of you will be lost; only the ship will be destroyed. (Acts 27:22)

I eagerly expect and hope that I will in no way be ashamed, but will have sufficient *courage* so that now as always Christ will be exalted in my body, whether by life or by death. (Phil. 1:20)

d. Encouraging Others

We can encourage others in the Lord because we are ourselves encouraged by the victory. The Greek word translated "spur" in Hebrews 10:24 is *paroxusmos*, which means "inciting stimulation." We are to serve as a stimulus for our brothers and sisters to move forward in love and good deeds. The word *encourage* is from the Greek word *parakaleo*, which literally means "to urge one to pursue some course of conduct." It always refers to "looking to the future." Thus we are always encouraging each other to move only *forward*, never to stop or go backward. We are not like Lot's wife who stopped to look back at the country and kingdom she was leaving behind, but like Abraham, who looked ahead for a city whose builder and maker was God (Heb. 11:10). We thus encourage one another toward our heavenly home and a "better" country.

> As iron sharpens iron, so *one man sharpens another.* (Prov. 27:17)

> *And let us consider how we may spur one another on toward love and good deeds.* Let us not give up meeting together, as some are in the habit of doing, but let us encourage one another—and all the more as you see the Day approaching. (Heb. 10:24-25)

> Josiah celebrated the Passover to Yahweh in Jerusalem, and the Passover lamb was slaughtered on the fourteenth day of the first month. He appointed the priests to their duties and encouraged them in the service of Yahweh's temple. (2 Chron. 35:1-2)

> Therefore *encourage each other* with these words. (1 Thess. 4:18)

> *Therefore encourage one another and build each other up,* just as in fact you are doing. (1 Thess. 5:11)

> *But encourage one another daily,* as long as it is called Today, so that none of you may be hardened by sin's deceitfulness. (Heb. 3:13)

> But everyone who prophesies speaks to men for their strengthening, *encouragement* and comfort. (1 Cor. 14:3)

> We have different gifts, according to the grace given us. If a man's gift is prophesying, let him use it in proportion to his faith. If it is serving, let him serve; if it is teaching, let him teach; if it is *encouraging*, let him encourage; if it is contributing to the needs of others, let him give generously; if it is leadership, let him govern diligently; if it is showing mercy, let him do it cheerfully. (Rom. 12:6-8)

> *Speak to one another with psalms, hymns and spiritual songs.* Sing and make music in your heart to the Lord. (Eph. 5:19)

> I long to see you so that I may impart to you some spiritual gift to make you strong—that is, that you and I may be mutually *encouraged* by each other's faith. (Rom. 1:11-12)

> For you know that we dealt with each of you as a father deals with his own children, *encouraging*, comforting and urging you to live lives worthy of God, who calls you into His kingdom and glory. (1 Thess. 2:11-12)

> And we urge you, brothers, warn those who are idle, *encourage* the timid, help the weak, be patient with everyone. (1 Thess. 5:14)

2. Sulking, Pouting and Fearfulness

These negative characteristics result from the total absence of victory and joy. Because we are inturned and sullen, our spiritual vacuum fills with whining and crying, fussing and complaining. The child who sulks and pouts refuses to exercise faith. He listens to his flesh and the devil, and in his heart he judges and condemns others and even God. He blames God and others for his own failures. Like Cain, those who sulk and pout disregard the Word of God that would bring victory, choosing self-pity instead, convincing themselves that God or others have denied them the opportunity for victory that some they envy seem to have. The fear of God doesn't move them forward; but they fall back in cowardice, fearing to come into the light because they have judged God to be a "hard man" (Matt. 25:24). Thus they accept slander about God and His people— they believe a lie (2 Thess. 2:10-12). The sin "crouching at the door," which God clearly warns them against, then gets hold of their hearts, and they end up embittered and willfully blinded to the grace that could be theirs.

a. Sullenness

The word *sullen* is the translation of the Hebrew word *zaaph*, the root meaning of which is "to boil." It means almost "foaming at the mouth" with anger. It is "like a storm brewing within a person until it gives way to rage." It is angry rebellion clothed in self-pity. It is a rejection and hatred of God's wisdom and His way of doing things. The sullen are always frustrated that their plans are not implemented in place of God's because they believe their way is so much wiser than God's.

> So the people *grumbled* against Moses, saying, "What are we to drink?". . .
> Then Moses led Israel from the Red Sea and they went into the Desert of Shur. For three days they traveled in the desert without finding water. When they came to Marah, they could not drink its water because it was bitter. (That is why the place is called Marah.) (Exod. 15:24, 22-23)

> Some time later there was an incident involving a vineyard belonging to Naboth the Jezreelite. The vineyard was in Jezreel, close to the palace of Ahab king of Samaria. Ahab said to Naboth, "Let me have your vineyard to use for a vegetable garden, since it is close to my palace. In exchange I will give you a better vineyard or, if you prefer, I will pay you whatever it is worth."
> But Naboth replied, "Yahweh forbid that I should give you the inheritance of my fathers."
> *So Ahab went home, sullen and angry because Naboth the Jezreelite had said, "I will not give you the inheritance of my fathers." He lay on his bed sulking and refused to eat.*
> His wife Jezebel came in and asked him, "Why are you so sullen? Why won't you eat?"
> He answered her, "Because I said to Naboth the Jezreelite, 'Sell me your vineyard; or if you prefer, I will give you another vineyard in

its place.' But he said, 'I will not give you my vineyard.'" (1 Kings 21:1-6)

And Abel brought of the first-born of his flock and of the fat portions. And Yahweh had respect and regard for Abel and for his offering.

But for Cain and his offering He had no respect or regard. *So Cain was exceedingly angry and indignant, and he looked sad and depressed.*

And Yahweh said to Cain, Why are you angry? And why do you look sad and dejected? If you do well, will you not be accepted? And if you do not do well, sin crouches at your door; its desire is for you, and you must master it. (Gen. 4:4-7, Ampl.)

But Jonah *was greatly displeased and became angry*. He prayed to Yahweh, "O Yahweh, is this not what I said when I was still at home? That is why I was so quick to flee to Tarshish. I knew that You are a gracious and compassionate God, slow to anger and abounding in love, a God who relents from sending calamity. *Now, O Yahweh, take away my life, for it is better for me to die than to live."*

But Yahweh replied, "Have you any right to be angry?"

Jonah went out and sat down at a place east of the city. There he made himself a shelter, sat in its shade and waited to see what would happen to the city. Then Yahweh God provided a vine and made it grow up over Jonah to give shade for his head to ease his discomfort, and Jonah was very happy about the vine. But at dawn the next day God provided a worm, which chewed the vine so that it withered. When the sun rose, God provided a scorching east wind, and the sun blazed on Jonah's head so that he grew faint. He wanted to die, and said, "It would be better for me to die than to live."

But *God said to Jonah, "Do you have a right to be angry about the vine?"*

"I do," he said. *"I am angry enough to die."*

But Yahweh said, "You have been concerned about this vine, though you did not tend it or make it grow. It sprang up overnight and died overnight. But Nineveh has more than a hundred and twenty thousand people who cannot tell their right hand from their left, and many cattle as well. Should I not be concerned about that great city?" (Jon. 4:1-11)

You have said, "It is futile to serve God. What did we gain by carrying out His requirements and *going about like mourners* before Yahweh Almighty?" (Mal. 3:14)

b. Whining, Crying, Fussing, Complaining

Those unhappy in submitting to God's wisdom and desiring nothing more than to have their own way will try any means to obtain their wants. They will persistently attempt to play upon the emotions and natural affections of their parents and others to manipulatively obtain their desires. They make an idol out of their will, putting it above God's will for their lives. Because their lives center in their selfish desires, they find it intolerable that anything should be denied them and so resort to emotional outbursts to place pressure on others through their obnoxious behavior.

They cry tears, never from a burden, but only because their own will has been frustrated. This crying resembles the "worldly sorrow that brings death" (2 Cor. 7:10). It isn't, in other words, the sorrow of repentance or of a burden for others but the sorrow of the flesh when denied its will. It is self-idolatry because it attaches more value to its own desires than to what pleases God. This isn't the crying that Yahweh heard and took pity on when the children of Israel were enslaved in Egypt. Nor is it the tears Jesus wept for Lazarus. The crying we're talking about here elicits no pity from God because He knows that pity only fuels it and so leads to death.

A life centered in self and not in God and His purpose and plan can never constitute an acceptable offering to God. Such a person will always worry and fret that too much will be asked of them or that things may not go according to their own plan. In Luke 10:41, Jesus told Martha she was "worried and upset" about many things. "Worried" is the English translation of the Greek word *merimnao*, which derives from *merimna*—the word translated as "worry" and "anxiety." According to Thayer, *merimna* comes from *merizo*, which means "to be drawn in different directions." Martha "fussed" because she felt pulled apart in her life. This is also the meaning of anxiety. But instead of seeking the oneness in the Spirit that could bring harmony to her life, as Mary did, Martha blamed her circumstances and others for her frustrations. So in the previous verse, Luke mentions that Martha was "getting worried" or "distracted" with all her preparations (Luke 10:40, Wms., NASU). Rienecker tells us that "getting worried" in this case is to be "pulled or dragged away." Thus life becomes frustratingly fragmented and ends up only in more and more fussing and frustration. Our works are centered in ourselves, our own plans, our own schedules, rather than in the timing of the Lord. We become inflexible and unresponsive to the Spirit, upset at anything that changes the course we set for ourselves. Yes, God gives us routines and schedules that we should normally meet, but we shouldn't fret and fuss when God changes a plan, not at least if we're truly motivated by His burden and love; we only fuss if we're moving under our own self-centered burden and direction.

All whining, crying, fussing and sighing in complaint, if not uprooted from children's hearts, will eventually harden their hearts. They will then rebel against the authority of God in their life, complaining that God has not been fair to them.

Strong says that the Hebrew word *telunnah*, translated "grumbling," means "obstinacy." The root of this word is *lun*, which means "to stop" or "to stay." So to grumble and complain literally means to stubbornly refuse to move forward. In the New Testament, the Greek word *gogguzo*, translated "complain," literally means, according to Rienecker, "to murmur, to complain, to give audible expression to unwarranted dissatisfaction. It contains the idea of a judgment and a condemnation of God by man who, instead of giving God thanks and showing obedience, sets himself up as a judge over God." To complain against God is to declare the great lie, that our ways are higher than His.

> Refrain from anger and turn from wrath; *do not fret*—it leads only to evil. (Ps. 37:8)

> Then Samson's wife *threw herself on him, sobbing, "You hate me! You don't really love me.* You've given my people a riddle, but you haven't told me the answer."
>
> "I haven't even explained it to my father or mother," he replied, "so why should I explain it to you?" *She cried the whole seven days of the feast.* So on the seventh day he finally told her, because *she continued to press him.* She in turn explained the riddle to her people. (Judg. 14:16-17)

> Then she said to him, "How can you say, 'I love you,' when your heart is not with me? You have deceived me these three times and have not told me where your great strength is." And it came about when *she pressed him daily with her words and urged him, that his soul was annoyed to death.* (Judg. 16:15-16, NASV)

> As Pharaoh approached, the Israelites looked up, and there were the Egyptians, marching after them. *They were terrified and cried out to Yahweh. They said to Moses, "Was it because there were no graves in Egypt that you brought us to the desert to die? What have you done to us by bringing us out of Egypt? Didn't we say to you in Egypt, 'Leave us alone; let us serve the Egyptians'? It would have been better for us to serve the Egyptians than to die in the desert!"* (Exod. 14:10-12)

> The rabble with them began to crave other food, and again the *Israelites started wailing* and said, "If only we had meat to eat! We remember the fish we ate in Egypt at no cost—also the cucumbers, melons, leeks, onions and garlic. But now we have lost our appetite; we never see anything but this manna!" (Num. 11:4-6)

> But Martha was distracted by all the preparations that had to be made. She came to Him and asked, "Lord, don't you care that my sister has left me to do the work by myself? Tell her to help me!"
>
> "Martha, Martha," the Lord answered, *"you are worried and upset about many things,* but only one thing is needed. Mary has chosen what is better, and it will not be taken away from her." (Luke 10:40-42)

> In the desert the whole community *grumbled against Moses* and Aaron. The Israelites said to them, "If only we had died by Yahweh's hand in Egypt! There we sat around pots of meat and

ate all the food we wanted, but you have brought us out into this desert to starve this entire assembly to death." (Exod. 16:2-3)

Moses also said, "You will know that it was Yahweh when He gives you meat to eat in the evening and all the bread you want in the morning, because He has heard your *grumbling against Him*. Who are we? *You are not grumbling against us, but against Yahweh.*"

Then Moses told Aaron, "Say to the entire Israelite community, 'Come before Yahweh, for *He has heard your grumbling.*'"

While Aaron was speaking to the whole Israelite community, they looked toward the desert, and there was the glory of Yahweh appearing in the cloud.

Yahweh said to Moses, "*I have heard the grumbling of the Israelites.* Tell them, 'At twilight you will eat meat, and in the morning you will be filled with bread. Then you will know that I am Yahweh your God.'" (Exod. 16:8-12)

So *they quarreled with Moses* and said, "Give us water to drink."

Moses replied, "Why do you quarrel with me? Why do you put Yahweh to the test?"

But the people were thirsty for water there, and *they grumbled against Moses*. They said, "Why did you bring us up out of Egypt to make us and our children and livestock die of thirst?"

Then Moses cried out to Yahweh, "What am I to do with these people? They are almost ready to stone me.". . .

And he called the place Massah and Meribah because the Israelites quarreled and because they tested Yahweh saying, "Is Yahweh among us or not?" (Exod. 17:2-4, 7)

Now *the people complained about their hardships* in the hearing of Yahweh, and when He heard them His anger was aroused. Then fire from Yahweh burned among them and consumed some of the outskirts of the camp. (Num. 11:1)

Now there was no water for the community, and *the people gathered in opposition to Moses and Aaron. They quarreled with Moses* and said, "If only we had died when our brothers fell dead before Yahweh! Why did you bring Yahweh's community into this desert, that we and our livestock should die here? Why did you bring us up out of Egypt to this terrible place? It has no grain or figs, grapevines or pomegranates. And there is no water to drink!" (Num. 20:2-5)

But the men who had gone up with him said, "We can't attack those people; they are stronger than we are." (Num. 13:31)

That night all the people of the community raised their voices and wept aloud. *All the Israelites grumbled against Moses and Aaron*, and the whole assembly said to them, "If only we had died in Egypt! Or in this desert! Why is Yahweh bringing us to this land only to let us fall by the sword! Our wives and children will be taken as plunder. Wouldn't it be better for us to go back to Egypt?" And they said to each other, "We should choose a leader and go back to Egypt."

Then Moses and Aaron fell facedown in front of the whole

> Israelite assembly gathered there. Joshua son of Nun and Caleb son of Jephunneh, who were among those who had explored the land, tore their clothes and said to the entire Israelite assembly, "The land we passed through and explored is exceedingly good. If Yahweh is pleased with us, He will lead us into that land, a land flowing with milk and honey, and will give it to us. Only do not rebel against Yahweh. And do not be afraid of the people of the land, because we will swallow them up. Their protection is gone, but Yahweh is with us. Do not be afraid of them."
>
>   But the whole assembly talked about stoning them. Then the glory of Yahweh appeared at the Tent of Meeting to all the Israelites. (Num. 14:1-10)
>
> And do not *grumble*, as some of them did—and were killed by the destroying angel. (1 Cor. 10:10)
>
> *Do everything without complaining or arguing.* (Phil. 2:14)
>
> *Don't grumble against each other, brothers*, or you will be judged. The Judge is standing at the door! (James 5:9)
>
> These are murmurers, *complainers*, walking according to their own lusts; and they mouth great swelling words, flattering people to gain advantage. (Jude 16)

This attitude causes us to view everything from the perspective of self. Nothing can then satisfy us or give us pleasure, especially doing God's will.

c. Fearfulness

The Bible speaks of two kinds of fear. One fear is negative, the other positive. One kind hinders us from doing God's will, and the other helps us do it. Negative fear causes us to "shrink back" from the light (Heb. 10:38). The New Testament Greek word translated here as "shrink back" can also be translated as "to cower" in "timidity." It means we stop moving toward the light and move backward into the darkness. The Israelites who wouldn't move forward into the Promised Land stopped because they were afraid of the giants (Num. 13:31-33, KJV). The man who hid his talent in the earth did so because he, too, was "afraid" (Matt. 25:24-25). Peter stopped walking on the water toward Jesus when he became "afraid" (Matt. 14:29-30). The "fear of man" is a "snare" (Prov. 29:25). This fear destroys the motivation to move forward in God. So it makes us prey to our spiritual enemy; it imprisons us. The book of Hebrews records that the "fear of death" brings us into "bondage" (Heb. 2:15, Ampl.). We're "bound," unable to move forward in the Lord. Ultimately, this fear causes us to forever fail to reach the goal of salvation (Rev. 21:8, KJV).

God doesn't pity any fear that prevents us from walking in His light. Such fearfulness cloaks a rejection of, and a rebellion against, His Word. It stems from a refusal to believe God and receive the grace Jesus died to give us. Someone who cowers in fearfulness chooses to believe the lie that God exercises His authority as a "hard taskmaster." The fearful person refuses to recognize that God gives us grace to fulfill all that He calls and ordains us to do and that He asks us to carry our responsibilities in His purpose for our blessing and to do so with a measure of dignity and courage.

> But the just shall live by faith [that is, My righteous servant shall live by his conviction respecting man's relationship to God and divine things, and holy fervor born of faith and conjoined with it]; *and if he draws back and shrinks in fear, My soul has no delight or pleasure in him.* (Heb. 10:38, Ampl.)

> He answered, "I heard You in the garden, and *I was afraid* because I was naked; *so I hid.*" (Gen. 3:10)

> Announce now to the people, "Anyone who *trembles with fear* may turn back and leave Mount Gilead." So twenty-two thousand men left, while ten thousand remained. (Judg. 7:3)

> But when he saw the wind, *he was afraid* and, beginning to sink, cried out, "Lord, save me!" (Matt. 14:30)

> Then the man who had received the one talent came. "Master," he said, "I knew that you are a hard man, harvesting where you have not sown and gathering where you have not scattered seed. *So I was afraid* and went out and hid your talent in the ground. See, here is what belongs to you." (Matt. 25:24-25)

> When they came to Jesus, they saw the man who had been possessed by the legion of demons, sitting there, dressed and in his right mind; and *they were afraid.* Those who had seen it told the people what had happened to the demon-possessed man—and told about the pigs as well. Then the people began to plead with Jesus to leave their region. (Mark 5:15-17)

> *Fear of man will prove to be a snare*, but whoever trusts in Yahweh is kept safe. (Prov. 29:25)

> Then Saul said to Samuel, "I have sinned. I violated Yahweh's command and your instructions. *I was afraid of the people and so I gave in to them.*" (1 Sam. 15:24)

> For this is the way the holy women of the past who put their hope in God used to make themselves beautiful. They were submissive to their own husbands, like Sarah, who obeyed Abraham and called him her master. You are her daughters if you do what is right and *do not give way to fear.* (1 Pet. 3:5-6)

> I also will laugh at your calamity; I will mock when your fear comes; when your fear comes as desolation, and your destruction comes as a whirlwind; when distress and anguish comes upon you. (Prov. 1:26-27, KJV)

> For you did not receive a spirit that makes you a *slave again to fear*, but you received the Spirit of sonship. And by Him we cry, "Abba, Father." (Rom. 8:15)

For God did not give us a spirit of timidity, but a spirit of power, of love and of self-discipline. (2 Tim. 1:7)

Since the children have flesh and blood, He too shared in their humanity so that by His death He might destroy him who holds the power of death—that is, the devil—and free those who all their lives were *held in slavery by their fear of death*. (Heb. 2:14-15)

We've said that the fear* of the Lord never causes us to move backward. Noah "moved with fear" to bring the ark to completion (Heb. 11:7, KJV). The fear he knew didn't paralyze him but spurred him on. Because Abraham feared God, he was willing to step forward in obedience to make the supreme sacrifice. And through his reverential fear of God, Abraham received the promise that through his offspring salvation would come to the whole world (Gen. 22:12, 15-18). Likewise, we're to "carry out . . . the goal and fully complete" our salvation with "fear and trembling" (Phil. 2:12, Ampl., NIV). The fear of the Lord is the "beginning of wisdom" (Prov. 9:10), the beginning from which we move toward perfection; and we're told to bring holiness to perfection "in the fear of God" (2 Cor. 7:1, KJV). We also read that the fear of the Lord "leads to life" (Prov. 19:23). Ultimately the fear of the Lord is something that will bless us forever (Ps. 19:9).

"Do not lay a hand on the boy," he said. "Do not do anything to him. Now I know that you *fear God*, because you have not withheld from Me your son, your only son." (Gen. 22:12)

By faith Noah, when warned about things not yet seen, *in holy fear* built an ark to save his family. By his faith he condemned the world and became heir of the righteousness that comes by faith. (Heb. 11:7)

Yahweh Almighty is the one you are to regard as holy, He is the *one you are to fear*, He is the *one you are to dread*. (Isa. 8:13)

Therefore, my dear friends, as you have always obeyed—not only in my presence, but now much more in my absence—continue to work out your salvation *with fear and trembling*. (Phil. 2:12)

The *fear of Yahweh is the beginning of wisdom*, and knowledge of the Holy One is understanding. (Prov. 9:10)

The fear of Yahweh leads to life: Then one rests content, untouched by trouble. (Prov. 19:23)

The fear of Yahweh is the beginning of knowledge, but fools despise wisdom and discipline. (Prov. 1:7)

Do not be wise in your own eyes; *fear Yahweh and shun evil*. (Prov. 3:7)

To fear Yahweh is to hate evil; I hate pride and arrogance, evil behavior and perverse speech. (Prov. 8:13)

---

* See pp. 30-35.

The fear of Yahweh adds length to life, but the years of the wicked are cut short. (Prov. 10:27)

He who fears Yahweh has a secure fortress, and for his children it will be a refuge. The *fear of Yahweh is a fountain of life*, turning a man from the snares of death. (Prov. 14:26-27)

Better a little *with the fear of Yahweh* than great wealth with turmoil. (Prov. 15:16)

The fear of Yahweh teaches a man wisdom, and humility comes before honor. (Prov. 15:33)

Through love and faithfulness sin is atoned for; *through the fear of Yahweh a man avoids evil*. (Prov. 16:6)

Do not let your heart envy sinners, but *always be zealous for the fear of Yahweh*. (Prov. 23:17)

Although a wicked man commits a hundred crimes and still lives a long time, I know that *it will go better with God-fearing men, who are reverent before God*. (Eccles. 8:12)

Now all has been heard; here is the conclusion of the matter: *Fear God and keep His commandments*, for this is the whole duty of man. (Eccles. 12:13)

But select capable men from all the people—*men who fear God*, trustworthy men who hate dishonest gain—and appoint them as officials over thousands, hundreds, fifties and tens. (Exod. 18:21)

Now *let the fear of Yahweh be upon you*. Judge carefully, for with Yahweh our God there is no injustice or partiality or bribery. (2 Chron. 19:7)

Serve Yahweh with fear and rejoice *with trembling*. (Ps. 2:11)

The fear of Yahweh is pure, enduring forever. The ordinances of Yahweh are sure and altogether righteous. (Ps. 19:9)

Yahweh confides in those who fear Him; He makes His covenant known to them. (Ps. 25:14)

How great is Your goodness, which *You have stored up for those who fear You*, which You bestow in the sight of men *on those who take refuge in You*. (Ps. 31:19)

But *the eyes of Yahweh are on those who fear Him*, on those whose hope is in His unfailing love. (Ps. 33:18)

I will give them singleness of heart and action, so that they will always fear Me for their own good and the good of their children after them. I will make an everlasting covenant with them: I will never stop doing good to them, and *I will inspire them to fear Me, so that they will never turn away from Me*. (Jer. 32:39-40)

And He said to man, "*The fear of the Lord—that is wisdom*, and to shun evil is understanding." (Job 28:28)

He will be the sure foundation for your times, a rich store of salvation and wisdom and knowledge; *the fear of Yahweh is the key to this treasure*. (Isa. 33:6)

Wherefore we receiving a kingdom which cannot be moved, let us have grace, whereby we may *serve God acceptably with reverence and godly fear.* (Heb. 12:28, KJV)

You shall follow Yahweh your God and fear Him; and you shall keep His commandments, listen to His voice, serve Him, and cling to Him. (Deut. 13:4, NASV)

You who fear Yahweh, praise Him! All you descendants of Jacob, honor Him! Revere Him, all you descendants of Israel! (Ps. 22:23)

Show proper respect to everyone: Love the brotherhood of believers, *fear God,* honor the king. (1 Pet. 2:17)

Who will not fear You, O Lord, and bring glory to Your name? For You alone are holy. All nations will come and worship before You, for Your righteous acts have been revealed. (Rev. 15:4)

And now, O Israel, what does Yahweh your God ask of you but *to fear Yahweh your God,* to walk in all His ways, to love Him, to serve Yahweh your God with all your heart and with all your soul . . . ? (Deut. 10:12)

But be sure to fear Yahweh and serve Him faithfully with all your heart; consider what great things He has done for you. (1 Sam. 12:24)

But with You there is forgiveness; therefore *You are feared.* (Ps. 130:4)

He did this so that all the peoples of the earth might know that the hand of Yahweh is powerful and so *that you might always fear Yahweh your God.* (Josh. 4:24)

He said in a loud voice, "*Fear God and give Him glory,* because the hour of His judgment has come. Worship Him who made the heavens, the earth, the sea and the springs of water." (Rev. 14:7)

Then those who feared Yahweh talked with each other, and Yahweh listened and heard. A scroll of remembrance was written in His presence *concerning those who feared Yahweh and honored His name.* (Mal. 3:16)

But as for me, I will come into Your house in the multitude of Your mercy; *in fear of You I will worship toward Your holy temple.* (Ps. 5:7)

In *the council of the holy ones God is greatly feared;* He is more *awesome* than all who surround Him. (Ps. 89:7)

Moses said to the people, "Do not be afraid. God has come to test you, *so that the fear of God will be with you to keep you from sinning.*" (Exod. 20:20)

Having therefore these promises, dearly beloved, let us cleanse ourselves from all filthiness of the flesh and spirit, *perfecting holiness in the fear of God.* (2 Cor. 7:1, KJV)

Yahweh delights in those who fear Him, who put their hope in His unfailing love. (Ps. 147:11)

As a father has compassion on his children, so *Yahweh has compassion on those who fear Him.* (Ps. 103:13)

Then Peter began to speak: "I now realize how true it is that God does not show favoritism but *accepts men from every nation who fear Him and do what is right.*" (Acts 10:34-35)

His mercy extends to those who fear Him, from generation to generation. (Luke 1:50)

But from everlasting to everlasting *Yahweh's love is with those who fear Him*, and His righteousness with their children's children. (Ps. 103:17)

Praise Yahweh. *Blessed is the man who fears Yahweh*, who finds great delight in His commands. (Ps. 112:1)

He will bless those who fear Yahweh—small and great alike. (Ps. 115:13)

You who fear Him, trust in Yahweh—He is their help and shield. (Ps. 115:11)

He fulfills the desires of those who fear Him; He hears their cry and saves them. (Ps. 145:19)

The fear of Yahweh adds length to life, but the years of the wicked are cut short. (Prov. 10:27)

Teach me Your way, O Yahweh, and I will walk in Your truth; give me an undivided heart, *that I may fear Your name.* (Ps. 86:11)

But sanctify the Lord God in your hearts, and always be ready to give a defense to everyone who asks you a reason for the hope that is in you, *with meekness and fear.* (1 Pet. 3:15)

Eat the tithe of your grain, new wine and oil, and the firstborn of your herds and flocks in the presence of Yahweh your God at the place He will choose as a dwelling for His Name, so *that you may learn to revere Yahweh your God always.* (Deut. 14:23)

Come, my children, listen to me; I *will teach you the fear of Yahweh.* (Ps. 34:11)

Then the church throughout Judea, Galilee and Samaria enjoyed a time of peace. It was strengthened; and encouraged by the Holy Spirit, it grew in numbers, *living in the fear of the Lord.* (Acts 9:31)

The Spirit of Yahweh will rest on him—the Spirit of wisdom and of understanding, the Spirit of counsel and of power, the Spirit of knowledge and of the *fear of Yahweh—and he will delight in the fear of Yahweh.* He will not judge by what he sees with his eyes, or decide by what he hears with his ears. (Isa. 11:2-3)

CONCLUSION

"Be ye perfect," Jesus urged, "as your heavenly Father is perfect." God's Spirit empowers us to ever strive to conform to the ultimate image of perfection (Rom 8:29, KJV). And God's Word defines that image. The preceding pages have sought to provide a Spirit-directed mosaic of that definition. So the goal cannot merely be victory in isolated aspects of the characteristics discussed above. God calls us to perfection, and He will remain steadfast, unswerving from His purpose until it is accomplished. So, too, your goal must be total victory, a life and character fully integrated in oneness with God, completely reflecting His image. We cannot rest until not only our children but also we conform to the positive characteristics in the previous pages and are thus freed from all the negative characteristics that destroy human lives (Isa. 62:1-7).

Yet in our press toward total victory, we should rejoice in and give thanks for every small step forward along the way. Remember, every victory is a supernatural gift of grace and must be received and appreciated as such. Remember also that mercy triumphs over judgment (James 2:13) and that the Lord's long-suffering is our salvation (2 Pet. 3:15, KJV). So while not compromising in any way the standards of God's Word, we always strive to see mercy triumph over justice (James 2:13). In this way, encourage your children to proceed forward unswervingly to total victory, and encourage yourself as well. For we can work with the assurance that—if we will persevere—

> He who began a good work in you will carry it on to completion until the day of Christ Jesus. (Phil. 1:6)

With this assurance, we can faithfully pursue the course laid out for us. We can strain forward, as Paul did, following his example. We, too, can say:

> Not that I have already obtained all this, or have already been made perfect, but *I press on to take hold of that for which Christ Jesus took hold of me.* Brothers, I do not consider myself yet to have taken hold of it. But one thing I do: Forgetting what is behind and *straining toward what is ahead, I press on toward the goal to win the prize for which God has called me heavenward in Christ Jesus.*
> All of us who are mature should take such a view of things. And if on some point you think differently, that too God will make clear to you. Only let us live up to what we have already attained. (Phil. 3:12-16)

In this spirit, let us run, and train our children and ourselves to run, the course God has given us, the pilgrimage into the promised land of our life in Christ. Fixing our eyes on Jesus, we will not grow weary or lose heart, but we will move forward steadfastly until we can also proclaim with Paul:

> I am already being poured out like a drink offering, and the time has come for my departure. *I have fought the good fight, I have finished the race, I have kept the faith.* Now there is in store for me the crown of righteousness, which the Lord, the righteous Judge, will award to me on that day—and not only to me, but also to all who have longed for His appearing. (2 Tim. 4:6-8)

Notes

1. Richard Chenevix Trench, *On the Study of Words: Lectures*, 17th ed. (London: Macmillan and Co., 1878), p. 328; Robert Alexander Webb, *Christian Salvation: Its Doctrine and Experience* (1921; reprint, Harrisonburg, Va.: Sprinkle Publications 1985), pp. 149-50; Adrian Room, *A Dictionary of True Etymologies* (London: Routledge and Kegan Paul, 1986), p. 17; Roger E. Olson, *The Westminster Handbook to Evangelical Theology* (Louisville Ky.: Westminster John Knox Press, 2004), p. 149; Walter W. Skeat, *An Etymological Dictionary of the English Language*, rev. and enl. (Oxford: Clarendon Press, 1935), p. 37.

2. Daniel Goleman, "What We Can Do about Emotional Illiteracy," in *The Power of Character: Prominent Americans Talk about Life, Family, Work, Values, and More*, ed. Michael S. Josephson and Wes Hanson (San Francisco: Jossey-Bass, 1998), p. 319.

3. Goleman, "What We Can Do about Emotional Illiteracy," p. 319.

4. Goleman, "What We Can Do about Emotional Illiteracy," p. 319.

5. Goleman, "What We Can Do about Emotional Illiteracy," p. 318.

6. Goleman, "What We Can Do about Emotional Illiteracy," p. 318 (emphasis in original).

7. Goleman, "What We Can Do about Emotional Illiteracy," p. 318.

8. Goleman, "What We Can Do about Emotional Illiteracy," p. 319 (brackets in original quoted material).

9. William Gouge, *Of Domesticall Duties* (Norwood, N.J.: Walter J. Johnson, 1976), p. 429.

10. Gouge, *Of Domesticall Duties*, pp. 428, 430 (emphasis added).

11. *The NIV Study Bible: New International Version*, ed. Kenneth Barker et al. (Grand Rapids, Mich.: Zondervan, 1985), p. 788n.

12. *NIV Study Bible*, p. 68n.

13. Barbara W. Tuchman, *Stilwell and the American Experience in China, 1911-45* (New York: Macmillan, 1971), p. 67.

14. Wayne C. Booth, *The Rhetoric of Fiction*, 2nd ed. (Chicago: University of Chicago Press, 1983), pp. 52-53.

15. Miguel de Unamuno, *Tragic Sense of Life*, trans. J. E. Crawford Flitch (Mineola, N.Y.: Dover Publications, 1954), p. 193.

16. George Lakoff, *Don't Think of an Elephant! Know Your Values and Frame the Debate* (White River Junction, Vt.: Chelsea Green Publishing, 2004), p. xv (emphasis added).

17. Lakoff, *Don't Think of an Elephant!* p. xv (emphasis in original).

18. Lakoff, *Don't Think of an Elephant!* p. xv (emphasis added).

19. *Webster's New World Dictionary*, 2nd college ed., s.v. "familiarity."

20. Urie Bronfenbrenner, *Two Worlds of Childhood: U.S. and U.S.S.R.* (New York: Pocket Books, 1973), pp. 105, 112, 120-21, 156; Raymond S. Moore et al., *School Can Wait* (Provo, Utah: Brigham Young University Press, 1979), pp. 49, 60-61.

21. Raymond S. Moore, "Research and Common Sense: Therapies for Our Homes and Schools," *Teachers College Record*, Winter 1982, p. 366.

22. Moore, *School Can Wait*, p. 32.

23. Moore, *School Can Wait*, p. 32.

24. Stanley Milgram, *Obedience to Authority: An Experimental View* (New York: Harper and Row, Harper Colophon Books, 1974), pp. 114-15.

25. "The Harris Poll #58," *Harris Interactive*, 8 October 2003, http://www.harrisinteractive.com/.

26. Radomîr Hubálek, "While We Have Enough Men," *Human Life Review*, Spring 1981, p. 74.

27. Hubálek, "While We Have Enough Men," pp. 74-75.

28. Hubálek, "While We Have Enough Men," p. 74.

29. Francis Brown, S. R. Driver and Charles A. Briggs, *The New Brown— Driver—Briggs—Gesenius Hebrew and English Lexicon* (Peabody, Mass.: Hendrickson Publishers, 1979), p. 1071; Samuel Prideaux Tregelles, trans., *Gesenius' Hebrew and Chaldee Lexicon to the Old Testament Scriptures* (Grand Rapids, Mich.: Baker Book House, 1979), p. 867.

30. William D. Mounce, D. Matthew Smith and Miles V. Van Pelt, eds., *Mounce's Complete Expository Dictionary of Old and New Testament Words* (Grand Rapids, Mich.: Zondervan, 2006), p. 506.

31. X. J. Kennedy, "In a Prominent Bar in Secaucus One Day," in *In a Prominent Bar in Secaucus: New and Selected Poems, 1955-2007*, by X. J. Kennedy (Baltimore: Johns Hopkins University Press, 2007), p. 12.

32. Joseph Conrad, *Heart of Darkness and The Secret Sharer* (New York: New American Library, A Signet Classic, 1950), p. 94.

33. Everett Ferguson, *Backgrounds of Early Christianity* (Grand Rapids, Mich.: William B. Eerdmans Publishing Co., 1987), pp. 331-33; William

Barclay, trans., *The Gospel of John*, vol. 2 (Philadelphia: Westminster Press, 1956), pp. 278-80; Will Durant, *Caesar and Christ: A History of Roman Civilization and of Christianity from Their Beginnings to A.D. 325*, part 3 of *The Story of Civilization* (New York: Simon and Schuster, 1944), p. 571.

34. *The American Heritage Dictionary*, 4th ed., s.v. "neat."

35. *Webster's New World Dictionary*, 2nd college ed., s.v. "neat."

36. Everett Fox, *The Five Books of Moses: Genesis, Exodus, Leviticus, Numbers, Deuteronomy*, vol. 1 of *The Schocken Bible* (New York: Schocken Books, 1995), p. 13.

37. Fox, *Five Books of Moses*, p. 12.

38. *Webster's New World Dictionary*, 2nd college ed., s.v. "initiative," "initiate" and "initial."

39. Heini Arnold, *In the Image of God: Marriage and Chastity in Christian Life* (Rifton, N.Y.: Plough Publishing House, 1977), p. 85.

40. Arnold, *In the Image of God*, p. 86.

41. *Webster's New World Dictionary*, 2nd college ed., s.v. "smirk."

42. W. B. Yeats, "These Are the Clouds," in *The Collected Poems of W. B. Yeats*, ed. Richard J. Finneran, rev. 2nd ed. (New York: Simon and Schuster, Scribner Paperback Poetry, 1996), p. 96.

43. John Murray, *The Epistle to the Romans* (London: Marshall, Morgan and Scott, 1967), p. 125 (emphasis added).

44. W. E. Vine, *An Expository Dictionary of New Testament Words*, in *Vine's Complete Expository Dictionary of Old and New Testament Words*, by W. E. Vine, Merrill F. Unger and William White Jr. (Nashville, Tenn.: Thomas Nelson Publishers, 1985), p. 136.

45. Vine, *Expository Dictionary of New Testament Words*, p. 136.

46. Andrew J. McKenna, *Violence and Difference: Girard, Derrida, and Deconstruction* (Urbana, Ill.: University of Illinois Press, 1992), pp. 1, 3, 107-108, 204; Gil Bailie, *Violence Unveiled: Humanity at the Crossroads* (New York: Crossroad, 1995), pp. 6-7; Cesáreo Bandera, *The Sacred Game: The Role of the Sacred in the Genesis of Modern Literary Fiction* (University Park, Pa.: Pennsylvania State University Press, 1994), pp. 21-22; James G. Williams, *The Bible, Violence, and the Sacred: Liberation from the Myth of Sanctioned Violence* (San Francisco: Harper Collins Publisher, Harper San Francisc, 1991), pp. 6-7; Raymund Schwager, *Must There Be Scapegoats? Violence and Redemption in the Bible*, trans. Maria L. Assad (San Francisco: Harper and Row Publishers, 1987), p. 18; Robert G. Hamerton-Kelly, *The Gospel and the Sacred: Poetics of Violence in Mark* (Minneapolis, Minn.: Fortress Press, 1994), p. 6.

47. James D. G. Dunn, *The Epistles to the Colossians and to Philemon: A Commentary on the Greek Text* (Grand Rapids, Mich.: William B. Eerdmans Publishing Company, 1996), p. 153.

48. Frederick William Danker, ed., *A Greek-English Lexicon of the New Testament and Other Early Christian Literature*, 3rd ed., based on the sixth ed. of Walter Bauer's lexicon, trans. W. F. Arndt, F. W. Gingrich and F. W. Danker (Chicago: University of Chicago Press, 2000), p. 946 (emphasis in original); James Swanson, *A Dictionary of Biblical Languages with Semantic Domains: Greek New Testament*, electronic ed. (Oak Harbor, Wash.: Logos Research Systems, 1997).

49. Vine, *An Expository Dictionary of New Testament Words*, p. 196.

50. Jean Bottéro, *Mesopotamia: Writing, Reasoning, and the Gods*, trans. Zainab Bahrani and Marc Van De Mieroop (Chicago: University of Chicago Press, 1992), pp. 186, 189, 192-93, 236-39; Henri Frankfort, *The Birth of Civilization in the Near East* (Garden City, N.Y.: Doubleday and Company, Doubleday Anchor Books, 1956), p. 64; 1 Enoch 7:1-2.

51. 1 Enoch 8:1-2.

52. 1 Enoch 69:9-10, 1 Enoch 8:1-3.

53. 1 Enoch 69:6-8.

54. Jubilees 11:2-3.

55. Jubilees 11:4-5.

56. Bottéro, *Mesopotamia*, pp. 215, 247; Frankfort, *The Birth of Civilization in the Near East*, p. 64.

57. Ralph H. Abraham, *Chaos, Gaia, Eros: A Chaos Pioneer Uncovers the Three Great Streams of History* (San Francisco: Harper Collins Publishers, Harper San Francisco, 1994), pp. 146-47.

58. Abraham, *Chaos, Gaia, Eros*, pp. 147-48; Hermann Gunkel, "The Influence of Babylonian Mythology upon the Biblical Creation Story," in *Creation in the Old Testament*, ed. Bernhard W. Anderson (Philadelphia: Fortress Press, 1984), p. 27.

59. *Webster's New World Dictionary*, 2nd college ed., s.v. "calumniate."

60. Carol Bly, *The Passionate, Accurate Story* (Minneapolis: Milkweed Editions, 1990), p. 30.

61. Bly, *Passionate, Accurate Story*, p. 30.

62. Bly, *Passionate, Accurate Story*, pp. 30-31.

63. Bly, *Passionate, Accurate Story*, p. 31.

64. C. John Cadoux, *The Early Christian Attitude to War: A Contribution to*

the History of Christian Ethics (New York: Seabury Press, A Vineyard Book, 1982), pp. 229, 231, 235-36, 244-45; Ernst Troeltsch, *The Social Teaching of the Christian Churches*, vol. 1, trans. Olive Wyon (New York: Harper and Brothers, Harper Torchbooks, 1960), pp. 123-25; Gerrit Jan Heering, *The Fall of Christianity: A Study of Christianity, the State, and War*, trans. J. W. Thompson (New York: Garland Publishing, 1972), pp. 12, 21-32; James Turner Johnson, *The Quest for Peace: Three Moral Traditions in Western Cultural History* (Princeton, N.J.: Princeton University Press, 1987), pp. 51, 65-66; Jacques Ellul, *Violence: Reflections from a Christian Perspective*, trans. Cecelia Gaul Kings (New York: Seabury Press, 1969), pp. 9-10.

65. Paul Johnson, *Intellectuals* (New York: Harper and Row Publishers, 1988), p. 24.

66. Ellul, *Violence*, p. 84.

67. Max Weber, *The Theory of Social and Economic Organization*, trans. A. M. Henderson and Talcott Parsons, ed. Talcott Parsons (New York: Oxford University Press, 1947), pp. 154-55 (emphasis added).

68. Kenneth Kaunda, *The Riddle of Violence*, ed. Colin M. Morris (San Francisco: Harper and Row Publishers, 1980), p. 41.

69. Kenneth R. Westphal, "Hegel's Phenomenological Method and Analysis of Consciousness," in *The Blackwell Guide to Hegel's "Phenomenology of Spirit,"* ed. Kenneth R. Westphal (Malden, Mass.: John Wiley and Sons, Wiley-Blackwell, 2009), p. 30 (emphasis in original).

70. Weber, *Theory of Social and Economic Organization*, p. 155; William H. McNeill, "Violence and Submission in the Human Past," *Daedalus*, Winter 2007, p. 5.

71. Derek H. Davis and Matthew McMearty, "America's 'Forsaken Roots': The Use and Abuse of Founders' Quotations," *Journal of Church and State*, Summer 2005, p. 470.

72. R. J. Rummel, *Death by Government* (New Brunswick, N.J.: Transaction Publishers, 1994), pp. 4, 9; R. J. Rummel, *Lethal Politics: Soviet Genocide and Mass Murder since 1917* (New Brunswick, N.J.: Transaction Publishers, 1990), p. xi; Wolf Blitzer, introduction to *Century of War*, by Luciano Garibaldi (New York: Friedman/Fairfax Publishers, 2001), p. 6.

73. James Hefley and Marti Hefley, *By Their Blood: Christian Martyrs of the 20th Century* (Milford, Mich.: Mott Media, 1979), pp. 478, 589.

74. John R. W. Stott, *The Message of the Sermon on the Mount (Matthew 5-7): Christian Counter-Culture* (Downers Grove, Ill.: Inter Varsity Press, 1978), p. 40.

75. Ernest Becker, *The Denial of Death* (New York: Macmillan Publishing Co., Free Press, 1973), pp. ix, 15-17.

76. Paul Johnson, *Modern Times: The World from the Twenties to the Nineties* (New York: Harper Collins Publishers, 1991), pp. 403-404, 424-26.

77. James J. Thompson Jr., "In Praise of Southern Manners," *Southern Partisan*, Spring/Summer 1981, p. 23.

78. Thompson Jr., "In Praise of Southern Manners," p. 23.

ACKNOWLEDGMENTS

We would like to thank the following people whose assistance made the production of this book possible:

Production coordinators: Denny and Camille Allensworth

Editing: Denny Allensworth, coordinator; Regina Adams, Joel Stein

Typesetting: Gail Gardner, coordinator; Rachel Mawk

Checking: Camille Allensworth and Lisa Bradford, coordinators; Gretchen Deines, Kaitlin Tindell

Proofreading: Marcia Bench, coordinator; Kerry Matthews

Research and references: Deanne Ballerino and Marian Smith, coordinators; Alyse Loree, Ruth May, Omie Muir, Teresa Tittley

Scripture references: Denny Allensworth, coordinator

Graphics: Doyle Borman, coordinator; Gail Gardner

Cover design: Doyle Borman, Gary Linzer

Printing and binding: Howard Wheeler and Denny Allensworth, coordinators; Evan Birdsong, Jacob Klingensmith